CAUCASUS MONS

SARMATIA ASIATICE PARS

Albaniae portae

Soanae fl.

Chabala
Chobota
Thiauna
(Thiaula)
Thabilaca
(Cabalaca)
Thilbis
Gerrhi fl.
GERRHI
Gelaeba urbs

L B A N I A

Caesii fl.

Boziata
Misia
Gerda
Gerrhi fluvii ostia

Albani fl.
Alamus
(Amalus)

Chadacha
(Chandaca)

Caesii fluvii ostia

...mechia○
(...mechia)
ALBANA

...TARA○

Albani fluvii ostia

...ca
...ra)

Cyrus fluvii ostia

HYRCANIUM   CASPIUM   MARE   PARS

Araxes fluvii ostia

...sarata

...UM MONS

MEDIA   PARS

...outa

Tigranoama
(Tigranuana)

UDACESPES MONS

S

MAP OF ARMENIA BY PTOLEMY

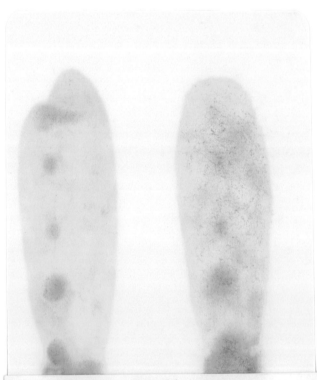

ARMENIA: CRADLE OF CIVILIZATION

ARMENIA

CRADLE OF CIVILIZATION

SECOND EDITION, CORRECTED

BY

David Marshall Lang

Professor of Caucasian Studies
University of London

London
GEORGE ALLEN & UNWIN
Boston   Sydney

FIRST PUBLISHED IN 1970

© *George Allen & Unwin (Publishers) Ltd, 1970 and 1978*
ISBN 0 04 956008 5

British Library Cataloguing in Publication Data

Lang, David Marshall
   Armenia. – 2nd ed
   1. Armenia – Social life and customs
   I. Title
   956.6'2   DS171   77-30625

   ISBN 0-04-956008-5

PRINTED IN GREAT BRITAIN
in 11 on 13 pt Plantin type
BY JOLLY & BARBER LTD
HILLMORTON ROAD, RUGBY

Dedicated with Respect
to

HIS HOLINESS VAZKEN I
Supreme Catholicos of All the Armenians

PREFACE

'The earth like a living thing has its own spirit, and without one's native land, without close touch with one's motherland, it is impossible to find oneself, one's soul.'

MARTIROS SARIAN

The ancient land of Armenia is situated in the high mountains immediately north of the great plains and rivers of Mesopotamia. Although Mesopotamia, with its ancient civilizations of Sumeria and Babylon, is usually considered together with Egypt as the main source of civilized life in the modern sense, Armenia too has a claim to rank as one of the cradles of human culture.

To begin with, Noah's Ark is stated in the Book of Genesis to have landed on the summit of Mount Ararat, in the very centre of Armenia. From the Ark, Noah's descendants and all species of living beasts, and birds are supposed to have issued forth to people the globe. Whether or not we attribute any importance to the Book of Genesis as a historical source, none can deny the symbolic importance of its account of Noah's Ark, which is cherished by both believers and unbelievers all over the world.

Again, Armenia has a claim on our attention as one of the principal homes of ancient metallurgy, beginning at least five thousand years ago. Later on, Armenia became the first extensive kingdom to adopt Christianity as a state religion, pioneering a style of Church architecture which anticipates our own Western Gothic. In these and other respects, Armenia has enriched the civilized world to an extent for which this long forgotten and much ravaged land is seldom given credit.

My own acquaintance with Armenia goes back fully quarter of a century, to the days at the close of World War II when I was stationed in Tabriz as British Vice-Consul. From the north-western corner of our consular district, the twin caps of Mount Ararat were clearly visible, with their majestic summits covered in perpetual snow. Tabriz cannot be regarded as a city with a gay social life, but the Armenian community there were our best friends. I well remember many talks with the venerable Archbishop Nerses Melik-Tangian, who told me tragic stories of the 1915 massacres, and the promises of a new Great Armenia given by President Woodrow Wilson, but never fulfilled. These stories were corroborated by my wise and experienced chief, Sir Reader Bullard, then H.M. Ambassador in Tehran, who had begun his diplomatic career around 1910 with consular postings to Bitlis, Erzurum and Trebizond, and witnessed the harrowing events which led up to the Ottoman genocide of the Armenians.

A planned repatriation of Armenians from Iran to their national home in Soviet Armenia began in 1946. Soon afterwards I returned to Cambridge. It was not until twenty years later, in 1966, that I had my next glimpse of Mount Ararat, this time from the uplands around Lake Sevan in Soviet Armenia. Since then, my studies have brought me increasingly into contact with Armenian communities all over the world.

I was encouraged to undertake this book by my friend Mr Philip Unwin, of the publishing house of George Allen & Unwin, and by Mr Robert Gulbenkian and Mr Vahram Mavian, of the Calouste Gulbenkian Foundation in Lisbon. In acknowledging the generous financial assistance and moral support of the Calouste Gulbenkian Foundation, I wish to make it absolutely clear that this organization has never attempted to influence my judgement in the slightest degree. Any reflexions on the rights and wrongs of the 'Armenian Question' are my own, and I take responsibility for them.

I would like to express grateful thanks to many Armenian friends, who have supported and aided me in writing this book. In Paris, I have to mention especially my teacher and counsellor, Professor Sirarpie Der Nersessian, formerly of the Dumbarton Oaks Research Library in Georgetown, Washington. Among my Armenian friends in London, a word of praise is due to Mr Asatur Guzelian, the well-known Armenian man of letters, who has been tireless in his good offices. The Armenian Mekhitarist Fathers both on San Lazzaro island in Venice, and in Vienna, have been extremely kind in welcoming me amongst them in 1967, and unveiling the treasures of their museums and manuscript collections.

Naturally it is in Soviet Armenia that one finds the best resources for research in Armenian culture and history. I have to thank here several of my hosts and advisers at the Armenian Society for Friendship and Cultural Relations with Foreign Countries, who have twice invited me to Erevan and given me facilities rarely accorded to overseas visitors. Mrs Bersabe Grigorian and Mr Ruben Parsamian, successive Presidents of the Society, were exceptionally constructive and helpful, as was Mr Robert Vardanian, Deputy Chairman, and our beloved and much regretted guide, the late Mr Willy Meserian.

It is my good fortune to be on intimate terms with several of the outstanding masters of Armenian history and archaeology. I have in mind such friends as Academician Suren Tigranovich Eremian, the expert on Armenia in classical and feudal times; Academician Babken Nikolaevich Arakelian, discoverer of the hidden riches of the ancient palace of Garni; Professor Ervand Lazarovich Sarkissian, the authority on modern Armenian history; and Dr Konstantin Oganesian, Director of the Department of Ancient Monuments, and consultant architect to the Urartian buildings at Erebuni (Arin-Berd). I would like to thank most warmly the distinguished philosopher Professor George Brutian, and the respective Directors and staff of the Erevan Matenadaran Manuscript Library, and of the Armenian State Historical Museum for their great kindness on many occasions.

A number of British and Armenian friends and colleagues have kindly supplied photographs and illustrations for this book. Several have preferred to remain anonymous; but to all I express grateful appreciation. I also have to thank Miss Rose O'Connor, who typed the major part of my manuscript with great care.

DAVID M. LANG

School of Oriental and African Studies
University of London, W.C.1. December 21, 1968

PREFACE TO THE SECOND EDITION

The welcome accorded to the original edition of this book on its appearance in 1971 came as a pleasant surprise. Later that year I was asked to attend the Armenian Book Fair held at Watertown, near Boston, in the United States. The following May my wife and I visited Paris, where the ladies of the Armenian community graciously presented me with the Prix Brémond. At Marseilles in March 1973 I delivered a lecture on Armenian culture to the large local community.

Visits to the Armenian communities in Romania and Bulgaria followed. Both in Bucharest and in Moldavia there are Armenian monuments of unusual interest. The Armenian contribution to Bulgarian civilization goes back to medieval times and a noted Bulgarian tsar, Samuel, was of Armenian extraction. Until 1976 an Armenian High School functioned at Plovdiv.

After an absence of nine years, I returned to Soviet Armenia in June 1977. The progress in economic, industrial and artistic development was truly impressive. Looking out of the train coming from Tbilisi in the middle of the night, I could see blast furnaces working full out and several railway stations recently rebuilt in a handsome style. In Erevan I explored a spacious new residential district on the north-eastern side of the city.

The classical temple at Garni, destroyed by an earthquake in the seventeenth century, has been expertly re-erected by Dr Sahinian and now looks much like the architect's sketch reproduced on plate 39 of this book. I also found a brand new Armenian Apostolic church functioning in the heart of Erevan, not far from the main food market. This is a rare phenomenon in the Soviet Union and witnesses the resurgence of Armenian traditional Christianity under Catholicos Vazken I. Returning from Erevan to Moscow by air, I landed straight into a special 'Week of Armenian Culture' being held in the Soviet capital.

I regret to record here the deaths of the painter Martiros Sarian, of the novelist Garegin Sevunts and also of Archbishop Habozian, head of the Mekhitarist community in Vienna.

Grievous loss to Armenian life and property has been sustained during the recent civil war in Lebanon. Many teachers and students of the American University in Beirut were scattered, including several Armenologists. We must also deplore the bombing of the Melkonian Institute High School in Nicosia during the barbarous Turkish invasion of Cyprus in 1974. Within Turkey Armenian monuments continue to disappear and decay, both from neglect and from wilful destruction.

Vigorous leadership, however, should be assured to Armenians in the Middle East by the young western-educated Archbishop Karekin Sarkissian, a scholar and dynamic administrator, who has been elected to succeed Catholicos Khoren as head of the Church of Cilicia at Antelias.

Here in England the outlook for Armenian community and cultural life is encouraging. Three Armenian Apostolic churches function in London, while gastronomic tastes are catered for by excellent Armenian restaurants. At London concert halls recitals are regularly given by Cathy Berberian, the versatile singer, and by the Chilingirian Quartet, while Loris Tjeknavorian, Master of the Music of the Shahinshah of Iran, has founded an Institute of Armenian Music. The Calouste Gulbenkian Chair of Armenian Studies does excellent work in Oxford. In Bloomsbury the British Library currently features exhibits of Armenian illuminated manuscripts and incunabula.

DAVID M. LANG

University of London
September, 1977

Grateful thanks are expressed to the following for kindly supplying photographs, or for giving advice on the choice of illustrations:

Academy of Sciences of the Armenian SSR; Armenian Society for Friendship and Cultural Relations with Foreign Countries; Dr R. D. Barnett; The Trustees of the British Museum; Michael Burrell, Esq; The Supreme Catholicosate of Holy Echmiadzin; M. Chahin, Esq.; Chester Beatty Library, Dublin; Jonathan Coad, Esq.; Professor Sirarpie Der Nersessian; Professor S. T. Eremian; Dr K. V. Golenko; Calouste Gulbenkian Foundation; R. Harcourt Williams Esq.; Mrs. Marilyn Heldman; Historical Museum of Armenia, Erevan; Professor Richard Hovannisian; Verlag Klinkhardt & Biermann; G. M. Meredith-Owens, Esq.; Novosti Press Agency; Mrs Gorky Phillips; Russian Historical Museum, Moscow; Dr S. Sardarian; Dr Ulrich Schurmann; Society for Cultural Relations with the USSR; The Tate Gallery; John Webb, Esq. (Brompton Studio); Mrs Marian Wenzel-Evans.

I wish to thank also Mr Ronald Eames and Mr Peter Lavery of the firm of George Allen & Unwin for their greatly valued help in many problems connected with the selection, preparation, and layout of the illustrations, as with the production of the book generally.

CHRONOLOGICAL TABLE

Abbevillian (Lower Palaeolithic) culture in Armenia	from 500,000 or earlier
Acheulean (Lower Palaeolithic) culture	from 400,000
Middle Palaeolithic (Mousterian) culture	approx. 100,000–40,000
Upper Palaeolithic cultures	approx. 40,000–12,000
Mesolithic cultures	approx. 12,000–6000
Armenian Neolithic culture	from 6000
Chalcolithic ('Copper-Stone') culture	from 4000
Early Bronze (Kuro-Araxes) culture	3200–2000
Khirbet Kerak pottery in Palestine	2600–2400
Indo-European immigration into Armenia	c. 2100
Armenian Middle Bronze Age	2000–1500
Late Bronze Age	1500–900
Hurrian and Mitanni kingdoms	c. 1400
Hayasa confederation flourishes	1400–1300
Salmanesar I of Assyria campaigns in Van district	1275
High point of Lchashen *kurgan* culture	1250
Fall of Hittite Empire	1200–1190
Iron Age in Armenia	from 900
King Aramé of Urartu (Ara the Fair)	c. 880–844
Sarduri I of Urartu, founder of Van	844–820
Foundation of Erebuni (Erevan) by King Argishti I	782
Foundation of Argishtihinili (Armavir)	775
Scythians and Cimmerians invade Armenia	from 730
Sargon of Assyria ravages Urartu	714
Sack of Nineveh	612
Fall of Urartu	590
Persian Achaemenid dominion over Armenia	546–331
Xenophon and his Ten Thousand traverse Armenia	401–400
Orontes I, founder of Orontid dynasty	401–344
Alexander the Great conquers Persia	331
Arsamosata founded by King Arsames	c. 250
Ervandashat founded by King Orontes IV	c. 210
Reign of Artaxias I, founder of Artaxiad dynasty	190–159
Tigranes the Great	95–55
Campaigns of Lucullus in Armenia	69–68
Pompey in Caucasia	66–65
Romans annihilated at Carrhae	53
Artavazd II deposed and murdered by Antony and Cleopatra	34
	B.C.

Distinguished architect Trdat flourishes	980–1000
Byzantine Emperor Basil annexes Vaspurakan	1021
Gagik II, last Bagratid king	1042–45
Constantine Monomachus annexes Ani	1045
Seljuq Turks destroy Artsn, near Erzurum	1048
Ani falls to the Seljuqs	1064
Battle of Manzikert: capture of Emperor Romanus Diogenes	1071
Armenian nobleman Ruben established in Cilicia	1080
Crusaders arrive in Cilician Armenia	1097
Georgians occupy part of Armenia	1123
Death of Catholicos Nerses Shnorhali	1173
Reign of Levon I in Cilicia	1186–1219
Death of Nerses of Lampron	1198
Georgian Queen Tamar captures Kars	1206
Death of Mkhitar Gosh, fabulist and lawgiver	1213
Reign of Hetum I in Cilicia	1226–69
Art of Toros Roslin	1260–70
Assizes of Antioch translated into Armenian by Constable Smbat	1265
Mamluks of Egypt ravage Cilicia	1266
Marco Polo in Armenia	1271
Fall of Hromkla to the Egyptians	1292
Life and career of philosopher Grigor Tatevatsi	1340–1411
Last king of Cilician Armenia, Levon V Lusignan	1363–64; 1374–75
Death of Levon V Lusignan in Paris	1393
Eminent Armenian physician Amirdovlat Amasiatsi	1416–96
Fall of Constantinople to the Ottoman Turks	1453
First Armenian printed book published in Venice	1512
Armenian church opened in Agra	1562
Julfa Armenians deported to Isfahan	1605
First Paris cafe opened by Pascal the Armenian	1672
Mkhitar of Sebastia, founder of Mekhitarist Order	1676–1749
Sayat–Nova, prince of Armenian minstrels	1712–95
First printing press at Echmiadzin set up by Catholicos Simeon	1774
First Armenian journal, *Azdarar*, published in Madras	1794–96
Khachatur Abovian, father of Armenian intelligentsia	1805–48
Lazarev Institute founded in Moscow	1815
Life and career of marine painter Aivazovsky	1817–1900
Life and career of dramatist Gabriel Sundukian	1825–1912
Annexation of eastern Armenia by Russia	1828

Scholarly journal *Pazmaveb* founded in Venice	1843
Life and career of poet Hovhannes Tumanian	1869–1923
Life and career of poet Avetik Issahakian	1875–1957
Birth of Martiros Sarian	1880
Scholarly journal *Handes Amsorya* founded in Vienna	1887
Massacres of Armenians by Abdul-Hamid	1895
Birth of Aram Khatchaturian	1903
Life and career of abstract painter Arshile Gorky	1904–48
Annihilation of Turkish Armenians by Young Turk junta	1915
Establishment of Armenian independence	1918
Soviet Armenia set up	1920
First congress of Soviets of Armenia adopts Constitution	1922
Première of opera *Almast* by Spendiarov	1930
Patriotic poet Eghishe Charentz liquidated	1938
Armenian Academy of Sciences founded	1943
Election of Supreme Catholicos Vazken I	1955
2750 jubilee of Erevan–Erebuni	1968

CONTENTS

17

ILLUSTRATIONS

20

MAPS

COLOUR PLATES

Chapter I

LAND AND PEOPLE

THE Armenian uplands are situated on the northern borders of the Near East, above Syria and Mesopotamia. They divide the Anatolian plateau to the west from the mountainous country of Iranian Azerbaijan and Kurdistan. The territory of historical Armenia occupies an area between latitude 37° and 41° 15′ north, and longitude 37° and 47° east. At its greatest extent, two thousand years ago, the area inhabited by the Armenian people amounted to well over 100,000 square miles. Of this territory, only 11,175 square miles are included within the Armenian Soviet Socialist Republic today. Most of the remainder now forms the eastern *vilayets* or provinces of the Turkish Republic. Other sections of historically Armenian territory form the Nakhchevan Autonomous SSR and the Mountain-Karabagh Autonomous District, belonging administratively to the Azerbaijan SSR.

The main Armenian plateau lies at an average height of between 4,500 and 5,500 feet above sea-level. There are a few points where it drops below 3,000 feet, as in the Middle Araxes plain, while at the extreme north, at Debedashen on the Georgian border, it falls to 1,200 feet. But almost everywhere, Armenia is higher than the countries which immediately surround it. Cut off from them on virtually all sides by barriers of lofty hills and mountain peaks, Armenia seems like some massive rock-bound island rising out of the surrounding lowlands, steppes and plains. To the west, Armenia shades off into the uplands of central Anatolia, while access to the Black Sea is blocked to the north-west by the Pontic Alps and the densely wooded slopes of Lazistan. To Armenia's north lies the land of the Georgians, running up to the Great Caucasian range. On the eastern flank, Soviet and Persian Azerbaijan cut Armenia off from the shores of the Caspian Sea. The southern marches of Armenia are inextricably entwined with the territory of her agelong adversaries, the Kurds, whose own tribal lands extend far south into Mesopotamia, the modern Iraq.

The geological structure of Armenia is unusually interesting, comprising elements from most phases of the earth's history, from the pre-Cambrian right down to the Quaternary epoch. At one stage, the entire territory of modern Armenia was covered by sea, which persisted longest in the territory of the middle Araxes valley. Long phases of relative stability were punctuated from time to

23

time by violent crustal disturbances, which threw up great folds and ridges made up from marine deposits which had accumulated on the sea bed over millions of years. These convulsions also threw up, from the inner depths of the earth's crust, vast quantities of lava and friable volcanic products.

According to exponents of the Continental drift theory, a general shift of land from the north towards the equator took place during the Tertiary period, perhaps fifty million years ago, bringing about the great belt of folding which extends from the Himalayas westwards to the Alps and to the Atlas Mountains in North Africa. Of this great belt the Taurus and the Ararat systems in Anatolia are but a small part. The final phases of these mighty upheavals resulted ultimately in the retreat of the ocean waters which had covered Armenia, and the extrusion of colossal mountain ranges in a succession of upward thrusts. These ranges only took shape in the Neogene or newer Tertiary period, around twenty-five million years ago – a comparatively modern phase in the formation of the earth's crust, the evolution of which is now confidently charted over a period of some three milliard years. The severe earthquakes to which Armenia is subject even today, culminating in the disastrous tremors which laid waste Varto, Hinis and several other towns near Lake Van in 1966, show that even now, the terrain of Armenia has by no means settled down into geological quiescence.

These processes left the whole of Armenia and Eastern Anatolia studded with extinct volcanoes in various states of decay. The sheets of lava which flowed down from them in the remote past have built tablelands often much higher than the plains which form their foundation, and the limestone downs surrounding them. This lava supplies the pink and black tufa stone which is such a feature of Armenian architecture. Variety is given to the otherwise monotonous landscape by a few ranges of non-volcanic origin, which protrude through the drab volcanic overlay.

The upper reaches of the main rivers which rise in the Armenian highlands sometimes meander across the plateaux, and sometimes occupy canyons cut through the lava obstructions, or else make circuitous detours to avoid these. In their lower courses, these rivers flow through tremendous gorges, especially where they have carved a passage from north to south across one of the non-volcanic mountain ranges. The most important of these rivers are the Tigris and the Euphrates, with their numerous tributaries, all rising in the former Turkish Armenia, and criss-crossing an enormous area centred on Lake Van and the Kurdish Taurus.

The most famous natural feature of Armenia is Mount Ararat, legendary resting place of Noah's Ark, and situated about halfway between Lake Van to the south-west, in Turkish Armenia, and Lake Sevan to the north-east, in the Armenian SSR. The *massif* of Ararat rises on its north and east sides out of the rich alluvial plain of the River Araxes, which flows here at between 3,000 and 2,500 feet above sea level. On the south-west, it sinks down into the plateau of Bayazid, about 4,500 feet high, on the frontier between Persia and Turkey. On the north-

Looking towards Mount Ararat *(after Lord Bryce)*

. Garni landscape

west of Ararat, a *col* nearly 7,000 feet high connects it with a long ridge of volcanic mountains running further westwards into Asia Minor. Out of the Ararat *massif* rise two peaks, their bases merging at a height of 8,800 feet, their summits standing about seven miles apart. Great Ararat is a huge broad-shouldered mass, more like a dome than a cone; Little Ararat is an elegant pyramidal cone, rising with smooth, steep, regular sides to a comparatively sharp peak. On the north and west, the slopes of Great Ararat are covered with glittering fields of *névé*. There is a glacier on the north-east side, at the bottom of a great chasm running far into the heart of the mountain. The permanent snow line begins at the unusually high level of some 14,000 feet: this is due to the small rainfall, and to the upward current of dry air from the plain of the River Araxes. Both Great and Little Ararat consist of volcanic rocks, notably andesites and pyroxene andesites, with some obsidian. In medieval times, the lower slopes of Ararat were wooded, but now they are stark and bare.

Mount Ararat stands today just within the frontier of the Turkish Republic. Over the Soviet border, to the north-west of Erevan, the immense bulk of Alagöz (Aragats) extends across the horizon. This massive group of extinct volcanoes occupies a space forty miles long, from close to Lake Sevan westwards to the Arpa Chai, a tributary of the Araxes. Alagöz rises on the northern fringe of the level tracts of the Araxes valley to a height of 13,410 feet, the snowy fangs of its shattered crater forming the dominant feature on the Russian side. On its lower slopes is the world-famous astro-physical observatory of Byurakan, which has achieved international renown under the direction of Academician V. A. Ambartsumian.

Other notable mountains of Armenia include the mighty Bingöl Dagh, 'mountain of the thousand tarns', directly south of Erzurum. This volcanic mass, also known as Bingöl Koch, or 'cauldron of a thousand pools', is the parent mountain both of the Araxes and the principal tributaries of the Euphrates. Its highest peak rises to 10,770 feet. Even more grandiose is the volcanic peak of Suphan Dagh (14,540 feet), close to the north-western shores of Lake Van, with its enormous extinct crater covered perpetually with snow and ice, though mounds of volcanic rock protrude gauntly through the white overlay. In summer, the upper slopes of Suphan are beautiful with turf, forget-me-not, pink daisies, buttercups, campanulas and sweet-scented arabis. Another ancient volcano of topographical interest is Nemrut or Nimrud Dagh (9,900 feet), close to Tatvan at the south-western corner of Lake Van. Nemrut Dagh played an important part in determining the present conformation of Lake Van: thick streams of lava flowing out of Nemrut Dagh in the remote past blocked up a former branch of the Murat Su, and gradually confined the waters of the present lake behind a natural dam of volcanic deposits.

The formidable bunch of peaks, including Boz Dagh, Ala Dagh, Tendürük Dagh and Hama Dagh, combine with the Ararat *massif* to divide Armenia into two halves, the south-western Vannic area (historical Vaspurakan), and the north-

3. Crossing the Euphrates
4. Bullock cart near Lake Van
5. Farming near Lake Van

eastern Araxes plain, Lake Sevan and Karabagh region (historical Siunia), most of which now forms the Armenian SSR. The existence of this great barrier and consequent difficulty of communications, played a role in the division of Armenia into rival feudal principalities, and hindered the creation of a United Armenian state. Within Soviet Armenia, the range of the Lesser Caucasus runs up to the north-west from above Lake Sevan, and forms a natural barrier between the cultural sphere of the Hayk (Armenians) and the Kartvelian peoples, the Georgian nation of today.

Lake Van, which played a central role in the cultural evolution of Urartu in Assyrian times, lies at a height of 5,640 feet above sea level. It is about eighty miles long from east-north-east to west-south-west, and thirty-five miles across between Suphan and Gevash, where it is widest. Roughly triangular in shape, it covers 1,460 square miles; its waters, rich in sodium carbonate, are unpleasant to the taste. The lake is bordered by fertile arable plains on the north and east sides; these are hemmed in by lava deposits which have impinged on their edges. The cultivated land is also punctured by volcanic thrusts, now surrounded by cones. The ruins of the ancient city of Van, and the new Turkish town nearby, stand on the eastern shore of the lake. Three main streams drain into Lake Van from the east: Bendimahi, Kara Su, and Hoshap. These are the surviving upper reaches of rivers drowned by the Lake when the Nemrut natural dam was formed in the remote past. The southern rim of Lake Van differs from the others in that it rises steeply to a divide which at one place is no more than three miles from the indented shoreline. The rocks composing this southern rim are marbles and schists, instead of the usual shales, lavas and sandstones.

Rather different is the character of Lake Sevan, known in Turkish as Gökche, or 'the Blue Lake', and to the Ancients as the Lychnitis. On the north, Sevan is confined by the long ridge of mountains which cuts off Armenia from Georgia and Azerbaijan; to the south, by the volcanic plateau of Akhmangan, which rises in places to a height of close on 12,000 feet. The lake itself stands at a level of 6,340 feet; its waters are sweet, and yield delicious salmon trout known as *ishkhan* or 'prince fish'. Sevan has only one outlet, the river Zanga or Razdan, now harnessed to a system of hydroelectric stations which supply a major portion of the energy of the entire Armenian SSR. For travellers approaching Armenia by road from Tbilisi in the north, Sevan with its grandiose backcloth of mountains forms one of the first vistas to greet the eye after cresting the lofty pass above the health resort of Delijan. Fresh from the lush, wooded slopes of Delijan, with its streams and orchards, the voyager is brought face to face with a stark and uncompromising landscape which leaves an indelible impression on the beholder.

Both Lake Van and Lake Sevan have ancient island monasteries. About two miles from the shore at the south-eastern corner of Lake Van is the small island of Aghtamar, on which the tenth century King Gagik Ardsruni of Vaspurakan built his royal residence, complete with palace, church and extensive gardens. Gagik's

. Boating on Lake Sevan

. Town scene in Erevan

magnificent palace church was erected and decorated between 915 and 921 AD Its exterior is carved with friezes representing a wide variety of biblical scenes and secular motifs, and the church is recognized as one of the earliest and finest examples of Romanesque architecture in the Byzantine world and in medieval Christendom generally, a precursor of the great Romanesque churches of the Mediterranean; it also preserves many decorative features characteristic of Sasanian Iran, and the Umayyad civilization in Islam. For several centuries, Aghtamar was the centre of an independent Armenian Catholicosate, a rival to the mother Church at holy Echmiadzin and in Sis, but now the island is deserted and its former Armenian community long since dead or dispersed.

The Sevan monastery stands on a peninsula – until recently, an island – at the north-west corner of the lake. Founded in AD 874 by Princess Mariam of Siunia, the monastery originally contained three churches, built in the usual cruciform pattern with a central dome and cupola. The two surviving churches, in blackish stone, are dedicated to Saint Karapet, and to the Holy Apostles respectively. The site is popular as a summer resort, and can be reached by a modern electric railway from Erevan.

With its mighty mountains topped by eternal snow, two great lakes, and count-less ravines and canyons, almost two thirds of the territory of historical Armenia must be classified as unfit for settled habitation. Large tracts of the Armenian plateau can yield only a scanty living to nomads and their herds. Although its territory once equalled that of England and Wales together, Armenia has never supported a population of more than five or six millions. In recent years, modern industry and cultivation methods have worked wonders in that portion of the land now under Soviet control, though the former Turkish Armenia remains, since the great massacres, largely sterile and waste.

Typical soils encountered in Armenia are the following:

(a) The light brown alluvial earth of the Ararat valley and Araxes plain, set at an average height of 2,500 to 4,000 feet above sea level. This soil is rich in marl but poor in humus, and has been irrigated, manured and cultivated over many centuries. Much of this area is taken up by cereal and vegetable crops, cotton, vineyards and orchards. Parts of the region are still occupied by salt flats and marshes.

(b) The rich brown soil of the drier hill country, lying in the south between 4,000 and 5,000 feet above sea level, in the north-east, between 1,200 and 2,500 feet, where we find all kinds of crops, ranging from corn to valuable plantations of fruit and nut trees.

(c) The mountain black-earth districts, occupying a large portion of the higher steppes of the Armenian uplands, at heights between 4,500 and 7,000 feet. Covered in snow for a great part of the year, and littered with loose stones, this land is susceptible of vast improvements. It can be made to yield excellent crops of hardier varieties of cereals and vegetables during the brief spring and summer season.

(d) The higher meadow lands, covering the slopes of Armenia's great hill and mountain ranges, between 5,000 and 10,000 feet, in the sub-alpine zones. These rugged highland meadows or *yailas*, often steeply sloping, yield little apart from hay and fodder for flocks and herds, but play an essential part in the country's economy by providing summer pasture for sheep and cattle. The rearing of these is traditionally associated with the Kurdish and Tatar tribes, who have led a nomadic life throughout the region since time immemorial.

Much of Armenia's soil is formed in part from the detritus of volcanic lava, and is rich in nitrogen, potash, phosphates and other useful chemicals. Where irrigation is available, and surface stones and debris cleared away, fertile fields can be formed even from quite unpromising terrain. But much labour is usually required for farming in Armenia. The novelist Garegin Sevunts truly remarked to the present writer that, through the ages, the Armenian people has literally had to wrest its bread from among the stones.

In much of Armenia, the severity of economic conditions is aggravated by the harsh climate of the mountainous and upland areas. Over the exposed plains of Erzurum, Kars and Ardahan, the winter wind blows with freezing intensity. Snow falls on between fifty and sixty days annually in the north, and lies up to seven months in places. In these regions, the Armenian peasantry was forced from ancient times to build semi-underground houses and burrows to survive the winter seasons, when temperatures can fall to 40° below freezing point. A notable exception to these conditions is provided by the Araxes valley, where winters are mild, though summer heat here is trying, and temperatures reach 90°. Climatically, the most agreeable areas of Armenia are those lying around Lake Van, and in the north, the wooded mountains and hills of Lori, Zangezur and the Karabagh, where trees give shade in summer, as well as protection from winter gales.

The flora and vegetation of Armenia are as varied as the climate and landscape. Forests cover only about one-tenth of the region, and these have suffered much from indiscriminate felling and depredations by the flocks and herds of nomads. At present, a concerted effort is made in Soviet Armenia to restore the country's wooded covering and prevent soil erosion. Common trees are the oak, the beech and the hornbeam, which are often found growing side by side, and also in association with the lime, the ash and the maple. The woods of Armenia also contain the plane tree, the yew, the walnut and the hawthorn, while in northern regions, small forests of pine and spruce occur. There are birch woods mixed with barberry, wild currant, wild rose, and mountain ash. Armenia is rich in wild fruits of many kinds, including the vine, the cornelian cherry, the wild pear, crab-apple, damson, medlar, cherry, raspberry and dew-berry. Botanists agree that as well as being a natural habitat of the vine, Armenia and neighbouring Georgia are the original home of many trees, bushes and plants now found all over Europe in cultivated state.

Even the unpromising, dried-up steppe land in the neighbourhood of the ruined medieval city of Ani yields rich booty to the naturalist. In 1912, for instance, a Swiss botanist, Dr Martin Rikli, identified and listed thirty-seven species of flowers and plants which he found in the vicinity of Ani railway station on the Erevan-T'bilisi line. These included such items as *Asparagus officinalis*, *Aster Amellus*, *Delphinium divaricatum* and *Scabiosa linifolia*, while further searches in the nearby ravine of the Arpa Chai yielded another dozen items of interest. The Araxes valley, on the other hand, favours sub-tropical growths, such as cotton and tobacco, and bushes like the olive, the oleander and the mulberry.

The volcanic peaks, such as Ararat, Suphan and Nemrut, have climatic conditions incompatible with an abundant plant life. The porous and loose volcanic soil reduces the ground moisture available for plants. The lower slopes of these peaks are covered mainly with steppe grasses, well suited to dry conditions, and with thorny, shrubby milk-vetches. Uncultivated parts of the middle Araxes valley tend to be covered with brushwood and salt steppe and marshes, with camel thorn and other plants tolerant of such conditions. Sand steppes found in higher reaches have wormwood, spurge, and everlasting flowers such as Xeranthemum and Helichrysum. Between 4,000 and 6,000 feet, wild rye and several other grasses flourish, while river gorges favour bistort, juniper, and prickly cushions of a type of sea-lavender *(Acantholimon glumaceum)*. Above 7,000 feet, ground is often stony and vegetation sparse, except for a few alpine meadows which are beautiful in spring time. Northern types of plant able to survive intense cold are characteristic of these higher reaches.

The variety of Armenia's landscape and vegetation is matched by a wide range of animal life. In Soviet Armenia alone, 454 species of vertebrates – animals, birds and fish – have been classified, about 10,000 kinds of insect, and over 1,000 invertebrate creatures. The vertebrates include 76 species of mammal, 304 kinds of bird, 44 varieties of reptile, 6 sorts of amphibious animals, and 24 species of fish. The mammals comprise insectivorous types, such as the mole and the hedgehog, cheiroptera, such as the bat, and various beasts of prey, such as the leopard, panther, porcupine, hyena, polecat and wild-cat, several species of rodents, not to speak of a vast range of domesticated animals ranging from the horse to the rabbit. The wolf and the jackal are fairly common, even in the quite densely populated Soviet Armenia, and there are a few bears and badgers left. Armenia was once a hunter's paradise, and there are still the occasional wild-boar, roe-buck, mountain goat, moufflon and mottled deer, though these are now rare. Fur-bearing animals include the squirrel, marten, otter, fox, and also the coypu. The weasel takes toll of mice and other small rodents, but hares are common. In remote districts south of Lake Van, wild sheep are found on open uplands, and ibex on crags and cliffs. Grey bear and wild pig abound near Shatak, and lynxes lurk in the deep gorges.

Among freshwater fish, the most notable are the *ishkhan* salmon trout of Lake Sevan, also the whitefish, the carp and the barbel. Birdlife is varied, and includes the raven, crow, vulture, hawk, falcon, owl, Caucasian grouse, partridge, quail, hazel-grouse and snipe, also the rare *Ular (Tetraogallus caspius)*. The pigeon and the dove are common, and there are plenty of water-fowl, such as the coot, the teal, the pochard and sundry species of duck. Flies and mosquitoes, both disease carriers, are troublesome in marshy ground, though in Soviet Armenia a successful anti-malaria campaign has been carried through. Poisonous snakes and scorpions are fairly frequent. In Turkish Armenia, swarms of locusts from the Kurdish hills may ravage the eastern plains in April and May.

The unique geological features of the Armenian highlands help to account for the land's unusual richness in metals, minerals and a wide range of stones useful for industrial purposes. The fusion of vast floods of liquefying magmas with the subsoil of Armenia in remote epochs resulted in rich deposits of copper, molybdenum, aluminium, lead, zinc, mercury, gold, silver, iron, chrome and other metals, as well as quartzite and asbestos and various other minerals with fire-resisting properties and industrial uses. Volcanic action left behind several types of stone with high-grade constructional qualities – tufa of several colours and shades, basalt, andesite, pumice, slag and granite. These are currently much employed in building and construction in Soviet Armenia, and are exported to other regions of the Soviet Union. The fact that Armenia was for millions of years covered by sea water led to the precipitation and solidification in sedimentary form of lime, dolomite, gypsum, rock salt, high-grade clays, phosphorite, diatomite and many other substances useful in agriculture and industry. The crystallization of limestone has produced a high-grade marble, famed for its constructional and decorative qualities. Soviet Armenia has a flourishing cement industry.

Mines of precious metals, notably gold and silver, and also copper and iron mines, were exploited in antiquity, gold and copper being refined in Armenia from around 3,000 B.C. In Soviet Armenia, the metallurgical industry is in a flourishing and rapidly expanding condition. Prospecting for new mines and sources of metals and minerals is constantly carried on. In Turkish Armenia, even those mines, particularly copper and silver, which were well known in ancient times and the Middle Ages, are now in a languishing condition, due to the disappearance of the once industrious Armenian population.

Petroleum and natural gas have not yet been discovered in Armenia in commercial quantities. Soviet Armenia is easily supplied with these from Baku, the great oil town in nearby Soviet Azerbaijan. Prospecting for oil and natural gas is going on actively in Soviet Armenia, and there are signs that strikes may soon be made. In the meantime, supplies of electric energy are assured by the series of hydroelectric stations built along the River Razdan (Zanga), which flows out of the north-western corner of Lake Sevan. Armenia is rich in hot springs and mineral waters, the most famous being those of Jermuk, Arzni, Ankavan,

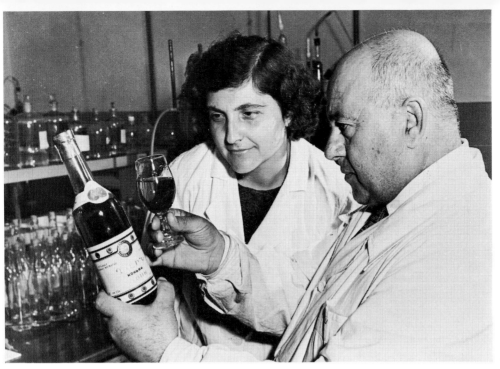

8. In the State Cognac
Factory

9. Synthetic rubber plant
in Erevan

Delijan, Martuni and Sisian. There are a number of spas and health resorts at these mineral springs and elsewhere.

Though Armenia is the source of several renowned rivers of the East, including the Tigris and Euphrates, also the Araxes and the Kura, she has never enjoyed regular access to fully navigable waters. The upper Tigris and Euphrates could be navigated downstream by special rafts of timber and brushwood, usually lashed by tamarisk or willow bark, and supported on inflated sheepskins, the necks of which are tied with liquorice fibre or hemp. These *keleks*, described by Herodotus in classical times, were made from between 200 and 800 skins, and the largest could carry over 30 tons of merchandise. Below Diyarbekir on the Tigris, the Kurds used to levy blackmailing tribute on all who passed downstream, in default of which they would fire on the *keleks*, killing the passengers and crew, or else perforating the skins and forcing the rafts to put in to shore. Fishing boats have sailed Lake Sevan, and ferry boats Lake Van, since time immemorial, but these have only local importance.

The great seas of the Near East – the Black Sea, the Caspian, the Mediterranean and the Persian Gulf – have been accessible to the Armenian people only on rare occasions and for short periods, as during the reign of Tigranes the Great in the first century BC, or when the Rupenian dynasty ruled at Sis in Cilician Armenia during the era of the Crusaders. Soviet Armenia has no direct access to the sea at all. Consequently, the Armenians, with all their commercial acumen, have almost always had to use the ships of other powers to furnish them with the physical basis for maritime trade. It is no accident that many of the main centres of Armenian emigration overseas have been in great ports of the world, such as Bombay and Calcutta, Singapore and Rangoon, Boston and San Francisco, Marseilles and Amsterdam, Beirut and Istanbul.

Armenia has a number of renowned cities, both ancient and modern. Greatest of them is Erevan, capital of Soviet Armenia, which was founded in 782 BC by the Urartian king Argishti I, who gave it the name Erebuni. Erevan is now a flourishing and fast growing town of over 900,000 inhabitants, with modern factories, a busy railway station and marshalling yards, airport, University and Academy of Sciences with a series of research institutes, as well as the Philharmonic Hall, Opera House, and many theatres and cinemas. Another large modern town with an ancient history is Leninakan, the former tsarist town and military base Aleksandropol (Gumri), from which a railway line runs into nearby Turkey. Leninakan is now an important industrial town of 150,000 inhabitants. The third largest city of Soviet Armenia is Kirovakan, north of Erevan; it is a health resort and centre of the chemical industry.

Apart from these, the Middle Araxes valley has a number of ancient sites which served successively as capital of Armenia at different periods of her chequered history. Chief among these are Armavir, important during the Urartian and Hellenistic periods; the once royal city of Vagharshapat, now Echmiadzin,

35

residence of the Supreme Catholicos of the Armenians, about 15 miles west of Erevan; Artashat, 20 miles south-west of Erevan, a low-lying and rather swampy site which once served as the residence of the Armenian Artaxiads; and more salubrious Dvin, 3 miles north of Artashat, to which the capital was moved during Sasanian and Arab domination. Especially famous is the now ruined Bagratid capital of Ani, 'City of 1,001 Churches', built in triangular form on a rocky peninsula overhanging the rapid waters of the Arpa Chai, on the present Soviet-Turkish frontier. Towards Persia, we must not overlook Nakhchevan and Julfa within the Nakhchevan Autonomous SSR; both of these were notable trading centres up to the time of the Safavi shahs, and retain interesting monuments of medieval Persian architecture.

The former Turkish Armenia contains the renowned city of Van, like Erevan an ancient Urartian foundation, dating back at least 2,800 years. The old town with its narrow winding streets lay at the foot of the citadel, on which are important Urartian inscriptions carved into stone slabs. This old town was wrecked and depopulated during the 1915 massacres and the military campaigns of World War I. A new Turkish township has now been built farther away from the lake shore. South-west and west of Lake Van are two once prosperous towns, Bitlis and Mush, where a mixed population of Armenians, Kurds, Turks, Arabs and Syrians lived in comparative harmony prior to the terrible events of the late nineteenth century and World War I. Bitlis occupies a strategic position on the caravan route from Erzurum to Baghdad, and was once a bustling commercial centre of 50,000 inhabitants. Now that the Armenian population has been exterminated, and trade and industry have declined, both Bitlis and Mush are insignificant townships, offering to visitors a couple of squalid 'hotels' apiece, where tourists are harassed by vermin and by hostile gendarmes. Much the same applies to the fortress towns of Kars and Ardahan near the Soviet border, the former being once the capital of an independent Armenian kingdom, Vanand.

There are a number of other sites in Turkey, lying further to the west and south-west, where important Armenian cities existed at various epochs in history. Such, for instance, was Tigranokerta, the present Farkin (Mayyafariqin), where Tigranes the Great built his grandiose capital, which he occupied for only a few years before being overwhelmed by the legions of the Roman general Lucullus in 69 BC. Nor must we overlook the cities and castles of Cilician Armenia, where the Rupenian dynasty reigned from the time of the crusaders until the area fell to the Mamluks of Egypt in the fourteenth century. Among the most important Armenian centres at this period were Sis, capital of the Rupenid kings, and Hromkla, for a time residence of the Supreme Catholicos.

The Armenian highlands lie at the crossroads of the Iranian, the Greek, and the Eurasian worlds. In fact, a glance at a map of the globe shows up the central position of Armenia in the entire world scene: the country is seen to be almost equidistant from the Cape of Good Hope and the Bering Straits, and roughly halfway from the Pacific to the Atlantic Ocean. Archaeologists hold that several migrations of Stone Age peoples into Europe began in or near Armenia. From the Early Bronze Age onwards, Armenia was a focal point on the southward spread of the Indo-Europeans from their original habitat, which was evidently somewhere in Poland or south Russia. In Urartian times, early in the Iron Age, Armenia witnessed a death struggle between the ancient civilizations of Anatolia and Mesopotamia and warlike interlopers from the northern steppes, as a result of which the vestiges of old Near Eastern cultures were absorbed or readapted by bearers of the new.

The origin and racial affinities of the Armenians remain somewhat mysterious. At one time, it was thought that they immigrated *en masse* from the Balkans and the Aegean region, less than a thousand years before Christ. However, recent research indicates that the modern Armenian nation is in fact the product of a process of ethnic mingling which has been going on for thousands of years in Transcaucasia and the mountains and valleys of the Ararat-Vannic region. The Armenians of today are generally stocky in build, rather below middle height, and often distinguished by having heads of unusual shape, straight at the back and tapering towards the top. The flattened occiput is often associated with a prominent nose, sometimes hooked or aquiline, sometimes rather bulbous in shape. Certainly the Armenians are physically closer to the ancient inhabitants of Asia Minor, as depicted on Hittite and Urartian friezes, than they are to representations of Scythians and other Indo-European steppe nomads from southern Russia, as preserved by archaeological finds. The predominant type of Armenian has black or dark brown hair, usually straight, and dark eyes. It is interesting to note, however, that ancient Armenian legends tell of blond, blue-eyed giants, a vanished race of Armenian supermen. These may well be reminiscences of tribesmen from the north – Sarmatians, Cimmerians and Scythians – who overran Armenia repeatedly from about 730 BC onwards.

The Armenian language can provide only a partial answer to this question of the origin and affinities of the Armenian people. Experience in the United States of America and elsewhere teaches the scholar to guard against confusing ethnic origins with linguistic affinities, except where these have been correlated by research. Armenian is an independent, one-language family within the Indo-European group, being thus comparable with Celtic, Germanic and Slavic. It is no longer classified as an Iranian language, though it has a great number of Iranian loan-words. Within Indo-European, Armenian is one of the so-called 'satem' languages, the others being Baltic, Slavic, Indo-Iranian, and Albanian. This binary division into 'satem' and 'centum' languages turns on the evolution of the word for 'hundred'. It probably represents a dialectal cleavage in the so-called 'period of unity' prior to the great Indo-European migrations. (The distinction, R. H. Robins has kindly explained to me, relates to differing treatment by the 'satem' and 'centum' languages of the hypothecated Indo-European velar, labio-velar and palatal plosive consonants.)

37

Through long evolution side by side with Georgian, Armenian has further acquired a consonantal system of great complexity, having much in common with the Kartvelian group of Caucasian languages; these are, of course, not Indo-European at all. The question of the affinities of Armenian with the Urartian or Vannic language, which is a form of Hurrian, is also receiving increasing attention from philologists.

It must always be remembered that by the time the first Indo-European arrived in Asia Minor, human civilization already had its own ancient tradition in the regions of Lake Van and Mount Ararat. Herodotus, who knew Armenia and the Armenians as part of the Persian Empire in the fifth century BC, thought that the Armenians were colonists from Phrygia.[1] It is often stated that the Armenian and Phrygian languages are closely akin, though so little remains of Phrygian that comparison is difficult. The Greek authority Strabo links the Armenians with Thessaly in northern Greece; he adds that a Thessalian, Armenus, visited the country in company with Jason and the Argonauts, and gave it his name.[2] As for the Phrygians, Strabo says that they were Thracian in origin, and entered Asia Minor from present-day Bulgaria after the Trojan War. These semi-legendary indications are of some interest, as they enable us to link the ancestors of the Armenians with the mysterious 'Sea Peoples', who swept into Asia Minor about 1200 BC and put an end to the Hittite Empire. Certain of these 'Sea Peoples' undoubtedly penetrated far eastwards into Anatolia and settled down between the River Halys and the upper reaches of the Tigris and Euphrates. In course of time, these invaders, numerically inferior, were evidently absorbed by the original inhabitants of eastern Asia Minor, who later helped to form the nucleus of the Armenian people. However, before the immigrants mingled with the ancient local population, they had time to impart and transmit their expressive, sonorous and well-constructed language, together with other features of their Indo-European cultural heritage.

Armenia's strategic position has exposed her to repeated invasion. Situated immediately to the south of the Caucasian corridor, the Armenian highlands must be traversed or skirted by northern peoples driving south from the Eurasian steppes, or by any Near Eastern power moving north to control the Black Sea and Caspian littorals. Equally, Armenia must necessarily feature in rivalry between any dominant power in Asia Minor and the Bosphorus, and forces controlling Iran and Central Asia. From the time of Darius and Xerxes, this political tug-of-war has been an ever-present factor in Near Eastern affairs, to which the arrival of tsarist and soviet Russia on the scene has merely added a new dimension. In all such clashes of empires, the Armenians have found themselves between two warring camps, to the detriment of their economic and social development.

[1] Herodotus, *Histories*, VII. 73.
[2] Strabo, *Geography*, XI. iv. 8.

To survive in such a maelstrom demands rare qualities of physical and mental endurance and adaptability. That great student of Armenia, H. F. B. Lynch, once remarked that the distinguishing characteristic of the Armenians is *grit* – toughness and endurance – to which they owe their continued existence as a people. An excellent modern example of this quality is provided by the Soviet elder statesman Mr Mikoyan, with his amazing powers of survival.

Many of the neighbours of the Armenians in antiquity have vanished from the map, like the Hittites and the people of Mitanni, once mighty rivals of the Egyptian Pharaohs, as well as the Caucasian Albanians; relapsed into barbarism, like the Kurds, descendants of the proud Medes; or else shrunk into obscurity, like the modern Assyrians. Only the Armenians like their neighbours, the Georgians, have forged a national and cultural unity which has stood the test of centuries of alien domination. This unity, based on a common language, civilization and religious faith, and backed by uncommon personal tenacity and courage, has survived persecutions which were intended to result in the nation's total extermination. The Armenians of today are among the most dynamic of the peoples of the Soviet Union, with an outstanding economic growth rate, and standards in education and medical science on a par with the nations of Western Europe.

Despite the massacre of one million and a half Armenians in 1915, and the depopulation of vast areas of Turkey's eastern *vilayets* (formerly comprising Turkish Armenia), estimates made in 1965 give the number of Armenians living in the Soviet Union, including the Armenian SSR, as 3,200,000, and those living abroad, in Western Europe, North and South America, India, the Arab countries and elsewhere, at around 1,200,000. The total population of the Armenian SSR, including non-Armenian elements, is given as 2,200,000.

These estimates are, if anything, probably too conservative. The ethnic picture of the USSR itself is complex, and there is a great deal of overlapping. Whereas a substantial proportion of the population of the Armenian SSR is made up of Russians, Kurds, and Azeri Turks, it must be remembered that the Armenians still make up a large part of the urban element of Tbilisi, capital of the Georgian SSR, and Baku, capital of Soviet Azerbaijan. Armenians are numerous, if not an absolute majority, in the Nakhchevan Autonomous SSR, which forms an enclave between Armenia and Iran, and in the Mountain-Karabagh Autonomous District, which contains a number of ancient Armenian townships, but is now incorporated into the Azerbaijan SSR. Many Armenians living abroad have lost their separate identity, or been forced to adopt other religious faiths, notably Islam. If we take the number of Armenians or persons of Armenian extraction in the world today as between five and six million, we should not go far astray.

The events of their national past have had a marked effect on the national characteristics of the Armenians. Originally proud and warlike, they have often had to bow to an alien yoke, and cultivate qualities of diplomacy and guile to ensure physical survival. They are first-rate farmers, and outstanding craftsmen, excelling in every branch of handicraft, sculpture, and fine work in precious metals and textiles. Sober and industrious, they will work without respite for long hours. Armenians are extremely sociable and hospitable, and faithful to family and community ties. They have a truly Scottish regard for thrift and honesty, though they know how to drive a hard bargain.

Armenians are no cowards. In his autobiography, published in 1933, a British friend of Armenia, Sir Robert Windham Graves, praises the warlike qualities of those Armenians who volunteered for service with the Allied forces in World War I, adding:

'I mention this incident [of Armenian courage] in order to help in correcting the entirely erroneous impression which still lingers in some British circles that the Armenian is, like Canning's "Needy Knifegrinder", a "spiritless outcast" – a "wretch whom no sense of wrongs can rouse to vengeance", whereas I have known him for many years as a stout and intelligent fighter, able if given a fair chance to hold his own with those of any of the surrounding nations. This foolish notion exists chiefly in military and naval circles, and is a relic of the Crimean War when "bono Johnny" the Turk was our ally, and the Eastern Christian who generally sympathized with our enemies, not without reason, was regarded as a dog and son of a dog, no allowance being made for his having been the under-dog during centuries of oppression, when he had not the right to bear arms even in self-defence, and was too often driven to do the best that he could for himself in occupations which were parasitic or otherwise discreditable.'

When these words were written, Armenians had already shown what they could do as soldiers and administrators in the service of the sultan, of the khedive of Egypt, and of the nineteenth-century tsars. It is enough to recall the role of Nubar Pasha in Egypt, the heroism of General A. A. Tergukasov (1819–81) in the Russo-Turkish war of 1877–8, and the even more renowned name of Count M. T. Loris-Melikov (1825–88), the noted soldier and Minister of the Interior of Russia under Tsar Alexander II. At the close of World War I, the partisan general Andranik performed prodigies of valour against Turkish armies of overwhelming strength. During World War II, no less than 106 Armenian soldiers, sailors and airmen won the title of Hero of the Soviet Union, while sixty officers of Armenian descent rose to be admirals, generals or marshals of the Soviet Union. Best known of these are Marshal I. Kh. Bagramian, Admiral of the Fleet I.S. Isakov and Marshal of Aviation S. A. Khudyakov (Armenak Khanferiants).

In the town of Pazardjik in Bulgaria, on the railway line from Istanbul to Western Europe, there is a street named after a certain Ovanes Sevadjian. This Sevadjian was the local station master and cipher officer during the Russo-Turkish war of 1877–8, which freed the Bulgarian people from the Turkish yoke. When the Russian forces drew near, the Turkish commander-in-chief ordered the

10. Mr A. I. Mikoyan
11. Marshal I. Kh. Bagramian

military commandant in Pazardjik: 'Set fire to the town and deport the population.' This order came over the telegraph in code at a moment when high ranking Turkish officers were actually in Sevadjian's office, where the messages were received and dealt with. At the risk of his life, Sevadjian deciphered the telegram in the opposite sense, namely that the town and citizens were to be spared. To prevent verification, he put the original message in his mouth, chewed it up and swallowed it. A little later, Russian troops entered the town, which had been spared from destruction by an Armenian's courage and presence of mind.

Armenians in the Soviet Union, in Western Europe and in America have risen to the top of all the liberal and scientific professions. In medicine and physics, in school and university teaching and research, in literature, the cinema and radio, Armenians are found in key positions. William Saroyan is world-famous as novelist and story-teller; the name of Aram Khatchaturian is a household word in operatic and orchestral music; while Charles Aznavour is among the most popular figures in light music and song. The London musical scene is enriched by the violinist Manoug Parikian and by the talented music criticism of Felix Aprahamian; while the European and American operatic stages pay homage to the voices of prima donnas Lynne Dourian and Luisa-Anaïs Bosabalian. Henri Troyat is eminent as a literary historian and biographer.

The late Calouste Gulbenkian rivalled if he did not surpass the Rothschilds in the field of international finance, and set up by his testament a foundation which supports worth-while cultural and educational projects all over the world.

Other examples of Armenian enterprise and practical success are too numerous to mention individually. Readers of the *San Francisco Examiner* for December 3, 1967 could see on the front page a photograph of Mr Kirk Kerkorian – 'Croesus in the Desert' – in conjunction with the following article, which had been transmitted from Las Vegas by special correspondent Frank Purcell:

'A publicity-shunning San Francisco Bay Area financial genius disclosed yesterday he is gambling $80 million that he can pioneer a "Second Strip" of plush hotels and casinos for this gambling mecca.

'Kirk Kerkorian, fifty, native of Fresno, now majority stockholder in the big Trans-International Airline Corp., headquartered in Oakland, thus stands second only to Howard Hughes, the brooding multimillionaire industrialist, in the no-limit game of buying and building that has brought Las Vegas into a period of unprecedented prosperity.

'Kerkorian, owner of the Flamingo Hotel and landlord for Caesar's Palace, two multimillion dollar showplaces on the exciting "strip", disagrees with those who contend this southern Nevada City may already have moved to the brink of saturation . . . '

After comparing the Howard Hughes and Kerkorian plans for developing Las Vegas, the *San Francisco Examiner* columnist concludes:

'When Kerkorian peeled $12.5 million from his bankroll to buy the Flamingo, and added another $2.5 million for an expansion program now under way, he was the largest stockholder in Trans-International Airlines Corp., with 1,822,000 shares. These were valued at $92 million. His land acquisition here and assorted financial odds and ends rounded out his tidy package.

'The airline now is in the process of being transferred into the gigantic Transamerica Corp., based in San Francisco, one of the world's largest holding companies.

'When the transaction is completed Kerkorian will own the biggest single block of stock in Transamerica.'

Truly one of the epic success stories of our time. But it would be wrong to conclude that the Armenians worship wealth and material success. They are deeply attached to their national church, which has long been a rallying point for the nation, the more particularly since the Bagratid kingdom of Ani was destroyed during the eleventh century, and the Cilician kingdom perished in the fourteenth. The Armenians certainly have a pronounced religious bent, and can often seem serious and subdued in manner. However, Armenian humour is also proverbial. Not for nothing does there exist in the Soviet Union a whole body of light-hearted jokes and sayings, which are popularly attributed to a fictitious source known as 'Radio Erevan'. The famous 'kinto' or Georgian Cockney humour of old Tbilisi was largely Armenian in origin.

Armenians are argumentative, quarrelsome, and great 'know-alls'. An Armenian officer in the old Ottoman army once remarked that he preferred to be in charge of a battalion of Turks than one made up of his fellow Armenians: the Turks obeyed without question, but each Armenian would have his own ingenious plan of campaign, and none would attack until they had all been discussed and tried out. In the Ottoman Empire, posts requiring intelligence and initiative were regularly filled by Armenians, especially in the fields of government administration and banking. Foreign residents in Turkey prior to 1915 regularly employed Armenian girls as maids and nurses, and men as porters, because of their trustworthy qualities. It was said in Istanbul: 'If you want something built, get an Armenian; if you want something destroyed, call a Turk.'

The fiery patriotism of the Armenian nation finds expression in the popular epic known variously as *David of Sassoun* or sometimes, *Sassna Dzourer*, 'The Daredevils of Sassoun'. A recent translator of the epic, Leon Surmelian, explains that this word *dzour* means 'twisted', 'mad', 'cracked' or even 'wacky', and has overtones of courage and heroism, of reckless adventures by daring fellows.

'The Armenian is *dzour* to begin with, he is mad, and he has survived by breaking the rules of history. He is a wild rebel by nature, a wild rebel with a dream. In Armenia we have the Don Quixote of nations. Armenians everywhere have taken to heart these indomitable and unpredictable screwballs of Sassoun who symbolize the magnificent crazy streak in the nation. These mountain giants deviate from the normal, the straight path is not for them, they will not play it safe, they will not do the conventional thing – and this quality has endeared them to other Armenians, who often had to bow before the inevitable, even if their submission to brute force was temporary and the national spirit was never wholly broken. The history of Armenia has been a series of insurrections and resurrections.'

The Armenian is one of nature's individualists, a leaven for the conformist mass of the human race. Logically he should have given up the struggle and lain down to die long ago. But he refused and still refuses to surrender, and here lies the key to understanding the nature of this dogged, invincible, little people, whose contribution to human civilization is out of all proportion to its numerical strength.

Chapter II

EARLIEST MAN IN ARMENIA

IN recent years, a fairly clear picture has begun to emerge of the oldest forms of human life in the Armenian uplands – a picture which provides a scientific background to the stories enshrined in such ancient legends as that of Noah's Ark. This is a comparatively recent development. While Western archaeologists, using the evidence of finds made in France, were reconstructing the evolution of man through the various phases and cultures of the Palaeolithic, Mesolithic and Neolithic epochs, some experts in Near Eastern archeology doubted whether any human life whatever had existed upon the territory of Armenia during the Old Stone Age. As recently as 1909, Jacques de Morgan could hold that Armenia, as well as the neighbouring Iranian plateau, was completely uninhabited by man during the greater part of the Pleistocene period, which began about a million years ago, and includes the great glaciations known successively as Günz, Mindel, Riss and Würm. Failing to take account of the incidence of the inter-glacial periods in Armenia, de Morgan thought of this highland region as continuously covered with thick sheets of ice, without intermission, for hundreds of thousands of years, thus rendering human life impossible. According to de Morgan's hypothesis, man first penetrated into Armenia during the Mesolithic or early Neolithic period, when the final melting of the great glaciers had flooded Mesopotamia, and forced survivors from the lower Tigris and Euphrates basins to take refuge in the Anatolian mountains.

However ingeniously it may explain Noah's arrival on Mount Ararat, this theory does not withstand the scrutiny of modern archaeology. We now know that interglacial phases occurred during the Pleistocene in Caucasia as well as in western Europe, creating excellent conditions for human life over lengthy periods. A series of discoveries made over the last thirty years demonstrate that Armenia and Transcaucasia are indeed among the regions with the most ancient remains of our early forefathers' activity and industry. It is relevant to note that the Garesja desert region east of Tbilisi in Soviet Georgia, and close to the northern border of Armenia, is the site of the discovery of fossil remains of a distinctive variety of anthropoid ape, the so-called *Udabnopithecus* (from Georgian 'udabno', a wilderness). This creature occupied an intermediary position between the chimpanzee and the gorilla. The find was made in 1939 by Soviet geologists N. O. Burchak-

Abramovich and E. G. Gabashvili. The remains are extremely fragmentary – two teeth, one being a molar – but they represent the only ancient anthropoid ape remains found on the territory of the USSR. Some Soviet scholars regard this discovery as an indication that Transcaucasia was among the regions of the world where the transition from ape-man to *Homo faber* – pre-men, still slightly ape-like and not wholly men, but creatures who had nevertheless the gift of technical invention – took place during the early phases of the Pleistocene epoch.

In the absence of more substantial finds of fossil ape or ape-man from the Caucasus region, we are thrown back on the evidence of ancient stone implements or artifacts. Kenneth Oakley remarks in his classic monograph, *Man the Tool-Maker*,[1] that 'man is a social animal, distinguished by "culture": by the ability to make tools and communicate ideas'. Apes, it is true, may occasionally improvize tools or implements for the solution of some immediately visible problem: a chimpanzee has been seen to fit together two bamboo tubes in order to secure a bunch of bananas dangling beyond reach outside his cage; on another occasion, this chimpanzee fitted into one bamboo tube a piece of wood which he had specially sharpened for the purpose with the aid of his teeth. However, to conceive the idea of shaping a stone or stick according to a regular pattern, and for use in some imagined future eventuality, is beyond the mental capacity of any known apes. The systematic making of tools implies a marked capacity for conceptual thought, and it is on the basis of finds of such tools in Armenia and other parts of the Caucasus that we are able to postulate the existence of man in this area from very early times, not less than half a million years ago.

The problem of man's earliest stone industries is complicated, it is true, by what are known as eoliths – naturally fractured stones, which sometimes resemble the earliest hand axes chipped by man. In fact, naturally fractured stone probably served as the first implements ever used by our remote forefathers. Even at the present time, there are backward tribes who use bits of sharp stone, shells or sharks' teeth as tools. Australian aborigines will even cut down trees with an unflaked piece of stone which has an unusually sharp edge. Near Clermont (Oise), in strata dating from about fifty million years ago, the late Abbé Henri Breuil once collected a large batch of flints that at first sight resembled the earliest artifacts fashioned by primitive man. Further research showed that the flints thus fashioned in the shape of implements had been crushed between blocks of stone rolled along by moving glaciers. Under the influence of various natural phenomena – rupture by glacial pressure, the effect of heat, or sharp changes of atmospheric temperature – flints have often been shaped in such a way as to mimic the tools of prehistoric man. Such freaks are naturally valueless when it comes to proving the ancient presence of man upon the earth.

Accidentally formed eoliths are not rare in Armenia. However, we are also well supplied with genuine evidence of ancient Stone Age industries in this area, as

[1] 5th ed., London, 1965, p. 1.

46

also in Abkhazia, on the Black Sea coast. It is true that we have as yet nothing approaching the antiquity of pebble-tools found in several parts of Africa in deposits from the end of the Villafranchian stage, nor can Armenia rival such spectacular sites as the Olduvai gorge. Yet the presence of a large and flourishing Abbevillian (Chellean) culture in Armenia and western Georgia, dating back at least four or five hundred thousand years, has been demonstrated over the last twenty-five years by a group of Soviet archaeologists, and also by several Turkish and Western scholars working in the territory of former Turkish Armenia, who have between them revolutionized our notions of the earliest human settlements in the Caucasian region.

At the time when primitive man first appeared in Armenia, probably between half a million and one million years ago, the climate was comparatively mild and humid. Characteristic fauna were the hippopotamus, the elephant *(Elephas armeniacus, Elephas trogontherii pohlig)*, the rhinoceros *(Rhinoceros mercki)*, a prototype of the horse *(Equus stenonis)*, the camel *(Camelus knoblochi)*, the ox *(Bos primigenius)*, the sabre-toothed tiger, and the stag *(Cervus elaphus)*. These lower Pleistocene fauna of Armenia are well known from the fundamental study by L. A. Avakian,[1] who lists a number of rare animal remains found near Leninakan, including the species of rhinoceros known as *Dicerorhinus etruscus*, also the hardy *Mammuthus trogontherii*. Of the special interest are the numerous finds of animal bones made by A. K. Vekua in Lower Pleistocene lake deposits at the foot of the dacitic hill of Amiranis-mta near the Georgian town of Akhalkalaki, just north of the Armenian border. On this spot, it seems that a large number of animals were hemmed in by a violent volcanic eruption, covering their pasture and hunting grounds with sheets of molten lava, causing them to perish. Vekua identified several new species of fauna at Amiranis-mta, including the *Hippopotamus georgicus Vekua*, and a new variety of prototype horse, the *Equus hipparionoides Vekua*. The same scientist found on this site remains of another ancestor of the modern horse, *Equus süssenbornensis*. A. K. Vekua's findings, published in 1962, certainly strengthen the presumption that the Armenian highlands were one of the original habitats of the equine species.[2]

At that time, Armenia was thickly covered with plants and trees, including the oak *(Quercus iberica)*, the maple, the elm *(Ulmus foliacea Gilib.)*, the willow and the common berberis. Many sub-tropical evergreens, now found in the humid coastal regions of Lazistan and Mingrelia on the Black Sea, then flourished also on the Armenian plateau.

The earliest stone tools found in Armenia belong to an ancient primitive stage in human development: the Abbevillian or Chellean culture. Credit for their

[1] L. A. Avakian, *Chetverichnye iskopaemye mlekopitayushchie Armenii* ('The Quaternary fossil mammals of Armenia'), Erevan, 1959.

[2] A. K. Vekua, *Akhalkalakskaya nizhnepleistotsenovaya fauna mlekopitayushchikh* ('The Akhalkalaki Lower Pleistocene mammal fauna'), Tbilisi, 1962.

discovery – the most ancient remains of human activity in the territory of the Soviet Union – belongs to two Soviet archaeologists, S. A. Sardarian and M. Z. Panichkina, working on a site known as Satani-dar or Satan's Hill close to Mount Bogutlu (Artin), on the south-western slopes of Mount Alagöz (Aragats). This region is rich in obsidian, a glassy volcanic rock of acid composition, consisting of a combination of silica, aluminium, calcium, iron, potassium and sodium, extremely hard and brittle, and ideal for splitting into sharp-edged hand axes and similar tools. In this respect, the Abbevillian industries of Armenia differ from those discovered in 1958 by an expedition of the Georgian Academy of Sciences headed by N. Berdzenishvili, at sites in Abkhazia, on the Black Sea coast of Transcaucasia. The Abkhazian tools are fashioned from local flint, which is also good material for implement making, though less outstanding in quality than the volcanic obsidian characteristic of Armenia.

Many of the Abbevillian hand axes recovered by Sardarian and his colleagues can be seen in the Historical Museum of Armenia in Lenin Square, Erevan. They weigh up to $1\frac{1}{2}$ kilograms, and are usually about 15 centimetres long. They were made by selecting an oval lump of rock of approximately the desired size, which was then flaked all round the edges first in one direction, and then in the other, so that they became two-faced lumps (bifaces), roughly oval or pear-shaped in outline, with a sinuous or zigzag margin formed by the intersection of deep-biting flake scars. In France, the archetypal Abbevillian hand-axes made from flint nodules are found in the gravels of the 40-metre terrace of the River Somme, perhaps dating from a warm interlude, or interstadial, between two stages of the second, or Mindel glaciation. The Chellean hand-axes from Armenia have been compared by their finder, Sardarian, to specimens found by G. and A. de Mortillet in the Garonne estuary near Toulouse, and now preserved in the museum of St Germain-en-Laye.

These Abbevillian or Chellean hand-axes with deep flake scars were evidently made by a hard hammer stone, or on the edge of a heavy anvil-stone. They were general-purpose tools, and apparently not fitted with hafts. In fact, they were not really axes in the modern sense, but served mainly for cutting and scraping, as well as burrowing in the ground. Alongside these standard *coups-de-poing*, as they are termed, we also find roughly shaped tools of different sizes and shapes, which were improvised to meet the special needs of the moment.

Turkish archaeologists have also been investigating the hill country immediately north of the town of Kars, the fortress town close to the Turco-Soviet border. Implements of the Abbevillian and the later Acheulean type were found in the neighbourhood of Kisir Dagh. As this place is only about 50 miles away from the sites on Alagöz (Aragats), it is clear that we have a major complex of early workshops, straddling both sides of the Arpa Chai. A useful map of these sites was given by the Soviet archaeologist V. P. Lyubin in 1957.[1]

---

[1] See *Sovetskaya Arkheologiya* ('Soviet Archaeology'), Moscow, tom. XXVII.

The identification in Armenia of a distinctive local Abbevillian (Chellean) culture is of great interest; it links the Armenian highlands with a vast complex of such early centres of human activity, stretching from southern England, France and Spain through the Mediterranean, including the Sahara region and Egypt, also south and east Africa, Palestine and Syria, across to southern India and then on as far as north-eastern China. A glance at the world map shows the focal position of Armenia in this system of early tool-making cultures. V. P. Lyubin has pointed out that during the early Pleistocene epoch, the Murat-Su, a major tributary of the Euphrates, must have offered an unusually good environment for permanent habitation by early Palaeolithic man, due to its good climatic conditions, presence of natural rock shelters, and abundant fresh water. It seems likely that this river, which collects the waters of the peaks west of Mount Ararat, and runs north of Lake Van westwards deep into central Anatolia, already served as an important channel of cultural migrations between Caucasia and the Fertile Crescent region throughout the Palaeolithic period.

The next stage in Stone Age technology is known as the Acheulean culture, from St Acheul near Amiens, where flint implements of a distinctive type were found in 1834 by Rigollot in gravel-pits on the banks of the Somme. The Acheulean culture represents an evolution from the Abbevillian (Chellean) towards a more elegant and refined technique in preparation of stone implements. The *coup-de-poing* is better made, and a new oval form known as the ovate develops, sometimes with a kind of S-shaped twist along the sides of the tools. Some Acheulean flint artifacts receive the name of *limandes* or 'dabs', because they resemble the outline of a flat fish. Others are pointed or almond-shaped.

The Acheulean culture is well represented in Armenia, Sardarian's explorations on Mount Artin having yielded over 400 obsidian artifacts of various shapes and sizes. The Acheulean period, broadly speaking, extends from the end of the Abbevillian, perhaps around 400,000 BC, right up to the Middle Palaeolithic or Mousterian, which began around 100,000 BC. Cultural development was very slow, and these industries remained practically uniform over nearly one-fifth of the world. Many Acheulean hand-axes dug up in localities as widely separated as, for example, the Cape of Good Hope, Kenya, Madras and London, are virtually indistinguishable from those found in Armenia, except for their being made from different types of rock.

The Acheulean culture takes in the period of the Riss glaciation. The previous glacial period, known as Mindel, coincided with the end of the Abbevillian culture, and had severe effects on life throughout Europe. However, the Mindel glaciation did not affect so markedly the climate of Armenia, which lay to the south of the main belt of frost and ice. Thus, none of the arctic flora or fauna characteristic of the Mindel glaciation phase in northern Europe are found in Armenia.

This meant that human life in Armenia could go on with the minimum of disruption. Whereas hand-axe makers disappeared entirely from north-western

49

Europe during the maximum of the second (Mindel) glaciation, in Armenia their existence was scarcely interrupted, so that the transition from the Abbevillian to the Acheulean culture is less abrupt. Sardarian is able to classify the Acheulean obsidian tools from Satani-dar in consecutive stages of development, representing early-Acheulean, middle-Acheulean and late-Acheulean cultures.

In addition to the standard types of Acheulean worked cores, we also encounter in Armenia worked splinters of the type known as Clactonian (from Clacton-on-Sea, England), and Levalloisian (from Levallois, a Paris suburb). Levallois industries are marked by the preparation of cores resembling tortoises in general form. The idea was to shape a block of flint or obsidian in such a way that flakes could be struck from one facet, ready to use just as they came. Sardarian also assembled a fine collection of obsidian and also dacite knives, scrapers, choppers, borers and drills, fully comparable with those from sites in western Europe. Some of these implements also served as spear heads, darts and spikes. Though often found in conjunction with the larger Acheulean hand-axes, artifacts of the Clactonian and Levallois type represent a definite stage forward towards greater specialization in the making and use of stone tools and weapons, and are characteristic of the later phases of Acheulean culture.

Besides the Satani-dar site, Acheulean settlements have been located at other points in Armenia, notably in the vicinity of the health resort of Arzni, 18 kilometres north of Erevan. Here the River Razdan runs down from Lake Sevan towards the Araxes plain, forming convenient terraces and plateaux with plentiful supplies of river and mineral waters. Acheulean hand-axes made of black, red and grey obsidian were found in the area of Arzni as long ago as 1933, by the geologist A. P. Demekhin, and further explorations were made by the archaeologists S. N. Zamyatnin and M. Z. Panichkina. Taken together with numerous Acheulean sites between Gagra and Sukhumi on the Black Sea, and those located in southern Ossetia, immediately south of the main Caucasian chain, these Armenian settlements of the Acheulean era testify to the existence of a considerable, if scattered population throughout Transcaucasia at periods ranging between 400,000 and 100,000 BC.

During the middle phase of the Acheulean culture, Armenia was strongly affected by the Riss glaciation. Heat-loving evergreen trees and sub-tropical vegetation vanished, as did the sabre-toothed tiger and other mammals which flourish in hot climates. Other animals had to adapt themselves to cooler surroundings by growing protective woolly coats, so that we find the mammoth supplanting the elephant, and the woolly rhinoceros *(Rhinoceros tichorhinus)* replacing his cousin, *Rhinoceros mercki*. Heat-loving evergreens, such as are now found on the humid shores of the Caspian and Black Sea, retreated from the Armenian plateau, to be replaced by beech, oak and other deciduous trees.

Human life at this stage was, of course, highly primitive. Man hardly differed in outward appearance from the brute creation. People lived in small groups, without any fixed abode, subsisting on hunting and gathering wild fruits, nuts and berries. Edible roots were grubbed out with crude stone tools, and fruits and nuts growing high up in trees were knocked down by means of long sticks. Towards the end of the Acheulean culture, fire came into general use, and people began to clothe themselves in animal pelts.

Apart from Transcaucasia, the main centres of the Acheulean culture in the Soviet Union are the southern Ukraine, Kiik-Koba in the Crimea, and Turkmenia, on the eastern shores of the Caspian.

Our knowledge of early human life in Armenia broadens considerably when we reach the Mousterian – a term used by Soviet scholars to include the cultures dated from between about 100,000 and 40,000 BC, which Western archaeologists group more loosely under the rubric 'Middle Palaeolithic'. The Mousterian is the material culture of Neanderthal man, and has been found at many localities in western Asia, Europe, and North Africa. The earliest Neanderthalers with Mousterian culture, such as those of Ehringsdorf near Weimar, lived under the mild conditions which prevailed in Europe during the latter part of the third, or Riss-Würm interglacial period; their nomadic, out-door mode of life was similar to that of the Acheuleans. The later or typical Mousterian culture developed in Europe under the cold tundra conditions brought about by the fourth, or Würm glaciation, which also affected the climate of Armenia to a marked extent. The Neanderthalers adapted themselves to the rigours of the climate by using caves as dwellings, and wrapping themselves up in animal skins; they lit fires to keep warm and to drive away the fierce carnivores which prowled around their cavern doors. They were fearless and skilful hunters, and used wooden spears and stone missiles to hunt mammoth and woolly rhinoceros.

At the close of the Acheulean and during the Mousterian epoch, essential changes took place in the structure of the human body. The ancient ape-man or *Pithecanthropus* and his successors, *Homo habilis* or *Homo faber*, had gradually developed into people with recognizable human traits. These Neanderthalers, so-called after the site at Neanderthal near Düsseldorf where the most famous specimen was found, were of low stature, around 5 feet high, thickset, slightly stooping, and walking and running with a clumsy gait. They had bandy legs, low shoulders and a bent back. With his prognathous face, receding forehead, and eyes sunk deeply in their orbits and overhung by a large bony protuberance, our Neanderthaler was not a prepossessing individual. The head rested on a short thick neck, which formed a single whole, so to speak, with the flat back of the head.

The Soviet archaeologist G. A. Bonch-Osmolovsky studied the hand formation of a Neanderthal man from Kiik-Koba in the Crimea, and found it to be very powerful, rough and clumsy, with broad, stump-like fingers. Strongly developed muscles gave it immense strength, but it lacked the flexible mobility of the hand of modern man. Particularly interesting for the study of Neanderthal man in central Asia is the grave of an eight or nine year old boy, discovered in 1938 by A. P.

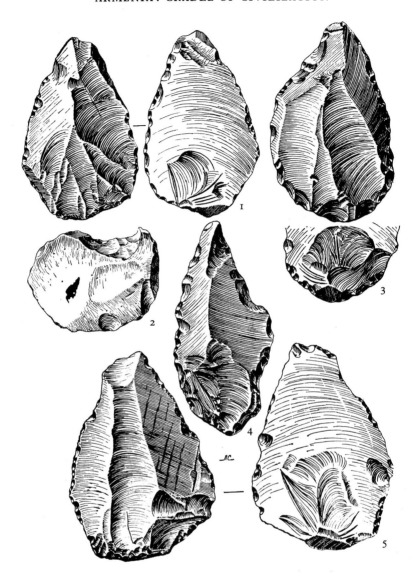

12. Primitive obsidian tools (Middle Palaeolithic)

Okladnikov in the Teshik-Tash grotto in south Uzbekistan, from which the sculptor M. M. Gerasimov made his well-known reconstruction. Father Teilhard de Chardin once divided Neanderthal man into two main groups, the 'savages' and the 'advanced' type. The 'savages' who lived in Java, Rhodesia and elsewhere, are those with the flattest cranium, the more receding forehead, projecting face, and generally ape-like appearance. The 'advanced' Neanderthaler, who lived in Palestine, western Asia, and Germany, were the more 'civilized' men of the epoch, with prominent cheek bones, a relatively tall forehead, a well-formed chin, and jaws less projecting than the average of the species.

Mousterian man in Armenia greatly improved the techniques of fashioning obsidian tools which had been evolved by his Acheulean forerunners. The Neanderthalers made side-scrapers, disc-cores, flake-tools, knives, spearheads and small points resembling arrowheads, as well as hand-axes or more traditional shapes. They sharpened the edges of weapons and implements by minute retouching and 'resolved' chipping, as the technique is called. They do not seem to have worked bone, though they selected large, hard bones such as those of bison for use as chopping blocks or anvils. Some of these Neanderthalers were cannibals; they were organized loosely into tribes or clans, often buried their dead with care, and covered themselves with manganese dioxide and red ochre for ritual ceremonies and magic rites.

The region just south of the Caucasus range, taking in Georgia, Abkhazia and Armenia, was a most important centre for the evolution and diffusion of the culture of the Neanderthal man during the Mousterian period. No less than twenty-five Mousterian sites are known on or near the Black Sea coast of Abkhazia and Mingrelia (the ancient Colchis), as well as five in the Rioni valley and twenty along the River Kura (Mtkvari) and its tributaries. Mousterian remains found in Kudaro cave in Ossetia contain bones of rhinoceros, chamois, marmot, badger, mole, otter, hamster, hare and weasel.

In Soviet Armenia, Mousterian sites are known in the same area of Mount Artin which had been inhabited by early man during the Abbevillian and Acheulean culture periods; also near the village of Pemzashen, immediately to the northwest of Mount Alagöz, and at Noemberian, on the Armenian-Azerbaijan frontier. Particularly important are the numerous finds from Arzni and other points along the valley of the River Razdan, as it runs down from Lake Sevan towards Erevan; these were first published by M. Z. Panichkina in 1950. The Mousterian artifacts from the River Razdan number over 340 items, of a wide variety of shapes and types, some resembling the Kiik-Koba cave finds from the Crimea, others comparable with the flint implements from Teshik-Tash in Uzbekistan, others again recalling Mousterian artifacts from Umm-Qatafa near Jerusalem, as published by R. Neuville in 1931.

In the former Turkish Armenia, Mousterian artifacts have been recovered at widely separated sites, including the River Borluk valley south of Kars, and also, fully 120 miles away, near the small town of Liz, west of Lake Van and north-east of Mush. Liz is close to the Murat-Su, thus strengthening the argument put forward by Lyubin, namely that this river valley served as an important cross-cultural artery between Armenia and the Fertile Crescent during many phases of Anatolian prehistory.

The next phase in human life in Armenia is the Upper Palaeolithic period, extending from approximately 40,000 to 12,000 BC, and often referred to as the

Reindeer Age. Throughout most of Europe and northern Asia the climate was still cold and, at the beginning of the period, very humid. The glaciers had scarcely moved since the heyday of Neanderthal man, and they still covered the greater part of northern Europe and Siberia. In Armenia, glaciers and frozen snow extended far down the sides of Ararat, Alagöz, Bingöl and the other great mountain peaks. A few hundred miles to the north, the perpetual snow line on the main Caucasian range, steady today at between 2,800 and 3,400 metres, was then as low as 1,200–1,300 metres. Mammoth, reindeer and woolly rhinoceros lived in more or less numerous herds, and are typical of the fauna of the epoch. In Armenia, we find remains of the mammoth, the ancestor of the horse *(Equus caballus)*, the bison and the stag *(Cervus elaphus)*.

Two milder, 'inter-stadial' phases are distinguished within this great Würm glaciation; during these the temperature became more clement. But soon the frost returned, and this time it was dry and more severe generally. Then to the animals aforementioned were added the aurochs, saiga antelopes, chamois, marmots and some jerboas. Many of these animals are known to us not only from their semi-fossilized remains, but from the wonderful cave paintings which extend from Altamira in northern Spain, through Périgord and other regions of France, right across to the Urals in Russia, thus testifying to the artistic mastery of these remote ancestors of modern man.

The earliest Upper Palaeolithic culture, formerly called Lower Aurignacian but now known as Chatelperronian, was already foreshadowed in Acheulean times. The Chatelperronian probably originated not far from Armenia. According to Oakley,[1] it spread, possibly from south-western Asia, to western Europe before the end of the Mousterian, so that in France, as in Palestine, there was some mingling of the two traditions. The Chatelperronians used a knife made from a blade of stone with one edge straight and razor-like, the other curved over to a point and blunted by abrupt trimming; such implements are by no means rare in Armenia – at least eighteen specimens were collected by Sardarian.

There is some dispute among scholars as to whether the early Upper Palaeolithic cultures, notably that known as Aurignacian after the great French type-station, evolved directly from the culture of Neanderthal man, namely the Mousterian. Most western archaeologists consider that the Aurignacian culture was introduced into Europe by some immigrant peoples coming from the east, and known as Cro-Magnon man. The Cro-Magnons were taller and more gracefully built than the crouching Neanderthalers. Western scholars would hold that the Cro-Magnons evolved independently from the Neanderthalers, whom they then ousted by superior intelligence and technical achievements. Soviet archaeologists, faithful to their evolutionary and environmental tenets, would assert that the Cro-Magnon, and indeed modern *homo sapiens*, are lineal descendants of Neanderthal man, who simply developed into a more efficient and

[1] *Man the Tool-maker*, p. 57.

54

aesthetically pleasing type of being by a process of natural development and selection.

The rich Middle Aurignacian culture is particularly well represented in Armenia and Georgia. Giorgi Nioradze (1886–1951) studied the Aurignacian cave camp of Devis-Khvreli in the Shorapani district of Georgia, where he found a human jawbone and many flint implements and animal bones, enabling him to make an impressive reconstruction of the life of Upper Palaeolithic man in Georgia. For Armenia, we have to rely mainly on obsidian tools made on Mount Artin and in the Razdan valley. Plans exist for systematic exploration of the numerous caves and grottoes adjoining the River Razdan finds. By analogy with Georgia, and having regard to the severe climate of Aurignacian days, there is little doubt that Armenia too will yield evidence of extensive occupation of cave stations by the men of Aurignacian culture.

Tools and weapons of the Aurignacian culture are noted for their wonderful fluting technique, difficult to copy even today. Gone are the Mousterian side-scrapers with their 'resolved' chipping. Instead we have finely made end-scrapers, keeled or otherwise, in which percussion flakes rise fan-wise to a central point. Burins are often met with, also points having a sharp working edge and blunted back, developing from the Chatelperronian. Sometimes there are double-purpose tools, a graver at one end, and an end-scraper at the other. Tools were also fashioned from bone, and these are well attested in Armenian sites of this period. Well made dacite and obsidian knives from the Aurignacian culture are found on Mount Artin and at other points in Armenia. In fact, the recovery of part-worked slabs of obsidian and dacite, together with chippings and flakes lying about nearby, shows that Mount Artin was for thousands of years a veritable tool factory, from which ready-made implements as well as chunks of partly trimmed or unfinished rock were regularly exported to surrounding regions.

It is interesting to note that the Soviet archaeologist E. I. Krupnov[1] considers that there were considerable movement of Caucasian tribes into European Russia in the period of the Aurignacian culture. Comparisons have been made between a certain type of finely retouched flint arrow and dart head associated with the Georgian site of Gvarjilas-klde, and similar finds from Kostenki and Borshevo, in the Russian plain near Voronezh. The conclusion is that, during the Upper Palaeolithic epoch, tribes from Transcaucasia, and perhaps from as far south as Armenia, diffused specialized methods of fashioning stone implements in regions north of the Caucasus range, namely round about the Sea of Azov, and along the Don and the Volga.

On the basis of another group of obsidian implements from the Alagöz area, it has been suggested by Sardarian that a specialized Upper Palaeolithic culture, the Solutrean, was also represented in Armenia. Now the Solutreans, so-called after the type station of Le Solutré, Dordogne, were a local culture group, relatively

[1] *Voprosy Istorii* ('Problems of History'), No. 5, 1966, pp. 27–40.

small in number, and highly specialized in their flint technology. They invented a type of slender javelin head, known from its shape as the 'laurel leaf' point, and perfected a pressure technique for flint flaking, enabling them to retouch their implements all over, and not only at the edges.

The Solutreans are often said to have originated somewhere in Hungary, and to be a hybrid product of Neanderthal and Aurignacian man. Although they flourished at a number of points in south Russia, their existence in the Mediterranean and Near Eastern regions is usually denied. The appearance in Armenia of a genuine Solutrean culture would be a sensational event for Near Eastern archaeology. In the view of most other archaeologists, Sardarian has classed as 'Solutrean' the similar but much later products of the Neolithic age. The existence in Armenia of a genuine Solutrean culture seems for the moment to be ruled out.

In Armenia, as in many other parts of the inhabited world, prehistoric man of between 40 and 30 thousand years ago was already *homo sapiens*. His cerebral functions and even his moral and religious aspirations differed relatively little from what these were subsequently throughout the early historical period of human history, and still are today. Economic and social life was entering on a more advanced and better organized phase, now that men had lost their ape-like features, walked fully erect, and had the hands of modern human beings.

Though hunting and the gathering of fruits and berries remained the chief forms of Upper Palaeolithic man's economic activity, he also learnt how to fish and finally may even have begun to tame dogs and other beasts. Where no natural caves or shelters were to be found, he made tents out of skins and even elaborate semi-underground dwellings, roofed with logs and earth, as have been found in south Russia. Regarding his social organization, many Soviet scholars, led by M. O. Kosven, believe that the Upper Palaeolithic witnessed the formation of the institution of 'matriarchate', or the matriarchal clan system, which is also stated to have continued through the Mesolithic and Neolithic periods.[1] Certainly Upper Palaeolithic man, especially in Russia, had a marked propensity for carving statuettes of nude women, mostly with large bellies and heavy-sagging breasts, to symbolize the elements of fertility and child-bearing, though a number of slim and elegantly proportioned figurines are also found.

The Aurignacian culture era was followed by the Magdalenian, the last great phase of the advanced or Upper Palaeolithic phase in human prehistory. The Magdalenian culture takes its name from La Madeleine, a rock shelter near Les Eyzies in the Dordogne, though it also extends throughout many regions of Europe and western Asia. The Magdalenian began in the last recurrence of the Würm glaciation, and extended right into the milder post-glacial period. Tools made from bone, horn, antler and ivory are numerous and most beautifully made. The skill in bone-working of these peoples is indicated by their fine-eyed needles, with which they stitched themselves garments from skins and furs. It was now

[1] M. O. Kosven, *Matriarkhat. Istoriya problemy* ('Matriarchate. The history of the problem.'), Moscow, 1948.

that cave art, first manifesting itself in Aurignacian times, reached its highest level of development. Stone implements of this epoch from Europe as well as from Armenia and Georgia are most competently made, though the perfection of middle Aurignacian workmanship is seldom again attained. New types of stone implements included saw-blades, gravers (burins), double-ended scrapers, spoke-shaves, and ingenious tools designed to be fitted on to wooden or bone shafts and handles.

It is usually supposed that the Magdalenians were nomadic and that in rocky areas like the Caucasus, as in central France, they occupied the mouths of caves during winter, and followed migrating herds of game during summer. In the grasslands of southern Russia, the mammoth hunters built earth houses for winter use, while in summer they dwelt in tents and lightly built huts. Rings of stones marking the sites of skin huts of Magdalenian reindeer hunters have been found in north Germany. The Magdalenians hunted mainly with spears, and to judge from some of their cave paintings, they also drove their quarry into snares and traps.

In Armenia, traces of the Magdalenians are found at the old haunts of Stone Age man around Mount Alagöz at Mount Artin (Satani-dar), also at Ani-Pemsa on the lower reaches of the River Akhurian, and along the course of the River Razdan above Erevan. In many cases, these finds of Magdalenian artifacts are associated with scattered obsidian microliths, or miniature stone implements, classified as being of the Azilian type. This is a later phase of human culture, dating already from the Mesolithic or Middle Stone Age, perhaps around 10,000 BC. So far as we know at present, the Magdalenians do not appear to have left any outstanding monuments of Upper Palaeolithic art in Armenia, though it may be that discoveries await us in the future.

Much remains to be done before the study of Palaeolithic man in Armenia can be regarded as complete or even comprehensive. However, we have enough evidence to establish Armenia's right to rank as one of the cradles of human civilization. Over the last few decades, Soviet archaeologists have shown that areas in the Armenian highlands were inhabited for lengthy periods, first by the *pithecanthropus* or ape man, then by *Homo habilis* and man of the Neanderthal type, and finally by modern *Homo sapiens* – in all, a span of prehistory extending over at least half a million years. Therefore Armenia takes its place as one of the most ancient hearths of human culture, and a link in the continuous chain of the Palaeolithic cultures of southern Asia, the Mediterranean, central Europe and Africa.

Chapter III

EARLY FARMING, COMMUNITY LIFE AND TECHNOLOGY IN ARMENIA

BY the end of the Upper Palaeolithic period, the climate of Europe and of Caucasia was becoming steadily milder. The arctic conditions which prevailed throughout its middle phases had disappeared, the mean annual temperature was rising, and forests appeared where frozen steppes and tundra had been before. Most of the old Quaternary or Pleistocene fauna either became extinct or migrated to cooler regions farther north. The snow line on Mount Ararat and the Caucasian range receded to a higher level, and many glaciers melted away.

Magdalenian man with his wonderful culture and art disappeared, his place being taken by a number of different, more or less isolated peoples, who occupied most of Europe and parts of Asia until the arrival of the true Neolithic civilization. During this Mesolithic or Middle Stone Age, art and industry were in definite retreat, partly because the mellow climatic conditions removed much of the incentive, indeed stark necessity which had driven Upper Palaeolithic man towards higher achievement and artistic self-expression. Stone implements now consisted mostly of very small microliths, comprising crescents or lunates, triangles, blunted backs and the like, also small burins and borers. The men of the Mesolithic period discovered the advantage of composite tools, having the haft made of one material, such as wood or bone, and the working edges of another, such as flint or, in Armenia, obsidian. Thus a wooden or bone haft, which is light and handy, could be used to mount a series of pygmy knife blades or saw teeth, made of sharp, brittle stone.

The Mesolithic of Armenia and Georgia is reckoned to extend roughly from 12,000 to perhaps 6000 BC, though by the latter period, the pre-pottery Neolithic was well into its stride in areas of Armenia bordering on Anatolia and Iran. Owing to his semi-nomadic way of life, the physical traces of Mesolithic man tend to be dispersed and lost, though there are some interesting examples in western Georgia,

58

such as the lower layer at the Odishi camping site near Zugdidi in Mingrelia, explored by A. N. Kalandadze in 1936–7. Along with numerous microliths, comparable with contemporary specimens from Iran and Iraq, the Odishi site also yielded a number of more substantial implements, resembling those of the so-called Campignian early Neolithic culture, and including pestles, graters, and partly polished stone hoe and mattock heads. These discoveries indicate that Transcaucasia, like central Anatolia, was among the first centres of settled agriculture in the ancient world. Other Mesolithic remains were found by B. A. Kuftin at a cave site in the Barmaksiz gorge in Trialeti, south-west of Tbilisi, and not far from the northern borders of Armenia. Here, microliths predominate, along with obsidian knives, while finds of various wild animal bones, including horses, also occur.

An important advance in hunting technique took place during the Mesolithic with the spread of the bow and arrow. Many people became skilful fishermen, and the tame domestic dog was common. Food gathering afforded an ample subsistence for tribes inhabiting the Crimea and Caucasia, as the milder weather made edible shellfish, fruit and berries available to man in greater quantities. In Armenia, characteristic fauna now include the hare, the stag and an ancestor of the modern horse – *Equus caballus*, which had succeeded the earlier *Equus stenonis* of Palaeolithic times. The existence of these prehistoric horses in Armenia is of great significance for the vexed question of the original homeland of the modern horse, which a number of modern scholars are inclined to locate on the Armenian plateau.

Armenia was well to the forefront of human development during Mesolithic times. One of the most interesting Mesolithic cultures of the Near East, the Zarzian of the Zagros Mountains, is thought to have been introduced from the north, perhaps ultimately from the Russian steppes beyond the Caucasus. The occasional use of obsidian, the black volcanic glass, indicates links with the region north and west of Lake Van, whence this material was exported. The richest site of the Zarzian culture is Shanidar (layer B2), lying in northern Iraq, just south of the present-day Turkish border, where the Mesolithic layer is dated to between 10,000 and 9000 BC.

In Armenia proper, Mesolithic settlements are recorded at Areguni Blur on Mount Artin. Obsidian microliths intended as inserts for harpoons, spears and arrows are found both in fixed stations on Mount Artin, and as isolated deposits in scattered localities, thus attesting the nomadic life led by the inhabitants of the Armenian highlands in those days. Other clues to interpreting this way of life are provided by some very remarkable rock engravings met with in isolated recesses, rock shelters, and huge blocks of cliffs on Mount Alagöz, the hill chain of Geghaghmaghan, and the mountains of Siunia. These schematic figures picture hunting scenes, in which, for example, men armed with bow and arrow and spears, assisted by hounds, chase the chamois, wild sheep, roe deer and reindeer. The human and animal figures, unlike the Palaeolithic cave paintings of France and

Spain, are portrayed in miniature – rather as the full size stone implements of the Aurignacian and Magdalenian have by now given way to insignificant microliths. Although the technique is very simple and stylized, the impression of strenuous movement is well conveyed, while the animal drawings are accurate enough to permit identification of the species represented.

Great steps forward, which enabled man to break through the barrier between barbarism and civilization, occurred with the onset of the Neolithic or New Stone Age. The mode of life and general outlook of the folk of the New Stone Age was radically different from that of their Palaeolithic and Mesolithic forebears. In this 'Neolithic Revolution', at least five new discoveries or practices played a part:

1. Settled agriculture.
2. Domestication of animals.
3. Manufacture of pottery.
4. Tool-making by grinding and polishing technique.
5. Sewing, weaving and textile manufacture.

The first two of these by themselves would have enabled man to lead a far less precarious existence than formerly, for he could now store food against times of dearth. A country like Armenia could obviously support a far larger population under these new conditions than it could when hunting and food collecting were the sole means of subsistence. Family and corporate organization could now become far more permanent and settled. Communal existence in turn led to specialization in work and craftsmanship, and to fresh breakthroughs in arts and crafts, also to the growth of a wide variety of religious cults with their attendant priestly castes.

The manufacture of pottery was well developed in Anatolia by about 6000 BC and played an important part in the refinement of home life. Armenia did not lag far behind, and pots with simple decorations, made up of rows of dots or linear patterns arranged in herring bone fashion, make their appearance at an early stage. The surface of an unbaked pot cries out for decoration, and gives ample scope for imaginative treatment in variety of form of the vessel itself, and in the development of various forms of painting and glazing. Simultaneously, the perfection of grinding and polishing techniques enabled men to obtain a tough cutting edge on flint and obsidian implements, such as could not be effected by chipping methods alone. A chipped edge, though sharp, is extremely brittle. Now that more durable tools were available to the craftsman, carpentry and woodwork became a practical proposition.

Naturally the fully-fledged Neolithic cultures of the Near East and Trans-caucasia did not spring into existence in a few brief generations. They were the result of a process of evolution from the Mesolithic stage, lasting in the more advanced regions of the 'Fertile Crescent' from about 9000 to 7000 BC. By the latter date, we find agriculture well established in Egypt, Jordan, Iran and parts of Anatolia. Even without actual grain, the presence of querns and mortars, pounders and grinders, also storage pits and sickle blades, all tell the same story of a basic change in the economy. At the same time, we find the first traces of permanent settlements, frequently rebuilt by successive inhabitants of a given site. Cemeteries appear, and the graves now contain such luxury objects as beads and pendants, showing that man had leisure for other pursuits than merely appeasing his physical hunger. At such sites as Çatal Hüyük in south-western Asia Minor, art makes its appearance in the form of animal carvings and statuettes of the supreme deity or mother goddess. There is evidence of regular commerce and by the end of this phase, the first towns are built, surrounded by defensive walls, often of massive proportions. These developments have been particularly well studied at Jericho, by the Dead Sea; also at a place called Jarmo in Kurdistan, not far south of the borders of ancient Armenia; and at Tepe Asiab, in the Kermanshah plain in western Iran.

The date and precise location of the very earliest settled farming communities is still a matter of active discussion among archaeologists. On March 14, 1967, the *Daily Telegraph* published a report issued by the Egyptian Antiquities Administration, claiming that the Nile valley was the first place in the world where agriculture was practised, and that ancestors of the Egyptians cultivated the land 14,000 years ago – when the rest of the world had scarcely entered the Mesolithic stage. This conclusion was based on excavations in Nubia by a team of American, Polish and Egyptian archaeologists over a period of six years. Hitherto it had been thought that agriculture was first practised some 9800 years ago, at Jericho and the hill sites of Iraq and southern Turkey. However, investigations at the Nubian villages of Toshka, Esna and Efdu, on the west bank of the Nile, produced striking new evidence. One well near Toshka was shown by Carbon-14 dating to have been sunk about 12,500 years ago. Thousands of flint tools and weapons and some grain grinders were found, and dated by Carbon-14 and electronic microscopes to around 12,000 BC onwards. A large number of human skeletons dating back between twelve and fourteen thousand years from the present day were also recovered at these villages. About 40 per cent of the males had been murdered by pushing small hard stones through the mouth and rectum, doubtless in the course of savage struggles over possession of narrow strips of scarce cultivated land. Farmers of this remote period still dwelt in caves or under some primitive, flimsy shelter, for no remains of permanent constructions were found at these Nubian sites.

Armenia itself is a land of some importance for the earliest history of farming. Scarcely any area in the world can boast of so wide a variety of wild and cultivated grains as can Transcaucasia: in her book, *The Neolithic Revolution*[1], Mrs Sonia Cole shows Armenia and Georgia among the original homelands of modern cereal plants. Armenia features among the areas where the hardy primitive wheat known as Einkorn was originally found, also as a homeland of wild two-row barley.

[1] 3rd. ed., London, 1965, p. 7.

Carbonized remains of various cereals are found widely distributed over a number of Neolithic sites in Armenia and Georgia; Neolithic pottery from Odishi near Zugdidi in Mingrelia actually has ornamental motifs portraying ears of corn.

As well as the usual stone and wooden digging implements and hoes, mattocks and picks of animal bone, fitted with wooden handles, were in use in Armenia. Reaping was done with wooden and bone sickles, furnished with small sharp teeth made from flint or obsidian. Finds of saddle querns, pestles and mortars show us how the ancestors of the Armenians ground their corn and prepared it for baking. Simple pottery storage jars, cooking pots and earthenware dishes, with rudimentary decoration in the form of patterns of dots or lines, also help to fill in the outline of what home life was like in Armenia seven or eight thousand years ago.

Tool making became more specialized, and formed the basis of a regular export industry. Many years ago, Jacques de Morgan located an obsidian tool factory in the region of Mount Alagöz. Other Neolithic tool industries existed at a number of points near Vagharshapat, the modern Echmiadzin, also at Eylar, some 15 kilometres north-east of Erevan, and around Nor-Bayazid, immediately south of Lake Sevan. As well as the usual ground and polished celts, axes, borers and end scrapers, Soviet archaeologists have remarked on the incidence in Armenia of a tool of unusual shape, rather like a bird's beak. The important site of Tilki Tepe or Shamiramalti near Lake Van, excavated by Belck as early as 1899, was inhabited from the beginning of the Neolithic onwards, and yielded up obsidian tools in vast numbers, as well as ornaments and cult figurines made from the teeth of wild beasts.

During the Neolithic period, man experimented with various methods of ploughing and tilling the soil. At first, he did little more than scratch the surface, sprinkle the seed about, and send his womenfolk to gather the ears of corn when they ripened later on. Subsequently, people felt the need for more intensive methods of cultivation. Man learnt by trial and error that ground deeply turned over yields better crops than earth that is merely cleared and lightly raked. The first deep digging tool was doubtless a simple wooden stake. Later on, stone heads were fixed to wooden shafts, and then, tips of copper and later, bronze. It is interesting that long after the invention of the plough, a primitive two-pronged fork was in constant use on hilly strips of land in such provinces as Sassoun, and is still found today in remote mountain districts. Called in Armenian *Erkmatni paytat*, and in Georgia, *Ortokhi*, this implement is handy for deep cultivation of small plots on rugged hillsides where ox teams cannot work. Large and massive in size, the tool has to be operated by a team of three men, two of whom together press down upon the footrest, while the other exercises leverage on the top of the handle. This implement, as S. T. Eremian points out, is a lineal descendant of the sharp wooden stake of Neolithic times.

The effect of recent archaeological discoveries by such investigators as Kathleen

Kenyon, R. J. and L. S. Braidwood, James Mellaart and others has been to extend our knowledge of Neolithic civilization in the Near East into a more distant past than was conceived of only a few decades ago. In fact, the old technological-evolutionary stages of 'Mesolithic', 'Neolithic', 'Chalcolithic' and so forth are losing their once sharp outlines, now that we see how they merge with and overlap one another in the various parts of the region. However, it is useful to have before one James Mellaart's suggested chronological sequence of the main culture phases as applied to the most advanced areas of the Near East, bearing in mind that the Armenian highlands probably lagged behind chronologically by several centuries:

Mesolithic, *c.* 10,000–9000 BC (frequently called 'Final Upper Palaeolithic')
Proto-Neolithic, *c.* 9000–7000 BC (instead of 'Mesolithic')
Neolithic, *c.* 7000–5600 BC
Early Chalcolithic, *c.* 5600–5000 BC
Middle Chalcolithic, *c.* 5000–4000 BC
Late Chalcolithic, *c.* 4000–3500 BC or later.

The southern parts of Armenia round about Lake Van benefited from contact with the sophisticated and advanced 'Halaf culture', which flourished from about 5500 to 4400 BC. Tell Halaf, which gives its name to the culture, is in northern Syria, but the best polychrome pottery comes from Arpachiyah in northern Iraq. In Mellaart's view, the Halaf culture was produced by newcomers from the north, and its homeland probably lies in the upper valleys of the Tigris and Euphrates, the region which later formed part of Greater Armenia. Early Halaf pottery is decorated in red or black on an apricot ground, and highly polished; it is notable for naturalistic representation of human beings, birds and animals. In the middle phase a cream slip is applied, and more elaborate shapes are found, with sharp flaring rims. In the final phase, large polychrome plates with sophisticated centre-pieces, featuring rosettes or Maltese crosses, are produced, to become one of the outstanding products of Near Eastern pottery. The Halaf people were great corn growers, and built houses of an original shape, set along paved roads; each house consisted of a round domed inner room and a rectangular ante-room, and was built from mud-pads on stone foundations. Similar houses are also found in parts of Armenia.

Though centred on northern Syria and Iraq, the Halaf culture had important and fruitful links with the Vannic region of Armenia. Indeed, beads, plaques and vessels cut from Armenian obsidian are an outstanding feature of Halaf culture; the Halaf people used native copper and lead, also from the Armenian region, as well as gold. Trade between the Halaf people and Armenia was well organized and extensive, and there was continual exchange of products between the Mediterranean and the Persian Gulf and Indian Ocean areas. An important Halaf trading post functioned at Tilki Tepe (Shamiramalti) close to Lake Van, where excellent

Halaf pottery has been found. The importance of Armenia as an entrepôt of international trade is further evidenced by finds of conch shells fron the Indian Ocean, which occur in Georgian sites such as Sagvarjile Cave, while Armenian obsidian occurs at sites not only in western Asia Minor, but even along the Lower Volga basin and in the Ukraine.

The Neolithic stage in human culture is succeeded by the Chalcolithic – a term derived from the Greek words *chalkos* 'copper', and *lithos* 'stone' and denoting the stage when men began to experiment with implements made of native copper, used alongside the older stone tools and weapons.

In Armenia as in other parts of the Near East, many villages established in the Neolithic period continued to flourish right through the Chalcolithic and well into the Bronze Age and later. In Persia and Turkey, such sites form large artificial mounds, to which the name *tepe* is given, the corresponding word in Armenian being *blur* or 'hill'. These mounds, built up from the debris of mud brick houses, rubbish and even human burials, had risen over the centuries to a level considerably higher than that of the surrounding plain. In countries where water and shade are at a premium, the innate conservatism of villagers tended to keep successive generations concentrated round some pleasant spot, with a spring of fresh water, fertile fields, orchards, and later, irrigation channels to assure a regular supply for crops. Thus it is that these hummocks, rising to 50 or 60 feet above the bedrock or natural soil level, preserve in their various strata the humble relics of village life going back occasionally as far as Neolithic times.

Among the richest sites of this type is the hillock of Kül-Tepe or 'ash-hill' situated in the Nakhchevan ASSR, 8 kilometres north-north-east of the ancient Armenian city of Nakhchevan, and on the left bank of the Nakhchevan-Chai. (This Nakhchevan Kül-Tepe is not to be confused with the better known Kül-Tepe or Kanesh in Cappadocia, hundreds of miles west of Armenia.) E. A. Lalayan first carried out a small dig here in 1904, yielding up a number of interesting finds from the Chalcolithic and Bronze Age. Since 1951, systematic excavations have been carried out at Nakhchevan Kül-Tepe by Academy of Sciences of the Azerbaijan SSR in Baku jointly with the Institute of Archaeology of the Soviet Academy of Sciences in Moscow, and the results were published in a series of interesting articles and monographs by O. A. Abibullaev.

Before excavations began, Nakhchevan Kül-Tepe measured 150 metres from north to south, and 100 from west to east. It rose to a maximum height of 14 metres above the surrounding flat ground. The local population had for years been in the habit of carting off loads of rubble and ashes from the mound to fertilize their fields, so that in places the hillock was almost levelled to the ground. The Kül-Tepe could in other spots be excavated to a depth of as much as 22 metres from its highest point, until remains of human life ceased and natural soil and bedrock were encountered.

Nakhchevan Kül-Tepe contains four main occupation layers, ranging from early Iron Age at the surface, down through Late and Middle Bronze Age (layer III), Early Bronze (layer II), then Chalcolithic (layer IB), and finally Neolithic (layer IA). Levels II and IB are separated by an intercalated layer of sterile earth between 15 and 40 centimetres thick, indicating that the village was abandoned for many years between the Chalcolithic and Early Bronze phases.

Although little remains of the actual buildings of the original Neolithic settlement forming layer IA, and the Chalcolithic houses of IB, it was possible to identify thirteen circular or roughly rectangular dwellings of these periods, built of clay and stone. The round houses were between 6 and 8 metres in diameter, while one of the rectangular ones measured 4 × 3·3 metres. The outer walls were between 35 and 55 centimetres thick, and the floors were of mud.

Layer II of the Nakhchevan Kül-Tepe contained remains of thirty-nine homes, both round and rectangular in plan, built of cobble-stones, clay and mud bricks. Each dwelling had in the centre a large flat stone or else a small hole in the floor, on which to stand the central pillar which held up the conical roof. These Layer II houses were heated either by a circular clay brazier (*mangala*) set into the floor, or else by a clay stove built close to the outer wall. Horseshoe-shaped hearth props are another special feature. These Kül-Tepe Early Bronze Age houses present points of similarity with dwellings familiar from Burton Brown's excavations at Geoy Tepe near Rezaieh in Persian Azerbaijan, and Charles Burney's at Yanik Tepe, near Tabriz.

The lowest occupation layer at Kül-Tepe contained no less than seventy-three human burials, mainly from the Neolithic period. Burial pits were hollowed out between the houses themselves, or even underneath the floor. No attempt was made to lay out the bodies in any particular direction. The bottom of each burial pit was smoothed over and smeared with clay. The corpses of the deceased were laid on their side or on their back, in a doubled up or contracted position. Their arms were folded with the hands close to the face or lain upon the chest, or else pulled straight down along the side of the body. Often a small stone or fragment of a pot was found in position beneath the skull. Some of the skeletons had been daubed with red ochre. Fragments of reeds and rushes lying by the skeletons suggest that the corpses were enveloped in a rough shroud of reed matting before being consigned to the ground. These primitive husbandmen were mostly too poor to bury any articles of value with their dead. In only twenty-five out of the seventy-three cases were any grave goods found, consisting of small beads of various coloured stones, bone pendants, obsidian knives, and crude handmade pots fashioned from clay with an admixture of straw and chaff. In two graves, skeletons of dogs were found. Most burials contained a single corpse, but a few had two, three or even four.

Particular interest attaches to pottery of various types found in the Neolithic and Chalcolithic occupation layers at Nakhchevan Kül-Tepe. The Neolithic is the usual plain, soft-baked ware, reddish brown or grey, and fashioned from straw-tempered clay irregularly fired. In the Chalcolithic stratum (IB), alongside crude local wares, some high-quality sherds turn up, moulded with refined technique from clay with an admixture of sand, well baked, and painted in red, brown, yellow and grey. The finely burnished surface is decorated with rather sophisticated geometrical patterns, executed in black, brown and red paint. These fine wares were probably imported from Iran or Anatolia, and a parallel has been suggested with the Persian painted ware of Siyalk III, usually dated to about 4000 BC. Local Kül-Tepe pottery of the Chalcolithic period is made from straw-tempered clay of a reddish colour, which was then burnished and painted with simple geometrical patterns – rows of lines and blocks of chevrons – in black, red and yellow. Finds of similar pottery have been made at other sites in Transcaucasia, notably in the Shusha district of Karabagh.

When we come to the Early Bronze period at Kül-Tepe, the dominant type of pottery is the well-known 'Kuro-Araxes' black, brown or red burnished ware. From about 3000 BC onwards, we note the use of an individual type of lug-handle, applied to the body of the vessel as a clay boss, and then pierced with a hole. It is often accompanied by finger-depressions or 'dimples' on both sides. This so-called 'Nakhchevan lug' originated not far from Kül-Tepe itself and was in use for many centuries, being attested at a number of sites in eastern Anatolia, Georgia, Armenia and Azerbaijan. Clay animal figurines also became common from the beginning of the Bronze Age.

The Nakhchevan Kül-Tepe provides a few valuable clues as to the origins of copper and bronze metallurgy in Armenia. From the top of the Chalcolithic occupation layer, four small copper objects were recovered: a borer, a bead, and two unidentifiable fragments. Chemical analysis shows that two of the objects are of unalloyed native copper, while two have an insignificant proportion (0·4 per cent, 0·7 per cent) of arsenic. In the Early Bronze layer, dated from after 3000 BC, we have a wide variety of articles in both native copper and then in tin bronze, together with clay moulds for casting copper and bronze axe-heads.

Progress has lately been made in narrowing down the chronological sequence of these early cultures at Kül-Tepe and elsewhere in Armenia. Use of Carbon-14 dating methods has begun to yield helpful results. Thus, a sample Carbon-14 dating made by the Leningrad laboratory of the Institute of Archaeology of the Soviet Academy of Sciences gave the result of 2920 ± 90 BC for a piece of charcoal from the Early Bronze layer at Kül-Tepe, taken from a depth of $8\frac{1}{2}$ metres. In 1966, the Soviet scholars Kushnareva and Yakobson reported a Carbon-14 dating of 3810 ± 90 BC, obtained from a depth of about 19 metres, or 3 metres above the bottom of the earliest occupation layer. This seems to indicate that during the Chalcolithic period, accumulation of rubble was causing the level of the hillock to rise by a metre every century or less. If this is the case, then the foundation of the original Neolithic settlement at Kül-Tepe should be placed around 4200 BC.

By this time, the culture of Neolithic man had of course been flourishing in Armenia for many centuries.

The Neolithic and Chalcolithic periods in Armenia as elsewhere saw a tremendous improvement in human living standards and the amenities of life generally. With the perfection of speech and language, sustained conversation was possible, the invention of writing only a matter of time. A cosy and relatively secure home and community life could be led in the more advanced and favoured localities. With the institution of family life and more settled marital arrangements, domestic cares no doubt beset the father and mother of the family, even in those remote days. Fortunately, the Armenian paterfamilias or matriarchs could drown their sorrows in drink, since Armenia was certainly among the earliest centres for the cultivation of the grape and the making of wine. One older authority, Victor Hehn, declared in 1888, in his book *The Wanderings of Plants and Animals* that the true home of the vine was 'the luxuriant country south of the Caspian Sea . . . . in Colchis on the Phasis, in the countries lying between the Caucasus, Ararat, and Taurus . . . . From these regions the vine accompanied the teeming race of Shem to the lower Euphrates in the south-east, and to the deserts and paradises of the south-west.'[1]

The wild vine, *Vitis vinifera silvestris*, from which the cultivated vine of the Old World is derived, has been established in Armenia, as in the Balkans and parts of western Europe, since Tertiary times, that is to say, over a million years. Grape-pips in a carbonized or petrified state are found at a number of Neolithic sites in Caucasia, particularly round about the Black Sea. Mr Edward Hyams considers that the use of naturally fermented grape juice may be even older than the Advanced Neolithic cultures of Anatolia and Caucasia. A bunch of grapes put aside for a few days in this warm climate would naturally begin to ferment, since yeasts are present in the bloom of all wild grapes. 'Sooner or later some thirsty member of a food-gathering community, not long after the first invention of pottery, would have taken a drink from a vessel which, two or three days earlier, had contained grapes, but which *now* contained – wine.'[2]

On the question of the Armenian origins of the cultivated grape, archaeologists and experts in viniculture can find support in Holy Writ. The Book of Genesis (IX. 18-29) records that one of Noah's first actions after alighting from the Ark on Mount Ararat was to plant a vine, which was in fact shown to pilgrims on the slopes of the mountain until the nearby village and monastery were destroyed in the disastrous earthquake of 1840. The consequences of Noah's overindulgence in the juice of the Armenian grape were momentous for the human race. Indeed, bigoted South African clerics, in order to justify the permanent subjection of the negroes, descendants of Ham, still quote from the Book of Genesis the following account of the incident:

[1] As cited by Edward Hyams, *Dionysus*, London, 1965, p. 86.

[2] Edward Hyams, *Dionysus*, p. 20.

'And the sons of Noah, that went forth of the Ark, were Shem, and Ham, and Japheth: and Ham is the father of Canaan.

'These are the three sons of Noah: and of them was the whole earth overspread.

'And Noah began to be an husbandman, and he planted a vineyard:

'And he drank of the wine, and was drunken; and he was uncovered within his tent.

'And Ham, the father of Canaan, saw the nakedness of his father, and told his two brethren without.

'And Shem and Japheth took a garment, and laid it upon both their shoulders, and went backward, and covered the nakedness of their father; and their faces were backward, and they saw not their father's nakedness.

'And Noah awoke from his wine, and knew what his younger son had done unto him.

'And he said, Cursed be Canaan; a servant of servants shall he be unto his brethren.

'And he said, Blessed be the Lord God of Shem; and Canaan shall be his servant.

'God shall enlarge Japheth, and he shall dwell in the tents of Shem; and Canaan shall be his servant.

'And Noah lived after the flood 350 years.

'And all the days of Noah were 950 years: and he died.'

Now both Babylonia and ancient Egypt had an advanced viticulture by about 3000 BC. As neither of them had any local wild vines, they must have acquired both the plants and the art of cultivating them from elsewhere. Since we have abundant evidence of trading in obsidian, ceramic ware and other commodities between Armenia and Egypt, Syria and Mesopotamia from at least the fourth millennium BC, merchants from the great cities of the plain had ample opportunity to bring back useful plants from Transcaucasia for their own use and further cultivation, as the Greeks later did from Colchis. Within Armenia itself, techniques of vine dressing and wine making reached a high pitch of sophistication by Urartian times, from around 800 BC. The evidence of Karmir-Blur, near Erevan, and other sites, shows that no Urartian garrison post was without its finely appointed wine cellars, with their long rows of *pithoi* or large wine jars, buried in neat rows up to the neck, and stamped with the vintage and quality of the wines inside. In the time of Herodotus (*Histories*, I. 194), a tremendous business was being done by merchants operating barges of wood and hides on the Tigris, on which they brought palmwood casks of wine down from Armenia for sale to wine traders and consumers in Babylon.

We have already spoken of the 'Neolithic Revolution', which enabled men to change over from hunting and food gathering to the settled life of village agricultural communities. A comparable leap forward occurred when men mastered the craft of metal-working, first the cold-forging of unalloyed copper, and then its fusion with tin, arsenic or antimony to form bronze.

The alloy of copper with tin was the first metallic compound in common use by mankind, and gives its name to a whole epoch of human history – the Bronze Age. Prior to this, copper was used by itself, but, since it is relatively soft, stone implements had to be retained for use when something harder was required. Native copper, sometimes termed by miners malleable or virgin copper, occurs as a mineral having all the properties of the smelted metal. It is a brilliant substance, of a peculiar red colour which assumes a pinkish or yellowish tinge on a freshly fractured surface of the pure metal, and is purplish when the metal contains cuprous oxide. It has a specific gravity ranging from 8·4 to 8·9; it takes a brilliant polish, is in a high degree pliable and ductile, and in tenacity it falls short only of iron, excelling in this respect both gold and silver. The molten metal is sea-green in colour, and at very high temperatures it vaporizes and burns with a green flame. Copper is not affected by exposure in dry air, but in a moist atmosphere, containing carbonic acid, it becomes coated with a green basic carbonate known as verdigris. When heated or rubbed it emits a peculiar, disagreeable odour. The word 'copper' itself is connected with the name of the island of Cyprus: according to Pliny, the Roman supply was chiefly drawn from there, and so it became known as *aes cyprium*, and then corrupted into *cuprum*, whence comes the English word 'copper', the French *cuivre* and the German *Kupfer*.

The origins of copper and bronze working have long engaged the attention of archaeologists. From around 5000 BC, the most advanced civilizations of the world, such as the Sumerians, Egyptians and Babylonians, used the metal in increasing quantities in its unalloyed form. However, copper ore is not found locally in sufficient amounts in southern Iraq, Syria and Egypt, and it is thought that it was imported in crude form from other regions to the north, notably Armenia. Among the specialists who have given attention to this problem are Henri Frankfort, V. Gordon Childe and W. F. Albright, also A. A. Iessen in Russia[1]. One leading expert on ancient technology, R. J. Forbes, allots a central place to Armenia in his sketch map of the diffusion of the earlier metallurgical techniques. The only other region which provided a yet more ancient source of copper for the ancient world seems to have been Bactria in central Asia, comprising present-day Afghanistan and southern Turkmenistan. A feature here was the famous Anau culture (from Anau, near Ashkhabad), where copper was in regular use by 4000 BC.

The invention of bronze must originally have taken place in an area where native copper occurs side by side with deposits of tin, antimony and arsenic. Only in such conditions could the primitive metallurgist stumble on the fact that copper mixed with one or other of these alloys acquires, as bronze, qualities of hardness

---

[1] A. A. Iessen. *Iz istorii drevnei metallurgii Kavkaza* ('From the history of ancient metallurgy in the Caucasus'), Moscow, Leningrad, 1935.

and strength altogether superior to those of pure copper by itself. Armenia and Georgia, with their rich deposits of copper alongside arsenic, antimony and also tin, provided ideal conditions for such a discovery.

From Armenia and Asia Minor, it seems that both the secrets of metallurgy and supplies of the metals themselves percolated down into the plains of Syria and Mesopotamia. Skilled artisans, some of them evidently of Caucasian and Anatolian origin, plied their craft in the cities of the south, and were regarded as possessing esoteric, magical powers. At Byblos in Phoenicia, these metal-workers, some possibly from Armenia, would deposit samples of their latest creations in bronze apparel and jewellery as offerings in the temple. Professor Claude Schaeffer expresses the view that 'given the complexity of special knowledge demanded by these crafts, and also their difficulty, it is probable that the birth of local bronze metallurgy was due to the arrival in Syria and Palestine of prospectors, miners and bronzeworkers who were natives of Asia Minor'.[1] The same authority adds that this migration was probably due to a series of earthquakes which disrupted the Armenian copper mines around 2000 BC and caused unemployment and consequent emigration among the mineworkers. More recent archaeological study of the area suggests that any such emigration may also have been caused by the arrival of the waves of Indo-European barbarians from north of the Caucasus, who put an end to the Transcaucasian Early Bronze Age, and spread panic among the local settled population of Armenia.

Recent excavations in Armenia, Azerbaijan and Georgia show that copper was certainly known there by 3500 BC, and probably as early as 4000 BC. At first it was treated as a precious metal, rather like gold, and not widely employed for industrial purposes.

From 3000 BC onwards, intensive metallurgical operations were carried on at Metzamor, in the Araxes plain. The evidence of the Nakhchevan Kül-Tepe and other sites shows that local artisans had by 3000 BC fully mastered the art of combining copper with various alloys to form bronze of different qualities. For instance, Layer II of Kül-Tepe yielded bronze objects containing up to 6 per cent of arsenic alloy. For this reason, the Armenian Early Bronze Age is now held to have begun around 3200 or 3000 BC, and not as late as 2500–2000 BC, as was previously maintained by most scholars. The terms 'Eneolithic', 'Chalcolithic' or 'Copper Age', if used at all, should properly be reserved for the period prior to the third millennium BC.

This fact is of importance when we come to consider that great phase in Armenian cultural history – the so-called 'Kuro-Araxes' Early Bronze Age culture, which in fact took in most of the third millennium BC. The unity of this enormous cultural zone, centred on Armenia but extending far to the north, the south, and the south-west, is manifested in a distinctive type of pottery, handmade, usually black or dark grey burnished. This pottery first attracted attention by its

---

[1] *Stratigraphie comparée de l'Asie occidentale*, Oxford, 1948, pp. 544–5.

style of decoration, in patterns consisting of ribs in low relief applied to the surface, and also in incised geometrical designs. A distinctive feature found in Armenia and Georgia is the double spiral, resembling a pair of spectacles. The texture of this Eastern Anatolian and Transcaucasian Early Bronze Age ware – termed 'Kuro-Araxes' because the culture centres on the Kura and Araxes river valleys – varies with the type of vessel. The core is usually black or grey, and both surfaces – inside and out – may be the same; however, it is common for the vessel's interior to be light in colour, and in the case of large jars, unburnished. The striking black finish was obtained by impregnating the clay with a solution of soot before the final firing. The burnish was normally applied direct to the surface, though there is sometimes a slip; the finer specimens are highly polished. Jars and deep bowls are the commonest forms, and handles are rather rare, except for the triangular ledge-handle and also the 'Nakhchevan lug', which is characteristic of pottery from the eastern half of the vast highland zone in which the Kuro-Araxes culture flourished.

This distinctive ware was encountered at Shengavit on the outskirts of Erevan, an important Early Bronze Age site where an ancient township was excavated by Y. A. Baiburtian in 1936–8. During World War II, in 1943–4, Turkish archaeologists reported finds of the pottery at Karaz near Erzurum, and then as far west as Erzinjan. Then it cropped up in various parts of Georgia, notably Trialeti, and even as far south-east as Geoy Tepe, near Lake Urmia in Persian Azerbaijan, a site excavated by the British archaeologist T. Burton Brown. The first comprehensive study of the Kuro-Araxes culture and its associated pottery was a brilliant monograph by the late B. A. Kuftin (1892–1953), published in the *Bulletin* of the Georgian State Museum in 1944. Other important Armenian sites of the period are Shresh-Blur near Echmiadzin, the ancient Vagharshapat, seat of the Supreme Catholicos of the Armenians; Eylar on the northern outskirts of Erevan, on the highway to Lake Sevan; and Kosi-Koter, near Kirovakan, a site discovered by E. V. Khanzadian and excavated by her from 1959 onwards, the results being first published in the journal *Sovetskaya Arkheologiya* for 1963.

Nor is this all. Far to the north-east, settlements with Kuro-Araxes black burnished ware were discovered right over the Caucasus range in remote Daghestan and Chechen-Ingushetia (Kayakent, Velikent, and Lugovoe near Grozny). Even more remarkable is the fact that the same ware, sometimes burnished in red, crops up as far from Armenia as in Syria and Palestine, where it goes under the name of 'Khirbet Kerak' pottery, after the village of this name situated by the Sea of Galilee, where specimens were first located. It also occurs in such famous sites as Ras Shamra.

In his *Archaeology of Palestine*, Albright describes the Khirbet Kerak ware as some of the most beautiful pottery ever made in Palestine: it is certainly among the most unusual in style and fabric, having none of the painted and incised decorations common in the local Palestinian cultures. Abandoning the potter's wheel, the makers of Khirbet Kerak ware worked entirely with their hands; decorative patterns were applied in high relief, and the finished article was finally coated with a thick slip and a red or black shiny burnish. Representative vessels of Khirbet Kerak ware include deep bowls with carinate, or keeled bodies, and outward-flaring rims, one-handled deep bowls, little one-handled jugs with flat bases, strange lids with knobs on top, trumpet-shaped stands and fireplace pot stands with human faces engraved or in high relief, as are found also in Early Bronze Age Armenia. As Emmanuel Anati points out,[1] Anatolian influences in Palestine of the third millennium BC are also known from earlier sporadic finds, such as the golden plaque discovered by Benjamin Mazar at Kinnereth, and the stone battle-axes of northern origin found by Judith Marquet-Krause at Ay. Crescent-shaped copper axes found at Jericho and Tell al-Hesi are identical in design to Anatolian and northern Mesopotamian tools of the same period.

The Khirbet Kerak culture is well known in inner Syria from Hama on the Orontes, from Aleppo, and also from the plain of Antioch, Ugarit and other sites along the coast. Excavations at Tabara al-Akrad, on the plain of Antioch, have revealed four major strata of Khirbet Kerak immediately following the Jemdet-Nasr period (3100–2900 BC). Here this Khirbet Kerak culture seems to have started earlier than in Palestine, which is yet another pointer to its northern, Anatolian origins. Between 2600 and 2400 BC the Khirbet Kerak ware temporarily displaced the regular wheel-made pottery long typical of those parts, before suddenly vanishing for ever. All this leads to the presumption that the makers of Khirbet Kerak pottery were alien intruders – perhaps the Hurrians, whose existence in Akkadian times is attested by tablets in their language from the Khabur valley. Since the appearance of the Khirbet Kerak ware in Syria and Palestine is accompanied by evidence of violent disturbance, suggesting actual invading groups, it can hardly have been carried there by normal trade relations. This leads several authorities, including Miss Kathleen Kenyon and Ruth Amiran, to hold that Khirbet Kerak ware was in fact introduced from the region of the Armenian and Georgian Kuro–Araxes culture by conquering hordes from eastern Anatolia or beyond – 'barbarous tribes', as V. Gordon Childe surmises, 'coming perhaps from Georgia'.[2] Speaking of the Khirbet Kerak ware found at Ras Shamra, Professor Schaeffer declares:

'Its appearance there coincides with the arrival of an alien ethnic element which installed itself in the city which had been ravaged by fire, as in a conquered land. There is no doubt that we are dealing here with the traces of an invasion originating in the mountainous zone of upper Syria and Anatolia in the north – an area always ready to spill over its excess population into the alluring lands of the south.'[3]

[1] *Palestine before the Hebrews*, London, 1963, p. 360.
[2] *New Light on the most ancient East*, p. 219.
[3] *Stratigraphie comparée*, p. 345.

All this evidence provides a picture of a vast Early Bronze Age culture, centred in Armenia and Georgia on the Kura and Araxes valleys, but stretching for hundreds of miles south-westwards to Palestine and Syria, and to the north-east, right up to the north Caucasian plain and the Caspian littoral. Comparable cultural unification was attained subsequently in Armenian history – and then for very short periods – only during the heyday of the Urartian kingdom about 750 BC, and then during the reign of King Tigranes the Great (95–55 BC).

We know also that Armenia bulked large in the consciousness of the Sumerians, and contributed to the cosmopolitan civilization associated with Ur of the Chaldees. Unusual interest attaches to a round-topped limestone relief of the third millennium BC discovered by Sir Leonard Woolley at the ancient sanctuary of Dublal-makh in Ur. This relief shows the god Ea, patron deity of the city of Eridu, whose ruins break the line of the horizon some twelve miles south-west of Ur itself. 'According to the old Sumerian convention the god is shown holding a vase from which two streams of water are pouring to the ground, while fish are swimming up and down in the streams; as lord of the Waters of the Abyss Ea holds the source from which rise the twin rivers Tigris and Euphrates, givers of life to the land of Mesopotamia.'[1] This eloquent passage shows that during the Third Dynasty of the Sumerian empire, the dwellers in the plain were conscious of their debt to the region around Lake Van and Mount Ararat, and that they knew that it was from Armenia that life-giving water flowed down to the Mesopotamian lowlands.

Armenia itself was thus no mere backwater in the Near East during the third millennium BC. It had emerged from isolation into full commercial and cultural relations with Iran, Mesopotamia and Anatolia. Mastery of the use of bronze and improved agricultural techniques led to a rapid increase in population, and vastly higher standards of living. Economic life was based on farming and stock raising, with emphasis on the rearing of cattle, sheep, goats, dogs and horses. Clay figurines of rams, oxen, barking dogs, and horses appear in large quantities, both as children's toys and, no doubt, as totems connected with various forms of animal worship.

Agriculture centred on grain and orchard crops and mixed plantings; harvesting and flour-making implements are found in large numbers. Wheeled transport was widely used, mainly ox carts with solid wheels, as are often met with in backward parts of rural Turkey to this day. Toy models of oxen have small hollows in the fore part of the trunk, showing that they were designed to be attached to model carts, the clay wheels of which, with projecting hubs, have in fact been preserved. There were the usual conventional female figurines. Some settlements of the Kuro-Araxes Early Bronze Age culture yield up numerous objects worked in metal, such as archaic shaft-hole battle-axes, tube-socketed axeheads, and trinkets of various kinds. These are usually encountered in graves in or near the more prosperous villages. Other communities, in poorer or more remote parts,

[1] C. Leonard Woolley, *Ur of the Chaldees*, London, 1929, pp. 199–200.

lagged behind in metal technology, and continued to rely mostly on implements of wood, flint and obsidian. Among the arts and crafts most commonly practised were weaving, pottery making and carpentry.

Many of the inhabitants of Armenia during the Early Bronze Age pursued settled lives in well-constructed houses made of stone, wood, reeds and sun-baked brick, or a combination of these. Buildings were erected above ground; dugouts and semi-dugouts, common in Armenia at later periods, are not characteristic of this particular era. A good example of an Armenian township of the 'Kuro-Araxes' culture is Shengavit, situated on an elevated promontory on the left bank of the Razdan (Zanga) River on the outskirts of Erevan. Even before excavations were begun by Y. A. Baiburtian in 1936, large circles with a diameter of about 7 metres could be distinctly made out on the surface of the ground, especially after rain. These proved to be remains of round central rooms of houses, to which rectangular out-buildings were adjoined, giving the effect of the type of 'tholos' found at Arpachiyah and other sites of the Tell Halaf culture in northern Iraq. The walls were of big, sun-baked bricks laid on a stone foundation.

The floors of the central rooms were paved with pebbles arranged in concentric circles. In the middle was a large stone which served as a base for the post supporting the conical wickerwork roof, a feature of Armenian houses since Neolithic times. Beside this stone would be a low, round, clay fireplace, about a metre in diameter, decorated with ornament in relief along its upper edge. Highly elaborate miniature hearths have also been found, decorated with fantastic zoomorphic motifs, and obviously designed for sacrificial purposes. Near the fireplace, handmills and large vessels filled with wheat and barley were often found, as well as highly ingenious clay pot stands made in the form of stylized animal and human figures. Very fine pottery *karases* or round storage pots have been found at Shengavit; they are in the burnished Kuro-Araxes ware, and have their shoulders decorated with incised triangular patterns, alternating with round knobs or bosses in relief. Implements of bone and flint are found in abundance, with ornaments and archaic tools of copper and bronze.

There is little evidence of social differentiation among the representatives of the Kuro-Araxes culture in Armenia, nor of the existence of any hereditary royal family or warrior class. The pattern seems to be of village communes, consisting of clans with local headmen or elders, or else of extended family units organized on a patriarchal basis.

There was lively interaction throughout the third millennium BC between Armenia and the Chalcolithic and Early Bronze Age cultures of the Ukraine and south Russia. Particular interest attaches to possible Armenian influences on the famous Tripolye culture which flourished in the basins of the Dnieper, the southern Bug and the Dniester, right down to the Black Sea. These Tripolye folk were excellent farmers and husbandmen, and lived in well constructed houses, as did their contemporaries in the Armenian Kuro-Araxes culture. They were wonderful

13. Child's clay animal toy (Early Bronze Age)
14. Bronze model war-chariot from Lchashen
15. Bronze Age wooden couch burial (Lchashen)

artists in ceramics, though their pottery was very different from Kuro-Araxes ware. The best Tripolye pottery is painted with circles, spirals and parallel lines; sometimes there are symbolic representations of the sun or of animals.

The Tripolye men were expert workers in copper and bronze, deriving some of their metal supply from the Caucasus. Large numbers of clay figurines of women occur in Tripolye sites, connected with the cult of fertility as symbolized in the image of woman, the mother. This is, of course, a common feature of early agricultural communities the world over, and can be paralleled in Armenia. Some Soviet scholars, for example, T. S. Passek, detect in the faces of these figurines specifically Armenoid traits, pointing to ancient immigration from Transcaucasia and other Near Eastern centres of settled agriculture. If this is so, it would indicate that tribes from Anatolia and Armenia combined with the local hunters of southern Russia to create this important Tripolye culture, which is more sophisticated than anything seen before, north of the Black Sea. It is also interesting to trace possible reciprocal influences, reflected in resemblances between the Tripolye pottery and the fine Trialeti and Lchashen ware of the Middle Bronze Age in Georgia and Armenia. The use of an undulating Tripolye-type 'snake' motif on a splendid jar from Kurgan XVII in Trialeti, as excavated by B. A. Kuftin, is one typical case in point.

Both the Kuro-Araxes and the Tripolye cultures broke up towards the end of the third millennium BC, evidently under the impact of Indo-European invasions from north Caucasia and from southern Russia respectively. These Indo-Europeans brought to Armenia what Marija Gimbutas[1] terms the Eurasian kurgan or barrow culture, represented by the Nalchik cemetery and the great Maikop barrow, in the Terek and Kuban valleys. This Maikop period of the Indo-European kurgan culture, extending from about 2300 to 2100 BC, is noted for its royal graves at Maikop and at Tsarskaya, with their mausoleums built of timber or of stone slabs, furnished with a fantastic quantity of turquoise ornaments, Iranian cornelian stone, Mesopotamian gold figurines and jewellery, beads from Phoenician Byblos, also archaic axeheads, similar to contemporary models from Armenia, and made of an alloy of copper and nickel, characteristic of some Anatolian bronze.

That some major movement of populations brought to an end the Armenian and Eastern Anatolian Early Bronze Age is suggested by the layers of ashes and other evidence of sudden disturbance which occur at several sites in this region. In Armenia we observe a shift of population from the fertile lowlands, with their settled village communities, to the upland pastures usually favoured by owners of the large herds and flocks which are a feature of the pastoral life of the early Indo-European tribes from the steppe. The arrival of the Indo-Europeans on the scene contributed to the formation of the magnificent local civilization centred on Trialeti and Lake Sevan. This culture is known from Kuftin's excavations in Trialeti, the district south-west of Tbilisi, watered by the River Khrami, and from

[1] *American Anthropologist*, 1963, p. 821.

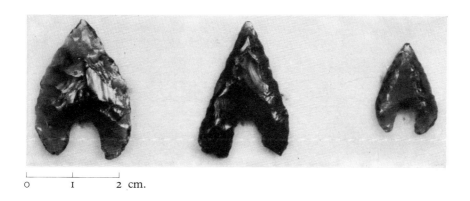

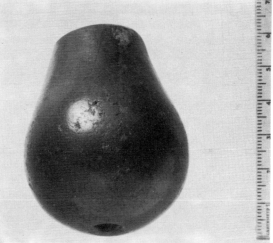

16. Obsidian arrow-heads (Bronze Age)
17. Stone mace-heads
18. Bronze Age spearhead and dagger

the Armenian Academy's work at Lchashen, on the banks of Lake Sevan. Discussing the evidence of the Trialeti and Armenian kurgans, Charles Burney writes:

'Interpretation of ethnic movements from pottery and other material can be very dangerous. Nevertheless, it is permissible to suggest that the arrival of newcomers from the northern steppes is demonstrated in Trialeti by the incised pottery and the cart in Barrow XXIX; a similar cart found at Shresh-Blur suggests that these newcomers reached the middle Araxes, since burial of carts is a habit of steppe-dwellers. The metalwork, with its profusion of stags and other animals, and with the spiral pattern on a cup from Barrow XVII, suggests, together with the painted pottery from the same tomb, strong influences from north of the Caucasus. The complete break with the East Anatolian Early Bronze Age tradition itself points to a change in population. Very possibly these newcomers were the first Indo-Europeans to enter Anatolia from the north-east, amongst whom were the Hittites, whose arrival in central Anatolia can be linked with the destruction of Kültepe II [Kanesh, in Asia Minor, not to be confused with Nakhchevan Kül-Tepe]. A date for their arrival in Trialeti during the century c. 2100–2000 BC is therefore plausible.'[1]

The Armenian Middle Bronze Age takes in the first half of the second millennium BC – from around 2000 to 1500 BC. Its history is basically that of the relations between the ancient local population – creators of the Kuro-Araxes culture, and makers of the Khirbet Kerak pottery, very likely of Hurrian and related stock – and the Indo-European invaders who brought down to Armenia elements of the Eurasian culture of the northern steppe lands. As time went on, elements of the advanced civilizations of Iran and India also made themselves felt increasingly throughout the Armenian highlands.

The local Hurrians joined forces with Indo-Iranian warrior castes to form two important kingdoms which reached their apogee in the fifteenth and fourteenth centuries BC. These kingdoms were the Hurrian monarchy proper, based on the region of Diyarbekir in south-eastern Anatolia, and the state of Mitanni, centred on Urfa, the classical Edessa, in northern Mesopotamia. The Indo-Aryan character of the ruling class in the Hurrian monarchy and in Mitanni is clearly indicated by the names of such rulers as Artatama, which is Iranian, and Mattiwaza and Tushratta, which are Indian, corresponding to the Sanskrit Mativaja and Dus-raddha. Even more striking are the names of the gods in the Hurrian and Mitannian pantheons. Here we encounter the deities Mitrasil, Arunasil, Indar and Nasat-tyana, which are to be equated precisely with the Indo-European gods Mithra, Varuna, Indra and Nasatya.

During most of this period, the dominant political power in Asia Minor was the Hittite kingdom, with its renowned capital at Boghazköy. The Hittite annals furnish some interesting data about a people called the Hayasa, who lived in the

[1] *Anatolian Studies*, VIII, 1958, p. 178.

region of the modern Erzinjan, near the upper valleys of the Euphrates. These 'Hayasa' cannot fail to attract our special interest, because their name closely resembles that used by the Armenians to refer to their own nation – the people being called 'Haik', the country of Armenia, 'Hayastan'. (The actual word 'Armenia' is of Persian and Greek origin, and comes into use much later.) In spite of the doubts of some scholars, there seems every reason to identify 'Hayastan' with the ancient 'Hayasa'.

At all events, we find the Hittite King Tudhaliyas III, who reigned about 1400 BC, campaigning against a king of Hayasa named Karannis, as well as against the nearby tribes of Azzi, who invaded eastern Cappadocia. The next Hittite king, Suppiluliumas (1375–1335 BC), was on friendly terms with the new ruler of the Hayasa, Huqqana by name. The Hittite royal family contracted marriage links with the Hayasa aristocracy, who absorbed many features of Hittite life and culture, including the sexual taboos and rules of social etiquette current among the Hittite ruling classes.

In this way, Hittite cults and rituals made themselves felt extensively during the Middle Bronze Age and a little later throughout the Armenian and southern Georgian highlands. A classic instance of Anatolian religious penetration of Transcaucasia is provided by a silver goblet from the Trialeti kurgans excavated by B. A. Kuftin.[1] This goblet has a frieze depicting a procession of masked hierophants in attendance on a high priest enthroned between an enormous goblet-shaped vessel and a sacred tree, possibly a cedar. It looks as though we have here a representation of a Hittite fertility cult, with the high priest and his acolytes preparing the magic potion of immortality. In the Araxes valley, idol worship was general in the Middle and Late Bronze Age, as attested by some grotesque stone images published by A. A. Martirosian in his important book on the Bronze and Early Iron Ages in Armenia.[2]

The material culture of Armenia during the Middle and Late Bronze Age reflects this mingling of ancient local cultures with new influences emanating from outside Caucasia. Many of the small, compact villages along the River Araxes valley, founded during the Neolithic and Early Bronze periods, continued to flourish. At the same time, the rich, rolling plateau lands were occupied by prosperous pastoral tribes, who introduced many of the ways of the steppe dwellers of the north. In spring and summer, they roamed over the uplands, where there is excellent grazing. In winter, they would descend once more into the valleys and take up winter quarters in the milder lowlands. Their way of life evidently resembled that of the Bakhtiari and Qashgai tribes of central Persia today. In personal wealth and splendour, their chieftains were the ancient equivalents of the rich Australian or Texas ranchers of modern times.

[1] D. M. Lang, *The Georgians*, London, 1966, Plate II.

[2] *Armeniya v epokhu bronzy i rannego zheleza*, Erevan, 1964, p. 181, fig. 74.

At this period, southern Georgia and Armenia formed virtually a single cultural zone. The kurgan burials of Trialeti, with their rich inventory in gold and silver cups, beautifully painted vases, and personal jewellery and ornaments, can be paralleled in Armenia notably by the Kirovakan barrow, excavated in 1948 by Professor B. B. Piotrovsky, now Director of the Hermitage Museum in Leningrad. The Kirovakan grave itself is a great pit, measuring over 30 square yards in area, and about 10 feet in depth. On the floor were found beautiful painted vases and other vessels, some of them adorned with an elegant pattern of triangular shapes, arranged like petals round the neck and shoulders of the vases. Four silver vessels were also found, and a fine gold cup with an engraved portrayal of three pairs of confronted lions, realistically snarling at one another. The chief's charred remains, partly cremated but not completely reduced to ashes, rested on a wooden catafalque decorated with bronze nails, each nail sheathed with silver. A rich necklace of cornelian and gold beads also lay on the catafalque, which stood in the centre of the grave. In addition, the Kirovakan burial mound contained a bronze pole-axe, a flat axe, three daggers and a spear-head. None of the big Trialeti and Kirovakan burials, of which more than forty have been excavated altogether, contain evidence that human sacrifices were made during the interment of an eminent person, as was common in the early kingdoms of Near East. The rich pastoral society to which the chiefs buried in the Trialeti and Kirovakan mounds belonged may not have had chattel slavery or well defined social classes; however, there was already a marked degree of distinction as regards property, as shown by the many ordinary, poor burials dating from the same period.

The techniques of metal working improved rapidly throughout the Armenian Middle and Late Bronze Age. The properties of specific alloys were well known, and were used in Armenia with conscious mastery to produce bronze of varying degrees of toughness and shades of colour and lustre. By the end of the Early Bronze Age, the properties of antimony and its influences on copper were already understood and exploited. Arsenical copper with an alloy of antimony is of a beautiful silvery colour, and possesses a fine lustre. Glossy antimony bronze ornaments are in fact a feature of Armenian burials around 2000 BC. Tin bronze came into general use somewhat later. By 1500 BC, many branches of advanced metal-processing were practised with great success in Armenia, including forging, chasing, cutting, stamping, grinding and polishing, as well as jewellery inlaying.

The variety of patterns and designs employed in bronze weapons and tools is truly astonishing. Plain and ornamental axes, battle-axes, and prototype halberds are a special feature, some of a sophisticated and subtly asymmetrical outline. Daggers, swords and javelins with sharp edges and finely incised geometrical patterns are found in great numbers. Even the humble instruments of toil – mattocks, hoes, buckets – were now available in bronze, and show a mastery of industrial design. The fact that the peasantry could use these metal articles quite freely,

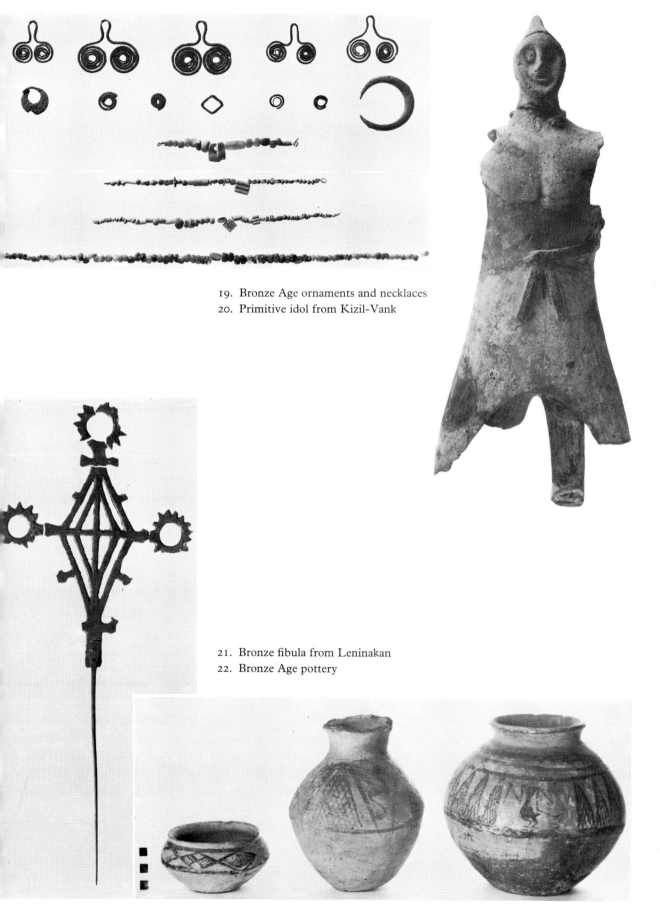

19. Bronze Age ornaments and necklaces
20. Primitive idol from Kizil-Vank

21. Bronze fibula from Leninakan
22. Bronze Age pottery

instead of cheaper wooden and stone tools and leather buckets, shows that a high level of prosperity prevailed in many regions.

Ceramics made steady progress in Armenia from the Middle Bronze Age onwards. The potter's wheel, scorned by the patient makers of the Kuro-Araxes burnished ware, was now in general use, and facilitated mass production of pottery vessels. These ranged from the beautiful urns and vases found in rich burials of chiefs, to domestic cooking pots of plain fabric and unpretentious design. However, even the latter are distinguished by sound craftsmanship and pleasant, if simple, geometrical ornament, either incised, or painted on the surface. In some cases, we even find fanciful human or animal figures prancing round the neck or shoulder of a vase, as in the case of some specimens from Eylar. A pot found at Delijan in northern Armenia in 1953 shows a ritual or perhaps a hunting scene, with a procession of goats or similar horned animals, and a two-wheeled chariot with a man standing upon it with outstretched arms, while another human figure nearby has his arms raised, as if holding up the rim of the vessel.[1]

The decoration of this remarkable Delijan pot brings us to another important feature of the Armenian Bronze Age – namely the country's very advanced position in the development of wheeled transport and military vehicles. The earliest chariots, with solid wheels, were in use among the Sumerians about 2500 BC, and they also had four-wheeled ox carts. The Sumerians then had the ingenious idea of adding a kind of metal rim or studded tyre, and by 2000 BC they were using metal axles as well. Carts with solid wheels are then found in Hungary from 1700; indeed, similar ones are still used by Turkish villagers today.

The ancestors of the Armenians had carts with solid wheels much earlier than 2000 BC, since the Early Bronze Age Kuro-Araxes culture yields up a large quantity of clay models of them, used as children's toys. The earliest wheeled vehicles in Anatolia were drawn by oxen, but horses were being ridden and harnessed to chariots from 2000 BC. Horse-riding is mentioned in Sumerian proverbs from 2100 BC, and it is interesting that the Sumerians refer to the horse as the 'ass of the mountains', as if they associated it with Iran and the hills of Kurdistan and Asia Minor. The people of Mitanni were very much at home with horse-breeding, while the Hittites wrote an important treatise about the rearing of horses. Later on, King Ashurbanipal of Assyria (668–626 BC) had at his disposal very large numbers of horse-drawn carts and chariots.

Against this background, great significance attaches to the finds of wooden chariots and wagons recovered from 1956 onwards at a site called Lchashen on the shores of Lake Sevan. These remarkable vehicles came to light when the lake's level was lowered in connection with the River Razdan hydroelectric scheme. Many great burial pits, walled and roofed with stone, were found in this area, for centuries buried deep under the lake waters. But for the mud and water which covered them, the wooden bodies and cart wheels would long since have

[1] Martirosian, *Armeniya v epokhu bronzy i rannego zheleza*, p. 99, fig. 46.

crumbled into powder. As it is, some twenty-five of the vehicles have been skilfully reconstructed by the architect G. K. Kochoyan of Erevan, and four specimens can be seen in the front hall of the Historical Museum of Armenia in Lenin Square, Erevan. One has a finely carved end panel and in general the standard of work-manship is high. Though dating from about 1250 BC, the four-wheeled covered wagons are modern in appearance, having arched roofs of bent wooden strips, over which an awning or canopy of felt or skin could be draped, exactly like the American covered wagons of pioneer days. There are also carts with square bodies, and two-wheeled war chariots from the Lchashen finds. Although the wagons and carts have solid wheels, the chariots have finely made wheels with a surprisingly large number of spokes.

Professor Stuart Piggott of Edinburgh University and Dr Richard Barnett of the British Museum are among the Western archaeologists who have examined these Armenian Bronze Age vehicles on the spot. In a lecture given in London in February 1967, Professor Piggott remarked that such discoveries as these led one to rethink the conventional evaluation of Bronze Age Caucasia as a technologi-cal backwater. For instance, there were vehicles from Trialeti in Georgia with tripartite disc-wheels, made of three planks of wood joined by means of dowels. The dowel-holes can hardly be cut out without a narrow chisel or gouge, and the earliest known examples of such tools are, in fact, found in the area stretching from Slovakia in the West to Hissar in northern Iran, and practically nowhere else in the ancient world at this time. The Armenian chariot wheel from Lchashen not only has an exceptionally large number of spokes, but has fellies made by bending a single continuous hoop, and joining it in one place only. This technique only became widespread in other regions during the Early Iron Age. These Armenian war chariots may be regarded as the prototype of those portrayed on carvings at the Persian royal palace of Persepolis, fully 750 years later.

We have now reached the beginnings of the Armenian Iron Age, which mark the opening of the era of modern technology. Iron smelting began in Asia Minor around 1400 BC, and the finished product was exported thence to Babylonia. There is a well known letter, written about 1275 BC by the Hittite King Hattusilis III to a royal contemporary, probably the king of Assyria, announcing the despatch of an iron dagger blade as a special gift. The Hittite iron smelting centre was in a district called Kizzuwatna, which was in Cilicia, the area later incorporated in the medieval kingdom of Little Armenia. Later, the techniques of iron and steel manufacture were perfected by the tribe of the Chalybes, who dwelt in Lazistan along the southern shore of the Black Sea. Probably akin to the Georgians, the Chalybes gave their name – in the Greek form, *khalyps* – to the metal which they worked with such success. By 1000 BC, iron was coming into general use in Armenia alongside bronze, though the latter was still cheaper and more readily accessible. By 750 BC, iron was in common supply for both weapons and agricultural tools and other implements. W. F. Albright once made the interesting suggestion that the name of the Babylonian god Ninurta could be interpreted alternatively as 'Lord of Armenia' (i.e. Ararat, Urartu), or as 'Lord of Iron'.[1]

In the cuneiform records of the Vannic kingdom of Urartu, there are few specific references to iron. This may indicate that it was by now a cheap and common substance: references to gold, silver and bronze are quite frequent. However, when King Sarduri II of Urartu conquered Colchis in the campaigns of 744–741 BC, we read that he had a special iron plaque made to commemorate his victory over the Colchians, and set up memorial inscriptions in prominent places in their townships.

[1] *Journal of the American Oriental Society*, 1918, pp. 197–201.

Chapter IV

URARTU—ARMENIA'S FIRST NATION STATE

THE Armenian national chronicle attributed to Moses of Khorene tells (Book I, chap. 16) the story of Queen Semiramis of Assyria (Shamiram), and her fruitless passion for the Armenian prince Ara the Fair, for love of whom Semiramis invaded Armenia with a countless army. Ara was killed in battle, rather than yield to the queen's impetuous desires. After Ara's death, the despairing Semiramis left the fertile valley of the Araxes and retreated towards the south. At length she arrived on the eastern shore of a great salt lake – Lake Van – where she caught sight of a high rocky hill running from east to west, its northern side sloping gradually to the plain beneath, its southern edge rising towards heaven, rugged and precipitous. At the foot of this great hill were streams of fresh water, and a number of flourishing villages.

The chronicler tells of how Semiramis fell in love with this spot, and built there a magnificent city with stone houses, public baths and wide streets, while the suburbs were rich in gardens, orchards and vineyards. A network of irrigation channels assured the townspeople and villagers ample supplies of water. The inner town was surrounded by a strong wall, with bronze gates.

Semiramis herself selected a site on the summit of the lofty crag, where the remains of the citadel now stand. There she built the royal palace, 'secret, and awesome to the view', grander than all the other splendid edifices of her capital. None was privileged to view the inner treasures of this palace, Moses of Khorene tells us; however, the visitor could see upon the sheer cliff face the entrances to the queen's temples and apartments, which had been carved in the solid rock. There were many inscriptions carved into the rock face and relating the exploits of Queen Semiramis. These were written in a script which no man living could read or decipher.

Such is the medieval, half-legendary story of the foundation of Van. Prince Ara the Fair can be identified with the historical King Aramé or Aramu of Urartu

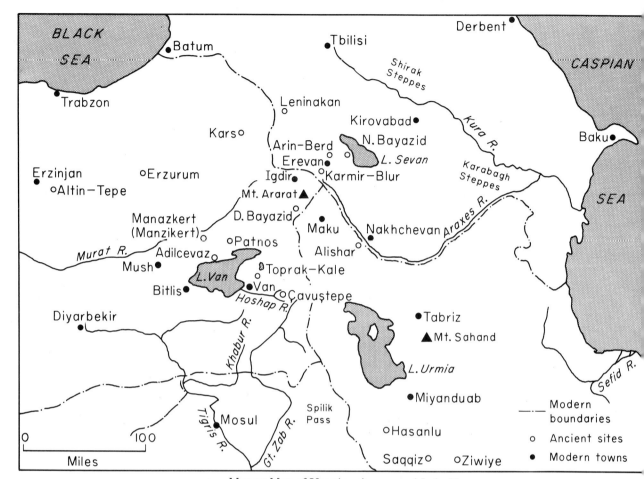

Map I: Map of Urartian sites around Lake Van

(*c.* 880–844 BC), who was in fact a contemporary of Semiramis (Shammur-amat), consort of the Assyrian monarch Shamshi-adad. Although historical records fail to confirm that Semiramis ever invaded Armenia or attempted to make love to Ara the Fair, none the less Moses of Khorene's account gives a chronologically accurate date for the foundation of Van and the Urartian kingdom. Indeed, considering that Moses of Khorene could have had no knowledge of the Assyrian or the Urartian sources, he shows in this passage more historical insight than he is often credited with.

Moses of Khorene was one of the first Armenian writers to become known to Western scholars. Early in the nineteenth century, this passage in his *History of Armenia* fired the imagination of the French orientalist Jean Antoine Saint-Martin, who was instrumental in persuading the Société Asiatique and the French government to lend official support to a project to explore the 'city of Queen

Semiramis'. A young German professor from Giessen, Friedrich Eduard Schultz, volunteered for this mission, and set off for eastern Turkey in 1827, just as the Russian war against Persia, and subsequently Turkey, was in full swing.

The dauntless Schultz reached Van safely, and even gained entrance to the citadel, which was officially kept closed to visitors. He found the fortress occupied by one aged janissary with a tame bear, and some brass cannon more suited for a museum than for active service. On the cliff below, Schultz located the priceless Urartian cuneiform inscriptions which he had come to record. Schultz had himself hoisted up the vertical rock face. Without knowing a word of the language in which they were written, he made faithful and painstaking copies of all the cuneiform texts carved there in stone. These copies, forty-two in number, were duly forwarded to the Société Asiatique in Paris, in whose journal they were published in facsimile in 1840. Meanwhile, Schultz had been treacherously murdered in 1829 by Kurds in the wild regions east of Lake Van, a tragedy which cut short one of the most heroic chapters of exploration in the Near East.

The next eminent name in the history of Urartian studies is that of Sir Henry Layard, 'Layard of Nineveh' (1817–94), who visited Van in 1850, and published plans and sketches of the royal cliff apartments, at the entrance to which was to be seen the long cuneiform inscription containing the chronicle of King Argishti I. Layard deciphered an Old Persian inscription of King Xerxes, son of Darius, also carved on the cliff overlooking Van, and found another text inscribed in Assyrian on the corner-stone of a colossal cyclopean wall at the cliff foot. However, the language of the inscriptions of the Urartian kings remained still an enigma.

From 1877 to 1880, some amateurish diggings were carried out at Toprak-Kale, on behalf of the British Museum, by Layard's former assistant, Hormuzd Rassam. Toprak-Kale is another palace-citadel of the Urartian kings, also quite close to the old town of Van. These diggings, which were continued by local consuls and missionaries, had more the character of treasure hunts than of regular excavations. Objects in bronze and precious metals were stolen by local peasants as fast as they were dug up, and then sold to dealers in Van, through whose agency some of them reached museums and private collections in Russia and western Europe. Only a part of what was recovered reached the British Museum, where the material lay largely forgotten until sorted out and published by Dr Richard Barnett.[1] A letter written by an Armenian antique dealer of Van in 1884 to Professor K. Patkanov in Moscow gives a lurid account of the disorderly state of affairs at the Urartian citadel and palace ruins on Toprak-Kale:

'Last year the English did a fair amount of digging in these extensive ruins, at the expense of the British Museum. A beautiful building resembling a palace was discovered. But in spite of the great expense incurred, they extracted only one shield and a little figurine, similar to my own, to which discoveries the British

[1] See the journal *Iraq* for 1950 and 1954.

press attached very great importance. They intended to investigate this site in detail.

'Once there was discovered in these ruins a quantity of magnificent objects, such as an incredibly large throne, all covered with cuneiform writing and gilding, but it is painful to relate, that when I returned from Europe, I learnt that it had been split up and destroyed. I remember in my youth what a vast amount of different figures were found in these ruins; but the natives, taking them for the accursed work of devils' or djinns' hands, beat them to pieces with a hammer and broke them up to make bronze vessels, shovels or plough shares . . . '[1]

The first systematic attempts to decipher the language of the Vannic inscriptions were made by the Oxford scholar Professor A. H. Sayce, whose studies appeared in the *Journal of the Royal Asiatic Society* over a period of half a century, from 1882 up to 1932. Since the Urartian kings shared with their Assyrian neighbours a taste for pompous proclamations and boring boasts about their conquests and spoils of war, together with fearsome threats against their foes, it was possible to collate the stereotyped formulae encountered in the Urartian inscriptions with parallel phrases from the Assyrian ones. This led to the building up of considerable vocabulary of Urartian words, and the discovery that the language itself is akin to Hurrian.

Particular interest attaches to the work of Professor C. F. Lehmann-Haupt, who began digging at Toprak-Kale in 1898, in collaboration with Dr W. Belck. These excavations were far more scientific than those of Hormuzd Rassam. Lehmann-Haupt's three-volume work, *Armenien einst und jetzt* (1910–31) is unsurpassed for its wealth of original material on all periods of Armenian history, including that of the Vannic kingdom of Urartu, in spite of Lehmann-Haupt's insistence that the Urartians were immigrants from western Asia Minor, which today appears a highly dubious proposition. Just before World War I, in 1911–2, Iosef Orbeli, later Director of the Hermitage Museum in Leningrad, also carried out excavations at Toprak-Kale, which were later continued in 1916, after Van had been occupied by the Russian army.

Following World War I, valuable work on the decipherment of the Urartian inscriptions was done in Germany by the late Professor Mikheil Tsereteli and by Professor Albrecht Goetze, later of Yale University, who both elucidated many obscure words in the Vannic texts. The results of this pioneer work are contained in the corpus of Urartian inscriptions by Giorgi Melikishvili of the Georgian Academy of Sciences, of which the first edition appeared in Moscow in 1953–4. This corpus, together with a historical monograph entitled *Nairi-Urartu* (Tbilisi, 1954), won its compiler a Lenin Prize. Soon afterwards, in 1955, there appeared at Graz the *Handbuch der chaldischen Inschriften* by Professor F. W. König, of the University of Vienna. It is unfortunate that König, following Lehmann-Haupt,

[1] Quoted from Dr R. D. Barnett's report in *Iraq*, XVI, 1954, p. 17.

.. Castle of Old Van

.. Old Van. The Citadel

perpetuates the misnomer of the Urartians as 'Chaldians', after the name of their chief god, Chaldis or Haldi. This leads to endless confusion with the quite separate and distinct Chaldeans of Babylonia, familiar to readers of the Old Testament; there is also risk of further confusion with the 'Chaldia' of Byzantine times, which designated the province around Trebizond.

So far the attention of excavations had centred on the capital of the Urartian kingdom, Van, or Tushpa, as it was originally called, and the nearby royal residence of Toprak-Kale. A new chapter in Urartian studies opened during and after World War II, with the systematic excavations of B. B. Piotrovsky and K. L. Oganesian at two sites on the outskirts of Erevan – Karmir-Blur, and Arin-Berd (Erebuni). The latter turned out to be the original emplacement of the city of Erevan, founded in 782 BC by the Urartian King Argishti, son of Menua, who also founded the city of Argishtihinili on the site of the modern Armavir. These facts were established with the aid of Urartian cuneiform inscriptions found on the spot. Karmir-Blur, or Teishebaini, to use the Urartian name, was founded nearly a century later by King Rusa II, son of Argishti II, and gradually supplanted the nearby Erebuni, which fell into decline.

Karmir-Blur means 'Red hill' in Armenian; the original Urartian name Teishebaini means 'city of the god Teisheba'. The city became a formidable military and administrative centre on the north-eastern marches of Urartu, and contained military barracks, store houses, temples and royal apartments. With its combination of military, civil and religious functions, Karmir-Blur can be compared with some British district centre on the North-West Frontier of India in the time of the viceroys. For the archaeologist, the site retains special interest, because it was overwhelmed by the Scythians very suddenly in a night attack early in the sixth century BC. The entire town was burnt down, thus covering all the military equipment, treasury and stores with a thick layer of debris and ashes. Neither the attackers nor treasure hunters in the Middle Ages troubled themselves to dig through all this in their search for booty. Much of the stores and larders, though occasionally charred, remained intact. Whole rows of wine jars could thus be uncovered, with grape skins and dried up dregs still lying on the bottom; also vessels full of scorched and petrified corn, and a wide variety of bronze dishes, shields and helmets, many of them stamped with the monograms of the Urartian kings themselves.

The results of these excavations have been published by Piotrovsky and Oganesian in a series of monographs issued by the Armenian Academy of Sciences in Erevan. Professor Piotrovsky has published two excellent general outlines of Urartian history and culture: *Vanskoe Tsarstvo* ('The Vannic kingdom', 1959), and *Iskusstvo Urartu* ('The Art of Urartu', 1962). The second of these appeared in London in 1967, translated into English by Peter Gelling.

During the last few years, several new Urartian sites have been explored in eastern Turkey. Since 1959, Tahsin Özgüç and his colleagues have been active at the grandiose site of Altin-Tepe ('Golden hill'), east of Erzinjan. Preliminary findings were published in the Turkish historical journal, *Belleten*, in 1961. C. A. Burney and G. R. J. Lawson published in *Anatolian Studies* (vol. X, 1960) a series of measured plans of no less than eleven Urartian fortresses in the Van region. The great urban and military centre of Kayalidere, close to the Murat Su, not far from the town of Varto, was first investigated thoroughly by a British expedition headed by Professor Seton Lloyd in summer, 1965. Meanwhile, between 1961 and 1964, excavations were carried out at Urartian sites near Patnos, north-west of Lake Van, by a Turkish team financed by the Ataturk University of Erzurum, with excellent results presented in a lecture given by Professor Kemal Balkan of Ankara University at the London University Institute of Archaeology on October 13, 1966. At the same Institute, on February 21, 1967, Dr Baki Öğün gave an account of recent Turkish excavations at the Urartian site of Adilcevaz, on Lake Van, at the foot of the Suphan Dagh. Interest in Urartian studies is also shown in Sweden, as evinced by Carl Nylander's study of the Urartian acropolis at Zernaki Tepe.[1]

The early political history of Urartu can best be followed in the annals of Assyria, which provide us with a fund of dynastic and chronological data on the Vannic kingdom. Since Van (Tushpa) is less than 200 miles from Nineveh, it is remarkable that the two empires could subsist for so long side by side, frequently at war it is true, but never able to destroy one another completely. From the rise of the Assyrians as a great power, their might was challenged constantly by the war-loving people of the northern hill country, but for whom the rulers of Nineveh would have been undisputed masters of the entire Near East.

The inscriptions of King Salmanesar I of Assyria (1280–1261 BC) already make mention of campaigns against tribes living in the region of 'Uruatri', to the south of Lake Van. 'At the commencement of my divine sovereignty the lands of Uruatri rebelled against me,' Salmanesar complains. 'To Ashur and the great gods my masters, I upraised my hands, and I mobilized my forces. I climbed up the crags of their mighty mountains . . . and subjugated eight provinces together with their armed forces. I destroyed and burnt down fifty-one villages and led their inhabitants into slavery, carrying off all their possessions. All the lands of Uruatri I made to bow down to the feet of Ashur, my lord. I made a selection from their offspring for my service, and laid upon them heavy tribute for evermore.' This is so far the earliest known mention of the people of Uruatri. It indicates that during the thirteenth century BC, they had not yet formed themselves into a centralized kingdom; rather, they lived as separate social units, with their individual tribal chieftains and local village organization.

Salmanesar's son, Tukulti-Ninurta I (1261–1218 BC) also campaigned against the tribes of the Van region, who in his time are called the 'people of Nairi'. As many as forty-three 'kings' or petty chieftains of the Nairi conspired together to

---

[1] Published in *Orientalia Suecana*, XIV-XV, 1966.

rebel against the Assyrian king, who vanquished them and led away many of the local rulers in chains of bronze to the royal city of Ashur. Among the royal titles assumed by this Assyrian monarch we find 'king of all the lands of Nairi'.

In the list of princes conquered by Tukulti-Ninurta I there figures a certain ruler of Alzi, who may have some connection with the region of Azzi, prominent in the Hittite annals. The Azzi were always associated with the Hayasa district, on the eastern border of the Hittite realm. The name of Hayasa, of course, may plausibly be linked in turn with 'Haik', 'Hayastan', used by the Armenians to designate their own people and land.

These Assyrian campaigns against the tribes of the Van region were renewed with added vigour by King Tiglath-pileser I (1115–1077 BC). This ruler began his long reign with annual campaigns to the north of his domains, into various regions of Greater Armenia. First he attacked the Mushki, ancestors of the south-west Georgian tribe of the Meskhians. These Mushki had taken advantage of the collapse of Hittite power in Anatolia to swarm into the upper Euphrates region, along the river Murat-Su, in the districts of Alzi (Azzi) and Purulumzi, where Tiglath-pileser defeated them in 1113 BC, subduing five Mushki 'kings' and their twenty thousand men.

During the next few years, Tiglath-pileser concentrated his attacks on the region of Lake Van, or 'sea of Nairi', as the Assyrians called it. 'Twenty-three kings of the land of Nairi ordered their chariots and warriors to assemble, and rose against me for war and battle. I moved against them in the fury of my dread armaments and, like the flood of Adad, I annihilated their numerous hosts . . . Sixty princes of the land of Nairi, together with their allies, I drove with my spear as far as the Upper Sea [? the Black Sea]. I captured their great towns and carried off their booty, wealth and property, and burnt down their villages with fire.' The Assyrian royal annals add that the Nairi kings were pardoned on condition that they handed over their sons as hostages, together with tribute of 1200 horses and 2000 head of cattle.

Analysis of these Assyrian sources provides much useful data on the military organization and economic life of Armenia round about 1000 BC and even earlier. They show, for instance, that the local peoples were well equipped with war chariots, and that even after a series of disastrous defeats, they could muster over a thousand good quality steeds to hand over as tribute to the victorious Assyrians. The comfort-loving Tiglath-pileser complains bitterly about the rugged terrain which he had to traverse in Armenia, and the vigorous resistance of the natives, who lured him into 'difficult places, as sharp as a dagger's point', where the monarch himself had to stagger along on foot, engaging the enemy at close quarters and 'stabbing the foe to the heart' until the mountain side was covered in an ocean of blood – 'as if draped in scarlet wool'.

The immediate successors of Tiglath-pileser were kept occupied in repelling Aramean tribes who invaded Syria, though occasional Assyrian sallies into the

Van region are still recorded in the annals. From about 1000 BC onwards, new political and social forces were at work among the petty principalities and clans which made up the Nairi-Urartian federations. The need to organize corporate resistance against Assyrian aggression, coupled with the spread of absolutist ideology from the great kingdoms of Mesopotamia, led gradually to the emergence in the Vannic region of a single dominant line of rulers. These dynasts eventually forged a great kingdom out of the scattered tribal units encircling Lake Van – the country of Biaini, as the Urartians called it – and built up their capital of Tushpa close to the modern Van, on the eastern shore of the lake. Soon we begin to encounter place names which are in current use even today, such as that of Van (Biaini) itself, and then, from 782 BC, that of Erebuni (Erevan).

The survival into modern times of a substantial number of Urartian place names provides strong evidence for the continuity of the Urartian and early Armenian monarchies and civilizations generally. The Urartians themselves were predominantly of local, Hurrian and Anatolian stock. Strong resemblances between certain items of Urartian and Etruscan bronze work led older generations of Urartologists to speculate on the possible immigration of the Urartians and their culture from Thrace or Phrygia, via western Asia Minor. There are other instructive parallels with contemporary metal work from Cyprus and Phoenicia. In particular, the fantastic Urartian bronze tripods and cauldrons are found very far afield and are the subject of an extensive literature.[1] But it must be remembered that Urartu kept up constant relations with such Mediterranean trading cities as Tyre and Sidon, which acted as entrepôts for Urartian metal work and other works of art, which were disseminated thence throughout the Mediterranean world.

The creation of a strong unified state in the wilds of Armenia and eastern Anatolia demanded unusual qualities of stamina and determination. It is not always realized that the climate of much of the Urartian territory is more akin to that of Siberia or southern Canada than to that of nearby Mesopotamia. The winters are long and severe, with snow lying to a depth of several feet for at least four months, with consequent immobility of the population and comparative isolation of each community from its neighbours. In winter, both attacks from outside, for instance, from Assyria, and also effective administration from the capital at Tushpa (Van) would have been impossible. At the present time, winter journeys are avoided in those parts unless absolutely essential. A feature of the modern village at Kayalidere, the important Urartian site west of Lake Van first excavated by a British team in 1965, is the use of wooden sledges instead of wheeled carts, even in the summer. The Mush plain is also notoriously cold in winter, though some districts immediately adjoining Lake Van are moderately sheltered, in spite of the fact that they are 1,750 metres above sea level. The relatively temperate

[1] A convenient summary of the evidence is given by Hugh Hencken in his book *Tarquinia and Etruscan Origins*, in the 'Ancient Peoples and Places' series (London, 1968).

Araxes valley was annexed by the Urartians only at a later stage in their history.

There is no question here of a sun-drenched land running continuously in milk and honey, and shaded by date-palms and fig-trees. The often harsh climatic conditions imparted to the Urartians vigour and endurance, which enabled them to vie with their more advanced southern neighbours dwelling in the fertile if enervating plains and river valleys of Mesopotamia and Babylonia. Recent archaeological finds in chased metal and carved stone work vividly portray these stocky, tough little men, with large heads and eager, peering eyes, often shown in violent motion on horseback or in chariots, engaged in hunting and fighting, or else stationary in acts of worship before their gods. Prudent husbandmen and methodical men of affairs, some of them were forerunners of Armenian merchants and collective farmers of today.

Over a broad arc of territory, extending some 200 miles to the west, north and north-east of Lake Van, these great engineers dotted the landscape with their fortresses, towns and aqueducts. By choice and strategic necessity, they nearly always built upon hills and mounds; where none were found, they piled them up artificially. On top of these hills they built their settlements, combining military, commercial and religious edifices, and up the hills they made broad, curving approach roads for chariots, carts and beasts of burden. Long before the Athenians, the kings of Urartu developed the classic architectural complex of the acropolis, as an entity uniting the nerve centres of the official cult, of military power and of civic activity, and also providing refuge for the mass of the people in time of war and disaster.

The founder of the unified Urartian kingdom was evidently King Aramé or Aramu, mentioned in Assyrian inscriptions of King Salmanesar III under the years 860, 858 and 846 BC, and no doubt to be identified with the half-legendary Armenian king, Ara the Fair, loved by Queen Semiramis. According to the late Nicolas Adontz, Aramu's reign is to be dated from 880 to about 844 BC. Aramu was the first to bear the title 'Erili Erilaue', or 'King of Kings, Shahinshah'. The Armenian chronicler Moses of Khorene regards the Urartian king Aramu as the eponymous ancestor of the Armenian nation. It is likely that his names lives on in that of the ancient province of Aramili (or Amarili, Armarili), which corresponds to the medieval Armenian province of Apahunik.

Aramu's capital, the first royal city of Urartu, was called Arzashkun, and was captured during one of the campaigns of King Salmanesar III, in the course of which the Assyrian king 'washed his weapons in the sea of Nairi (Lake Van)'. Adontz plausibly identifies this site of Arzashkun with the well-known medieval town of Manazkert or Manzikert, north of Lake Van, on the river Arsanias, and an important road junction commanding access routes to Van, Mush, Erzurum and Erevan. In AD 1071, Manzikert was the scene of the defeat and capture of the Byzantine emperor Romanus Diogenes by the Seljuq Turks.

The following is the chronological series of the kings of Urartu who are known to history, following the calculations of Nicolas Adontz and B. B. Piotrovsky:

1. Aramé or Aramu (880–844 BC). Evidently deposed during a campaign which he undertook against some barbarians in the north.
2. Sarduri I, son of Lutipri (844–828). He removed the royal capital from Arzashkun to Van, where his inscription is carved on the citadel, and is mentioned in accounts of the Assyrian monarch Salmanesar III's campaign of 834 BC.
3. Ishpuini, son of Sarduri (828–810). For a time reigned jointly with his son and successor.
4. Menua I, son of Ishpuini (810–785). A great builder, under whom Urartu became the largest state in western Asia; famous for his canals and irrigation works.
5. Argishti I, son of Menua (785–760). Annexed large tracts of northern Armenia and founded the cities of Erebuni, modern Erevan (782 BC) and Argishtihinili, medieval Armavir (775 BC).
6. Sarduri II, son of Argishti (760–730). Mentioned in the annals of Tiglath-pileser III of Assyria under the years 743 and 735 BC. Urartu was pillaged by the Assyrians and national decline began to set in.
7. Rusa I, son of Sarduri II (730–714). Committed suicide following Sargon of Assyria's victories over Urartu in 714, culminating in the sack of the shrine of the gods Haldi and Ardini at Musasir, the modern Sidikan, situated between Rowanduz and Ushnu in Kurdistan.
8. Argishti II, son of Rusa (714–685).
9. Rusa II, son of Argishti II (685–645). Completed the building of the great citadel of Teishebaini at Karmir-Blur close to Erevan.
10. Sarduri III, son of Rusa II (645–625). Under this ruler, Urartu became a satellite of Assyria.
11. Erimena (625–605). This sovereign is known only through a few inscriptions of his son:
12. Rusa III, son of Erimena (605–590). Contemporary of the prophet Jeremiah, who mentions Urartu as foe of Babylon. The last Urartian monarch to have left cuneiform inscriptions telling of the events of his reign. Following Rusa III's death, Urartu disintegrated and was overwhelmed and annexed by the Medes and Persians.

An interesting feature of the above series of Urartian monarchs is the strong dynastic principle evinced in the transmission of the throne from father to son. This hereditary principle later became marked among the Armenian dynasties from the Orontids onwards, and among the Georgians under the long-lived dynasty of the Bagratids, who flourished for over a thousand years – from AD 780 to 1810. The Urartian rulers used the title 'King of Kings' – as it were, chairman of a group of tribal princes, the senior among a group of equals. There is no suggestion of a divine, infallible autocrat, trampling on a rabble of abject slaves. Indeed, the Urartian rulers were far from claiming any divine attributes for themselves, and ascribed their victories to the favour of their supreme deity, the god Haldi.

During the zenith of the Vannic kingdom, the Urartian monarch was suzerain of all the minor rulers of eastern Anatolia, and parts of the present-day Persian and Soviet Azerbaijan. The clan chiefs would pay him tribute in the form of gold and silver, agricultural products, cattle and sheep. Alongside the hereditary chieftains, there were provincial governors appointed directly by the king and responsible for the military and fiscal administration of each province. Many of these governors became permanent rulers of the districts which their sovereigns had appointed them to administer on behalf of the Urartian crown. As the Urartian kingdom grew from the original nucleus around Lake Van, and came to embrace regions as far apart as the Gulf of Alexandretta, the eastern side of Lake Urmia, and the plains around Erzinjan and Erzurum, the role of the central government's direct agents became proportionately enhanced. City-citadels such as Karmir-Blur on the outskirts of Erevan, and Altin-Tepe near Erzinjan, were manned by contingents of Urartian picked troops and colonists under a royal viceroy, with orders to keep the local inhabitants under surveillance and political control.

Apart from political and military objectives, the expansion of Urartu followed well defined economic aims. Chief among these figured possession of the iron, silver and gold mines of the Taurus region; control of local transit of goods between Phoenicia, Syria and Asia Minor; and domination of the international trade route between east and west. To reach the Mediterranean lands, goods from India, central Asia and even China had to pass either through Mesopotamia in the south, or Anatolia and the Van region in the north. In addition, the north-south trade route between the Black Sea region, particularly prosperous Colchis, and Mesopotamia and Elam, passed straight through Urartu. With good management, the economic hegemony of the country through which all this trade passed would be assured.

Urartu itself was a supplier of cochineal dyestuffs to the lowlands of the Fertile Crescent, which it also furnished with metal goods and ores. It was an entrepôt for spices from India, and silk from China. Fragments of silk textiles found near Van have been dated to 750 BC, and are among the oldest remnants of the eastern silk trade. Choice Egyptian scarabs and amulets with hieroglyphics recovered in the same region, also Assyrian seal cylinders and beads, gold and pearl ear rings and a silver jug from Phoenicia found at Karmir-Blur in Soviet Armenia, all combine to show that Urartu's commercial links extended to the banks of the Nile and beyond.

The period of Urartu's greatest territorial expansion coincided with the reigns of Argishti I and his son Sarduri II, from 785 to 730 BC. The kingdom's frontiers were extended north of the Araxes, and Utupurshi, ruler of the Diauehi

1 St John the Evangelist, from a medieval Armenian manuscript
(British Museum)

II Mount Ararat
Rough Mountain country, Lake Van

(medieval Tao or Taik), was dethroned. In the south, around 766, Urartian armies under Argishti I penetrated as far as the outskirts of the Assyrian capital, Nineveh. During the next reign, Sarduri II advanced right through the modern Kurdistan, and annexed the southern shores of Lake Urmia. The rulers of Melitene (Malatya) and Kummukh (Commagene) in southern Anatolia were reduced to vassal status, thus ensuring for the Urartians free passage to the Mediterranean sea-board.

Reaction set in after the accession of the energetic Assyrian conqueror Tiglath-pileser III (745–727 BC). This monarch began his reign with a series of campaigns against the Vannic state. The Urartians were soon worsted at Arpad on the Euphrates, in northern Syria, thereby losing control over Commagene, Sophene (the Kharput district) and regions adjoining. In 736, Tiglath-pileser appeared at the gates of Tushpa (Van) itself, Sarduri II's capital, and subjected the city to a prolonged but unsuccessful siege. Eventually the Assyrians withdrew, after erecting as a sign of arrogant defiance a statue of their monarch, Tiglath-pileser III, before the city walls.

From now on, the Urartians were obliged to concentrate on civilizing and developing the territories remaining to them around Lake Van and to the north, beyond Ararat. The Urartians were superb engineers and builders of irrigation works. Supreme in this type of enterprise was King Menua (810–785), who has left fourteen inscriptions telling of his construction of a great canal, 40 miles long, to bring water to Van from the Artos range, near the River Hoshap. While credit for this feat of engineering work properly belongs to Menua, it is actually known in Armenian popular tradition as 'Shamiram Su', or Stream of Queen Semiramis. Starting about a mile from the village of Mzenkert or Mechinkert, it passes by an aqueduct over the River Hoshap and then runs westwards towards Lake Van, watering on the way no less than twenty-five villages in the large and otherwise arid tract of land known as *Hayotz dzor* or 'Valley of the Armenians'.

This great waterway, shored up by enormous blocks of cyclopean masonry, and once guarded by a series of small forts, is used to this day, as is the one which runs close to Karmir-Blur, on the outskirts of Erevan. Other canals watered the land south of Lake Van, known in the Urartian sources as Aidu-ni ('Aiadu' in Assyrian), also the regions of Berkri and Menuaskert, modern Manzikert, the original Arzashkun. The region of Van is especially dependent on irrigation, since the lake waters are bitter and salty, and so unsuited for drinking or for growing crops. Rusa I (730–714), the builder of Toprak-Kale, also constructed an artificial lake or reservoir 15 miles east of Van, known as 'Rusai sue' or 'Rusa's lake', the modern Keshish-göl.

The appearance of the Urartian guard-forts, which protected the canals and other installations from sabotage and attack, is known from a bronze model from Toprak-Kale now in the British Museum and another discovered more recently at Altin-Tepe in eastern Turkey. They were remarkably like the O'Brien and

O'Flaherty castles so common in western Ireland, having three stories, battlements, windows, turrets and embrasures.

The renown of the Urartian rulers and their public works spread throughout the Near East. The narrative of King Sargon of Assyria's expedition of 714 BC tells of the vineyards and rich fields of Aiadu, south of Lake Van, which excited the envy of Sargon himself. Many of the irrigation works were dedicated to the Urartian god of fertility and crops, Kuera, after whom the Urartian town of Kuerahinili was named. In addition to canals, the Urartians also made use of underground *qanats* or channels, such as are commonly found in Persia. These have the advantage of preventing evaporation until the water emerges above ground close to where it is to be used.

The Urartians were ingenious in manufacturing agricultural implements. Over half a century ago, Lehmann-Haupt found at Toprak-Kale a wide range of farming tools made of iron. Among these were three-pronged forks, iron ploughshares, and mattocks and hoes. The heavy Urartian wooden plough, with its iron ploughshare, was hauled by a team of two or four oxen, and guided by up to three men. Large quantities of stone pestles, mortars, grinders and mill stones of various sizes have been recovered in Urartian town and village sites, showing that the population was well supplied with bread.

Having solved many of their agricultural problems, the Urartians turned their attention to town planning and urban organization. Their expertise in this field had already become apparent from the excavations of Rassam, and then of Belck and Lehmann-Haupt at Toprak-Kale, even though this site was soon wrecked by amateurs and treasure-hunters. The measured plans of Urartian citadels in Turkish Armenia, published by Burney and Lawson, are full of interest in this connection. Most comprehensive of all is the information provided by the unearthing of the two virtually intact Urartian fortified cities of Arin-Berd and Karmir-Blur, on the outskirts of Erevan.

Evidence of Urartian buildings and public works in the Erevan region had been provided as early as 1901, when a basalt stele with an Urartian inscription was discovered, mentioning extensive improvements carried out by King Rusa II in the Kuturlini valley, on the banks of the River Razdan, opposite Karmir-Blur. In this inscription, Rusa writes: 'I planted this vineyard, fields with their crops, orchards did I create there, and with them I surrounded the towns. The canal from the Ildaruni (Razdan) river I built.' The canal referred to, which remains in use today, passes through a large tunnel hewn in andesite-basalt rocks. This tunnel, rebuilt more than once in the Middle Ages, now serves as a passage for the Echmiadzin canal; it is referred to in the archives of the Armenian Supreme Catholicos at the Echmiadzin monastery. Thus King Rusa's tunnel has brought life-giving water to the local people for over 2,600 years, a rare record of public utility.

The next stage in these explorations was the chance discovery, by a geologist

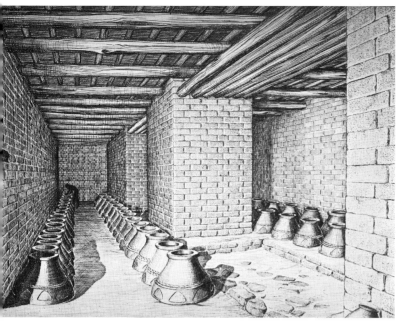

25. Urartian wine-cellar, Karmir-Blur

26. Steatite jar lid showing the Tree of Life and fantastic
    creatures

27. Van. Castle of Toprak-Kale

called A. P. Demekhin, of a fragment from an ancient stone wall, with a cuneiform inscription also mentioning the name of Rusa, son of Argishti – that is to say, King Rusa II of Urartu, who reigned from 685 to 645 BC. This inscription led Soviet excavators straight to the site of Urartu's main outpost in the Erevan region – Karmir-Blur – where excavations began in 1939 under B. B. Piotrovsky's direction. Soon the expedition came upon a ring from a bronze doorbolt, still in place at the entrance to a store room, and bearing an Urartian inscription saying: 'Arsenal of the town of Teishebaini, belonging to Rusa, son of Argishti.' This shows that the town was named after the Urartian god of war, thunder and storms, Teisheba, corresponding to the Hurrian deity Teshub. A bronze figure of Teisheba, which adorned a battle standard, was actually found on Karmir-Blur later on.

When finally uncovered, the Urartian town of Teishebaini on Karmir-Blur was found to cover a considerable territory, about 40 hectares, and was protected by a substantial rampart, with foundations of roughly hewn masonry of massive proportions. The upper portions of the walls, as in other Urartian centres, were of unbaked mud brick and have long since crumbled away. The town was built according to a prearranged plan, and formed an orderly urban ensemble far in advance of many shambling Near Eastern provincial towns of today. In Teishebaini, there were long, fairly wide streets, with living quarters along each side. These quarters did not consist of separate houses, but of a long, single structure with a continuous roof covering a whole row of almost identical dwellings, built to a standard pattern comprising an open or semi-open yard, and two living and sleeping rooms. The fact that there are no cattle or animal sheds near the living premises, and that the store rooms are all communal ones, indicates that the inhabitants received rations from the state, and that the individual families did not have to fend for themselves by farming and stock-raising.

The population of Teishebaini consisted of Urartian warriors and their families, numerous artisans working in the citadel workshops, and agricultural workers cultivating the state domains and orchards, as mentioned in King Rusa II's inscriptions. Many of these were doubtless slaves of the state, and vassals of the royal family personally. Official records of the Urartian kings show that the nearby and earlier town of Arin-Berd (Erebuni – the modern Erevan) was populated after its foundation in 782 BC by 6,600 prisoners transferred from the lands of Khate and Supani, in northern Syria, and from the upper reaches of the Euphrates. Archives of clay tablets with Urartian cuneiform inscriptions, and also remains of papyrus scrolls with Aramaic characters, provide data on the fiscal and administrative system prevailing in these Urartian citadel towns. Some of these documents are requisitions for supplies, others assignments of labourers for specified work.

Within these fortress cities close to Erevan, the thrifty Urartians accumulated great quantities of grain, grapes and fruit. The Soviet excavations uncovered remains of coarse-milled flour, plums, apples, pomegranates, and water-melon seeds. Cut apples and pressed grapes show that dried fruit was already being preserved – an industry which is well developed in Soviet Armenia today. In three huge wine cellars at Teishebaini, enormous vessels of the type called 'karas', each of about 1000 litres capacity, were buried up to their shoulders in the earthen floor, and arranged in four parallel rows. The first storeroom contained eighty-two such vessels, the second seventy, and the third twenty. The vessels were marked with hieroglyphic signs and cuneiform inscriptions, indicating the capacity of each one; sometimes the quality and age of the wine would be shown. The three main cellars at Teishebaini alone contained over 170,000 litres of wine – enough to provide a thousand men with half a litre each per day for nearly a year. Nearby was a storeroom where red polished clay wine-jugs were stocked, over a thousand of them, and many absolutely intact. Other Urartian quartermasters' stores contained iron and bronze implements, and various kinds of fabric and yarn – including remnants of a roll of cloth which must originally have been about 20 yards long.

Although Teishebaini is 150 miles from Van, the Urartian kings evidently liked to visit the city frequently, and treated it as one of their royal residences. Many personal relics of the Urartian monarchs were stored in the royal arsenal. A wide range of finely wrought bronze articles bear inscriptions of most of the Urartian kings of the eighth century BC, many of them transferred from the earlier royal city of Erebuni (Arin-Berd) only a few miles away. Eleven large bronze shields found early in the Soviet excavations bore inscriptions showing that they had belonged to Argishti I: the shields are up to three feet in diameter, with a bulge in the middle, and turned-up edges. Two shields were richly decorated with images of oxen and lions, arranged on three concentric belts of ornamental design. Bronze quivers, with inscriptions of Argishti and Sarduri II, are ornamented with pictures of Urartian chariots and horsemen. The images are finely chased, showing details of clothes, harness, and even the ornaments on the chariots, the human and animal figures overflowing with energy and movement.

Urartian arrowheads of bronze or iron were recovered in large numbers. We know that the Urartians were outstanding archers. An inscription from Van states that King Argishti II himself set up a national record for archery, shooting an arrow a distance of 950 cubits, or 494 metres.

Several bronze helmets of a distinctive shape came to light at Karmir-Blur. These had also belonged to Urartian monarchs, namely Menua and Argishti I. Hemispherical at the base, these helmets taper at the top into a high point, which provided good protection in battle. As they were liable to jerk off when the wearer was riding over rough ground, or to catch on overhanging trees or low arches, the practical Urartians usually fitted them with chin straps. These Urartian helmets are covered with artistic pictures in repoussé work, including war chariots, animals, and sacred trees and stelae flanked by acolytes and attendant deities. They were highly prized throughout the Near East; a specimen purchased by the British Museum in 1964 came from as far away as Luristan, in central Persia.[1] This particular type of helmet seems to derive from the Assyrian pattern. There is also an earlier style, represented on bronze figurines from Toprak-Kale, having a crest along the top of the helmet. The crest is formed from a brush of hair mounted on a curved comb and then fixed to the top of the helmet itself. This earlier and more original style of Urartian helmet was much imitated in Greece, where it became the standard pattern in the sixth century BC.

Also of outstanding interest is a royal coat of armour found at Teishebaini in 1952, made of bronze plates decorated with salient rosettes. The buttons are inscribed with dedicatory formulae in the name of King Argishti I. This monarch's father, Menua, had deposited here his richly decorated horse's harness, including also the bridle, plates for shielding the forehead, circular armour plates, and bells. The Urartians, like most of the Anatolian peoples, were outstanding horsemen. Long ago, a stone with a cuneiform text was found near Tushpa (Van), recording that from the place where the stone was erected Artsibi, King Menua's steed, jumped 22 cubits, about $11\frac{1}{2}$ metres, with his master on his back. It is a curious fact – even if no more than a coincidence – that this horse's name, Artsibi – in the form *Artsivi* – means 'eagle' in both modern Armenian and in Georgian.

Besides beautiful costume jewellery and gold trinkets, the finds of bronze bowls, vessels, goblets and other items of high quality metal work at Karmir-Blur are numerous and important, and supplement those earlier found at Toprak-Kale. For instance, over one hundred bronze bowls were found neatly packed in piles at Karmir-Blur. Most of them have a schematic picture of a turret with a tree sticking up at the top, and a lion's head underneath, together with a brief cuneiform inscription recording the name of the reigning monarch, constituting a form of hallmark.

These recent Soviet finds, together with those made at Toprak-Kale and at various Urartian sites in eastern Turkey, support the prescient judgment of Professor A. H. Sayce. Over forty years ago, before the distinctive qualities of Urartian civilization were fully appreciated, Sayce wrote in the fourteenth edition of the *Encyclopaedia Britannica*:

'The best extant metal work of the late Assyrian period has been found at Wan, the ancient capital of the kingdom of Urartu, on the shore of Lake Wan. Realistic bronze bulls' heads, a figure of a god in the Assyrian style, couching sphinxes with inlaid human heads (now lost), a snake monster with inlaid black and white roundels, and a model of a wall with a gateway, apertures for archers, towers and battlements, may be cited as typical; the finest individual object is a round shield, quartered, with repoussé figures of animals. Some authorities would see in Armenia the centre from which such work was inspired elsewhere, and the commencement of a style continued in Achaemenian Persia . . . '

---

[1] Illustrated in *The British Museum: Report of the Trustees*, London, 1966, plate XIIa.

28. Urartian helmets, from time of King Argishti I

29. Detail of bronze shield of Sarduri II

30. Urartian wall painting, Erebuni

While much of Urartian art is ceremonial and military in character, it is also of paramount importance for the study of Urartian religion. Like almost all Near Eastern peoples of antiquity, the Urartians evolved a complicated system of faith and ritual. The official pantheon of Urartu at one time comprised no less than seventy-nine gods, goddesses and satellite deities. These are listed on a cuneiform inscription found at the so-called Mher-Kapusi or 'Mher's Gate', on the Zimzim-Dagh not far from Van. The inscription, carved shortly before 800 BC, enumerates the tariff of sacrifices which had to be offered to each god by way of propitiation. Expressed in terms of specified numbers of bulls and sheep, the size of the offerings destined for each god indicates his relative seniority in the religious hierarchy. Thus, the senior god, Haldi, receives 17 bulls and 34 sheep, while Teisheba, god of war, thunder and storms, is offered 6 bulls and 12 sheep. Third in the hierarchy came Shivini, the sun god, who received 4 bulls and 6 sheep; Shivini is equated with the gods Adad and Shamash of the Assyrian pantheon.

As well as animals, human beings were sometimes sacrificed to the Urartian gods. Lehmann-Haupt discovered at Toprak-Kale a large number of human and animal skeletons all heaped together in a storeroom, evidently part of a sanctuary. The human skeletons had all lost their skulls, from which it may be concluded that the victims were beheaded during the ritual sacrifice. Again, an Urartian seal in the possession of Professor K. V. Trever in Leningrad portrays an altar by the side of which lies a beheaded human body.

Haldi, the supreme deity, had a consort, the goddess Arubani (Arubaini, Uarubani). Teisheba, the Hurrian Teshub, had as his spouse the goddess Khuba – Hurrian name, Khebat or Khepa. The moon was worshipped in the person of the god Shelardi, corresponding to the Assyrian deity Sin.

Like the ancient Sumerians and Hittites, and the medieval Georgians, the Urartians paid a special cult to sacred trees and plants – notably, the Tree of Life and of Immortality. A number of seals and articles of metal work show worshippers paying homage to a holy tree, shown sometimes in conjunction with up to three stelae or tall upright stones. On one seal from Toprak-Kale, the sacred tree has a temple watering pot standing close by it.

Upright stones with rounded tops, some of them cult stelae from Urartian times, are still seen in the Van area. At other sites in Armenia vertical stones are found carved into the shape of an enormous phallus, having a bulbous top, these being of course associated with ancient fertility rites. The border region between Georgia and Armenia is rich in single free-standing megaliths or menhirs, often carved with representations of animal or bird totems. Many of these belong to the beginning of the first millennium BC, especially the conspicuous megaliths carved with the emblem of a fish or sea-dragon – the so-called *vishaps* – often found on hillsides on the Armenian and Georgian marchlands. These *vishaps* were connected with ancient Urartian irrigation systems, as their attendant spirits and patrons. They are often found on high hills from which canals flowed down into the valleys, notably in the Trialeti and Ararat regions. In some cases, the original *vishaps* are definitely pre-Urartian, as for example one seen by this writer at Garni, near the palace of the Armenian kings; in this instance, the carved head had an Urartian inscription carved on top of the original dragon-like effigy.

The Urartian cult of fishes and sea monsters is further evidenced by the discovery at Karmir-Blur of clay statuettes in the form of bearded male figurines, surmounted with the effigy of a fish head. These figurines were painted pale blue. Another statuette from Karmir-Blur has a scorpion's tail, and bears traces of four different colours of paint. These small portable idols have Assyrian and Sumerian parallels.

No study of Urartian religion would be complete without some account of burial customs. These can best be studied by reference to three tombs discovered at the Urartian fortified town of Altin-Tepe ('Golden hill') situated on a steep hill 60 metres high and 500 metres long, 20 kilometres east of Erzinjan on the main road to Erzurum. Since 1959 a Turkish expedition has explored three sets of tombs, all evidently belonging to a single princely family or clan of the period of King Argishti II (714–685).

One of these tombs was virtually intact. To construct it, a shaft or tunnel 7 metres wide and over 8 metres long had been driven into the slope of the hill, and the monumental stone sepulchre built deep underground. For protection against robbers and landslides, the funerary chambers themselves were enclosed in a wall of large stones and covered over with thick layers of soil, before the tunnel itself was finally filled in.

The Altin-Tepe tombs each contained three chambers. In the present case, behind a large stone slab and a pile of heavy stone blocks at the north-eastern end there was a door 3 feet wide, and then an entrance vestibule 4 feet long. The first room or antechamber, measuring 12 by 4 feet, contained a large bronze cauldron, inside which were crammed a folded bronze belt, two bronze discs, bronze parts from a war chariot, horse trappings, statuettes depicting horses for fitting to the end of chariot poles, as well as the decayed remains of iron weapons. Two stools with silver-plated wooden legs had been placed on the floor between the entrance door and the cauldron. A table had been piled with pottery vessels, horse bits, harness, three bells, and a few bone trinkets and other objects. From this first chamber, a door led to a second room measuring 13 by 8 feet, and containing two trough-shaped stone coffins with curved lids, which could be readily opened and shut. The coffins bore no form of decoration or inscription; one contained the remains of a man, the other that of a woman. Outside the coffin of the male corpse were lying some gold, silver and bronze buttons which had been sewn on to a garment; there were also some iron arrow heads lying around. The woman's corpse had been buried fully clothed, the gold buttons and spangles of her costume being fully preserved, along with a necklace of gold and precious stones. A faience vase, of Assyrian make, pottery vessels, trinkets, bone tools, also a stool and some now decayed wooden objects had been deposited in an orderly fashion on the tomb floor. From this main funerary chamber, a narrow door led to the third and smallest room, measuring only 8 by 6 feet. Cut into each wall of this chamber was a niche; on the floor had stood a wooden couch reinforced with eight pairs of bronze rings, also a substantial table on four legs, four pottery vessels, and a rod of solid silver 17 centimetres long, decorated with a lion's head at each end. This Altin-Tepe grave is built of carefully cut and dressed stone, erected deep within the side of the hill. Earthquakes have subsequently caused the flat roof to collapse. It is evident that the general layout of these sepulchres was modelled on that of the rock-cut funerary chambers carved out of the citadel wall at the royal city of Tushpa in Van.

These Altin-Tepe tombs provide valuable insight into Urartian domestic and ceremonial styles. Furniture was strong and elegant, but squat in proportions, the stools and tables found here not exceeding 50 centimetres in height. The chairs are backless, and are really elaborate stools; they have wooden legs enclosed in bronze casings usually shaped like bull or lion paws. The bases of table and chair legs are often of silver, and conical in form. Furniture legs are joined and strengthened by wooden crossbars, adorned with double volutes in bronze. Neatly fitted metal corner pieces enable many pieces of furniture to be accurately restored, even when the original woodwork has long since crumbled away. Many of these pieces would have done honour to a French Empire salon, or to a British Regency drawing room.

The gold and silver treasures brought to light in the various funerary chambers at Altin-Tepe were in fact more numerous than all those ever found previously over the whole of Urartu, taken together. The technical mastery, and the virile and energetic treatment of human and animal figures by the craftsmen working for this provincial outpost of Urartu, is a noteworthy feature. Winged gods mounted on winged bulls, or on winged horses, are characteristic, and strikingly foreshadow the Greek cult of Pegasus. Centaurs, lions running with open jaws, speeding goats, hybrid lion and bull figures are favourite motifs. The horsemen are shown with great attention to detail, wearing tapering, pointed helmets such as those belonging to the Urartian kings, covering the ears and nape of the neck. The riders wear long robes with short sleeves. The winged centaurs are depicted in the act of shooting arrows, and the bulls and lions in furious movement, rushing forward to attack with all their might.

One of the Altin-Tepe tombs, as already mentioned, had a bronze cauldron standing close to the door, containing a number of articles crammed tightly together. Many of these had been deliberately crushed, bent or mutilated in such a way as to be unusable in the future. While this could be interpreted in part as an attempt to deter grave robbers, it also had a ritual, religious significance, deriving from the burial practices and beliefs of earlier Anatolian Bronze Age civilizations. In his book on the Chalcolithic and Early Bronze Ages in the Near

East and Anatolia[1], Dr James Mellaart describes a tomb at Horoztepe in Asia Minor, dating from the Early Bronze Age. Here excavators found two copper tables supported by legs shaped like human feet and legs wearing short boots, and bent double. With these was a mass of copper vessels, all bent and folded for magico-religious reasons. 'The bending or breaking was believed to make the object "harmless" to the dead. Furniture was frequently taken to pieces, swords bent or broken, and vessels crushed, . . . to make sure that the dead were not disturbed.'

Whereas Altin-Tepe gives us an excellent idea of the burial customs of the Urartian upper classes, for the tombs of humbler folk we have to go to another site – that of Malaklyu near Igdyr, on the northern slopes of Mount Ararat, where some excavations were carried out by P. F. Petrov in 1913. Published by B. A. Kuftin in 1944 in the *Bulletin* of the Georgian State Museum in Tbilisi, the results of Petrov's investigations were later made available in English translation by Dr Richard Barnett.[2] Petrov unearthed what Kuftin rather misleadingly termed a 'columbarium' (Latin: a pigeon-cot), but was in reality an urn-field or cemetery, containing bodies both inhumed and cremated, and laid to rest in clay urns. These urns were then placed in rock crevices, and covered with large stones. Grave-goods consisted of iron knives, spear- and arrow-heads, copper vessels and ornaments, placed in separate heaps beside the urns. However, the most numerous class of grave-goods were beads, consisting of stone, glass, nephrite, paste and bronze, very seldom, shell. Cornelian and agate beads also featured.

Cremation burials in urns, as evinced at Malaklyu, is a rite usually considered alien to the southern Caucasus at this period. The absence of wood-ash shows the burning was done with fuel of dung bricks, trees being rare in this locality. The bodies were burned still clothed and wearing ornaments, such as beads, which were found in the urns together with the ashes. All urns were of standard type – handleless, round vessels with a narrow neck and red polished surface, covered over with a saucer made of the same clay ware, placed base upwards. The urns were provided with a hole at one side, presumably to let the soul emerge. The character of this cemetery, so unusual in Transcaucasia at this date, shows that it was left by an alien, intrusive population, possibly members of an Urartian military garrison with their families. This interpretation is supported by finds of Urartian seals in this Malaklyu urn-field; such seals are otherwise almost unknown in poorer class burials in Armenia during the early Iron Age.

We have left until now one of the most distinctive Urartian contributions to architecture and structural engineering – namely the remarkable temples, many dedicated to the supreme Urartian god Haldi, and others of the so-called 'Susi' type, which are a feature of all the main Urartian urban centres so far excavated. Some of their main features have been known for many years from a bas-relief originally adorning the palace of the Assyrian King Sargon II at Khorsabad: this

[1] Published at Beirut in 1966: pp. 185–8.
[2] *Anatolian Studies*, XIII, 1963.

depicted the sack by the Assyrians of the great temple of Haldi and Ardini at Musasir in Kurdistan (714 BC). The notable fact about this picture is that the building is covered by a gabled roof. The low, squat proportion of the façade as shown on the relief could well be due to restrictions of space imposed on the sculptor, by the conventional system of depicting all the scenes of the reliefs between the upper and lower borders of one single register. In fact, reconstructions of these temples made on the basis of actual archaeological evidence show that they were originally surmounted by tower-like structures of considerable height, built of mud brick. This applies to the example at Toprak-Kale, of which Rassam's original drawings were found in 1951 in the archives of the British Museum, and also the sites at Erevan, at Altin-Tepe near Erzinjan, and the shrine at the Urartian acropolis at Kayalidere in the Varto area, first excavated by a British expedition in 1965.

The general plan of Urartian temples is square, with wide but shallow buttresses at each of the four corners. Inside, the sanctuary itself consists of a single square compartment, windowless, and hardly wider than the thickness of the immensely heavy walls surrounding it. These walls are built to about a man's height in neatly cut ashlar masonry, sometimes with a dedication incised in cuneiform in prominent positions; above this, the walls are carried up to a considerable height in sun-dried brickwork. There is a single entrance, frequently facing south, and with recessed jambs. Usually, an altar faces the door and stands up against the back wall of the sanctuary inside; there is a built-up offering table outside as well. The building was surrounded by a paved court, partly covered over by a flat roof supported by pillars. The compact inner sanctuary, measuring between 40 and 50 feet across when taking in the thickness of the walls, was too cramped to accommodate large bodies of worshippers, but would hold only a select band of priests and acolytes.

The inner walls of the shrine were painted with magnificent and imaginative frescoes in a variety of colours, in which blues, reds and black predominate. The Haldi temple at Arin-Berd near Erevan has wonderful wall-paintings, including a striking portrayal of a deity standing on the back of a lion; another section of the wall is painted with rosettes laid out in diagonal patterns, like the pieces on a chess board. Similar techniques were used to decorate palaces and public buildings, often with highly sophisticated effect. In deference to the god Haldi's warlike attributes, the spearhead motif is commonly found in temple frescoes as well as in bas-reliefs; spears were commonly offered up by the worshippers as tribute to the god.

King Sargon's Khorsabad relief shows cauldrons on tripods standing before the Urartian temple at Musasir, and also decorative spears and shields used as wall ornaments. All these items have now been discovered *in situ* in the course of archaeological operations, thus confirming the accuracy of the Assyrian sculptor's portrayal.

31. Urartian bronze cauldron
32. Cast bronze figurine of winged bull
33. Bronze horse's head (Karmir-Blur)
34. Urartian figure of The god Teisheba

The importance of these Urartian temples for the history of world architecture is considerable, as also for the later history of architecture in medieval Armenia itself. Lehmann-Haupt has drawn parallels between Urartian temples and those erected at a slightly later date in Paphlagonia, further westwards in Asia Minor. Ernst Herzfeld once pointed out that the façade of the Musasir temple, with its geometrical motifs, foreshadows well-known Phrygian models.

However, the most important diffusion of Urartian architectural influence was towards Iran. The monumental layout of a tower-like structure combined with a lower, central building with a gabled roof, characteristic of Urartian Haldi temples, was later imitated by the Medes and Persians, the sixth-century tomb of Cyrus at Pasargadae providing a good example. One of the public buildings at Altin-Tepe clearly anticipates some features of Achaemenid architecture. This was a plain rectangular assembly hall, some 45 metres in length, its roof supported on eighteen wooden columns arranged in three rows. This is the prototype of the Achaemenid royal reception hall or *apadana*, familiar from such sites as Pasargadae, Susa, Persepolis and Ecbatana. At Arin-Berd, close to Erevan, the Medes and Persians adapted the outer colonnade of an old Urartian temple to form an *apadana*, following their annexation of the country. According to K. L. Oganesian, there were originally twelve pillars supporting the outer portico and adjacent covered area of this Arin-Berd shrine: the Medes then added eighteen further columns and roofed over the entire edifice, thus creating an impressive thirty-pillared assembly hall.

Such structures as the Haldi temple at Arin-Berd are also instructive for study of the much later Christian architecture of Armenia. As reconstructed by Oganesian[1], with its square central area and four corner buttresses, we see here the distant ancestor of the cruciform-domed church which came into prominence in Armenia and Georgia from AD 600 onwards. It required only the invention of the squinch and the pendentive to make possible the erection of a lofty drum, resting on buttresses and columns above the quatrefoil of the nave and transepts. In these developments, as we shall see, the Christian peoples of the Caucasus were to prove well to the fore.

The kingdom of Urartu survived the downfall of its constant political rival, Assyria, for in 612 BC Nineveh was destroyed by the united forces of Babylon, the Medes and Scythian hordes from the north. The fact that Urartu was still in precarious existence at this time is mentioned in Babylonian chronicles relating to the years between 609 and 605 BC. In a portion of the Book of Jeremiah dated to 594 BC, the Urartians still feature as enemies of Babylon, but these were the closing years of the Vannic kingdom. Around 590 BC it was finally overthrown by the Medes. Outlying strongholds, cut off from the support and authority of Van itself, were soon overrun and pillaged one by one, by local subject tribes or by Scythian and Cimmerian bands who had long waited for their opportunity.

[1] *Arin-Berd*, tom. I, Erevan, 1961, fig. 27.

The relevance of Urartu for the history of civilization in Armenia and the ancient world generally is clearer today than ever before. Its high accomplishments, military and administrative prowess, and distinctive art and culture, have until recently been consistently underrated. As Professor Seton Lloyd writes:[1]

'Urartu is now being presented to us as a nation – and in its time a very great nation – whose history and even identity seem to have been completely expunged from the records of human memory for two-and-a-half thousand years. Yet today, everything about it – its racial characteristics, political and economic history and its art – constitute one of the most intriguing problems in Near Eastern archaeology.'

[1] *Early Highland Peoples of Anatolia*, London, 1967, p. 122.

Chapter V

THE FORGING OF THE ARMENIAN NATION

MANY of the older historians give a rather over-simplified account of the origin of the modern Armenian nation. According to Herodotus, the Armenians entered Asia Minor from the west in company with the Phrygians, to whom he regarded them as closely allied ethnically. The fact that the Armenian language is an Indo-European one might seem to give support to a migratory hypothesis, and there is no doubt that considerable ethnic disturbance did take place in the Van and Araxes regions at various times during the second and also the first millennium BC.

However, the findings of modern archaeology and linguistics show that a simple migratory theory cannot fit the facts. Many features of Urartian civilization in particular are perpetuated in ancient Armenian culture. The very name 'Urartu' lived on in various forms long after the ruin of the Vannic kingdom. Indeed, 'Urartu' is only a different form of the name of Mount Ararat, a focal point of Armenian national consciousness to this day. The name 'Urartu' is also preserved in the ethnic term 'Alarod-(ians)', a people often referred to by classical geographers from Herodotus onwards. These Alarodians formed a special contingent in the grand army of the Persian Great King Xerxes, had their own language (no doubt based on Urartian), and continued to occupy a large area in the Armenian heartland long after the disappearance of the Urartian kingdom itself.

The name 'Urartu', in the form 'Urashtu', still occurs in 520 BC in the Babylonian inscriptions of King Darius, while the parallel Persian text from Behistun already carries the term 'Armina'. The ethnic term 'Urashtu' occurs for the last time in the inscriptions of King Xerxes, early in the fifth century BC, again referring to the territories which we know as Armenia. However, Hecataeus of Miletus, the pioneer Greek geographer and historian, writing about 500 BC, was already familiar with the term 'Armenioi'. One of the first kings of Urartu was called

112

III Collective farm, Soviet Armenia
    Kindergarten, Soviet Armenia

IV Erevan, general view
Erevan, Lenin Square

Aramé or Aramu: Moses of Khorene includes this monarch in his list of ancient kings of Armenia, as the sixth descendant of the Armenian eponymous ancestor Hayos. Some scholars see a connection between the Urartian name 'Aramé', and the ethnicon 'Armenia(n)'.

It is of interest to quote the opinion of Dr Richard Barnett, who considers that the last king of Urartu, Rusa III (605–590), 'son of Erimena', was in fact an Armenian usurper; instead of 'Rusa, son of Erimena', in fact, his title should properly be read as: 'Rusa the Armenian'.

The Urartian ruling class, as we have seen, used a form of Hurrian as their official language, which they wrote down in cuneiform characters modelled on Assyrian and Babylonian models. With the passing of the Vannic kingdom, the people of Armenia lost the habit of writing in their local language. This is not to say that they became illiterate. For nigh on a thousand years – until the invention of the Armenian alphabet by St Mesrop Mashtotz in the fifth century AD – the Armenians kept state records in the leading international languages, Iranian, Aramaic and Greek. However, the absence of written records in the vernacular does certainly add to the difficulty of tracing the genesis of the Armenian nation, as we know it today.

We may be certain that the indigenous population of Urartu and Armenia generally did not vanish from the face of the earth when overrun by the Medes and barbarian tribes around 590 BC. In his partly legendary biography of King Cyrus of Persia, the *Cyropaedia*, Xenophon gives an interesting account of how Cyrus pacified Armenia, and acted as mediator between the Armenians proper and the followers of Haldi, that is, the descendants of the Urartians. The Armenian king, whose name is given as Tigranes, becomes a Persian vassal. King Cyrus finds the Armenians occupying the fertile valleys and arable land, and the followers of Haldi refugees in the mountains. Cyrus persuades the Armenian king to invite the people of Haldi to come down to the valleys and cultivate the vacant fields, on payment of suitable dues and tribute money. In return, the followers of Haldi (Urartians) promise to allow the Armenians to pasture their cattle in the hill country. Cyrus then takes measures to preserve peace between the two communities by building forts in Armenia at strategic points, and installing his own garrisons with their commanders.

In his study of the art of Urartu, B. B. Piotrovsky compares the physical appearance and style of dress of Urartian envoys at the court of the Assyrian king Ashur-bani-pal, and Armenians shown on the stone reliefs of Xerxes at Persepolis, nearly two centuries later.[1] In 654 BC, after Ashur-bani-pal's victory over the Elamites, King Rusa II of Urartu sent envoys to Arbela to congratulate the Assyrian ruler. The reception of the Urartian envoys is represented on a relief from the royal palace at Nineveh. The Urartians are shown as undersized, and they wear cloaks over long fringed garments. On their feet they have high l

[1] *Urartu*, trans. Gelling, London, 1967, pp. 12–13, fig. 3.

boots, details of similar boots being represented on clay beakers in the form of footwear found at Karmir-Blur in 1959. The Urartian envoys wear hats of soft felt with tassels, which may be compared with the hats worn by the Armenians on the reliefs of Xerxes at Persepolis. An interesting feature is that the Urartians are shown as short and stocky, compared with other races depicted; many Armenians of today are also on the short side, especially compared with their Iranian, Kurdish or Tatar neighbours.

As mentioned, the Armenians term themselves 'Haik', and their land 'Hayastan'. There seems good reason to connect this ethnic name with the old eastern Hittite province of Hayasa, in mountainous western Armenia, along the upper reaches of the River Euphrates or Kara-Su. The Hayasa people's language was evidently related to the ancient Indo-European languages of Asia Minor, namely Hittite, Luvian, Lydian, Lycian and Phrygian, and this is important in view of the affinities of Armenian with the other Indo-European languages. The inclusion of the Hayasa tribes within the borders of the Hittite empire certainly contributed to the further evolution of their language and culture patterns.

After the fall of the Hittite empire, the name 'Hayasa' disappears from historical record, and is not found either in Assyrian or in Urartian official inscriptions. It is replaced by references to a land named 'Sukhmi' or 'Sokhmi', located between the upper reaches of the Euphrates, and the River Aratsani or Murat-Su.

In the south-western portion of the Armenian highlands, west of Lake Van, lay the Hurrian land of Shupria. In an Urartian inscription of Sarduri II (mid-eighth century BC), this territory receives the name of 'Arme' (or 'Armini'). During the next hundred years, as a result of the weakening of Urartian central authority, the people of Arme evidently assumed leadership of most of the minor tribes of the south-western Armenian hill country.

Up in the north, in the old land of Hayasa, the remnants of the Hayasa people formed a tribal federation, whose name gave rise to the forms 'Haik', 'Hayastan' used by the Armenians today. The name 'Sokhmi', also applied to tribes living along t'   er Euphrates, seems to be perpetuated in the medieval and modern
                        as a name for the Armenians in general – 'Somekhi', meaning
                  and 'Somkheti', or 'Armenia'. Following the fall of Urartu and
                  sion, there was further fusion and intermingling of all these
                  ', 'Arme' and 'Sokhmi' became more or less synonymous. The
                  ves adopted the form 'Hai', the Georgians 'Somekhi', while
                  r the form 'Armina', which in Greek or Latin turns into the

                  raditions speak of a race of blond, blue-eyed supermen
                  and wrought great deeds of prowess and valor. These
                  he migrations of the Indo-European peoples, which
                  ene in Armenia as well as in Iran during the Bronze

Age. In several parts of Asia Minor, including the Hittite realm, an Indo-European aristocracy imposed its language and state organisation on a local population largely Anatolian in ethnic character. This is what happened in the southern marches of historical Armenia, in the case of the Mitanni kingdom, for a time a powerful rival of the Hittites and the Pharaohs of Egypt. As Manfred Mayrhofer has shown,[1] the kings of Mitanni all bore Indo-Aryan names; their gods were those of the Indo-Aryan pantheon; and they used Indo-European terms for all matters concerned with horse breeding and training. However, the bulk of the population was Hurrian, as is shown by the names of the queens, and the government of Mitanni carried on official correspondence with the Egyptian pharaohs in the Hurrian tongue.

Long after the fall of Mitanni, there took place a whole series of invasions by Scythians and Cimmerians from the Russian steppes and the Eurasian plain. The Cimmerian invaders descended on Colchis about 730 BC from the direction of the Sea of Azov, skirting the Black Sea coast, to be followed shortly by waves of Scythians surging over the Daryal Pass in the central Caucasus and along the Caspian shore past Derbent and the modern Baku. Besides the testimony of Herodotus, the presence of large numbers of these nomads in Georgia and Armenia is attested by Scythian burials and finds of Scythian arrowheads at the Samtavro burial ground in Mtskheta, also in Trialeti south of Tbilisi, at Karmir-Blur in Armenia and elsewhere.

From their bases in Armenia, the Scythians and Cimmerians fanned out to the west, the south, and the south-east. They invaded Media, ravaged the Phrygo-Mushkian kingdom of King Midas in 696–695 BC, and later plundered the Greek colony of Sinope on the Black Sea. They stormed into Syria and Palestine, and even approached the borders of Egypt. They terrorized the people of Israel, as attested by references to Gomer (the Cimmerians) and Gog and Magog, by which are meant the Scythians, in the book of the prophet Ezekiel. They helped to prepare the downfall of both Assyria and Urartu.

The rule of the Scythians over large regions of Asia Minor, Armenia and northern Iran is said to have lasted about twenty-eight years, from 652 to 624 BC. The Scythians were finally crushed by a coalition made up of Medes, Persians and Armenians, which also dealt destructive blows to the declining power of Urartu and Assyria. The Armenian tribal federation of Armini–Shupria to the west of Lake Van temporarily took the side of the Medes. According to the partly legendary account of Moses of Khorene, a certain King Paruir of Armenia took part in the sack of Nineveh in 612 BC, alongside the Babylonians and Cyaxares and his Medes. As a reward, King Paruir was confirmed in office by the Medes as ruler of the first autonomous Armenian state.

The conquerors of Nineveh now divided the provinces of the former Assyrian empire between themselves. Syria with Palestine and the south of Mesopotamia fell

[1] *Die Indo-Arier im alten Vorderasien*, Wiesbaden, 1966, pp. 28–9.

to the Chaldean empire of Babylon; the Median king Cyaxares ruled over the greater part of Iran, Assyria and northern Mesopotamia, Armenia and Cappadocia. The Medes incorporated within their domains most of the old Urartian territories. The vigorous Medes were much feared by their neighbours, and the exiled Jews expected to see Babylon destroyed by them at any moment. In addition, the Book of the Prophet Jeremiah (LI. 24–9) specifically predicted that the Armenians and Urartians would contribute to Babylon's final downfall:

'And I will render unto Babylon and to all the inhabitants of Chaldea all the evil that they have done in Zion in your sight, saith the Lord.

'Behold, I am against thee, O destroying mountain, saith the Lord, which destroyest all the earth: and I will stretch out mine hand upon thee, and roll thee down from the rocks, and will make thee a burnt mountain.

'And they shall not take of thee a stone for a corner, nor a stone for foundations; but thou shalt be desolate for ever, saith the Lord.

'Set ye up a standard in the land, blow the trumpet among the nations, prepare the nations against her, call together against her the kingdoms of Ararat, Minni, and Ashchenaz; appoint a captain against her; cause the horse to come up as the rough caterpillars.

'Prepare against her the nations with the kings of the Medes, the captains thereof, and all the rulers thereof, and all the land of his dominion.

'And the land shall tremble and sorrow: for every purpose of the Lord shall be performed against Babylon, to make the land of Babylon a desolation without an inhabitant.'

For a time, the rulers of Babylon staved off the evil day. King Nebuchadressar strove to secure his kingdom against the menace from the north by building great fortifications, canals and walls. He succeeded in establishing a state of equilibrium for half a century, further secured by dynastic marriages. When the Mede Cyaxares attacked Lydia, the kings of Cilicia and Babylon intervened and negotiated a peace treaty in 585 BC, by which the River Halys, which runs close to Armenia's western fringe, was established as the frontier between the Lydians and the Medes.

This tenuous balance of power was shattered about 550 BC by the emergence of Cyrus and his Persians, a highland people dwelling to the south-east of the Medes, and like them of Indo-European speech and manners. The Persians were inspired by the new religious teaching of Zoroaster, and by a fresh concept of imperial responsibility, which distinguished their rule from earlier oriental despotisms. They soon put an end to the decaying power of Babylon, the last king of which, Nabonidus, perished in 539 BC.

Persian rule over Asia Minor and most of Armenia lasted from 546 to 334 BC. Like the rest of the immense empire, Asia Minor was administered in provinces or satrapies. According to Herodotus, Anatolia, Armenia and regions adjoining comprised the following satrapies:

I. The Ionian and other Greek coast cities from the Sea of Marmora to the Gulf of Antalya, with Caria and Lycia, and the adjacent islands, while these were under Persian control.

II. Lydia, with the interior of Anatolia from the Gulf of Adramyttium to the Cilician border.

III. Phrygia, which combined the frontage of the Marmora and Pontus with the plateau as far as the salt desert, and Cappadocia north of the Halys.

IV. Cilicia including the Taurus highlands and as far as the upper Halys.

V. Syria, immediately to the south-east of Cilicia, from the Amanus to the Arabian desert and Egypt.

X. Media with Ecbatana and large tracts of Western Iran.

XI. The Caspian provinces, including parts of Azerbaijan.

XIII. The Armenians, with the Pactyans and 'the peoples beyond as far as the Euxine Sea'; the capital of this satrapy was the city of Van.

XVIII. The Matieni and the Saspeiri (ancestors of the Georgians), and the Alarodians (remnants of the Urartians).

XIX. The Moschi, Tibareni, Macrones, Mossynoeci and Mares, tribes of Caucasian and Kartvelian stock, dwelling in the mountainous regions south of the Black Sea.

This distribution was essentially geographical, but it also took account of populations and former dynasties. Each province had its satrap or viceroy, over whose doings a royal secretary kept vigilant watch. There were local military levies with various forms of equipment; but the western coastguards were a separate command. Some provincial commands were hereditary fiefs; sometimes several were assigned to a single high commissioner from the Court. During the campaigns of Xerxes, the Armenians together with the Phrygians were placed under the command of Artochmes, a son-in-law of King Darius Hystaspes. On these same campaigns, the Alarodians (Urartians) and the Caucasian tribe of the Saspeiri were commanded jointly by a certain Masistius, son of Siromitres. Their weapons and armour resembled that of the Colchians, who themselves wore wooden helmets and carried little shields of raw oxhide, short spears, and knives.

The Persian empire was the greatest which the world had seen. Armenia lay on the northern borders of the empire's central heartland. The land was rapidly drawn into an immense network of international communications and trade routes. From north to south ran the highway connecting Colchis on the Black Sea with Media, via the Araxes River Valley. Thanks to this, the former Urartian city of Argishtihinili in present-day Soviet Armenia attained prosperity and importance; this city, under the name of Armavir, became capital of Armenia under the dynasty of the Orontids. The Armenian provinces south of Lake Van also gained strategic and commercial importance through their position on the Royal Road linking Susa with Ancyra, the modern Ankara, and with Sardis and western Asia Minor. According to Herodotus:[1]

'The truth about this road is as follows. All along it are royal post-stations, and very good inns, and it goes all the way through country that is inhabited and safe. So much of it as goes through Lydia and Phrygia is twenty post stages, a distance of ninety-four and a half parasangs [roughly 300 miles]. Where the river Halys flows out of Phrygia there is a gate which must be passed through to get to the river-crossing, and a great fortress stands beside it. Here the road goes into Cappadocia, and from there to the frontier of Cilicia is twenty-eight post stages and a hundred and four parasangs; and at that frontier you go through two gates and past two forts. From there the way through Cilicia is three post stages and fifteen and a half parasangs; and the boundary between Cilicia and Armenia is the navigable river called the Euphrates. In Armenia there are fifteen stages with inns, making fifty-six parasangs (over 180 miles), with one fort by the way. From Armenia the road runs into the land of the Matieni, where there are thirty-four stages, making a hundred and thirty-seven parasangs. This country is crossed by four navigable rivers, which you must pass over by ferry boat . . .'

This account by Herodotus confirms that the profession of inn and hotel keeping is an ancient one in Armenia – it is an occupation in which the hospitable Armenians excel. At this same period, enterprising Armenians and Assyrians were doing a brisk trade with Mesopotamia on inflatable rafts floating down the Tigris. The improved road transport and security system of the Persian empire certainly did much to improve Armenia's commercial position. However, the Armenians and Alarodians, together with neighbouring tribes forming between them the XIIIth and XVIIIth satrapies, had to furnish the Persian Great King with tribute totalling six hundred talents of silver, as well as horses, slaves and various military supplies in kind. This tribute certainly imposed a severe strain on the Armenian economy.

Farming, stock raising and wine growing remained the staple occupation of the bulk of the people. Herodotus describes Armenia as having a people 'rich in flocks',[2] and Xenophon calls it 'a large and prosperous province.'[3] Though little fresh engineering work seems to have been undertaken by the Persians the Van and Araxes regions continued to benefit from the tremendous canal systems of the old Urartian kings.

The classic account of Armenia under the Persian Achaemenid rulers is that of Xenophon, who crossed it with his Ten Thousand in 401–400 BC. Xenophon unfortunately arrived on the Armenian plateau in November, with the result that

[1] *Histories*, V. 52.
[2] *Histories*, V. 49.
[3] *Anabasis*, III. 5.

his men suffered terribly from the snow and the north wind's icy blast. Many died; others were blinded by the snow, and had their toes rotted off by frostbite. The hereditary satrap of Armenia at the time was Orontes, and his deputy, the lieutenant-governor of Western Armenia, was called Tiribazus. This latter was a personal friend of the Persian Great King; whenever Tiribazus was present, it was his exclusive privilege to help the supreme ruler mount his steed.

The satrap Orontes lived in a fine palace, while the ordinary houses in the surrounding township were surmounted by turrets. Elsewhere, in the more mountainous and exposed regions, houses were built largely underground, 'with a mouth like that of a well, but spacious below; and while entrances were tunnelled down for the beast of burden, the human inhabitants descended by a ladder. In the houses were goats, sheep, cattle, fowls, and their young; and all the animals were reared and took their fodder there in the houses.'[1] Such houses exist in Armenia and parts of Georgia to this day, though they are now being replaced by more modern dwellings. Their method of construction is described by Vitruvius, and is based on the principle of the corbelled cupola, tapering towards the summit. The Georgian variant of these dwellings is known as the *darbazi* house, and is often supported at its underground base by finely carved beams and pillars.[2]

Xenophon's Greeks captured the tent and household of Governor Tiribazus of Armenia, complete with a set of silver-footed couches, also drinking cups, and took prisoners some 'people who said they were his bakers and his cup-bearers'. The common people naturally did not pretend to such luxury, but even they were not badly off. Organized in village communes, they were ruled by their own headmen, who were in turn responsible to the satrap through the local deputy governors. These villagers gladly provided Xenophon's men with plenty of 'animals for sacrifice, grain, old wines with a fine bouquet, dried grapes, and beans of all sorts'. Sometimes they drank a kind of barley wine. 'Floating on the top of this drink were the barley-grains and in it were straws, some larger and others smaller, without joints; and when one was thirsty, he had to take these straws into his mouth and suck. It was an extremely strong drink unless one diluted it with water, and extremely good when one was used to it.'[3]

When Xenophon inspected his troops in bivouac, 'he found them faring sumptuously and in fine spirits; there was no place from which the men would let them go until they had served them a luncheon, and no place where they did not serve on the same table lamb, kid, pork, veal and poultry, together with many loaves of bread, some of wheat and some of barley. And whenever a man wanted out of good fellowship to drink another's health, he would draw him to the bowl, and then one had to stoop over and drink from it, sucking like an ox.' At another place, Xenophon draws a pleasing picture of his troops feasting in their quarters, 'crowned

---

[1] *Anabasis*, IV. 5.

[2] D. M. Lang, *The Georgians*, London, 1966, pp. 119–123.

[3] *Anabasis*, IV. 5.

with wreaths of hay and served by Armenian boys in their strange foreign dress; and they were showing the boys what to do by signs, as if they were deaf and dumb'. Thus we see that from their earliest years, the Armenian people have always been hospitable to strangers, who have not always repaid them as they deserved.

Xenophon further gives special praise to the quality of Armenian horses, which the local people used to rear specially for the Great King of Persia. 'The horses of this region were smaller than the Persian horses, but very much more spirited. It was here also that the village chief instructed them about wrapping small bags around the feet of their horses and beasts of burden when they were going through the snow; for without these bags, the animals would sink in up to their bellies.'

During the fraternal strife between Artaxerxes II and his brother Cyrus the Younger, for the Persian throne, in which Xenophon and his Ten Thousand played a prominent role, the Armenians seized their opportunity to reassert their country's autonomy. The satrap Orontes, who figures in Xenophon's *Anabasis*, was married about 401 BC to princess Rhodogune, daughter of Great King Artaxerxes II. Orontes took the side of his father-in-law Artaxerxes against Cyrus, who was defeated and killed.

Artaxerxes II turned out to be a feeble ruler, under whom the once mighty Persian empire fell into decay. Profiting by this, Orontes set himself up in Armenia as a virtually independent dynast, and became extremely wealthy, having a personal fortune of three thousand talents of silver. In later years, Orontes even turned against his father-in-law and overlord, Great King Artaxerxes, and led a revolt of the chief satraps which broke out in 366 BC. Eventually, Orontes submitted, was pardoned, and granted the satrapy of Mysia; he died in 344 BC.

The name Orontes is of Iranian origin, deriving from Avestan *aurand* ('mighty hero'), and closely related to Pahlevi *arvand*, with the same meaning. The Armenian forms of the name are Erwand, Arawan, and also Hrant. The Orontid dynasty is of great historical importance, since it spans much of the gap between the old Urartian kings (the first monarchy in Armenia), and the third Armenian monarchy of the Artaxiads in Classical times. The Orontids guaranteed the social and historical continuity of Armenia, as it evolved from its pre-Armenian phase and passed into the Hellenistic age.

Until recently, little was known about the offspring and successors of Orontes himself. The document that now allows us to establish the Orontids' existence as a regular dynasty is the funeral monument of Nimrud-Dagh in central Turkey, erected by King Antiochus I of Commagene (69–34 BC), himself a scion of the Orontid House. A series of Greek inscriptions on this mighty funeral hill commemorate the ancestors of Antiochus I, many of them rulers of Armenia. From this and other data, Professor Cyril Toumanoff of Georgetown University has compiled the following table of the Orontid monarchy in Armenia, several of the regnal dates being approximate only:[1]

[1] C. L. Toumanoff, *Studies in Christian Caucasian History*, Georgetown, 1963, pp. 293–4.

A. *Satraps of Armenia*

Orontes I, 401–344 BC

Orontes II, 344–331 BC

B. *Kings of Armenia*

Orontes II (continued), 331 BC

Mithranes, 331–317 BC

(Neoptolemus, satrap, 323–321 BC)

Orontes III, 317–260 BC

Samus, 260 BC

Arsames, 260–228 BC

Xerxes, 228–212 BC

Abdissares, *c.* 212 BC

Orontes IV, 212–200 BC

C. *Kings of Sophene*

Zariadris (Zareh), Strategos 200 BC; King 190 BC and after

Mithrobuzanes I, a contemporary of Artaxias I of Greater Armenia, around 170 BC

Orontes V, about 95 BC; annexation of Sophene by Tigranes II of Greater Armenia.

Under the last Persian kings of the Achaemenid dynasty, Armenia enjoyed peace and prosperity. The rulers of Iran now interfered little in Armenian internal affairs, and trade and agriculture flourished. This state of things was abruptly shattered by the invasion of Alexander the Great of Macedon. The battle of Arbela (Gaugamela) on October 1, 331 resulted in decisive victory for the Macedonians and Greeks over the last of the Achaemenids, Darius II Codomannus. Loyal to the last, the Armenians furnished 40,000 infantry and 7,000 horsemen to the Persian Great King, under the personal command of their own sovereign, King Orontes II. The Armenian cavalry made up the right flank of the Persian line of battle at Arbela.

During this catastrophic defeat, Orontes II apparently lost his life. At any rate, Alexander the Great celebrated his victory by sending Mithranes, a son of Orontes II, to be satrap of Armenia in his father's stead. It is interesting to note that this Mithranes was a former Iranian governor of Sardis in western Asia Minor, who had defected to the side of the Macedonians, and thus found himself ranged at the battle of Arbela on the opposite side to his own father. This is an instance of one of Armenia's perennial tragedies – of divisions of allegiance whereby father and son, brother and brother, through the ages would find themselves fighting on opposing sides, sometimes even against their own Armenian homeland.

Alexander the Great died at the zenith of his power, at the age of thirty-three. But his cultural and imperial heritage lived on. Far to the east, in Bactria, Parthia, Afghanistan, and at many sites in modern India and Pakistan, Greek or rather

Hellenistic cities grew up almost overnight. Stagnant, sleepy backwaters were revitalized, and decayed trade routes brought swiftly back into operation. Greek taste in building, sculpture and the arts, and knowledge of Greek literature and philosophy spread to out-of-the-way corners of Anatolia and central Asia. Greek science and technology produced rapid improvements in living standards, hygiene and sanitation, and in domestic amenities, at least for the select few. Greek ingenuity in engineering and construction left its mark over many regions of the old Persian empire.

Armenia, which lay close to Alexander's expansion route towards India, could not escape the impact of the new Graeco-Oriental world civilization which he helped to create. At the same time, in this new world of Hellenism, the vestiges of the earlier world of 'Iranianism' were not effaced, nor the elements of local advanced culture which were inherited from Urartu. Armenia now found herself in close touch with a number of Hellenistic countries, and thus open to new economic and social influences. The exclusively agricultural economy and rural existence of Achaemenid Armenia, where the use of coined money was scarcely known, were suddenly altered. The important overland route of transit trade, connecting China, India and central Asia with the Mediterranean world, passed through Armenia, while there was a parallel northern route through Caucasian Albania (Azerbaijan), Iberia and Colchis debouching on the Black Sea.

Great cities arose along these routes, which became homes of foreign merchants and centres of diffusion for Greek culture. The growth of a money economy and of urban life generally made for the decay of Armenia's traditional tribal-patriarchal society, and for the emergence of new patterns of urban stratification, including the growth of a town bourgeoisie and artisan class, and the commercial exploitation of slaves, though this latter institution never reached the massive proportions which it did in Greece and Rome. From the third century BC, Armenian royal authority grew more absolute, and the administrative machinery more complex, especially in regard to the royal court and the taxation and fiscal systems. The clan chiefs and rustic headmen began to turn into a more sophisticated courtier and squire class, enjoying greater luxury and ease, and demanding a higher standard of living.

A feature of this period of Armenian history is the foundation of a number of new cities, combined with the revival of towns which had flourished long before, under the Urartian kings. It is perhaps significant that Xenophon, traversing Armenia in 401–400 BC, fails to mention any cities of importance – though his route, which lay northwards from the plain of Mush, effectively passed well to the west of the Van region and the fertile Araxes valley, perhaps to avoid meeting any hostile city garrisons.

The Armenians, like the Urartians before them, used to name their main cities after the kings who founded them. This helps us to pinpoint the date of the foundation of many key Armenian towns. Now Orontes I, Xenophon's contemporary, had his capital at the ancient city of Armavir, north-west of Mount Ararat, in the fertile plain of the Araxes. From this site, King Orontes IV (212–200 BC) transferred his residence a few miles westward, to the new city of Ervandashat or Orontosata, which he named after himself, while Armavir still remained the religious centre of the Armenian kingdom. A few decades later, Artaxias I (190–159 BC) chose to reside further down the Araxes valley, at the rather malarial, marshy site of Artashat (Artaxata), also named after the reigning monarch. Artaxias is said to have built and adorned this capital with the aid and encouragement of the celebrated Hannibal of Carthage, who retired to Armenia after his defeat at the hands of Rome.

Far away to the west, towards the borders of Cappadocia, King Arsames (260–228 BC) built the renowned city of Arsamosata or Arshamashat, on the bank of the Aratsani, a major tributary of the Euphrates. This town became the capital of the independent Armenian kingdom of Sophene (in Armenian, Tsophk), and an entrepôt of international trade. Arsames inaugurated the regular striking of coins with Greek inscriptions, in the name of 'Basileos Arsames'.

At a later period, Tigranes the Great (95–55 BC) was the architect of the city of Tigranokerta – again named after himself – on the site of the present Farkin (Mayyafariqin). To complete this short list of royal foundations, we should recall that the most holy city of Armenia, Echmiadzin, residence of the supreme catholicos and within sight of Ararat, was originally called Vagharshapat, after Valarsh I (AD 117–40), himself a prominent member of the Arsacid dynasty which succeeded the house of Artaxias.

To appreciate Armenia's international position within the Hellenistic world, we must take stock briefly of the general situation in the Near East and Asia Minor. After Alexander the Great's sudden death in 323 BC, his generals quarrelled over the partition of his dominions. Ptolemy created a Greek kingdom in Egypt; Seleucus did the same in Syria and Mesopotamia, with his capital first at Seleucia, replacing ancient Babylon, and then at Antioch on the Orontes. Antipater conserved the old kingdom of Macedon, with its European dependencies as far as the Black Sea and also the Adriatic, with sovereignty over the city states in Greece. The attempts of Lysimachus to create a kingdom of the Bosphorus, with a capital on the Gallipoli peninsula, united his rivals against him, and failed at his death in 281 BC.

Hardly had Alexander's successors established an uneasy balance of power in the Near East and Aegean region, when new disturbances burst upon the civilized world from outside. Celtic tribes from the middle Danube shattered Macedon, devastated Thrace and Phrygia, and established themselves on the Asia Minor plateau to the west of Armenia, under the name of Galatians. Here they remained until Roman and Christian times, being the recipients of one of St Paul's epistles. Soon afterwards the Iranian-speaking people of Parthia overran the Persian plateau and deprived the Seleucids of their possessions east of the Euphrates.

The Parthians effectively separated the Seleucids of Syria, as well as the Armenians, from those eastern provinces of Alexander's realm which developed into the Greek kingdom of Bactria and also took in large regions of the Indus valley. These Eastern losses led the Graeco-Syrian kings of the Seleucid dynasty to seek compensation at the expense of Egypt to the south, and of Armenia and other independent states of Asia Minor to the north.

During the Seleucid period, Armenia became divided into several virtually independent kingdoms and principalities. The classification adopted at this epoch persisted, with certain changes, well into the Byzantine era. The most important region, of course, was Greater Armenia, situated east of the upper Euphrates, and including vast areas all round Lake Van, along the Araxes valley, and northwards to take in Lake Sevan, the Karabagh, and even the southern marches of Georgia. Lesser Armenia, on the other hand, was a smaller and less fertile kingdom, to the west of the upper Euphrates; it included the present-day districts of Sivas and Erzinjan, and bordered on ancient Cappadocia. To the south-west lay the two little kingdoms of Sophene and Commagene, separated from one another by the middle Euphrates, and having the fertile and desirable Melitene (Malatya) plain running between them. Sophene and Commagene often featured as buffer states between Parthia and Armenia on the one hand, and Syria and Rome on the other. Their royal houses had strong dynastic links with the Armenian Orontid house. Through their proximity to such great cities as Antioch and Palmyra, the kingdoms of Sophene and Commagene early became great centres of Hellenistic and then of Roman art and civilization, which they in turn helped to transmit eastwards into Greater Armenia and Transcaucasia.

The Seleucid kings never succeeded in asserting direct rule over Armenia proper. They collected tribute from local Armenian princes, whom they used to confirm in office by granting them the title of 'strategos', corresponding to the old Persian viceregal title of satrap. This situation changed somewhat under the Seleucid King Antiochus III, known as the Great (223–187 BC), an ambitious monarch who cherished dreams of restoring the empire of Alexander the Great. The Armenian King Xerxes rashly declined to pay tribute to Antiochus, who besieged him in his capital of Arsamosata and forced him to submit. Xerxes then received the sister of Antiochus in marriage. This lady, Antiochis by name, soon had the unfortunate Xerxes, her spouse, murdered, and united the Armenian kingdom of Sophene to the dominions of Antiochus III, her brother. The ill-fated King Xerxes has left some small coins bearing his portrait. We see on them a dignified, bearded, somewhat donnish-looking figure, wearing a pointed hat or tiara of unusual shape, with a peak in front and a streamer or tassels floating down the back. He has a thoughtful expression on his face, as if wondering how to cope with the political and marital troubles which eventually proved too much for him.

Antiochus III appointed a scion of the Armenian Orontids, Zariadris (Zareh) to be Strategos of Sophene in 200 BC. At this time, in Greater Armenia, the power of the main Orontid dynasty was drawing to a close. The last ruler of this line was Orontes IV (212–200 BC). Both he and his brother Mithras, High Priest of the Temple of the Sun and Moon at the city of Armavir, are mentioned in Greek inscriptions discovered there in 1927. One inscription contains an address of High Priest Mithras to his brother King Orontes; another evidently alludes to the king's tragic death. This event was the result of an uprising headed by a local dynast called Artaxias, son of Zariadris, and evidently instigated from Syria by King Antiochus III himself. Following this coup, Antiochus appointed Artaxias to be Strategos of Greater Armenia in place of the dead Orontes. The fact that the father of Artaxias was named Zariadris, as was the contemporary ruler of Sophene, prompts one to ask whether these two Armenian rulers may not have been father and son, though there is no proof of this.

Artaxias was the founder of the third and greatest Armenian monarchy, counting the Urartian kingdom founded by Aramé as the first (as does Moses of Khorene), and the Orontids as the second. The name Artaxias is the equivalent of the Persian Artaxerxes, and the Armenian Artashes. The accompanying table, showing the basic sequence of the Artaxiad line, is taken from the researches of the French numismatist Monsieur Henri Seyrig:[1]

The Artaxiad Dynasty

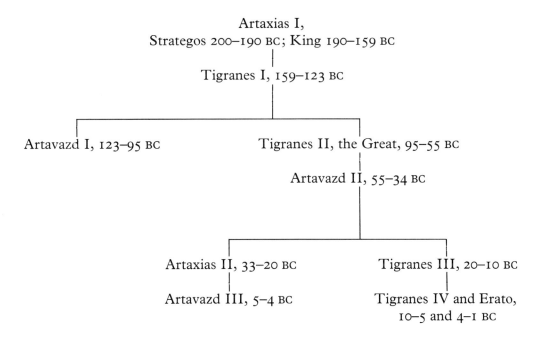

[1] See *Revue Numismatique*, 1955.

For a decade after being installed by Antiochus III, from 200 to 190 BC, Artaxias and his junior partner, Zariadris of Sophene, bided their time. Ultimately, Antiochus overreached himself by challenging the mighty Roman Republic to a trial of strength. No sooner had Antiochus sustained at Magnesia his great defeat at the hands of the Romans (190 BC) than Artaxias and Zariadris seceded from the Seleucid state. In the Peace of Apamea (188 BC) which sealed the Roman victory, the Senate in Rome granted them the status of independent rulers. This was Armenia's first juridical contact with the Roman Senate, which was glad to acquire two grateful allies in that strategic part of the world – pending completion of the usual preliminaries to swallow them up and annex their lands to the Roman republic itself.

Under this new-found Roman patronage, the two Armenian kingdoms of Greater Armenia and Sophene pursued a lively expansionist policy. From the Medes and Persians, Artaxias took Media Atropatena, the modern Azerbaijan, extending virtually to the banks of the Caspian Sea. From the Georgians he seized a broad slice of territory to the north-west of Lake Sevan. From the Chalybes, Mossynoeci and Taokhoi, the Armenians took much of the upland plateau round Erzurum, and some of the wild mountain country of the Pontic Alps. The province of Taron, round about the town of Mush, was cleared of remaining Seleucid garrisons.

One important result of this territorial growth was the cultural and linguistic consolidation of the Armenian people. Except for the Georgian marchlands, and for a few remote tribal districts such as Sassoun, Armenian became the dominant spoken language of the peasant masses, the hunters and tribesmen, and the townspeople except for those of Jewish and Greek birth. The Greek geographer Strabo (58 BC – AD 25) lays special stress on this result of the conquests of Artaxias and Zariadris. – Thanks to their work of unification, he says, 'all the inhabitants of these various districts today speak the same language.'[1] It must be remembered, however, that, prior to the invention of the Armenian national alphabet after AD 400, all works of literature, religious texts and government decrees were written down and transmitted in Iranian written in Aramaic characters, or else in Greek. The Armenian royal family and aristocracy were bilingual, speaking Greek or Iranian as well as Armenian.

An interesting passage in the History of Moses of Khorene relates how 'Artashes (Artaxias) ordered the borders of villages and farms to be marked out. For he multiplied the population of Armenia, introducing many immigrant tribes and settling them in the hills, valleys and plains. This is how he designed the boundary marks: he had rectangular stones carved, with a saucer-shaped cavity hollowed out in the centre. These were then buried in the ground, and four-cornered turrets fixed on top, projecting a little above ground level.' (*History of Armenia*, II. 56.) Three such stones have been found at various times not far from

[1] Strabo, *Geography*, XI. xiv. 5.

Lake Sevan, all carved with indentations at the top, as if to resemble a turret, and having inscriptions in an unusual form of Aramaic script. Although Professor A. Dupont-Sommer suggested that the stones commemorate a fishing expedition undertaken by King Artaxias in Lake Sevan, this explanation appears highly unlikely. There seems every reason to believe that these are three of the official boundary marks, so carefully and accurately described by the Armenian national historian, and that they embody in their Aramaic inscriptions the name of King Artaxias along with that of the local landed proprietor.[1]

It was during the ascendancy of the Orontids and the early Artaxiads that the complex edifice of Armenian paganism began to take shape. In addition to the famous temple of the Sun and the Moon at Armavir, the Armenians maintained a whole group of sanctuaries and shrines in the holy forest at Ashtishat (Acesilene), in the province of Taron, not far from Mush. There a row of resplendent temples stood, the most renowned dedicated to the goddess Anahit. A mighty golden statue of this patron and protectress of Armenia dominated an immense hall. When the Roman armies of Mark Anthony brought fire and sword to Armenia, the first soldier to lay a sacrilegious hand on the statue of the goddess was struck blind on the spot.

Anahit's father was Aramazd, the mighty Ahura-Mazda of the Iranians, corresponding in the minds of the ancient Armenians to Olympian Zeus of the Greek pantheon. From Armenia the cult of Ahura-Mazda spread northwards into Georgia, where the deity gave his name to the royal city and acropolis of Armazi, not far from Tbilisi.

The pantheon of ancient Armenia was an international, syncretic one. Native, local gods were worshipped side by side with deities imported both from Greek mythology and from the Iranian world, as well as survivals from the ancient cults which derived from the era of Urartu. Often there existed two or three embodiments of the same divine personage: Aramazd/Ahura-Mazda/Zeus is a case in point.

The ancient Armenians attached great significance to oracles and divination. Moses of Khorene (*History*, I.20) tells how Ara, great-grandson of Arma, left behind him a son who was called Anushavan, dedicated to the cult of the plane-tree, richly endowed and intelligent in word and deed. The child was consecrated to serve the cult of the plane-trees of Aramaneak, centred in Armavir. According to the rustling of their leaves, and their swaying in the breeze or in strong winds, and the direction of their movement, men used for long ages to carry on divination in the land of the descendants of Haik.

All this presents an illuminating parallel with the venerable oracle of Dodona in Epirus, seat of the most ancient of all Hellenic sanctuaries. The temple of Dodona was dedicated to Zeus. The method of gathering responses was by listening to the rustling of an old oak tree – perhaps a remnant of very primitive tree worship. Sometimes auguries were taken from doves cooing in the branches,

[1] See Trever, *Ocherki*, pp. 170–1.

the murmur of a fountain, or the clanging of brazen cauldrons hung – as also in the shrines of Urartu – round the tree or the temple building. It was from the oracle of Dodona that Lysander sought sanction for his ambitions, while the Athenians frequently appealed to its authority. Of additional interest is the discovery at Armavir of a Greek votive inscription mentioning a 'pinakion', which is a clay or pottery tablet on which questions to be put to the oracle were inscribed in advance. The same word exists in Armenian in the form *pnak*, meaning a saucer or dish.

Among the most universal cults of the ancient Armenians was that of Mithra, who was identified on the one hand with the Sun, or Helios, on the other, with Apollo and Hermes. Mithra was originally conceived of as a kind of angel, a power of light who fights on the side of Ahura-Mazda. This warlike characteristic he seems always to have retained. Names compounded of his, for instance, Mithra-dates, and also Buz-Mihr ('Great Mithra'), were common in both Armenia and Georgia. Mithra's festival, the Mithrakana, was celebrated in Iranian lands on the sixteenth day of the seventh month, and survived in modified form right up to Muslim times. Through Cilicia the cult of Mithra spread to Rome, and thence as far as London and other remote parts of the Roman empire. The typical bas-relief, which is found in abundance in the museums of Europe, represents Mithra in the form of a youth with a conical cap and flying drapery, slaying the sacred bull, the scorpion attacking the animal's genitals, the serpent drinking its blood, the dog springing towards the wound in its side, and frequently in addition, the sun-god, his messenger the raven, a fig-tree, a lion, a ewer, and torch-bearers. The head of the divine hierarchy of Mithra was Infinite Time; Heaven and Earth were his offspring, and begat Ocean. From Heaven and Earth sprang the remaining members of a circle analogous to the Olympic gods. Ahriman, embodiment of evil and darkness, was also the son of Time. Mithra was the most important member of the circle, the mediator between man and the supreme god.

The antiquity of the cult of Mithra in Armenia can be judged from the presence of a high priest of that name, a member of the royal Orontid family, at the shrine of Armavir around 200 BC; also by the prominence accorded to the composite deity Apollo/Mithra/Helios/Hermes, portrayed in the funeral monument of King Antiochus I of Commagene at Nimrud-Dagh. In the form 'Meherr', Mithra features later in the Armenian national epic *David of Sassoun* as the Great Meherr, Lion of Sassoun, who planted a splendid garden in Dzovasar and filled it with every kind of animal and fowl which God had created, and made his summer mansion there; he also founded a hermitage to which the sick, maimed and blind repaired for comfort and healing.

In political organization and statecraft, in culture and religious institutions, King Artaxias I and his associate Zariadris of Sophene were truly the architects of Armenia's greatness, which was to reach its apotheosis under the grandson of Artaxias, King Tigranes the Great.

128

Nimrud-Dagh: East Terrace,
showing head of Hercules

Nimrud-Dagh: West Terrace, showing Zeus

Chapter VI

TRIUMPH AND DECLINE—
TIGRANES THE GREAT AND AFTER

ARMENIA briefly attained a lofty pinnacle of imperial might and achievement during the reign of Tigranes the Great (95–55 BC). This ambitious, resourceful, and yet strangely erratic ruler is known to us largely through the hostile annals of his Roman foes, from his magnificent coinage, and from the silent, deserted ruins of his palaces and cities.

Tigranes the Great was the younger brother or perhaps, according to some sources, the son of King Artavazd I, grandson of the founder of the Artaxiad dynasty. Born around 140 BC, Tigranes spent some years as a hostage at the court of King Mithradates II of Parthia, who inflicted a signal defeat on the Armenians in 105 BC. On the news of the death of King Artavazd I in 95 BC, Tigranes purchased his freedom from the Parthians by ceding to them seventy fertile valleys in the Kurdistan area.

Tigranes ascended the Armenian throne at a singularly propitious moment. Roman power in Asia Minor was severely shaken by the warlike exploits of Mithradates Eupator, King of Pontus, who had consolidated his power over the Black Sea region, and threatened to drive the Romans out of Asia altogether.

Rome itself was on the threshold of the Social War, headed by the factions of Marius and Sulla. In Syria, the Seleucid dynasty was tottering towards anarchy and collapse.

From the moment of his accession, Tigranes set to work to enlarge his kingdom. He deposed and killed King Orontes (Arantes) V of Sophene, and entered into an alliance with Mithradates Eupator of Pontus, whose daughter Cleopatra he married. In 93 BC, Tigranes invaded Cappadocia in the interests of Mithradates, but was driven back by Sulla in 92. During the first full-scale war between Mithradates and the Romans, Tigranes supported the king of Pontus, though the astute Armenian abstained from interfering openly. For the time being, Tigranes was more interested in attacking the Parthians, whose empire was weakened by the death of Mithradates II (not to be confused with Mithradates of Pontus) in 88 BC. Parthia was now weakened by Scythian invasions and internal dissensions, enabling Tigranes to reconquer the seventy valleys which he had ceded and to lay waste large tracts of Media. The kings of Atropatene, Gordyene (now Bohtan), Adiabene (Assyria) and Osroene (Edessa) became his vassals, and attended him like slaves wherever he went. Tigranes also annexed northern Mesopotamia.

Syria itself fell to Tigranes like an overripe fruit. The last of the Seleucids were locked in civil strife, enabling the Nabataeans and other nomad tribes to rise in revolt. Anarchy threatened the existence of the Hellenized urban centres which had represented advanced civilization for several centuries past. An influential faction among the Syrian nobility and merchant class decided to call upon Tigranes to re-establish order, and invited him to invest himself with the crown of the Seleucid monarchs.

Tigranes required little encouragement. In 83 BC, the Armenians entered Syria, overran Cilicia and Phoenicia, and advanced into northern Palestine. Dividing his immense domains into 120 satrapies and provinces, Tigranes now took over from the Parthians the proud title of 'King of Kings', and from the Seleucids, that of 'God', 'the Divine' (*theos*), both of which appellations appear on his silver coinage. This silver coinage, the finest ever struck by an Armenian monarch, includes the large tetradrachms showing the effigy of Tigranes facing to the right, and wearing a five-pointed royal tiara decorated with a star and twin eagles. The reverse shows the *tyche* or city goddess of Antioch on the Orontes, with the river flowing by her feet. These splendid pieces were minted at Antioch and Damascus; later, Tigranes established his own mint, probably at Tigrano-kerta, where Lucullus the Roman conqueror later took possession of 8,000 talents of coined silver, equivalent to about ten million dollars. The coins minted in Armenia are markedly inferior to the Syrian issues.

In spite of charges made by his Roman enemies, Tigranes brought to Syria a brief era of political calm and economic revival. According to the Roman historian Junianus Justinus, and the more recent judgement of Theodore Reinach, 'Syria breathed again; for fourteen years she knew, along with the humiliation of foreign domination, peace, serenity and prosperity'.[1] Certainly, Armenian domination was in many ways preferable to that of Rome, which brought – along with good roads and general efficiency – economic exploitation, slavery and political subjugation.

The domains of Tigranes the Great stretched from the shores of the Caspian Sea to the Mediterranean, from Mesopotamia up to the Pontic Alps. The vast empire, formed of a varied mixture of diverse tribes, with their own dialects and cultures, could not be turned overnight into a cohesive, and durable political structure. Under the overlordship of Tigranes were united districts with a tribal or clan patriarchal structure, as well as semi-feudal countries belonging to the Iranian and Parthian tradition, and Hellenistic kingdoms and city states with their characteristic institutions. The neighbouring countries which acknowledged the suzerainty of Tigranes as 'King of Kings' were compelled to pay him a fixed tribute and send auxiliary troops in time of war. At the same time, each of these kingdoms and each of the autonomous Armenian principalities kept its own former laws and special status within the empire as a whole.

[1] H. A. Manandian, *Tigrane II et Rome*, p. 45.

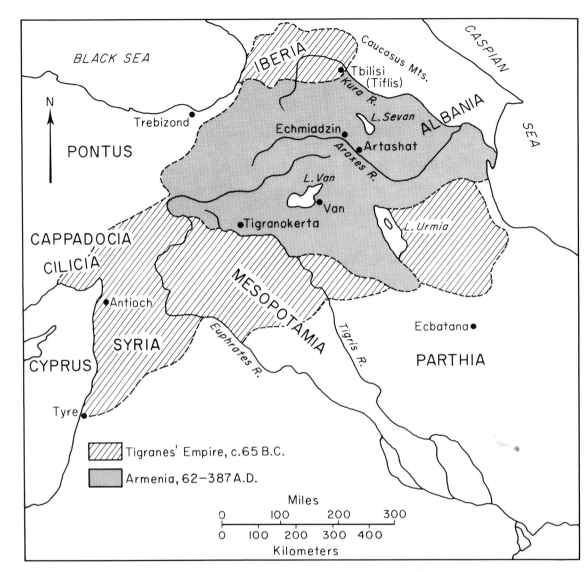

Map 2: Map of Armenia at the time of the Roman Empire

The leading role in Tigranes' system of government was played by the Armenian landed aristocracy, which formed his chief support, both in his victorious campaigns, and in public affairs. The king's brother Guras was appointed to the responsible position of governor of Nisibis, while the Armenian prince Bagrat was appointed governor of Syria. There is no doubt that the great feudal nobility of the *nakharars,* which was later to assume the initiative in national affairs and help to overthrow the Armenian monarchy itself, was already well established.

132

Alongside feudalism at home, there was widespread use of slave labour, in the form of captives taken in the course of Tigranes' many successful campaigns in the early part of his reign. To what extent chattel slavery formed the economic and social basis of the Artaxiad and later, the Arsacid monarchy, remains a matter of controversy. The most likely explanation is that a free native peasantry and herdsmen class existed side by side with slaves and serfs of largely foreign origin, who were employed both for domestic purposes and for building fortifications and other public works. Slaves were also used for mining and other arduous and unpopular forms of work, though their exploitation, partly through the nature of the terrain, never reached the level of ruthless efficiency characteristic of Greece and Rome. We may conclude that under Tigranes the Great, Armenia already had a hybrid social structure of transitional type, displaying survivals of clan organization, alongside the exploitation of slave labour for industry and public works. There were nascent elements of a feudalism deriving from Iranian and specifically Parthian models, and already showing some of the peculiarities of the *nakharar* system of the Arsacid period.

After having organized his vast realm, Tigranes began to build his capital Tigranokerta (near the modern Farkin in southern Turkey) which was to become the political, cultural and economic centre of the new state. (It is the Martyropolis of the early Middle Ages.) The former capital of Artaxata on the Araxes, and the Seleucid capital at Antioch, did not serve his purpose, since they stood on the north-eastern and western borders of his empire respectively. Antioch and other great towns of Syria had the further disadvantage that they would have caused the Armenian King of Kings to lose contact with his home base in Greater Armenia, which was the foundation of his power and military success.

The Greek and Roman historians who describe the campaigns of Lucullus in Armenia, and his capture of Tigranokerta, give us detailed information about the new capital. According to Appian's description,[1] Tigranokerta was surrounded by a wall 50 cubits high, which was so wide and thick that stables for horses were built inside it. Not far outside the actual city walls stood the royal palace, around which were laid out parks for hunting and ponds for fishing. Nearby was a strongly fortified castle. However, the city itself, unlike ancient Nineveh or Babylon, was relatively compact. In all likelihood, both in its plan and its mercantile and manufacturing character, it differed little from the usual type of Hellenistic cities of Asia Minor, Syria and Bactria.

To populate the new city with a suitable urban citizenry, Tigranes encouraged large numbers of Jews to migrate there, as well as forcibly transporting to it the inhabitants of the devastated cities of Cappadocia and Commagene which he conquered around 77 BC. According to Strabo:

'Tigranes the Armenian got the people into a bad plight when he overran Cappa-

[1] Appian, *Mithridatic War*, XII. 84.

133

docia, for he forced them (the population of Mazaca) one and all to migrate into Mesopotamia; and it was mostly with these that he settled Tigranokerta. But later, after the capture of Tigranokerta, those who could do so returned home'.[1]

In another passage of his *Geography*, Strabo states that Tigranes settled the peoples of twelve Greek cities in his new capital, while Appian estimates at 300,000 the number of inhabitants who were forcibly transported from Cappadocia and Cilicia. Plutarch mentions in addition the transfer to Tigranokerta of the population of the devastated regions of Adiabene, Assyria and Corduene. 'He transplanted also the Arabs, who lived in tents, from their country and home, and settled them near him, that by their means he might carry on the trade.' Plutarch adds that 'it was a rich and beautiful city, every common man, and every man of rank, in imitation of the king, studied to enlarge and adorn it'.[2]

Tigranes intended his capital to become one of the centres of Hellenistic science, art and literature. Amphicrates, the writer and rhetorician, was invited to Armenia when he was driven out of Athens. However, he ended his days in disgrace and starved himself to death; but he was accorded by Tigranes' queen, Cleopatra, honourable burial at a place called Sapha. Metrodorus of Scepsis, a philosopher and statesman from Pontus, called by Pliny 'Misoromaeus' or 'Hater of the Romans', was also a close adviser of Tigranes, and wrote a history of him which has not survived. He too was betrayed by Tigranes, who had him executed by King Mithradates of Pontus for some alleged political misdemeanour. When Lucullus captured Tigranokerta, he found a company of actors who had been recruited from all parts for the inauguration of a theatre Tigranes had built, and these the Roman conqueror made use of for celebrating his own triumphal games and spectacles. Tigranes can justly be called one of the founders of the Armenian national theatre, and his tastes were inherited by his son and successor Artavazd, whose original tragedies, written in Greek, are mentioned by Plutarch in his Life of Crassus.

So long as no external military threat existed, Tigranes' large though ramshackle empire stood apparently secure. Yet it contained within itself the seeds of its own destruction, not least of these being the discontent of the Greeks and Assyrians whom Tigranes had forced to migrate to his new capital. Many of these secretly yearned for the overthrow of their Armenian master. Again, Tigranes had bound up his own fate with that of his father-in-law, Mithradates, King of Pontus. As soon as this veteran combatant had passed the zenith of his success, the star of Tigranes was also bound to wane. With old age, too, Tigranes became increasingly ill-tempered and capricious. He executed two of his sons, whom he suspected of intriguing to depose him. In 70 BC, just before the invasion of Lucullus, he attacked Ptolemais in Phoenicia and took prisoner the local queen, Selene, also

---

[1] *Geography*, XII. ii. 9.

[2] 'Lucullus', in *Lives*, Everyman edit., II, pp. 219, 224.

134

7. General view of Garni

8. Bronze head of Anahit-Aphrodite from Satala (British Museum)

known as Cleopatra, whom he later beheaded. An irascible septuagenarian, Tigranes even executed the messenger who brought him the first news of the Roman invasion, so that nobody after this dared to give him any accurate information.

The pretext for a major Roman assault on Armenia was provided by Tigranes' action in sheltering his father-in-law, Mithradates Eupator of Pontus, following the latter's defeat at the hands of Lucullus in 72 BC. Lucullus sent an ambassador, Appius Claudius, to demand the extradition of Mithradates. Though unsuccessful in his principal mission, Appius Claudius was an extremely astute diplomatist, and secretly won over several of Tigranes' subject cities and vassal kings to the Roman cause. The clever Roman accurately sized up the weaknesses of Tigranes' personal character and the instability of his political position, reporting back to Lucullus that 'the Armenian government was an oppressive one, and intolerable to the Greeks, especially that of the present king, who, growing insolent and overbearing with his success, imagined all things valuable and esteemed among men not only were his in fact, but had been purposely created for him alone'.

Though coloured by anti-Armenian prejudice, the Roman reports, as reproduced by Plutarch and Appian, contain many valuable sidelights on daily life at the court of Tigranes. 'He had many kings waiting on him', Plutarch writes, 'but four he always carried with him as servants and guards, who, when he rode, ran by his horse's side in ordinary under-frocks, and attended him, when sitting on his throne, and publishing his decrees to the people, with their hands folded together; which posture of all others was that which most expressed slavery, it being that of men who had bidden adieu to liberty, and had prepared their bodies more for chastisement than the service of their masters.' Like many a modern colonial administrator, Lucullus and his envoy despised what they regarded as a disorganized, barbaric oriental state, and gratuitously insulted Tigranes by refusing him the customary title of 'King of Kings'. In his official replies, Tigranes responded by refusing to accord Lucullus his title of 'Imperator'.

The Classical sources contain highly coloured versions of the defeats inflicted by Lucullus on Tigranes near Tigranokerta in October 69 BC and again near Artaxata in the following year. In one battle, Plutarch states that the Armenians lost 'above a hundred thousand foot' and nearly all their cavalry, whereas 'of the Romans, a hundred were wounded and five killed'. These figures are subject to caution, and indeed show every sign of having been concocted by the Roman propaganda machine, which was as efficient at distorting facts and concocting statistics as many a modern totalitarian information agency. However, it is indisputable that the mighty city of Tigranokerta quickly fell to the Romans, largely because of the resentment felt by the Greeks and other forced settlers, who surrendered to Lucullus on being promised early repatriation to their former homes. This metropolis of over a quarter of a million souls rapidly declined to the status of a second-rate provincial town.

Tigranes was saved from complete disaster by a mutiny in the Roman army and the recall of Lucullus to Rome. There Lucullus gained renown as a gourmet and society host, giving sumptuous 'Lucullan' banquets which he financed by the fabulous spoils from the treasuries and temples of Armenia. The eclipse of Lucullus gave some respite to the aged Mithradates Eupator and his son-in-law, Tigranes, who even invaded Asia Minor once more. But meanwhile a son of Tigranes and Cleopatra, called Tigranes like his father, rebelled against him (as the old man had already killed two of his sons, the young Tigranes had reason enough to fear for his life), and found refuge with the Parthian King Phraates III, who supplied him with an army with which to invade Armenia. The elderly Armenian king now gave up all hope of resistance. He even determined to betray his father-in-law, Mithradates, and put a price upon his head. In 66 BC, when Pompey advanced into Armenia and joined forces with the younger Tigranes, the veteran monarch surrendered.

Reflecting that Tigranes the Great, now aged nearly seventy-five, could not put up further resistance to the Romans, Pompey cleverly changed his policy. He received old Tigranes graciously, and gave him back the remnants of his kingdom in return for a tribute of 6,000 talents of silver. As for Tigranes' rebellious son and heir, Pompey treated him coldly and took him back as a prisoner to Rome, where he was put to death in 58 BC. Tigranes II continued to reign in Artaxata as a harmless vassal of the Romans until his own death in 55 BC – a senile, abject client king of the Romans whom he had so long defied.

Scarcely less colourful in its way was the career and personality of Tigranes' son and successor, Artavazd II (55–34 BC), at once the most cultured and the most unfortunate of the Artaxiad line. A scholar, connoisseur and a man of cosmopolitan tastes, Artavazd was equally at home in the courts of Parthia and of the Graeco-Roman world. According to Plutarch, Artavazd was so expert in Greek language and literature, 'that he wrote tragedies and orations and histories, some of which are still extant'.[1] He continued to strike beautiful silver coinage, with Greek legends, after the style of his father Tigranes. The principal mint of Artavazd was at the capital, Artaxata, which now resumed its ancient status after the downfall of Tigranokerta. On many of his coins, which include a few rare tetradrachms but are mostly of smaller denominations, Artavazd assumes such titles as 'Great King', 'King of Kings', and even occasionally, 'The Divine'.

Artavazd played a crucial part in the disastrous campaign of Crassus against the Parthians, which culminated in the battle of Carrhae on May 28, 53 BC. Crassus received many warnings from his soothsayers, to avoid attacking the Parthians in the sandy wastes of Syria and Mesopotamia. 'But he paid no heed to them, or to anybody who gave any other advice than to proceed'. King Artavazd, faithful to the Roman alliance, promised Crassus a contingent of nearly 50,000 horsemen, cuirassiers and infantry. To quote Plutarch:

---

[1] 'Crassus', in *Lives*, Everyman edit., II, 302.

'He urged Crassus to invade Parthia by the way of Armenia, for not only would he be able there to supply his army with more abundant provisions, which he would give him, but this passage would be more secure in the mountains and hills, with which the whole country was covered, making it almost impassable to horse, in which the main strength of the Parthians consisted. Crassus returned him but cold thanks for his readiness to serve him, and for the splendour of his assistance, and told him he was resolved to pass through Mesopotamia, where he had left a great many brave Roman soldiers; whereupon the Armenian went his way.'

Seeing his advice unheeded and his goodwill unrequited, Artavazd struck up an alliance with the Parthians, which he cemented by marrying his sister to Pacorus, son of the Parthian monarch Orodes (Hyrodes) II. Following the annihilation of the Roman army by the Parthians at Carrhae, and the death of Crassus himself, the head and hand of the Roman commander were cut off and sent to the Parthian king just as Orodes was attending his son's marriage to the sister of the Armenian ruler. There followed a gruesome pantomime which formed a fitting epilogue to the Roman débâcle, as well as providing a sidelight on the barbaric splendours of the age. According to Plutarch, the betrothal ceremonies at Artaxata were very sumptuous, and various Greek compositions, suitable for the occasion, were recited before the two kings, both of whom were well versed in Greek literature.

'When the head of Crassus was brought to the door, the tables were just taken away, and one Jason, a tragic actor, of the town of Tralles, was singing the scene of the *Bacchae* of Euripides concerning Agave. He was receiving much applause, when Sillaces, coming to the room, and having made obeisance to the king, threw down the head of Crassus into the midst of the company. The Parthians receiving it with joy and acclamation, Sillaces, by the king's command, was made to sit down, while Jason handed over the costume of Pentheus to one of the dancers in the chorus, and taking up the head of Crassus, and acting the part of a bacchante in her frenzy, in a rapturous impassioned manner, sang the lyric passages –

"We've hunted down a mighty chase to-day,
And from the mountain bring the noble prey",

to the great delight of all the company . . . The king was greatly pleased, and gave presents, according to the custom of the Parthians, to them, and to Jason, the actor, a talent. – Such was the burlesque that was played, they tell us, as the afterpiece to the tragedy of Crassus's expedition.'

Though he was destined to reign over Armenia in peace and prosperity for twenty years, the ultimate fate of Artavazd was little better than that of Crassus himself. Artavazd's downfall was directly due to the overweening ambition, cruelty and greed of Antony and Cleopatra. In 36 BC, Mark Antony embarked on the fantastic plan of conquering Parthia with a grand army of 100,000 men, with which he entered Media and laid siege to the provincial capital of Praaspa, the modern Maragha. King Phraates of Parthia harried Antony's cumbrous columns at every step. The siege dragged on unsuccessfully, and had to be abandoned at the onset of winter. Artavazd meanwhile had given up all hope of a Roman victory, and had withdrawn with his contingent into Armenia. For Mark Antony, the retreat from Parthia was as disastrous as the retreat from Moscow was for Napoleon. He lost some 24,000 men, of whom most perished not in fighting the enemy, but through disease and starvation.

It is interesting to read Plutarch's account of the joy felt by the Roman soldiers when they finally crossed the River Araxes which divides Media and Armenia, and seemed, both by its deepness and the violence of the current, to be very dangerous to pass.[1]

'But when they were got over on the other side, and found themselves in Armenia, just as if land was now sighted after a storm at sea, they kissed the ground for joy, shedding tears and embracing each other in their delight. But taking their journey through a land that abounded in all sorts of plenty, they ate, after their long want, with that excess of everything they met with that they suffered from dropsies and dysenteries.'

Worsted in battle, Mark Antony and Cleopatra between them conceived the base scheme of compensating themselves at the expense of their Armenian allies, whom they affected to blame for the Roman defeat. Luring them to his camp by a pretence of friendship, Mark Antony carried off King Artavazd and his family to Alexandria, where Artavazd was forced to march in chains to grace the Roman 'triumph'. Artavazd and his queen and two of his sons were then handed over to Cleopatra's tender mercies, and pitilessly tortured to make them divulge the whereabouts of the Armenian royal treasury. Their fortitude and dignified bearing, Dio Cassius tells us, won them the sympathy and respect of many of the Romans at Cleopatra's court. Meanwhile, Mark Antony was enriching himself with the spoils of Armenia's cities, not sparing even the temple of the goddess Anahit. Giving up hope of breaking Artavazd's spirit, Cleopatra had him vilely murdered.

Those who think of Antony and Cleopatra only in terms of Shakespeare's romantic masterpiece should ponder this and other such iniquities committed during their infamous partnership, to which the triumph of Augustus put a well-deserved end in 30 BC. The history of Armenia during the next two centuries is largely concerned with the efforts by Rome and Parthia to place and maintain their own nominees on the Armenian throne, and to prevent the country from falling into the sphere of influence of their rivals. The Artaxiad dynasty petered out during the year before the birth of Christ, in I BC when the Emperor Augustus sent his grandson Caius Caesar to dislodge Tigranes IV and his sister-wife Erato,

[1] 'Antony', in *Lives*, Everyman edit., III, 303.

who ruled under Parthian patronage. It is interesting to note the brief appearance of this system of incestuous dynastic marriages in Armenia, no doubt under the influence of the Ptolemies of Egypt.

During the first century AD, the Romans consolidated their power to the north of Armenia, in Iberia. The excavations at Mtskheta-Armazi, in Iberia, not far from Tbilisi, combined with inscriptions, coin finds and the annals of Roman historians, give ample proof of this Roman dominance. The Romans found a willing ally in the King of eastern Georgia, Farsman I, whose brother Mithradates was placed on the throne of Armenia with the help of the Emperor Tiberius (AD 35). A Roman garrison was installed at Garni to maintain the unpopular Georgian against the local nobility and the pro-Parthian party. Some sixteen years later, in AD 51, Mithradates was treacherously murdered by his own nephew, Rhadamist, son of the ambitious Farsman of Iberia, who had dreamt of uniting Armenia with his own kingdom of Georgia, and founding a pan-Caucasian empire. This blood-thirsty dynastic struggle, which is recounted in the *Annals* of Tacitus, forms the subject of a celebrated tragedy by the French dramatist Prosper Jolyot de Crébillon (1674–1762). First performed in 1711, this play, entitled *Rhadamiste et Zénobie*, held the stage for a long period, though the plot is so complicated as to be almost incomprehensible. This tragedy in turn provided a libretto for Handel's opera, *Radamisto*. This Georgian intervention and the resulting popular discontent and disorders led directly to the inauguration of a new and important Armenian dynasty, that of the Arsacids, who ruled from AD 53, until their extinction in AD 428. The first Arsacid king was Tiridates I, brother of the Parthian King Vologases I. The two Parthian brothers invaded Armenia, occupied Artaxata and Tigrano-kerta, and had little difficulty in getting rid of the hated Georgian Rhadamist.

This Parthian incursion was the signal for fresh Roman intervention in the war-torn land. The young Emperor Nero's advisers appointed the seasoned general Corbulo to command the expedition charged with recovering Armenia. Corbulo found the eastern Roman legions in a deplorable condition, produced by decades of inactivity. He set himself to train them into a usable army, and the soldiers suffered nearly as much from his training as from the ensuing campaign. Two summers of drilling were followed by a winter under canvas in part of Armenia. In the piercing cold, frost-bite crippled the men, and sentries died from exposure at their posts. Deserters were executed.

During Corbulo's campaign of AD 58, Artaxata was captured. Next year, the Romans advanced on Tigranokerta, whose citizens closed their gates against him. To discourage them from a long resistance, Corbulo executed a captive Armenian noble in his camp, and fired the head into the town. It landed right in the middle of a council of war, and the townspeople promptly surrendered. A Roman nominee was placed on the Armenian throne, but Tiridates counter-attacked and defeated a fresh Roman army at Rhandeia (AD 62).

Nero prudently decided to compromise. Tiridates was to receive the crown of

Armenia, but from the hands of Nero in Rome. Though Tiridates was to be a client king of the Romans, Nero rightly judged that his investiture would satisfy the honour of the Parthians as well. Three years later, Tiridates made the journey to Rome. As a *magus* or priest of the Zoroastrian religion, he had to observe the rites which forbade him to defile water by travelling upon it, so he proceeded all the way by land. At Rome, in ceremonies of great pomp, Nero placed the Armenian crown on the head of Tiridates amid general rejoicing (AD 66). The Senate voted a special grant for the occasion, and sumptuous feasts and games took place, in which Tiridates himself excelled. The temple of Pompey was specially gilded for the occasion. Nero accorded Tiridates a subsidy of 50 million sestertii, perhaps worth 2 million dollars today, and sent him home with a squad of Roman masons and architects to rebuild Artaxata after the ravages of Corbulo, who was soon afterwards disgraced and forced to commit suicide in AD 67.

The long and prosperous reign of Tiridates I marks a return to an eastern, Parthian orientation in Armenian culture and religion. The period of his brother Vologases I, who reigned in Parthia until about AD 80, saw the rise to prominence of certain oriental features in Parthian public life. For the first time, Aramaic lettering is used instead of Greek on the royal coinage. A fire altar now appears among the designs of the official coin issues, which had wide currency in Armenia. There is a Zoroastrian religious tradition which attributes the collection of the surviving manuscripts and traditions of the sacred book of the Avesta to a Parthian king Valarsh (Vologases), who may be the same as Vologases I, brother of the founder of the Armenian Arsacid dynasty.

This resurgence of Iranian ways and beliefs under Tiridates I helped to undermine the Romanizing trends which had been in evidence in Armenia and Parthia during the preceding century. After the Hellenistic and Romanizing phase of Armenian history, stretching from the Orontids to the advent of the Arsacids in the first century AD, a new phase of 'Iranianism' was now entered into by Armenian society. In this new phase, the Armenian aristocracy began to pattern itself on the Iranian, exactly as the Arsacid monarchy of Armenia tended to become institutionally a mirror of the Parthian empire. Instead of the autocratic centralism characteristic of the Roman Empire, the Armenians adopted the more flexible system of feudal allegiances which had been characteristic of Iranian state structure since Achaemenid times. Unlike the formidable army of bureaucrats, tax gatherers and provincial governors on which the Roman emperors depended, the Armenian kings tended to rely on the loyalty of the great aristocratic houses, over whom from time to time the Armenian kings set viceroys of their own to strengthen the wavering allegiance of their vassals. Great offices of state became hereditary in certain noble families. Thus, the Bagratids, claiming descent from Kings David and Solomon of Israel, received from King Valarsh I of Armenia (117–40) the dignity of head of the royal cavalry, along with that of *tagadir* or hereditary coronant of the Armenian kings. Other noble families shared the remaining chief offices of state. These included the posts of Seneschal, Grand Chamberlain, and also High Constable. According to Moses of Khorene, King Valarsh appointed two royal secretaries, one of whom was deputed to remind him of deeds of beneficence and patronage to be fulfilled, the other of acts of vengeance to be carried out. The patronage secretary was also instructed to restrain the king from excessive severity, and to recall him whenever possible to a mood of mercy and magnanimity.

Under Tiridates I, who died about AD 100, Armenia remained a more or less docile buffer state. Nero and his immediate successors showed sense and moderation in maintaining Armenia as a neutral bastion against inroads both by nomads of the north Caucasian steppe, and by the Parthians themselves. An abrupt change in policy occurred under Trajan. Motivated, as Dio Cassius opines, by a sheer 'passion for glory', Trajan marched against Parthia in AD 113, and dethroned and killed the Armenian king, Parthamasiris. The scene is shown on an issue of Roman bronze coins, as well as on a relief reproduced on the triumphal arch of Constantine in Rome. Trajan advanced into Parthia and captured Ctesiphon, while Armenia groaned for three years under the yoke of a Roman legate. After Trajan's death in 117, the more prudent Hadrian handed back Rome's eastern territories to their old rulers and to client kings. The throne of Armenia was now occupied by another Arsacid monarch, Valarsh I, builder of Vagharshapat, the modern Echmiadzin.

There is little point in chronicling the futile wars against Armenia and Parthia undertaken by such emperors as Marcus Aurelius, Septimius Severus and Caracalla, which led to two further sackings of Ctesiphon (AD 165 and 198), and also did untold damage to the economic life of Armenia and of Rome's own eastern provinces.

The Roman emperors failed to grasp the fact that in setting up a kind of Iron Curtain against Parthia, and constantly trying to impose direct Roman rule over Armenia, they were weakening Rome itself. The Assyrian, the Neo-Babylonian, the Persian and the Seleucid empires had each, in succession, kept the Fertile Crescent united politically, from the eighth to the second century BC, so that Phoenician businessmen could trade freely as far as the Indus basin in one direction and the Atlantic coast of Europe and North Africa on the other. The Roman decision to break up the Seleucid empire and keep it broken was unfortunate both for Rome and for the Fertile Crescent, and particularly for buffer states such as Armenia. The decision kept the Fertile Crescent partitioned politically as well as economically for seven centuries, until the Arabs united it at last. The policy condemned Rome and then Byzantium to maintain, on the east, a difficult frontier which ran too close for comfort to the Mediterranean shore, and left lower Mesopotamia on the wrong side from the Roman point of view. The Persian Gulf and the sea trade to India were controlled by the Iranians, to Rome's economic detriment.

Of course, there were long periods of relatively peaceful co-existence, when such cities as Hatra and Dura Europos became centres of international trade and a flourishing syncretistic Graeco-Oriental art and culture. But, in the end, the implacable hostility of Rome towards the Parthians, and her failure to leave well alone in Armenia, helped to precipitate the rise of a much more dangerous and militant power, in the shape of the Sasanian kingdom. The culmination of this agelong struggle was the defeat and capture of the Emperor Valerian by the Great King Shapur I in 260, after which the power and prestige of the Roman Empire in the East were never the same again.

The rebellion which was to overthrow the Parthian Arsacids began in Persis (Fars) province, theoretically a Parthian vassal kingdom, early in the third century AD. One tradition holds that Sasan, ancestor of the Sasanid line, was a high priest of Anahita – the Armenian goddess Anahit – at Istakhr, near Persepolis. Another tradition makes Sasan a petty ruler of Parsis, whose kingdom was inherited by his son Papak and so eventually by Papak's son Ardashir Papakan (the name Ardashir is a later form of Artaxerxes). About 220 Ardashir broke into open revolt against his overlord, the Parthian King Artabanus V. Ardashir's allies included the Medes, the ruler of Adiabene (Assyria), and a King Domitian of Kirkuk. Artabanus was killed in 226. Ardashir had himself crowned king in Ctesiphon, commemorating the defeat of Artabanus by carving a great rock relief near Firuzabad. Under the new Sasanid dynasty, which claimed descent from the Achaemenids, firm government, prosperity and high cultural standards were to return to Iran for over four centuries right up to the Arab conquest.

The advent of the Sasanids to power in Iran had far-reaching results in Armenia. The Armenian Arsacids were of course a junior branch of the old Parthian royal house. From being close allies of the reigning dynasty of Iran, as had been the case during the epoch of the last Parthian kings, the Armenian Arsacids were transformed into sworn foes of the new ruling dynasty of Persia, the Sasanids. From the Sasanian viewpoint, the Armenian Arsacids represented the last offshoot of a hated and superseded dynasty, whom it was the duty of the Sasanians to root out. Hence the virulent hatred between the ruling houses of Armenia and Iran from about AD 226 onwards, and the Roman orientation which several later Armenian kings were forced in self-defence to adopt. This implacable hostility between the Sasanid ruling dynasty and the royal house of Armenia also helps later on to explain the curious phenomenon of an Armenian king of Parthian lineage, Tiridates III, being the first monarch in the world to establish Christianity permanently as the state religion of a large and durable kingdom.

During continual wars, the Armenian royal capital at Artaxata (Artashat) was several times razed to the ground. Excavations there, which will no doubt yield rich historical material, are planned by the Armenian Academy of Sciences. The other Arsacid capital of Vagharshapat is now largely covered by the modern town of Echmiadzin, so that we must wait for some future time before excavations reveal the town built by Valarsh I in the second century AD.

There is, however, one superb site of the Arsacid period which has been excavated by an expedition headed by Professor Babken Arakelian, and is now included on the regular tourist route for visitors to Soviet Armenia. This is the spectacular summer palace of the Armenian kings at Garni, eighteen miles east of Erevan. Garni is perched high up in the hills, overlooking the Azat River which flows down from the snow-covered peaks close to Lake Sevan. The village of Garni is renowned for its fruit, including grapes (from which are made the excellent Garni *vin rosé* served in Armenian restaurants), also apples, pears, apricots, and nuts.

From prehistoric times, man has made his dwelling on the Garni promontory which juts out high above the Azat River. This triangular promontory is impregnable for about four-fifths of its circuit, being joined to the upland slopes and orchards by a narrow and easily defensible causeway. Though harsh in winter, the climate is ideal in summer. Garni is well above the 5,000 feet mark, and is temperate even in July, when Erevan and the Araxes plain are sweltering in temperatures around 90 degrees.

Professor Arakelian's excavations in Garni have laid bare the remains of round houses from the Early Bronze Age, about 2500 BC. An Urartian inscription records that the Vannic kings also used Garni as an outpost and probably a summer residence. Enormous blocks of finely carved grey basalt surround the perimeter of ancient Garni, on the side which communicates with the hinterland. The lowest courses of these massive fortifications were laid down during Urartian times. No cement was used, but the blocks are fitted tightly together with consummate skill and art. Later, in the time of the Orontids and Artaxiads, the fortress walls were raised to a greater height, and the stone blocks clamped together with iron and lead braces. Fourteen massive turrets and bastions were added.

Garni became a favourite summer residence of the Artaxiad and Arsacid monarchs. When Artaxata, down in the Araxes lowlands, became unbearable in the sweltering, malarial summer heat, the Armenian kings could relax and also transact affairs of state in Garni, where such cultivated rulers as Artavazd II found time to compose plays and literary works. Garni is mentioned by Tacitus in connection with the civil wars of AD 52–3 in Armenia, involving the Georgian pretender Rhadamist. An important Greek inscription found at Garni, opening with an invocation to Helios, records that King Tiridates I, founder of the Arsacid dynasty, built a palace for his queen and restored the citadel here, in the eleventh year of his reign (AD 77).

The most famous feature of Garni is the Classical temple, built of grey basalt in the second half of the first century AD, and largely destroyed in an earthquake in 1679. Many European travellers visited the site during the nineteenth century, and in 1834 Dubois de Montpéreux drew an outline reconstruction of the temple,

39. Garni Temple, north façade (reconstruction by Buniatian)

40. Silver tetradrachms of King Tigranes the Great

41. Fallen capital from the Temple of Garni

which accords in its general features with the later and more systematic recreation by Professor N. Buniatian (1933). The temple was on a raised platform, at the highest point on the Garni promontory. A flight of nine steps led up to the front portico of the shrine, which was surmounted by an elegant triangular pediment. The rectangular inner cella or naos was surrounded by a peristyle of twenty-four Ionic columns. The dimensions of the cella, which apparently housed an image of Mithra, were modest – 5·14 by 7·92 metres. At each side of the front stairway was a massive pedestal, adorned with a bas-relief depicting the figure of Atlas holding up the pillars of the universe; evidently these pedestals once supported some kind of altar. All round the pitched roof ran a richly carved frieze, in which many specifically Armenian motifs were mingled with Hellenistic ones. Here we see carved luxuriantly in stone the conventional acanthus leaf, along with the pomegranate and the vine.

From 1966 onwards, the project of rebuilding the Garni temple has been under discussion in Soviet Armenia. It is calculated that nearly 80 per cent of the original masonry and ornamental friezes are still lying about on the site, in sufficiently good condition to be utilized in the proposed reconstruction. Each stone is being systematically numbered, and funds for the project have been voted by the Armenian Soviet government, as well as by Armenian charitable foundations abroad.

Fifty metres to the north-west of the Hellenistic temple stand the remains of a remarkable Roman bath, which dates from the third century AD. This bath was built on the usual Roman plan, with cold, tepid and hot chambers. The furnace and steam heating systems were highly elaborate. The layout of the bath is similar to that in the royal city of Armazis-Khevi, close to the modern Mtskheta, in Georgia.[1]

A particularly interesting feature of the bath at Garni is the partly destroyed mosaic floor, which adorned the vestibule of the bath. The outer pink frame encloses an allegorical scene based on marine mythology of the Classical world. The blending of blues and greens gives a subtle illusion of the movement of the sea. In the centre we see a male figure, symbolizing Ocean, and a female one who is Thalassa, the sea. On the four sides of the central area are hybrid creatures each having the torso of a fish, the front end of a horse, as well as certain human features. These marine centaurs carry Nereids on their back, including Thetis, the mother of Achilles. There are also lively representations of dolphins, fishes and fishermen. At the top of the mosaic is a Greek inscription, the sense of which is: 'We worked without receiving any reward'. The significance of this remark is hard to seize, unless it is a complaint about bad conditions of work and poor pay. Perhaps it means that the work of the bath-house staff resulted in nothing more tangible than water and hot air, which ran away and evaporated, leaving no durable result behind.

[1] Plan in D. M. Lang, *The Georgians*, fig. 19.

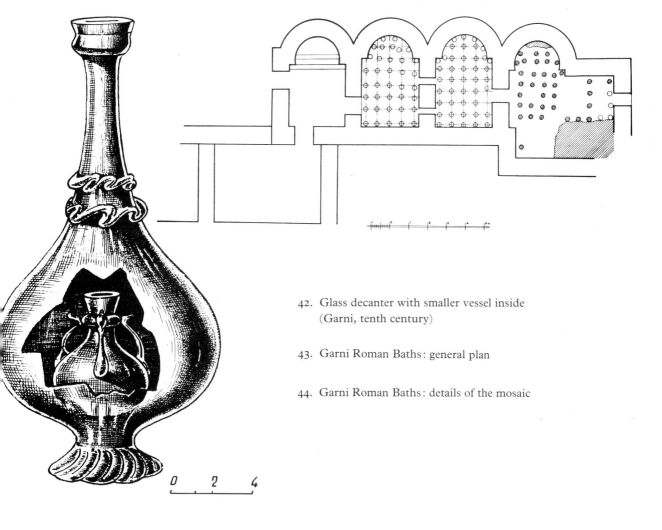

0   2   4

42. Glass decanter with smaller vessel inside
   (Garni, tenth century)

43. Garni Roman Baths: general plan

44. Garni Roman Baths: details of the mosaic

One of the most fascinating problems of Armenian civilization in the pre-Christian period is the nature of Armenian paganism. We have already outlined in the previous chapter the origins of ancient Armenian mythology, with its Greek, Phrygian and also Mithraic roots, which began to take shape under the Orontids and the Artaxiads. Undoubtedly Hellenistic religion and the pantheon of the Classical divinities were popular among the upper classes during the later Artaxiad and early Arsacid periods. We have also seen how Tigranes the Great, in his inscriptions, occasionally laid claim to possessing a divine nature, though we do not know how seriously this was taken by his more sophisticated subjects.

As time went on, the gods and goddesses of Hellas became hopelessly intermingled in Armenia with those of the Iranian and even the Babylonian world. According to Strabo,[1] temple prostitution was practised at the shrines of Anahit, the mother of Armenia, doubtless in imitation of Babylonian and Syrian custom. The goddess Astghik, sister of Anahit, corresponded on the one hand to the Assyrian Ishtar, on the other to the goddess Venus.

Astghik's lover was the Iranian god Verethragna, god of war and victory, known in Armenian as Vahagn. Venerated in the guise of Hercules the dragon slayer, Vahagn was also identified with Ares, the Greek god of battle, son of Zeus and Hera. In the opinion of Professor S. K. Chatterji,[2] Vahagn was a solar deity, in support of which one may cite an Armenian pre-Christian song which runs:

> In travail were heaven and earth,
> In travail, too, the purple sea!
> The travail held in the sea
> The small red reed.
> Through the hollow of the stalk came forth smoke,
> Through the hollow of the stalk came forth flame,
> And out of the flame the little boy ran!
> Fiery hair had he,
> Ay, too, he had a flaming beard,
> And his eyes, they were as suns!

Another prominent Armenian god was Tir, from whose name derives that of Tiridates given to several Armenian kings. Tir, originally Tishtrya, is another Iranian deity, leader of the Stars of Ahura-Mazda against the Planets of Angra-Mainyu, the Spirit of Evil. Tishtrya was identified with the star of Sirius and he brought rain regularly to the earth, after conquering the Demon of Drought. Among the Armenians, as Professor Chatterji has established, Tir became a God of Oracles and of Dreams, and was a defender of the arts and letters. Later on, he became associated with Apollo and Hermes of the Greek pantheon. He acted as the scribe or recording angel of Aramazd. To this day, Armenian folklore assigns to Tir the task of registering when a man is about to die.

[1] *Geography*, XI. xiv. 16.
[2] *Journal of the Asiatic Society*, Calcutta, I, 1959, p. 205.

Special herds and flocks were kept for the purpose of affording sacrifices to the gods and goddesses of the Armenian pantheon. We have an illustration of this in Plutarch's *Life of Lucullus*, where we read of the crossing of the Euphrates by the Roman general and his army.[1] Lucullus met with a lucky omen on landing on the Armenian side of the river:

'Holy heifers are pastured on purpose for Diana Persia [Anahit] whom, of all the gods, the barbarians beyond Euphrates chiefly adore. They use these heifers only for her sacrifices. At other times, they wander up and down undisturbed, with the mark of the goddess, a torch, branded on them; and it is no such light or easy thing, when occasion requires, to seize one of them. But one of these, when the army had passed the Euphrates, coming to a rock consecrated to the goddess, stood upon it, and then, laying down her neck, like others that are forced down with a rope, offered herself to Lucullus for sacrifice'.

We have few idols or images surviving to testify to the character of Armenian paganism of the Hellenistic type. The early Armenian Christians took the Biblical prohibition of graven images very seriously, and melted down or otherwise disposed of virtually all the fine statuary left over from the Classical phase of Armenian civilization. All the more interest attaches to a singularly fine bronze head of Aphrodite/Anahit, which has been in the British Museum Greek and Roman Gallery for nearly a century. This head, which is about one and a half times life size, is from a colossal statue of Aphrodite/Anahit, reputedly from Satala, the modern Sadagh, in eastern Anatolia, not far from Erzinjan. This place is notable as the site of the Emperor Trajan's encampment in Armenia during his campaign of AD 113.[2] It was here that Trajan deposed the Armenian King Parthamasiris, who was soon afterwards treacherously murdered by the Romans.

It might be expected that the accession of a Parthian king in the person of Tiridates I would herald a rejection of the Graeco-Roman pantheon in favour of purely Iranian gods. Certainly Tiridates himself was a Magian, and rode for nine months round the Mediterranean to Nero's court at Rome, rather than pollute the elements of the sea by undertaking a voyage by boat. However the Arsacids never enforced full Zoroastrianism.[3] The Sasanians would not recognize either the Parthian or the Armenian Arsacids as true believers, and indeed it is only with the persecutions of Yezdegird in the fifth century that a sustained effort was made to convert Armenia to official, state Zoroastrianism.

The Parthians were a tolerant nation. They indulged in a fairly widespread cult of the deified monarch, who was sometimes called 'Brother of the Sun and Moon'. At the same time, the *magi* were respected by the king, and each Arsacid had a royal fire burning continually for him. Parthian coins also show an abundance

---

[1] *Lives*, Everyman edit., II, 222.
[2] Freya Stark, *Rome on the Euphrates*, London, 1966, pp. 205–6.
[3] Malcolm Colledge, *The Parthians*, London, 1967, pp. 98–114.

of Greek deities – Victory, Tyche, Zeus, Artemis, and so on. Jews were numerous in Armenia and Parthia, and proselytized without hindrance. In Bactria and the eastern provinces, Buddhism had a strong foothold.

It may be that in Armenia, as in Parthia, Greek religion and culture were largely a preserve of the upper classes and urban bourgeoisie. But worship of the Greek gods and goddesses was widespread and pervasive. Hymns to Apollo were engraved at Susa. Statuettes of Zeus, Heracles, Athena, Aphrodite and other deities have been found in many Parthian city sites. But whenever Greek cults are involved in the Parthian and Armenian context, we must ask, with Dr Malcolm Colledge[1], whether they may not be oriental deities in disguise.

The arrival of Hellenism in the East, with Alexander the Great and his successors, started off a veritable symbiosis – the wholesale syncretism of Greek with oriental divinities – which affected both Armenia and Parthia. Henceforth Semitic, including Babylonian, also Iranian and Greek deities began to be considered identical and even interchangeable. Ahura-Mazda became the Iranian equivalent of Bel, Mithra of Shamash, and Anahit, the 'Mother of Armenia', of Ishtar or Nanai. In Armenia itself, Ishtar was worshipped in the guise of Astghik, sister of Anahit; Astghik was the voluptuous goddess of maternity and amorous delights. Nanai reappears as the Armenian Naneh, patron saint of warriors and of virgins.

This rather sophisticated mythology was not entirely comprehensible to the Armenian masses, especially the peasantry. But many feasts and festivals dear to the Armenian people have their roots in these pre-Christian days. Such is the festival of Navasart, when Anahit is worshipped in song, dances and an abundance of flowers and leafy blossoms. Again, the festival of Vardavar, 'the bearing of roses', celebrated in August, was marked by processions and dances in honour of the goddesses Astghik and Anahit. A vivid evocation of this festival occurs in the novel *Samuel* by the Armenian novelist Raffi, or Akop Melik-Akopian (1835–88).

The temples of pagan Armenia were numerous, both in the country and in the cities. There were special temple-towns, such as Ashtishat and Bagavan, containing several important sanctuaries. Christian churches and monasteries later succeeded to the wealth and the veneration belonging to those ancient sacred sites. These shrines, like Holy Echmiadzin today, were often the scenes of great concourses of people gathered for worship and religious festivities. Treasure houses were attached to each shrine, often exceedingly rich in images, gold and jewels. Hospitality was accorded to strangers, in the form of meat, flowers, fruit and even money. Agathangelos gives an account of the sacrifices offered up by one victorious monarch after a successful campaign:

'He commanded to seek out the seven great altars of Armenia, and he honoured the sanctuaries of his ancestors, the Arsacids, with white bullocks, white rams,

[1] *The Parthians*, p. 107.

150

white horses and mules, with gold and silver ornaments and gold embroidered and fringed silken coverings, with golden wreaths, silver sacrificial basins, desirable vases set with precious stones, splendid garments, and beautiful ornaments. Also he gave a fifth of his booty and great presents to the priests.'

The priesthood was hereditary in a well-organized caste. The high priest was sometimes of royal blood, and exercised political power as the repository of secret lore and wisdom, and of knowledge of omens and auguries. Two families, those of the Vahunis and the Spandunis, are mentioned as furnishing a cadre of qualified priests to the temples of pagan Armenia. The priests were certainly very wealthy, since we hear of the confiscation of great riches from them by St Gregory the Illuminator, after Armenia's conversion to Christianity. Priestesses were also much in evidence, especially in connection with such popular divinities as Anahit and Astghik.

Finds of ancient bronze statuettes with fantastic headdresses and mummers' costumes suggest that early pagan festivals were accompanied by elaborate mimes and dramatic spectacles. This helps to explain the hostility of the early Armenian Church to every manifestation of the drama and the theatrical arts.

Armenian popular superstitions and demonology, also cults connected with witchcraft, have their roots in the country's pagan past.[1] The *daeva* or demon spirit of the Avesta was feared in Armenia, as also in Georgia; the Armenian form is *dev*, the Georgian, *devi*. The devs haunted stony places and ruins; they appeared as serpents and in other monstrous forms, some corporeal, others incorporeal. Then there were the *druzhes*; like their Avestan counterparts, these were lying, perjuring and harmful spirits, believed to be of female sex. The *yatus* or sorcerers of the Avesta had their Armenian counterparts, who were even able to slay men. There were destructive female demons known as *parik*, whose husbands were called *kaj*. These *kajis* feature prominently in medieval Georgian literature, including Shota Rustaveli's romantic epic, *The Man in the Panther's Skin*.

Among ancient pagan superstitions may be mentioned fear of the evil eye. Moses of Khorene, for instance, records that King Ervand had so powerful an evil eye that he could break stones in pieces merely by gazing fixedly at them. The general belief was that people on whom the evil eye was cast pined away, without even knowing the cause of their ailment, and that nobody is safe from it. This superstition has persisted right up to modern times. It is said that the ancient Armenians had the same aversion for parings of nails and hair as was common among the Iranians, arising from the teachings of the Avesta. The sacred character of fire, of course, also had its roots in Iranian religious beliefs, as did the taboo on the defilement of water, particularly running water – a valuable sanitary precaution in the East.

---

[1] M. H. Ananikian, in James Hastings, *Encyclopaedia of Religion and Ethics*, I, Edinburgh, 1908, pp. 794–802; also *Armenian Mythology* by the same author, Boston, 1925.

Ancient Armenian literature and mythology contained frequent mention of *vishaps*. These were corporeal beings, acolytes of the huge stone dragon and fish-like monsters erected in Urartian and even earlier times in connection, it seems, with ancient irrigation systems. These *vishaps* could appear either as men or as serpents, and could soar away into the air with the help of oxen. They were fond of carrying away grain from the threshing floor, either by assuming the shape of mules and camels, or by real mules and camels of their own. In such cases, the fifth century Armenian writer Eznik tells us, the Armenians would call out: 'Kal, kal! (Stop, stop!)'. These *vishaps* would even suck the milk from cows. Some *vishaps* went hunting on horseback, and lived in comfortable mansions. They kept royal princes and heroes captive, among these being Alexander the Great and King Artavazd of Armenia. They sometimes appeared enormous and compelled men to do obeisance to them. They also entered into human beings, their breath was poisonous. There was a whole colony of them at the foot of Masis (Mount Ararat), with whom Vahagn fought; later these *vishaps* stole the child Artavazd and left an infant *dev* in his stead.

Allied to the *vishaps* were the *nhangs*, a term borrowed from Persian *nihang*, or 'alligator, crocodile'. They lived chiefly in the rivers, such as the Aratsani or Murat-Su. They adopted the form of mermaids, used their victims for their lust and then sucked their blood and left them dead. At other times they became seals, catching swimmers by the feet and dragging them to the bottom. On land, were-wolves were also to be feared.

Of a more kindly nature were the *shahapets*, or 'protectors of the homestead'. These are mentioned by the early historian Agathangelos as the protecting genii of graves. They appeared in the shape of men or of serpents, and also watched over the vineyards and olive trees.

Pagan Armenian burial customs seem to have had some resemblance to those of ancient Babylonia. The friends and relatives of the deceased came to the ceremony of wailing. At the funerals of the rich, professional mourners were employed, led by the 'mother of the dirge', who sang the story of the life and death of the deceased, while the nearest relatives tore their garments, plucked their hair and screamed. They cut their arms and faces. During the funeral they had music, produced by horns, violins and harps. Men and women danced facing each other, and clapped their hands. One ancient Armenian Christian writer, quoted by the historian Leonce Alishan, went out of his way to forbid 'wailing over the dead, cutting of the hair and other evil things'. When the deceased was a king or other great personage, servants and slaves committed suicide over his grave.

Ancient gravestones are found in the shape of horses and lambs, perhaps symbolic of sacrifices for the dead. The modern custom of distributing bread and raisins and strong drink after the burial is probably a survival of an ancient sacrificial meal. Today, in Soviet Armenia, sacrifices of animals are regularly made on festival days, even in the courtyards of the Cathedral of Echmiadzin. The Armenian and Georgian custom of spending Easter Monday eating and drinking in the graveyards, by the tombs of one's ancestors, clearly goes back to ancient pagan rituals.

Several Armenian legends concern the end of the world, and are entwined with ancient dragon myths. Such is the Armenian version of the Iranian legend of Thraetaona, who fought with Azhi-Dahaka, the demon-like dragon. After his defeat at the hands of Thraetaona, Azhi-Dahaka was chained up in a cave in the Elburz mountains by his victor. Thence he is to rise at the Last Day, and be slain by Sama Keresaspa.

In the Armenian recension, as recorded by Moses of Khorene (*History of Armenia*, I. 24–30), Azhi-Dahaka is transformed into a King Azhdahak of Media, who combats King Tigranes I of Armenia. In a later chapter, Moses of Khorene states that Azhdahak was fettered and imprisoned by Hruden in Mount Demavand, escaping only to be recaptured and guarded in a cave of that same mountain. Moses of Khorene likewise says that Azhdahak had once been kissed on the shoulder by an evil spirit, and that from this kiss had sprung serpents, who were fed on human flesh. Faustus of Buzanda, another early Armenian chronicler, tells a similar tale about the ill-fated Armenian King Pap.

This interesting legend seems to have contributed to another popular Armenian tradition, about the legendary King Artavazd, son of Artaxias or Artashes. This King Artaxias was much beloved of his people, and when he died, many citizens preferred to die too rather than live on without him.

Artavazd, son of King Artaxias, seeing that many people committed suicide over his father's grave, exclaimed:

'Thou didst depart and tookest with thee the whole country. Shall I rule over ruins?'

Thereupon the shade of his father cursed him, saying:

'When thou goest a-hunting up the venerable Masis, may the *Kajes* seize thee and take thee up the venerable Masis!
There mayest thou remain and see no light!'

Artavazd is said to have perished while on a hunting party near Masis (Ararat), by falling with his horse from a high precipice. One Armenian legend says that he is still chained in a cave of Masis, and two dogs, gnawing at his chains, try to set him free in order that he may bring the world to an end. The chains become very thin about the season of Navasart, the ancient New Year festivities in August. Therefore, in those days, the blacksmiths used to strike a few blows with their hammers on their anvils, in order to strengthen the chains that restrained Artavazd and save the world, a custom which continued into Christian times.

The legend has features which recall the story of Prometheus Bound, and also closely resemble the popular Georgian cycle of folk tales about Amiran, the titan who challenged Jesus Christ to a rock-hurling contest, and was also chained up in a cave for his temerity. The gnawing away of the chains by a dog, and the striking of blacksmiths' anvils as a precaution, are also paralleled in Georgia.

Chapter VII

EARLY CHRISTIAN ARMENIA

ARMENIAN national tradition is rich in information and in legends about the introduction of Christianity into the country. It is often said to have been preached here by the Holy Apostles, or the immediate disciples of the Apostles, notably St Bartholomew and St Thaddeus. However, these accounts are relatively late, and not generally regarded as historically authentic.

By the second and third centuries after Christ, the Christian religion was certainly making great headway in regions bordering on Armenia, being widespread there prior to Armenia's official conversion by St Gregory the Illuminator in AD 301. In particular, Armenia had regular commercial and cultural relations with the great city of Antioch. The apostolic church at Antioch played a central part in the early diffusion of Christianity. It was the home of the Gnostics Menander and Saturnilus also, while the writings of Theophilus, Bishop of Antioch, in the latter years of Marcus Aurelius and under Commodus, attracted the notice of the West. The existence of an organized school of Christian instruction in Antioch is further evidenced by the records of the council of bishops which met there in AD 269 to condemn the heresy of Paul of Samosata. All these tendencies had their echo in Armenia.

Even closer to Armenia proper was the ancient Christian centre of Edessa, royal city of the Christian King Abgar VIII (176–213); also the city of Nisibis and the region of Adiabene in northern Mesopotamia, where Christianity was well established in the third century. All these factors help to explain why it is that Armenian Church tradition has preserved the names of several saints and martyrs who bore their witness even before the official conversion of Armenia by St Gregory.

The story of this conversion is one of the most cherished traditions of the Armenian nation. Its fabulous details are not lightly to be called in question, even by historians of a sceptical turn of mind. Knowledge of these hallowed traditions is necessary for understanding the iconography of Armenian fresco and miniature paintings, for which they provide favourite themes.

St Gregory the Illuminator is described by national historians, such as Faustus of Buzanda and Agathangelos, as a member of the Parthian noble house of Suren-Pahlav, a branch of the Arsacid royal family, and thus a kinsman of the

Armenian monarchs themselves. According to legend, Gregory's father assassinated the Armenian King Khosrow I (about AD 238). During subsequent reprisals, Gregory's family was largely exterminated; the infant Gregory was carried off to safety in Cappadocia, where he grew up in a Christian environment in Caesarea.

Many years later, the murdered King Khosrow's son recovered the Armenian throne. As King Tiridates III, he was restored to his ancestral kingdom in AD 286 by the Emperor Diocletian, the inveterate foe of Christianity. By the Treaty of Nisibis in AD 298 the Sasanian Great King, after a severe defeat at the hands of the Romans, officially recognized the independence of Greater Armenia, under Roman protection.

Gregory also returned to the land of his fathers, and began to preach the the Christian faith. Tiridates discovered and identified him as the son of his own father's murderer. After suffering gruesome tortures, Gregory was cast into a dungeon in the royal castle of Artashat, where he languished for fifteen years. A charitable widow saved his life and provided him with food.

Tiridates III meanwhile reigned at Vagharshapat, where he brutally killed a group of thirty-seven Christian virgins, including a beautiful maiden named Hripsimé, whom he vainly wished to enrol among his many wives and concubines. The leader of the band of holy women, Gaiané, is revered equally with Hripsimé herself among the founder martyrs of the Armenian Church, their festival being celebrated on October 5th.

After this crime, Tiridates was deprived of his reason by divine retribution, and reduced to grovelling bestially upon the ground on all fours, like a wild beast. He was afflicted, it seems, with a form of violent lycanthropy. No doubt we have here an echo of the Old Testament legend of King Nebuchadnezzar. The cure and conversion of Tiridates likewise have traits reminiscent of the story of the prophet Daniel. The king's sister, Khosrovidukht, told Tiridates that she had had a vision of a man with a radiant face, who had declared to her that persecution of the Christians must cease forthwith. The princess was convinced that if Gregory was brought forth from his pit, he would cure the king of his dire affliction.

Tiridates accepted his sister's advice and released the saint from his dungeon. Gregory restored the king's health and sanity and then baptized him with all his household. No doubt political motives also played some part in this conversion, since it was now the policy of the Armenian Arsacids to resist in every way the ideological and cultural encroachments of Zoroastrian Iran.

One night, Gregory had a vision, in which he saw the firmament opened, and Jesus Christ descending from heaven surrounded by cohorts of winged figures, while the earth shone with resplendent light. Calling Gregory by name to witness the miracles which he was about to reveal, the Lord struck the earth with a golden hammer; an immense pedestal of gold emerged in the midst of the town of Vaghar-

45. Holy Echmiadzin: the Cathedral

46. and 47. Views of the belfries

shapat, on which arose a column of fire with a cloud as its capital, surmounted by a shining cross. Three other columns, red as blood, also surmounted with luminous crosses, rose around the pillar, on the spots where the martyred virgins were laid to rest. These four crosses formed an arch on which there rose aloft a grand temple with a cupola, on top of which again was a golden throne with a fiery cross.

Out of this wondrous edifice flowed abundant streams of water, flooding the plains beyond the town. In the firmament above were countless fiery altars, with crosses like stars in the night sky. Suddenly vast herds of black goats crossed the waters, and became white lambs which multiplied in numbers. Then half the lambs crossed the water again, and turned into wolves which attacked the lambs in a scene of bloody carnage. The slain lambs had wings, and joined the cohorts of the Lord; then fire descended on earth and burnt up the wolves. As dawn broke, the earth trembled and the vision ended. All this forms an allegory of the conversion of the pagan 'goats' of Armenia to be Christian 'sheep', then the backsliding of a part of them, and the association of these renegades with the wolves or heathen persecutors of the Christian faithful.

Following this vision, St Gregory built a reproduction of the mystical church which he had seen in his vision, at the place where the fiery column had come down to earth. He renamed the royal town of Vagharshapat as Echmiadzin, which signifies, 'the Only-Begotten has descended'. In the crypt of the present cathedral at Echmiadzin, archaeologists have uncovered the remains of a small stone church, which may date from these early times of the conversion of Armenia, which is usually assigned to AD 301. Nearby in the crypt are the remains of a pagan fire-temple, which apparently dates from the period of the Persian persecutions of the Armenian Church under the Sasanian King Yezdegird in the fifth century.

In recognition of Gregory's outstanding merits and feats of piety, the saint was unanimously elected Primate of the new Armenian state Church. He received episcopal consecration at the hands of Leontius, Archbishop of Caesarea in Cappadocia, in the year 302. Subsequently the Byzantine Church, jealous of the independence of the Armenian national Church, alleged that the see of Armenia was suffragan to that of Caesarea, and that the antagonism which divided the Greek and Armenian Churches from the fifth century onwards, should be ascribed to a schism on the part of the Armenians. However, it can well be argued that the Armenian Church is of apostolic origin, and that the consecration of St Gregory by the Archbishop of Caesarea arose from circumstances of a casual nature, through the fact that Gregory had received his early education in Caesarea. It should certainly not be used as an argument from which to infer a system of hierarchic relationship. To quote one good authority:[1]

'Armenia Major had been outside the pale of the Roman Empire and as such its ecclesiastical development could not have been influenced by Rome. The see of

[1] Aziz S. Atiya, *History of Eastern Christianity*, p. 321.

Armenia, like that of Persia or Ethiopia, grew independently outside Roman jurisdiction. Furthermore, if we study the subject of ecclesiastical relations of the sees in existence before the Council of Nicaea, it will be seen that none of them meddled in the affairs of the others. Advocates of the Byzantine or Roman viewpoint build up hypothetical arguments of no historical validity'.

Much of the bitterness which divided the Greek and Armenian churches is due more to political than to doctrinal causes. It stems from the dogged refusal of the Armenians to succumb to the worldly, empire-building ambitions of the Byzantine sovereigns, with their ecclesiastical satellites. Under the Byzantine Caesaro-Papist system, the Constantinople patriarchate was used only too often as a tool of military and political authority, with a view to assimilating all the smaller Christian nations under the guise of spreading religious unity. Also in Armenia's favour is the fact that she declared Christianity the state religion several years before Constantine the Great proclaimed the official conversion of the Eastern Roman Empire.

Naturally enough, the old pagan cults of Armenia did not succumb without resistance on the part of their followers and adepts. The ancient chroniclers enumerate the shrines and temples which were overthrown by the Christians, and the rich booty which accrued to the new church as well as to the royal treasury. Even after several decades, bishops and missionaries were still being attacked and even slain in outlying regions. Thus we hear of Saint Aristakes, assassinated by the satrap of Tsophk (Sophene); Saint Vrtanes obliged to flee before the pursuit of the mountaineers of Sassoun; Saint Hoosik dying under the scourgings of King Tigranes V, and Saint Daniel of Ashtishat, who had been nominated for the patriarchate, also meeting a similar fate.

An interesting and unusual feature of the early Armenian Church, long since discontinued, is that the chief bishops were often married, and that the headship of the Armenian Church descended from father to son, like any royal dynastic succession. This may possibly indicate some desire to emulate the ancient patriarchs of Israel. As Gregory the Illuminator approached the end of his life, he chose his second son Aristakes, who was celibate, to succeed him, and actually consecrated him in advance. Gregory himself died in 325, in which year Aristakes attended the Council of Nicaea as the chief representative of the Armenian Church. On the death of Aristakes in 333, the patriarchal throne of Armenia was occupied by his elder brother, St Vrtanes (333–341), who was married, and was succeeded by his son Hoosik, the catholicos who was put to death by Tigranes V. Hoosik's grandson, St Nerses, reigned from 353 to 373, and is venerated as one of the great fathers of the Armenian Church. Later, the son of Nerses, St Sahak or Isaac, completed a full half century upon the patriarchal throne, from 387 to 439, apart from a few intervals due to political troubles. With the death of Saint Sahak, the hereditary principle was extinguished, and the election to the catholicosate reverted to the assembly of king, people and clergy. Complete celibacy of bishops and monks soon became the rule.

St Nerses, known as the Great, is credited with widespread reforms and improvements in the organization of the Armenian Church. In 365, he summoned a synod at Ashtishat, to which both nobility and bishops were invited, for the settlement of uncertainties in regard to the law of the land, and also to the basic dogmas of the Christian faith. This council forbad marriage between first cousins, whereby the nobles sought to preserve their feudal estates from fragmentation. The council also tried to stamp out remains of pagan superstitions such as wailings and self-disfigurements over the dead, invocation of spirits and the use of amulets. A number of charitable institutions were set up, such as hospitals, refuges for lepers, homes for the blind, asylums for orphans and widows, and hostelries for travellers. Monasteries on the cenobitic model, like those in Egypt, the Byzantine Empire and western Asia, were established for the housing of ascetics and hermits.

These religious reforms took place against a background of increasing economic and social crisis at home, and military and political threats from without. The expectations of Tiridates III, namely that the establishment of Christianity in Armenia would lead to the creation of a strong, unified monarchy, were doomed to disappointment, especially under the rule of his less dynamic successors.

The reasons for the decline and ultimate fall of the Armenian monarchy of the Arsacids are complex. The Arsacid monarchy had its roots in the pre-Christian age of Greece and Rome and of Parthia. It was a national institution, supported by the adepts of Armenian paganism with their wealthy shrines, by the prosperity of many important towns, and by a large body of slaves dependent on the king. In encouraging the adoption of Christianity, the Armenian kings found that they had set up a state within a state. The battling bishops did not hesitate to criticize the policies and private lives of the kings, and many disagreeable conflicts took place. The great nobles took advantage of this to withdraw to their fastnesses. Aided and abetted by intriguing clerics, the *nakharars* or feudal princes could now set at naught the provincial viceroys appointed by the king; indeed, many of these viceroys themselves tended to become independent, hereditary satraps, and defied any attempts by the kings to remove them or deny succession to their sons. Territorial encroachments against Armenia by the Greeks and by Sasanian Iran meant that the kings no longer had fresh stretches of free territory to divide among their leading nobles and generals, to assure their loyalty and reward their prowess. Christianity preached the abolition of slavery. In many cases, the slaves and former prisoners became serfs and villeins, sometimes on the royal domains, but more often on the lands of the nobles and squires. Though domestic slavery apparently continued for several generations, the king was more and more dependent on his vassals when he needed to recruit an army, or mobilize labour for some important civil or military project or construction. Sometimes the nobles

8. Holy Echmiadzin: Interior of the Cathedral

9. Oshakan: Mesrop Memorial Church:
The Virgin and Child

refused to pay taxes to the crown, which imposed even greater limitations on the power of the monarch.

A crippling blow was struck to the edifice of royalty in Armenia when the Emperor Julian the Apostate was defeated and slain by the Sasanian Great King Shapur II in AD 363. Julian's successor, Jovian, signed a peace treaty with the Persians in which Rome's ally Armenia was abandoned to her fate. Led by a renegade Armenian noble, Meruzhan Ardsruni, the Persians stormed into Armenia and systematically besieged and sacked the principal cities and trading posts. King Arshak II and his loyal general, Vasak Mamikonian, were lured to the Persian court on pretext of peace negotiations and then put to death. Arshak's consort, Queen Parantsem, held out valiantly in a stronghold for over a year, until she too was captured and put to death after rape and torture.

Most serious and irreparable of all was the damage done to Armenian urban life. Towns in the Armenian highlands could only flourish in conditions of un-interrupted trade relations with foreign countries, internal security, and protection by the central monarchy. The Armenian urban class had been built up over the centuries by the deliberate encouragement of settlers from Syria, Asia Minor and Mesopotamia, and particularly, of Jews who took refuge in Armenia following the destruction of Jerusalem by the Emperor Titus. Great King Shapur was fully cognizant of the role of the urban municipalities in the structure of the Arsacid monarchy. His object was to raze as many of them as possible to their foundations, and deport all the citizens and burghers, especially the intelligent and hard-working Jewish bourgeoisie, to Persia. The Persian sovereign distributed part of the spoils to leading Armenian feudal magnates, whom he succeeded in winning over to his own side.

The fruits of this policy were soon evident. The great Armenian nobles, though nominally Christian, could not resist the privileges and other allurements held out to them by the aristocratic realm of the Sasanids. In AD 377, another ambitious Mamikonian prince, Manuel, dethroned and expelled the Armenian King Varazdat, who was a protégé of the Romans. It is interesting to note that Varazdat was then banished by the Emperor Theodosius to the 'Island of Thule', by which is meant the British Isles. Manuel Mamikonian concluded a bargain with the Persians, whereby he was recognized as regent of Armenia, in return for a promise of allegiance to the Persian Great King; tolerance for the Christian faith in Armenia was guaranteed by the Persian court.

Soon the weakness of Shapur II's successors encouraged Prince Manuel Mamikonian to transfer Armenia's allegiance back to the Eastern Roman Empire. Restoring to the throne two Arsacid brothers, the co-kings Arshak III and Valarshak, Manuel continued to rule over Armenia until his death AD 385. Thereafter, the co-operation of the Armenian crown and the feudal dynasts came to an end. Some of the *nakharars* revolted against the co-king Arshak, and appealed to the Persian court at Ctesiphon for another Arsacid prince to be appointed as their king. The Great King Shapur III sent Khosrow, son of King Varazdat, to seize Armenia at the head of an Iranian army. As King Khosrow III, this Arsacid prince soon occupied most of the realm of his ancestors, while his kinsman Arshak III was obliged to take refuge in Upper Armenia on the Roman frontier.

Both the Emperor Theodosius and the Persian Great King Shapur III seized upon this opportunity of achieving a peaceful settlement of their long-standing dispute over Armenia. In the peace of Acilisene (AD 387), the existence of two Armenian kingdoms, one under Roman, and the other under Iranian suzerainty, was ratified. Iran received the lion's share, the eastern region, the so-called Persarmenia. The Persian sphere was five times larger than the combined territory of the western region and the Sophene province retained by the Roman Empire since the Peace of Nisibis in 298. The frontier was a line passing roughly from Erzurum in the north to Mush in the south. When Arshak III, King of Roman Armenia, rather opportunely died in AD 389, the Romans allowed him no successor. The western part of Armenia was governed thereafter by Armenian feudal nobles under the supervision of a Greek *Comes Armeniae* or 'Count of Armenia', and later, under the authority of the *Magister Militum per Armeniam* or 'commander of the armies in Armenia'. These officials were, of course, appointed by the Byzantine emperors.

In the eastern province of Persarmenia, the Armenian Arsacids retained nominal power until the deposition of King Artaxias IV in 428. This event was provoked by a rebellion led by the principal nobles. In spite of the remonstrances of the Catholicos, St Sahak, the insurgents petitioned the Persian Great King Bahram V to abolish the Armenian monarchy altogether, which he readily did. From then on, the country was ruled by the local princes, supervised by a Persian *marzpan* or viceroy residing at the city of Dvin.

In an attempt to condone their selfish careerism, which culminated in the destruction of the last focus of Armenian national unity, the feudal lords and monkish chroniclers concocted a fabric of ridiculous allegations against the last sovereigns of the Arsacid line. Some of these are embodied in such otherwise reputable sources as the chroniclers Lazarus of Pharpi and Faustus of Buzanda, and repeated by serious modern historians. Thus, Faustus alleges that the ill-fated King Pap, who reigned from 369 to 374, was possessed by evil spirits in the form of white snakes who twined themselves round his body. Pap is also accused of murdering St Nerses the Great. This tissue of fabrication was evidently inspired by the fact that Pap closed down a few nunneries, declaring that the virgins would be of more use to the country if they were released from their vows and got married; he also subdued several rebellious feudal chiefs.

Similarly, King Artaxias IV (423–28), last of the Arsacid line, is accused of partiality for loose women. This charge was obviously concocted by Lazarus of Pharpi and his aristocratic and ecclesiastical sponsors to cover up the treason of the Armenian nobles who intrigued against their liege lord, and had him deposed by the Persians. The great St Nerses clearly saw the direction in which the feudal lords were dragging unhappy Armenia. In an interview with a group of *nakharars*, as recorded by Faustus of Buzanda, the saint had vainly reminded them of the favour which they had enjoyed from the hands of King Arshak II, and implored them not to play into the hands of the Persians by intriguing against their sovereign.

Another transparent calumny against the last Arsacids propagated by the pro-aristocratic chroniclers concerns the foundation of the city of Arshakavan by King Arshak II (351–67). According to Faustus of Buzanda and other sources, Arshak founded this city as a refuge for 'insolvent debtors, adulterers, refugees from justice and convicted criminals', promising them pardon and immunity if they settled in the new town. St Nerses is said to have denounced the new city and uttered an anathema against it, as a result of which the population was wiped out by an epidemic, or according to another version, by an attack by feudal barons who massacred the inhabitants.

The truth behind this naive fabrication is not hard to find. Arshak, hard-pressed both by the feudal nobles and the Persians, was aware that a king in such a situation can only triumph by the support either of a regular army, or of a loyal urban burgher class who will lend him money and uphold him against an insurgent nobility. (Such was the experience later of Louis XI in France and Henry VII in England.) His regular army being sapped by the disloyalty of the nobles, King Arshak felt the need to build up Armenia's urban centres, ruined by the Persians, and rally around himself any who were oppressed by the feudal lords and grasping bishops and abbots. Hence the furious denunciations by the prelates and princes, as embroidered by apologists for the feudal opposition such as Faustus of Buzanda, a slavish partisan of the Mamikonians, and also Moses of Khorene, the historian of the Armenian Bagratids.[1]

The following are the principal rulers of the Arsacid line, to whom Armenia owed the preservation of so much of her ancient glory:

ARMENIAN ARSACIDS

Tiridates I (53–100). Officially crowned by Nero, AD 66.

Axidares (100–113).

Parthamasiris (113–114). Deposed and murdered by the Emperor Trajan.

Parthamaspates (116–117).

Valarsh I (117–140). Founder of the city of Vagharshapat.

Sohaemus (140–178). Ranked as a Roman Senator and Consul.

Sanatruk (178–216)

Valarsh II (216–217).

Tiridates II, also known as Khosrow I (217–238).

Artavazd (c. 252).

Tiridates III (286–330). First Christian king of Armenia.

---

[1] This point is well seized by the Soviet historian G. Kh. Sarkisian, whose monograph on Tigranokerta (Moscow, 1960) is a valuable source-book on ancient Armenian towns and urban organization.

Khosrow II, called Kotak (330–38). Founder of the city of Dvin.
Tigranes V or Tiran (338–51).
Arshak (Arsaces) II (351–67).
Pap (369–74).
Varazdat (374–80).
Arshak III (380–89). Died as the last king of Roman Armenia. Originally co-
    king with –
Valarshak (380–86). King of Persarmenia.
Khosrow III (386–92).
Vramshapuh (392–414). Encouraged invention of the Armenian Alphabet.
Artaxias IV (423–28).

For five centuries following the abolition of the Arsacid monarchy, the political history of Armenia is largely that of the rival great houses of the feudal princes (*nakharars* and *ishkhans*). The most prominent Armenian princes at the time of the fall of the monarchy were those invested with the hereditary control of the four marches of the kingdom – notably the margraves (*bdeakhsh*) of Gogarene in the north, on the Georgian border, and of Arzanene in the south, as well as the Mamikonians of Taik, Taron, Bagravandene and Acilisene, this family being hereditary High Constables; the Bagratids or Bagratuni of Ispir, Kogovit and Tamoritis, hereditary coronants of the Armenian kings; the princes of Siunia in north-eastern Armenia, around Lake Sevan; the Kamsarakans of Shirak and Arsharunik; the Rshtuni ruling the southern shores of Lake Van; and the Ardsrunis who possessed the margraviate of Adiabene. In the Syrian march of Armenia, comprising the old kingdom of Sophene, there were the princes of Ingilene and of Greater and Lesser Sophene. Around the year 500, C. L. Toumanoff has calculated that there were in all Armenia as many as thirty-four states, and twenty dynasties.

The political and military weight of these great houses can be judged by the size of their respective cavalry contingents, formerly placed at the service of their suzerain, the king of Armenia, and later, of the Great King of Iran. According to Toumanoff's calculation,[1] Gogarene and Arzanene furnished 4,500 and 4,000 horse respectively; Ingilene, 3,400; Ardsruni, Bagratids, Mamikonians, Sophene, 1,000 each; Kamsarakan 600; Siunia, at a later period, up to 9,400. Several of these local dynasties devised for themselves exotic pedigrees. Thus, the Bagratids claimed Hebrew origin, from David and Solomon of Israel; the Mamikonians claimed kinship with the emperors of China; the Ardsrunis asserted a relationship with the ancient kings of Assyria.

What they lacked in political cohesion, these early medieval Armenian dynasts made up by their vigour, cunning, zest for living, and devotion to religion and the arts. Swashbuckling warriors, wily diplomats, great lovers, eaters and drinkers, strenuous sinners and pious penitents, theirs was the colourful world depicted in

[1] *Cambridge Medieval History*, IV, 1, p. 597.

the Armenian popular epic *David of Sassoun*. Some cool and calculating, others wild, mad figures, given to excesses both of wickedness and asceticism, they were patrons of literature, music and painting, protectors of the scribes who illuminated incomparably beautiful manuscripts, and organizers of the teams of architects and masons who produced the grandiose churches and cathedrals which still adorn Armenia's skyline. Born intriguers, they could sometimes sacrifice the interests of their homeland for the sake of some intrigue with the Byzantine and Sasanian courts, or later, at the emperor's court in Constantinople and the caliph's in Baghdad. At other times, they would lay down their life on the battlefield for the sake of the Christian faith and their Armenian national heritage.

Given the centrifugal tendencies in Armenian feudal society, it is probable that the Armenians would have finished by being assimilated or eliminated by one of the great powers which surrounded and alternately sought to dominate them, had it not been for the unifying force of the Christian faith. It was the Church, in the person of St Mesrop-Mashtotz, who gave Armenia her alphabet early in the fifth century, and opened the door to education and evangelical work in the vernacular. The pioneer work of St Mesrop also affected the neighbouring Christian countries of Georgia and Caucasian Albania. Both these countries adopted alphabets closely modelled on that devised by St Mesrop for Armenia.

Armenian cultural and religious hegemony made a strong impact on Caucasian Albania, now comprising part of the Soviet Socialist Republic of Azerbaijan. The Caucasian Albanians were once moon-worshippers, and are well known in Classical times from the descriptions of Strabo and other Greek geographers. The best account of early medieval Albania is the Armenian chronicle by Moses Daskhurantsi (or Kaghankatuatsi), written probably in the eleventh century, and translated into English in 1961 by Professor C. J. F. Dowsett of the University of Oxford. In the fifth chapter of his work, Moses describes this favoured country:

'Situated among the towering mountains of the Caucasus, the land of Albania is fair and alluring, with many natural advantages. The great river Kur flows gently through it bearing fish large and small, and it throws itself into the Caspian Sea. In the plains round about there is to be found much bread and wine, naptha and salt, silk and cotton, and innumerable olive trees. Gold, silver, copper, and ochre are found in the mountains. As for wild animals, there are the lion, the leopard, the panther, and the wild ass, and among the many birds the eagle, the hawk, etc. And it has the great Partaw as its capital'.

The Caucasian Albanians spoke a language which is imperfectly known, since virtually all literary texts have perished, and we depend mostly on inscriptions on stone and pottery sherds. The language was unusually rich in guttural sounds, and was described by Armenian missionaries as 'raucous, coarse and discordant'. However, the Albanian Christians, with their chief bishops residing at Partaw, near Ganja, proved a loyal support for the Armenian Gregorian church throughout

166

all its vicissitudes. They took part in the battles waged by the Armenians against the Sasanian kings, and followed the Armenians in their ecclesiastical polemics with the Byzantine and Georgian Orthodox Churches following the Council of Chalcedon (451) and the schism with Georgia (607). The Caucasian Albanians were largely annihilated or assimilated by the Seljuq Turks, though a few remnants are said to survive in the shape of the modern Udi, who dwell in two villages in the Shakki district.

Although previously respecting the local customs and institutions of Armenia, the Sasanian Great Kings took advantage of the abolition of the Arsacid monarchy in AD 428 to spread Iranian cultural and religious influences. In this they were thwarted, both by the local princes and Church hierarchy, and by the influence of such talented writers as the polemist Eznik of Kolb, whose tract, 'Against the Sects', is a clever and powerful exposure of the fallacies of pagan and heretical teachings. Open persecution of the Armenian Christians broke out under the Persian Great King Yezdegird II (439–457). Matters came to a head in 449, when Yezdegird promulgated an edict in Armenia and Caucasian Albania, requiring the immediate adoption of official Mazdaism by the entire population. The Persians sent trained Zoroastrian theologians, accompanied with troops, to every town and village, proclaiming:[1]

'If you voluntarily accept our law, you shall receive gifts and honours from the king, but if you will not accept willingly, we have orders to build fire-temples in the villages and hamlets, to place therein the Vahram fire, and to appoint magi and *mobads* as the country's lawgivers; and if any should rebel, he shall be put to death, and his wife and children shall be exiled.'

To this period of religious persecution we should probably assign the ruined fire-temple discovered in the crypt of the Patriarchal Cathedral in Echmiadzin, close to remains of an ancient Christian church. Among the Christians who endured a martyr's death at this time were St Atom Gnuni and St Manatjihr Rshtuni.

The Armenians appealed for help to Byzantium. However, the Emperor Theodosius II died in 450, and was replaced by Marcian, who was too much engrossed in internal difficulties and ecclesiastical polemics to send the Armenians any help. The Armenian bishops assembled at Artashat, and unanimously resolved to defend the Christian faith to the last. A group of leading Armenian nobles were summoned to the Persian capital at Ctesiphon, and given the choice of abjuring Christianity, or going into perpetual exile. They made a pretence of renouncing their religion, so as to be able to return to their homes and organize resistance there. The priests of the Zoroastrian religion, carrying their symbols aloft, escorted home in triumph the pretended renegades, but they were met and dispersed in the plains of Bagrevand by the armed populace, led by the Archpriest St Ghevond.

[1] *History of the Caucasian Albanians*, trans. Dowsett, p. 66.

A popular revolt broke out, led by Prince Vardan Mamikonian. Unfortunately, a group of princes, under Vasak of Siunia, withdrew from the struggle and made their peace with the Persians. When, on June 2, 451, at the battle of Avarayr, 66,000 Armenians, under Vardan Mamikonian, encountered an army of 220,000 Persians, reinforced by squadrons of armed elephants, a number of Armenian traitors reinforced the enemy's ranks. Vardan and eight other generals fell on the battlefield, and the Persians gained the day. So great was the carnage, however, that the Persians gave up their dream of subjugating Armenia. Ultimately an accommodation was reached, though not before a number of Armenian bishops and priests, including the Patriarch, St Hovsep, were carried off to the Persian court to suffer martyrdom for their cause. Vardan Mamikonian is numbered among the saints of the Armenian Church, and the anniversary of the Battle of Avarayr is among its main festivals.

It is interesting to note that the daughter of Vardan Mamikonian, the princess Shushanik, or Susanna, is also numbered among the saints, this time of the Georgian Church. Shushanik was married to the *bdeakhsh* or margrave Varsken, who governed the marchlands between Armenia and Georgia, on behalf of the Persian Great King, and resided at Tsurtav. Varsken abjured the Christian faith of his ancestors to win favour with the Persians, but Shushanik denounced his apostasy, and was put to death after several years of torture and ill-treatment.

The Life of Saint Shushanik, partly translated into English,[1] contains valuable details about family life and social conditions in early Christian Armenia and Georgia. Thus, it seems that the Armenian Christians deemed it unseemly for men and women to dine together at table, though this was acceptable among the Zoroastrian Persians. The saint's Life contains vivid word pictures of the behaviour of the renegade Varsken, who split open his wife's head with a poker, dragged her to and fro by her hair, 'bellowing like a wild beast and roaring like a madman', and later hauled her out of church through the mud and over the thorns – 'just as if they were dragging a corpse along' – before hitting her three hundred times with a stick. Such details remind us what it meant in those days to stand up for the Christian faith. Equally graphic is the description of the saint's last days in her noisome prison, 'incredibly infested with fleas and lice':

'In the summer the heat of the sun burns like fire, the winds are torrid and the waters infected. The inhabitants of this region are themselves afflicted with various diseases, being swollen with dropsy, yellow with jaundice, pock-marked, withered up, mangy, pimply, bloated of face and brief of life, and nobody attains old age in that district.'

Having withstood persecution at the hands of the Persian Mazdaists, the Armenian Church also had to defend its autonomous status and its doctrinal

[1] D. M. Lang, *Lives and Legends of the Georgian Saints*, London, 1956, pp. 44–56. It has also been staged in Tbilisi as a dramatic spectacle in 1968, with Vaso Godziashvili in the role of Varsken.

position in the face of encroachments by the Nestorian Church of Mesopotamia and Persia, and also from Constantinople. The Armenians were particularly sensitive to the threat of assimilation by the Nestorians, who founded an important school at Nisibis under Persian royal protection. They increased their activity still further after the Council of Chalcedon in 451, which they hailed as a doctrinal victory.

It is difficult today to appreciate the virulence of the theological quarrels which rent Eastern Christendom in the fifth century. To a great extent, these theological disputes masked political power struggles, just as today many of the quarrels between communist powers are carried on in theoretical, philosophical Marxist terms of a metaphysical character. The lettered public of those days, furthermore, derived much pleasure and zest from theological argument, especially as the Church had largely abolished gladiators, theatres and other profane spectacles, while newspapers, the radio, and football matches had not been invented. St Gregory of Nyssa even complained:[1]

'All places, lanes, markets, squares, streets, the clothes merchants, money changers and grocers are filled with people discussing unintelligible questions. If you ask someone how many obols you have to pay, he philosophizes about the Begotten and the Unbegotten; if I wish to know the price of bread, the salesman answers that the Father is greater than the Son; and when you enquire whether the bath is ready, you are told that the Son was made out of nothing.'

When the Council of Chalcedon assembled in 451, the Armenians were locked in the death struggle with the Persian invaders, which culminated in the carnage of the battle of Avarayr. Armenia was not represented at Chalcedon, nor could the decisions of that synod arouse interest at a time when the Armenian Patriarch St Hovsep himself was about to suffer martyrdom at the hands of the Persians (454) and the whole country was ravaged by internecine strife. Now the chief importance of Chalcedon was the definition of the nature of Jesus Christ, which has since been accepted as orthodox by the largest Christian Churches. The Chalcedonian creed recognized 'one and the same Christ, Son, Lord, Only-Begotten, proclaimed in two natures without confusion, without change, without division, without separation; the difference of the natures being in no way destroyed on account of the union, but rather the peculiar property of each nature being preserved and concurring in one person and one hypostasis – not as though parted or divided into two persons, but one and the same Son and only-begotten God the Word, Lord, Jesus Christ'.

This subtle formulation was aimed at reconciling the rival definitions of the nature of Christ, propounded by protagonists in a whole series of earlier synods and councils, many of them conducted in a spirit of great acrimony and even violence. The two extreme viewpoints were that of Nestorius, and that of the

---

[1] Cited by S. Der Nersessian, *Armenia and the Byzantine Empire*, Harvard, 1945, p. 28.

Monophysites, or believers in the single nature of Christ, as typified by Eutyches. Nestorius held that the divine and human natures of Christ remained complete and distinct after their union, each one retaining its specific properties, and acting according to them. This concept led to the recognizing of two Sons in Jesus Christ, since the person of Jesus Christ resulting from the incarnation was not absolutely identical with that of the Word, before the incarnation.

The Alexandrian school represented a conflicting point of view, and insisted more on the divinity of the Word incarnate, and on the intimate union of the two natures in His person. At the Council of Ephesus in 431, St Cyril of Alexandria professed 'one nature united of the two – one incarnate nature of the God-word'. A follower of Cyril, Eutyches, so emphasized the union, that the two natures in Christ were confused and the manhood seemed to be absorbed by the Godhead. Eutyches denied that the body of our Saviour was of the same substance as ours, and this naturally raised the question whether the manhood of Christ was true manhood at all.

Superficially, the Chalcedonian formula appears to come down on the side of the Nestorians, rather than on that of the Alexandrian school. This certainly was the view of the Nestorians themselves, who were jubilant. Instead of restoring peace, the council of Chalcedon in fact aggravated the antagonism between the opposing theological factions, and resulted in a schism in the Eastern Church, and notably the secession of the Syrian Jacobite Church from the Orthodox community. The emperors strove in vain to appease the opponents of Chalcedon. The conciliatory Henotikon promulgated by the Emperor Zeno in 482 declared the true manhood and the true Godhead of Christ, anathematized both the Nestorians and the Euthychians, and denounced those who at Chalcedon or any other synod thought differently from the Nicene creed, as completed at Constantinople. The Emperor Anastasius (491–518) even adopted an openly pro-Monophysite religious policy, later repudiated decisively under Justin and Justinian.

Such, very briefly, were the issues agitating Eastern Christendom, when Babken of Othmous became Patriarch of Armenia in 490. The Syrian Monophysites, who had remained faithful to the doctrines propounded at Ephesus in 431, were suffering from Nestorian pressure, and turned for support and guidance to the Armenians. Now the Armenians were known to have remained scrupulously faithful to the anti-Nestorian principles of St Sahak, and opposed to any compromise regarding doctrine. The Nestorians were relying on the authority of the Council of Chalcedon, the handiwork of the Emperor Marcian who had actually rebuffed the Armenian deputation which had come to ask his aid against Persian persecution on the eve of the battle of Avarayr. Beyond this, the Council of Chalcedon had been disavowed by Marcian's successors; and by the decrees of Basiliscus, of Zeno and of Anastasius, the Chalcedonian profession of faith had been officially set aside.

In these circumstances, one can readily surmise what would be the attitude of the Armenian prelates. The synod of Armenian, Georgian and Caucasian Albanian bishops, which assembled at Dvin in 506 under the presidency of Patriarch Babken, officially proclaimed the profession of faith of the Council of Ephesus (431), accepted the terms of Zeno's *Henotikon*, and rejected everything which savoured of Nestorianism, including the acts of the Council of Chalcedon. The following form of the Trisagion was adopted for the Armenian liturgy: 'Holy God, Holy and powerful, Holy and immortal, Who wast crucified for us'.

This did not mean that the Armenians underwrote the extreme Monophysite position typified by Eutyches. Indeed, the name of Eutyches, together with that of Arius, of Macedon, and of Nestorius himself, was officially condemned. This ruling was confirmed by the second Council of Dvin in 554, under the presidence of Patriarch Nerses of Bagrevand, which again attacked Chalcedon, and proclaimed the severance of the ties uniting the Armenian Church with the Constantinople patriarchate. The Armenian Church saw no reason 'to submit to the whim of the patriarchate of Constantinople, which had applied itself at Chalcedon towards the usurpation both of precedence and of superiority over other sees, by strengthening the basis of her plans through the instrumentality of secular power'.[1]

The Armenians marked their breaking off of relations with the Greek Orthodox Church by the inauguration of a national system of chronology, beginning from the year 552 and continuing in use right up to the present day. The Georgians, who had followed the Armenians into the anti-Chalcedonian camp, later seceded from union with them. In 607, the Georgian Catholicos Kyrion clashed with the Armenian Patriarch Abraham, and re-entered the Greek Orthodox Community of Churches, being excommunicated by the Armenians at the third Council of Dvin held in 608–9. This secession, motivated partly by political considerations, contributed to friction between Georgia and Armenia, which has not quite died out even today.

The fifth and sixth centuries, so rich in literary and religious life, witnessed continued political unrest in Armenia. The Byzantine Empire entered on a new period of expansion under Justinian (527–65) and Maurice (582–602), who fought a whole series of wars with the Persians for the purpose of extending their sphere of influence in Armenia. One of the leading generals of Justinian was the Armenian eunuch Narses (478–573), who was brought as a youth to Constantinople, and attained a footing in the *officium* of the Grand Chamberlain. Narses rose to be one of the three *chartularii*, a position involving the custody of the archives of the imperial household. In 532, the insurrection known as the Nika broke out in Constantinople, when for some hours the throne of Justinian seemed doomed to be overthrown. Justinian was saved partly by the bravery of his consort, Theodora, and partly by the timely largesse of Narses, who stole out of the capital and secured the loyalty of the 'Blue' faction with large sums of money. Narses later defeated

[1] Patriarch Malachia Ormanian, *The Church of Armenia*, p. 28.

the Ostrogoth ruler, Totila, in 552, with whom fell the last hopes of the Gothic kingdom of Italy.

The Emperor Maurice is popularly supposed to have been a simple Armenian peasant, who made his way to Constantinople on foot, and there worked his way up to the supreme dignity; a stone obelisk said to have marked his tomb is shown to visitors in the Armenian village of Oshakan, close to the memorial chapel of St Mesrop Mashtotz.

However, the treatment of the Armenian Christians by Justinian and Maurice was in some ways as bad as that meted out by the Persians. In 528, Justinian suppressed the remaining Armenian principalities in the Byzantine sphere of influence, which he organized in 536 as the provinces of First Armenia (the former kingdom), and Fourth Armenia (the former *Gentes* or principalities). The peace treaty of 591 (between Byzantium and Iran) pushes the Byzantine frontier roughly to the line between the lakes Van and Sevan, with Dvin in the reduced Iranian part.

Many Armenians now began to come into the Byzantine Empire, both as adventurers and as refugees. In 571, following an unsuccessful revolt against the Persians, numerous Armenian noblemen, headed by Prince Vardan Mami-konian, and accompanied by the Armenian catholicos and some bishops, fled to Constantinople. Vardan and his retinue entered the Byzantine army; the rest settled in Pergamon, where an Armenian colony is known to have existed in the seventh century. It was from this colony that Bardanes came who, as Philippicus, occupied the imperial throne from 711 to 713.

The Armenians, however, did not always enter Byzantium of their own accord. Sometimes they were forcibly removed from their homes and resettled in other regions of the Byzantine Empire. Justinian began this practice, though the numbers involved were then small.[1] Larger scale deportations took place under Tiberius II and Maurice. In 578, 10,000 Armenians were taken from their homes and settled in the island of Cyprus, which has an important Armenian community to the present day. The Armenians were valued for their hard-working qualities. The chronicler Evagrius Scholasticus remarked:

'Thus land, which had been previously untilled, was everywhere restored to cultivation. Numerous armies also were raised from among them, that fought resolutely and courageously against the other nations. At the same time every household was completely furnished with domestics, on account of the easy rate at which slaves were procured.'

An even vaster deportation was planned by Maurice who, in spite of his reputed Armenian origin, found the Armenians extremely troublesome in their own homeland. He even conceived a plan to co-operate with the Great King of Iran in removing all the main Armenian nobles and their followers from their

[1] P. Charanis, *The Armenians in the Byzantine Empire*, p. 14.

homes. According to the historian Sebeos, Maurice wrote to the Persian Great King that 'the Armenians are a knavish and indocile nation. They are situated between us, and are a source of trouble. I am going to gather mine and send them to Thrace; you send yours to the east. If they die there, it will be so many enemies that will die; if, on the contrary, they kill, it will be so many enemies that they will kill. As for us, we shall live in peace. But if they remain in their own country, there will never be any quiet for us'. The two rulers apparently agreed to execute this plan, but the Persian failed to co-operate fully. The Byzantines did carry out the deportations, whereupon many Armenians fled to Persia, which they found less tyrannical than Christian Byzantium. This deportation of Armenians to Thrace laid the foundations of the important communities which still flourish in modern Bulgaria, notably in Sofia and Plovdiv.

The reign of Khusrau II Parvez in Persia (590–628) was marked by violent fluctuations in the balance of power in the Near East. The assassination of the Emperor Maurice in 602 enabled the Persians to ravage Syria, capture Antioch and Damascus, and in 614, to raid Jerusalem and carry off the relic of the True Cross. At times, the Persians were encamped at Chalcedon, opposite Constantinople itself. The Emperor Heraclius (610–41) took some years to assemble the nucleus of a new military power. In 623, he took to the field, and during a series of campaigns, repaid the Persians with interest, capturing Tbilisi and most of Armenia and Azerbaijan, and compelling the vanquished Persians to restore the True Cross to the Holy City. A contingent of Armenian troops led by Mjej Gnuni was largely responsible for the success of these campaigns which led in 628 to the overthrow and murder of the Great King Khusrau himself.

It is interesting to note that following his victories, Heraclius conceived the idea of reuniting the Armenian and Greek Churches. Heraclius was one of the original proponents of the doctrine of a school of theologians known as 'Monotheletes' who, while otherwise orthodox, maintained that Christ had only one will. Their theory was an attempt to effect some kind of solution of the vital unity of Christ's person, on the basis of the now firmly established doctrine of the two natures. Heraclius supported the Monotheletes in the hope of winning back for the Church and the Empire the excommunicated and persecuted Monophysites or Euthychians of Egypt and Syria. In Egypt particularly, the Monophysite movement had assumed a nationalistic, patriotic character, which threatened complete secession from the Byzantine Empire.

In Armenia, while on his expedition against Persia, in an interview with Paul, head of the Severian Monophysites, there, Heraclius first broached the doctrine that the divine and human natures in Christ, while quite distinct in his one person, had but one single activity and operation. Sergius, Patriarch of Constantinople, was a strong upholder of this doctrine of one combined divine-human energy in Christ, and was the emperor's adviser on the whole christological question. This formulation appeared to Heraclius to offer a means of winning back the allegiance of the dissident Monophysites, without abandoning the Dyophysite position adopted by the Council of Chalcedon. In the event, it satisfied neither the Orthodox nor the Monophysites. The Monothelete dogma in fact led to such widespread controversy that the successor of Heraclius, Constans II, had to issue an edict forbidding all discussion of the questions of the duality or singleness of either the nature or the will of Christ.

Previously Heraclius, now master of Armenia, had summoned to his headquarters the Catholicos Ezr or Esdras of Parajnakert (630–41), and ordered him to submit to the theological dictates of the Greek Church, failing which Heraclius threatened to nominate a rival patriarch for Armenia, subject to Constantinople. Eventually Heraclius and Ezr hit on a formula based on the Monothelete doctrine, which appeared to be in conformity with the Armenian profession of faith, except that it passed over in silence the Council of Chalcedon itself. This concordat was approved at a special synod held at Karin (Erzurum), and solemnized in 633 by a mass at which Greeks and Armenians communicated together. The submission of Patriarch Ezr to the emperor's will incensed the Armenian bishops and people. Intense rancour was vented against Ezr, though the emperor's protection saved him from deposition. However, the indignation which his conduct excited has survived through the ages to such an extent that when his name figures on the list of Armenian patriarchs, it is written with the initial letter inverted.

These complicated questions seemed at the time to be of world shaking importance for Armenia and her neighbours. Within a few years, they were a matter of historical interest only. Weakened by religious schism and internecine strife, neither Byzantium, Sasanian Iran, nor Armenia itself was in any condition to resist the advance of a new world power – that of Islam under the Arab conquerors.

Chapter VIII

ARMENIA, BYZANTIUM AND THE ARABS

THE grim warfare and bitter theological strife that had convulsed the world
of Byzantium, Armenia and Sasanian Persia proved almost irrelevant to the
long term evolution of the Near East. Weakness engendered both by military
exhaustion and by ideological division gave the Arabs their chance to win hegemony over the entire Sasanian realm, and a good half of that of Byzantium at its
greatest. Weary of endless efforts to withstand the claims of the Constantinople
patriarch and the emperor, with his Caesaro-Papal pretensions, the Monophysites
of Syria, Palestine and Egypt were in no mood to oppose the advance of the
Bedouin from the Arabian peninsula. Indeed the new, militant faith of Islam, in
which the Oneness of God was the cardinal tenet, partly matched the Monophysite
belief in the Oneness of Christ, which they had long maintained against the Dyophysite ('Two-Nature') creed of the Orthodox. Nor were the Persians, laid low
by the Emperor Heraclius, in any position to offer effective resistance to the heirs
of Muhammad the Prophet.

The decisive battle between the armies of the Arab Caliph 'Umar, and those
of the Byzantine Empire, was fought by the River Yarmuk, a tributary of the
Jordan, in August 636. The Arab commander was Khalid ibn al-Walid, while the
Byzantine army was led by an Armenian named Vahan or Baanes. Shortly before
the battle, Vahan was actually proclaimed emperor by his troops. However, the
catastrophic defeat of his forces put an end to Vahan's imperial dreams, and he
later retired to Sinai and became a monk.

Byzantium's last organized attempt to defend the heritage of Rome, and to
hold the venerated sanctuaries of Jerusalem, ended with this disastrous collapse.
Heraclius, the valiant emperor who recovered the True Cross from the Persians,
is said to have exclaimed as he evacuated Syria for ever: 'Farewell, Syria! What a
good country for the enemy!' Five years later Heraclius was dead. Earlier,
Armenian princes in Constantinople had been plotting to overthrow him, and
place on the throne his illegitimate son, Athalaric. But in 641 it was the Armenian

Valentinus Arsacidus who enabled Constans II to assume the throne following the death of Heraclius, his father. Valentinus was then put in command of the troops in the east. But shortly afterwards Valentinus took part in a plot to seize the throne for himself, and was executed. After the violent death of Constans II in 668, another Armenian, the general Mjej Gnuni, was proclaimed emperor by the troops in Sicily. Though dislodged and killed the following year, Mjej Gnuni may be included in the series of emperors of Armenian descent who occupied the Byzantine throne.

Meanwhile, the Arab conquerors went from strength to strength. Between 639 and 641, they occupied the cities of Edessa and Harran in former Byzantine territory, and Nisibis and Sinjar in the Persian zone of upper Mesopotamia, while other contingents occupied Mosul, thus establishing a military line right along Armenia's southern border. Simultaneously, Caliph 'Umar's forces were pressing into central Iran from Basra and Ahwaz in the Persian Gulf. The final crushing battle between the Arabs and Sasanians took place in 642 at Nihawand, not far from Hamadan. The annihilation of the army of the Persian Great King opened the way to further Arab advances into central Asia, as well as into Azerbaijan and the Caucasus.

The Saracens began raiding Armenia from 640 onwards. Strangely enough, these years were a period of brilliant cultural efflorescence in Armenia, especially in the field of architecture. Such masterpieces as the church of Hripsimé in Echmiadzin were followed by the superb, three-storey circular cathedral of Zvartnotz built by Catholicos Nerses III of Ishkhan, surnamed *Shinogh*, or 'The Builder'. Nerses Shinogh occupied the patriarchal throne for twenty eventful years, from 641 to 661, though with interruptions due to the unsettled state of the country. His monogram, in Greek characters, is to be seen carved on the massive pillars of Zvartnotz, the grandiose ruins of which are a few miles from the modern Echmiadzin. The seventh century in Armenia also witnessed the scientific activity of Anania Shirakatsi, the famous mathematician, astronomer and geographer, a veritable Newton of early Armenia.

The Emperor Constans II made a determined attempt to recover Armenia for Byzantium in 647. However, the Armenian princes were aware of the uncertainty of the Byzantine position, of Greek bureaucratic high-handedness, and of their own religious separateness. They therefore turned, under the leadership of the High Constable and Patrician, Prince Theodore Rshtuni, to the invaders in the hope of securing advantageous terms for an Arab protectorate. A peace concluded by Theodore Rshtuni and the future Caliph Mu'awiya in 653 recognized Armenia as an autonomous tributary state. At the same time, the Iberian Patrician Stephen II accepted Arab suzerainty over eastern Georgia, as did also Juansher, the ruler of Caucasian Albania. The three Caucasian states now formed a single viceroyalty of the Arab Caliphate designated as *Arminiya*. Dvin was the seat of the Arab viceroys.

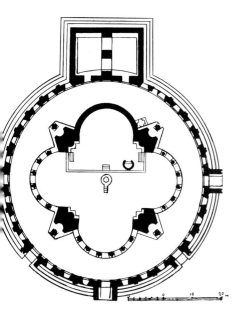

ZVARTNOTZ:
Cathedral ground-plan

Capital with Maltese cross

Eagle Capital

The following two centuries were marked by a fierce tug-of-war between Byzantine interference and Saracen reprisals with the presiding princes of Armenia wavering between the two allegiances. National consolidation was thwarted by ceaseless strife. Theodore Rshtuni, who had been presiding prince of Armenia on behalf of both the Byzantines and the Arabs, was deposed in 655. This marked the end of the power of this outstanding Armenian princely family of the Rshtunis. The chief princes of Armenia were now the Mamikonians, whose star was also gradually on the wane; the Ardsrunis, later kings of Vaspurakan, round about Lake Van; and above all, the Bagratids, who were later to reign in both Ani and in Tbilisi, and were a force in Caucasian politics for well over a thousand years.

The independent spirit of the Armenian dynasts several times impelled the Arab governors to suppress, and even to annihilate them. In 705, for instance, the Arab viceroy Muhammad ibn-Marwan decided to exterminate the Armenian high nobility. Several hundred Armenian lords with their families and retainers were inveigled into Nakhchevan and there locked up in churches and burnt, or crucified after torture. This atrocity sent many princes fleeing the country, to Georgia, and also to Byzantium, where career prospects were often very bright. The Nakhchevan massacre was one of the first steps trodden by the Armenian people on the road towards their Calvary at the hands of Muslim overlords, culminating in the Ottoman holocausts of 1895 and then of 1915. Revolts against Arab hegemony and the exaction of the caliphs' tax gatherers continued throughout the eighth century, leading to great destruction and loss of life, and the depopulation of large areas of Armenia. Many Armenian Christians, including numbers of monks and nuns, underwent cruel torture and martyrdom rather than win immunity and safety by embracing Islam.

Another menace with which the Armenians had to contend was a series of raids by Khazars and Huns from central Asia, often encouraged by the Byzantine emperors. These Khazars had been instrumental in capturing Tbilisi for the Emperor Heraclius in AD 627, at which time they had ravaged Caucasian Albania. Moses Daskhurantsi gives a lurid picture of the fear inspired by the Khazars among the Caucasian peoples:[1]

'Their terror increased at the sight of the ugly, insolent, broad-faced, eyelashless mob in the shape of women with flowing hair who descended upon them, and they trembled before them, especially when they saw their bent and well-aimed bows the arrows of which rained down upon them like heavy hailstones, and when they saw how they fell upon them in the lanes and streets of the town. Their eyes did not distinguish between the fair, the handsome, or the young among men and women, nor the weak and helpless. They spared neither the lame nor the old, neither did they feel pity, mercy, or compassion for the children who clutched their

[1] *History of the Caucasian Albanians*, trans. Dowsett, pp. 83–4.

murdered mothers and sucked blood from their breasts instead of milk. Like fire among straw, they entered in at one gate and emerged through another, and in their wake, they left work for the birds and beasts of prey.'

These invasions from the land of 'Gog and Magog' posed a constant threat to the Arab dominion in the Caucasus, which extended to Derbent and the mountains of Daghestan. The caliphs often found it expedient to depute one or other of the Armenian princes to defend the Caspian Gates against the Khazars. Subsequently, from about 914 onwards, the Varangians (Vikings combined with Russian adventurers) also penetrated as far as the northern borderlands of Armenia, sailing in from the Volga delta and over the Caspian Sea. Our Armenian source, Moses Daskhurantsi,[1] writes that 'a certain people of strange and foreign appearance, called Ruzik (Russians) attacked from the lands of the north, and rushing like a tempest over the inland sea of the east, the Caspian, they reached Partaw, the capital of Albania, in no more than three days'. Nobody could withstand these Varangians, and they plundered at will, returning to their own country laden with abundant loot.

During the Arab supremacy in Armenia, the chief town of the viceroy, Dvin, became one of the great cities of the Near East. Founded by the Armenian King Khosrow Kotak about 330 AD, Dvin was the ecclesiastical capital for several centuries, and witnessed the final separation of the Armenian from the Greek and the Georgian Churches. The Armenian patriarchs had several magnificent churches in Dvin, all of them now destroyed. However, the Dvin Archaeological Expedition of the Armenian Academy of Sciences headed by Professor Karo Kafadarian has uncovered the floor of the ancient patriarchal cathedral, which was a triple basilica built probably after the Syrian style. The cathedral was associated with a luxurious palace and extensive monastic buildings. The present author had the opportunity of visiting Dvin in 1966, and inspecting the local museum containing many remarkable finds.

The building of Zvartnotz, some thirty miles to the north-west, by Catholicos Nerses, somewhat impaired the importance of Dvin as an ecclesiastical capital, though synods and councils continued to assemble there in the period of Saracen domination. What really built up the international renown of Dvin was the concentration there of the military might, the commerce and administrative resources of the Arab viceroyalty of the Caucasus. This ensured regular access to the main Islamic centres of Damascus, Samarra and Baghdad; from these great cities, ceramic ware, metal work, and textiles were regularly exported to Dvin in exchange for local products. In addition, Dvin was an extremely important mint during the Umayyad and 'Abbasid caliphates; silver dirhams were struck there in large quantities in the name of the reigning caliph and of Muhammad the Prophet.

---

[1] *History of the Caucasian Albanians*, trans. Dowsett, p. 224.

Destroyed during the revolts and wars of the late seventh century, Dvin was rebuilt, according to the Armenian historian Ghevond, by 'Abd al-Aziz, governor of Armenia under the Caliph al-Walid (AD 705–15):

'But 'Abd al-Aziz, when he became the governor of our land of Armenia, pacified her by protecting her from all unjustified attacks, and by stern reproofs subdued the haughty arrogance of the sons of Ishmael (i.e. the Saracens). He built again the city of Dvin stronger and greater in size than it was before, he strengthened it with gates and bolts, surrounded the city walls with a dug out ditch, and filled it with water for the protection of the fortress.'

The excavations of Professor Kafadarian show that Dvin was a centre for extensive local manufactures, especially glassware and pottery, including faience. The magnificent coloured porcelain from Dvin preserved in the Armenian Historical Museum in Erevan, and inspected by this writer in 1966 and 1968, would honour the table of any modern king or millionaire, and is remarkable for its imaginative designs, wonderful colouring, often in greens and blues, and lustrous finish.

Dvin was destroyed by an earthquake in the second half of the ninth century; it was then rebuilt, and continued to be a key point in international transit trade. Professor H. A. Manandian[1] assembled a number of extracts from the writings of early Arab geographers, who all extol the wealth and importance of Dvin, which the Arabs knew as Dabil. Thus, in his *Book of Roads and Realms*, al-Istakhri writes:

'Dabil is greater than Ardabil [a famous city in north-western Iran]. This city serves as the capital of Armenia and in it is the palace of the governor, just as the palace of the governor of Arran [Caucasian Albania] is in Berdaa [Partaw], and the palace of the governor of Azerbaijan is in Ardabil. There is a wall around Dabil. Here there are many Christians, and the main mosque is next to the church. In this town are made woollen garments and rugs, cushions, seats, laces, and other items of Armenian manufacture. From here is also obtained the dye named 'kirmiz' [a form of cochineal], and cloth is dyed with it. I learned that this is a worm which weaves around itself a cocoon similar to that of the silkworm. In addition, I discovered that many silken cloths are manufactured here . . . . The city is always in the hands of the Christian nobility, and the Christians form the greater part of the population of Armenia, also known as "the kingdom of the Armenians".'

The Arab geographer Ibn-Haukal, who lived later than al-Istakhri, confirms the information on Armenia given in the *Book of Roads and Realms*, and adds that great quantities of silken garments were manufactured in Dvin, of higher quality than those made in Anatolia. Woven goods included the so-called 'butts', a large piece of silk worn on the head and falling beneath the shoulders, also seats,

[1] *The Trade and Cities of Armenia*, trans. N. G. Garsoian, Lisbon, 1965, pp. 143–4.

rugs, covers and cushions. 'There is none equal to them among the things of this world from end to end, and in all directions.'

Another leading Arabic authority, al-Muqaddasi, also devotes much attention to describing the town of Dvin, or Dabil:

'Dabil is an important city, in it are an inaccessible citadel and great riches. Its name is ancient, its cloth is famous, its river is abundant, it is surrounded by gardens (as is the case even today); the city has suburbs, its fortress is reliable, its squares are cross-shaped, its fields are wonderful. The main mosque is on a hill and next to the mosque is the church. The Kurds watch over the town. By the city is a citadel. The buildings of the inhabitants are made of clay or stone. The city has many gates such as Bab-Keydar, Bab-Tiflis and Bab-Ani (designating the cities lying along the respective roads from the town). Despite all its advantages the Christians are a majority there'.

The Arab inroads into Armenia and Anatolia, by sapping the civil and spiritual power of both the Orthodox and the Armenian Churches, helped to foster the growth of heresy and rebellious sects. Some of these were basically revivals of earlier pagan beliefs or philosophical systems, which had been suppressed by the Christian Church, and had, so to speak, 'gone underground'.

The most important Armenian 'opposition' sect of this period was that of the Paulicians, and their off-shoot the Tondrakites, whose activities extended all over the Byzantine Empire, and became a regular menace to the central government of Constantinople. The Paulicians were distant successors of early Christian nonconformists, such as the Gnostics, whose dualist beliefs had flourished widely in Asia Minor. The Gnostics had prepared a fertile ground for the spread of Manichaeism from Persia. The third-century Persian seer Mani had taught that there are two eternally opposite principles of good and evil: God, or spirit, represented by the Light, and Matter, represented by Darkness. This world was supposed by the Manichaeans to be a mixture of both opposing principles or elements, in which particles of light, the souls of men, are imprisoned by evil forces in the body, which is the darkness of matter. According to Mani, the divine Will intended the separation of light from darkness, and man should co-operate by refusing to propagate his kind and by practising an extreme asceticism which, unlike Christian asceticism, was aimed not at controlling the body but at destroying it.

Naturally, these doctrines led readily to antisocial practices. On the one hand, the Manichees inveighed against the multiplying of children, so that towns and countryside were threatened with depopulation. This aroused the apprehension and indignation of governments. Again, there was a tendency to channel sexual activity into forms which would not propagate the family unit. Later Manichaean movements, such as the Bogomils, were accused, not without reason, of favouring promiscuity or even homosexuality. The Manichees had an inner élite, known as

181

the Elect, as well as more numerous lay adherents, or 'Hearers'. All Manichees were vegetarians, but the Elect abstained from wine, from marriage and from owning property. Their obligation not to produce fresh life nor to take it was so absolute that it extended to the vegetable kingdom. They might neither sow nor reap, nor even break their bread themselves, 'lest they pain the Light which was mixed with it'.

Although they formally anathematized Mani, the Paulicians were in many respects successors of the Manichees. Their founder was a certain Constantine of Mananali, who lived in the sixth century. He took the name of Silvanus, after the Pauline Epistles, and organized many churches. These were particularly dangerous to both Armenian and Byzantine orthodoxy, because they permitted external conformity with the dominant Church, and held that Christ would forgive it. The Paulicians thus built up a secret network of underground conventicles, which might burst into open opposition to the established Church at any moment. At a later period, the Crusaders found them everywhere in Syria and Palestine, and corrupted their name to Publicani, under which name we find them scattered all over Europe during the ages following the Crusades. Edward Gibbon has a long and interesting account of them in *The Decline and Fall of the Roman Empire*.

The most exhaustive manual of Paulician doctrine is a comparatively modern document, called *The Key of Truth*, said to have been brought to Russian Armenia from Turkey by a group of Armenian refugees in 1828.[1] However, we have a number of much earlier references in Byzantine and Armenian sources, though these are all hostile, and make every effort to condemn and even to distort the tenets of the Paulician sect. The Armenian Catholicos-Patriarch and Saint, John III of Otsoon, known as the Philosopher (717–28), devoted his attention to refuting the heresy of the Paulicians; he states that already in the sixth century, Catholicos Nerses II (548–57) had chastised the sect, but ineffectually; after his death, they continued to lurk in Armenia.

In the ninth century, the Paulicians burst out of Armenia into western Anatolia, and became a real threat to Byzantine authority. They captured Ephesus in 867, after which an imperial ambassador, Peter of Sicily, was sent to treat with them for the release of Byzantine prisoners. Peter of Sicily made use of his embassy to compile a history of the Manichees, i.e. the Paulicians, which he dedicated to the archbishop of Bulgaria, where the Paulicians constituted a formidable element. He reported that their belief in the intrinsic evil of matter led them to deny the reality of Christ's incarnation. Thus they asserted that Christ's body was only the semblance of a real body. They rejected much of the written and oral traditions of the Church, including the whole of the Old Testament. They particularly venerated the Pauline epistles, possibly because of their ascetic teachings. The Paulicians further rejected the Eucharist, taking the words of the Gospels which

[1] It was published by the Oxford scholar F. C. Conybeare in 1898.

refer to it in a figurative sense. They had strong iconoclastic tendencies, smashing images and even crosses whenever they could.

In the year 872, the military resistance of the Paulicians was finally crushed by the destruction of their stronghold of Tephrike in western Armenia, and the annihilation of the forces of the Paulician chieftain Chrysocheir. The Paulician centres, which were now incorporated in the Empire, had been predominantly manned by Armenian settlers from further east, combined with Greek and local elements. Many thousands of these Paulicians were forcibly dispersed and deported, in many cases to Italy and also to Bulgaria, where they established themselves notably at Philippopolis, the modern Plovdiv, and helped to give rise to the later and equally dangerous heresy of the Bogomils.

The liquidation of the Armenian Paulician strongholds in Byzantine territory led to intensified efforts to build up the movement afresh within the Armenian homeland. Between 830 and 840, a certain Sumbat Zarehavantsi had begun his missionary work in the district of Apahunik, near the town of Manazkert, to the north of Lake Van. His headquarters were at the village of Tondrak, hence the name Tondrakites given to the later, Armenian branch of the Paulician movement. Sumbat Zarehavantsi was a well travelled man, familiar with the teachings of Mani and another early Persian religious and political leader, Mazdak, as well as with the ancient Greek philosophers and the teachings of the earlier Paulicians of Asia Minor.

As well as being a well organized religious sect, the Tondrakites were a formidable group of social reformers and rebels. Their Manichaean background led them to preach asceticism and renunciation of the riches of the world. They were hostile to feudal principalities and powers, and to the well-established Armenian Gregorian church hierarchy, with its enormous wealth and its control of the ideology, social life and culture of the population at large. The historian John Catholicos (fl. 898–929) complains that 'the lower orders aimed to be more competent than the upper class, and the servants planned, Solomon like, how their masters should wear sandals and go on foot, and how they themselves should sit on magnificent and prancing horses. They became proud and insolent, raised a great insurrection'.

The Tondrakites attacked the feudal privileges of the Armenian *nakharars*, who made common cause with the clergy in persecuting and suppressing them. Modern Armenian historians salute the Tondrakites as spiritual ancestors of present day communism. Certainly they provided a focus for the poor peasantry and the urban proletariat, for whom the prevailing social system held scant prospect of betterment or even, in some cases, of a tolerable subsistence for themselves and their families.

Faced with this well organized and deeply rooted movement of social protest, the Armenian princes for once made common cause with the Arab *amirs* or viceroys resident in Dvin. The Arab viceroy Abu'l-Ward embarked on a general campaign against the Tondrakites, with the support of the Armenian aristocracy of the Manazkert region. Sumbat Zarehavantsi was captured and put to death. However, the Tondrakite movement did not perish with its founder, but lived on throughout the tenth century, keeping a large area of Armenia and Caucasian Albania convulsed with civil strife and social protest.

The period of Arab domination in Armenia was marked by continued emigration of large groups of Armenians into the territory both of the Caliphate and of the Byzantine Empire. Sometimes this was the result of persecutions, but in many cases it was due to a desire for social and economic improvement. With Armenia divided into many rival feudal principalities, the opportunities for advancement for an able soldier from the lower ranks of society were much brighter in Constantinople, or in Damascus and Baghdad, than in the Armenian mountains. The growth of trade and manufactures within Armenia was slower than in the great centres of Byzantium and the Caliphate, so that merchants tended to migrate to the great markets of the Near East. This movement can be compared with that of the Scots after the suppression of their independence in 1715 and 1745. Having lost the freedom of their homeland, the Scots took revenge by assuming a preponderance in the professional and commercial life of their conquerors, the English, which they have not lost to this day.

To chronicle in detail the achievements of eminent Armenians in the military life of Byzantium, and also of the Arab caliphate, would be as monotonous as attempting to list the Macdonalds, the Macphersons, the Macmillans and others who have featured in the political, military and commercial life of Great Britain, Canada, Australia, and the United States of America. The role of the Armenians in Byzantium is chronicled by Sirarpie Der Nersessian in the first chapter of her *Armenia and the Byzantine Empire*, as well as by Peter Charanis in his monograph, *The Armenians in the Byzantine Empire*. Of special value is the collection of essays by the late Nicolas Adontz, collected and published at Lisbon in 1965, under the title *Études Arméno-Byzantines*. In the pages of these works, we meet a colourful array of Armenian generals and patricians, intriguers and courtiers, philosophers and rhetors, who managed to reach high rank in the Greek Orthodox world of Byzantium, though without losing their Armenian individuality, or renouncing completely their loyalty to the Armenian homeland.

From the eighth to the tenth century, Armenians were never far from the imperial throne in Constantinople. From 711 to 713, the Armenian Bardanes Philippicus actually reigned over Byzantium. Philippicus was a successful military leader, who was implicated in plots against the Emperor Justinian II. When the latter was murdered in 711, Philippicus assumed the purple, and summoned a conclave of Eastern bishops, which temporarily restored the doctrine of the Monotheletes. Their dogma had been favoured by the Emperor Heraclius, and was supposed to have certain affinities with the creed of the Armenian national Church, though the latter refused to adopt it. For two years Philippicus had to resist invasions by both the Bulgarians and the Saracens, and was then removed from the throne by a military conspiracy.

During the crucial reign of Leo III (717–41) Byzantium was virtually dominated by a group of ambitious Armenians. Leo III originated the Iconoclastic movement, designed to abolish the all-pervading cult of religious images which had undoubtedly become an abuse, and obscured the primitive teachings of the early Fathers. It has been suggested that the Armenians behind Leo's throne played some part in devising the doctrine and strategy of Iconoclasm, particularly since the cult of images, though not proscribed in the Armenian Church, is far from occupying in Armenia the central position which it does in Greece or in Russia. There is also evidence that Leo had contacts with the Paulicians, who were strongly opposed to image worship. However this may be, Leo III came to the throne with the active assistance of the Armenian general Artavasdus, commander of the Armeniakon Theme, or military province, in Asia Minor, and the bearer of an illustrious name recalling the glories of Tigranes the Great. Leo gave Artavasdus his daughter Anna in marriage, and Armenians played a prominent part in public affairs throughout his reign.

After the death of Leo III, his religious policy of Iconoclasm was carried on by his son Constantine V Copronymus, who was brother-in-law of the Armenian Artavasdus. Constantine soon had to set out from the capital to repel a force of Arabs who invaded Phrygia. Artavasdus saw fit to set himself up as champion of the religious images and traditional customs of the Orthodox Church, which Leo III and his son were trampling underfoot. With the help of his cousin Tiridates (another famous Armenian royal name), Vahtan the patrician, and other Armenians, Artavasdus seized power in 742, and crowned his son Nicephorus co-emperor with himself. His other son, Nicetas, was appointed general of the Armeniac Theme. In the following year, however, Constantine V staged a triumphal re-entry into Constantinople. Artavasdus and his two sons were blinded while the Patriarch Anastasius, who had taken an active part in the revolt, was flogged and publicly humiliated by being made to ride through the city seated backwards on an ass.

Several other Armenian claimants held power in Byzantium for brief periods: Alexius Museles in 790, Bardanes in 803, and Arsaber in 808. However, Leo V (813–20) is the only emperor who has been officially recognized as an Armenian by the Byzantine historians. 'As to his immediate origin', writes Georgius Monachus (Hamartolus), 'it is well known. He came from the country of the Armenians, whence, according to some, his obstinacy and his bad disposition.' Nicolas Adontz has shown that Leo V was a scion of the Armenian princely family of the Ardsrunis. His eldest son bore the Armenian name of Sumbat, which the emperor later changed to Constantine. Leo's reign was largely taken up with theological disputes regarding the cult of images, which he opposed, and with wars against the Bulgarians, who captured Adrianople and advanced to the walls of

Constantinople. An ancient Slavonic manuscript of the Byzantine Manasses chronicle preserved in the Vatican Library has a series of lively miniatures, one of which portrays Leo the Armenian on horseback, wearing a gold crown, and galloping in hot pursuit of the formidable Bulgar Khan Krum.

Leo the Armenian succumbed in 820 to a conspiracy headed by Michael Psellos, or 'the stammerer', who ascended the throne as Michael II (820–29). Michael was an old comrade in arms of Leo V, but had been accused of treason, and sentenced, by some quirk of Armenian humour, to be bound to an ape and cast into the furnace which heated the palace bath water. This verdict exasperated Michael's friends and partisans, who disguised themselves in clerical robes and entered the palace chapel on Christmas morning, 820, and there murdered Leo V in the middle of the Christmas service.

During the reign of Michael III (842–67), Armenians held the most important positions. Michael III was son of an Armenian empress, Theodora. One of the emperor's uncles, the Caesar Bardas, was the real ruler for a decade, from 856 to 866; another Armenian uncle, Petronas, led the imperial armies with distinction.

Ironically enough, it was another, rival group of Armenians who led the two bloody coups which resulted in the elevation of Basil I to the imperial throne in 867. Though called 'the Macedonian', Basil was in fact an Armenian of humble descent, from the Adrianople district. His family were taken prisoner by the Bulgarian Khan Krum, and deported to the region of the Danube. Basil later made his way to Constantinople, and rose from being an imperial equerry to the rank of Basileus or 'King'. Basil became a close favourite and confidant of Michael III whom he eventually betrayed and murdered. In spite of his modest origins and unprincipled character, Basil I turned out one of the ablest of the Byzantine emperors, and even distinguished himself as a legislator. Professor J. B. Bury remarked: 'He is one of the most remarkable examples of a man, without education and exposed to the most demoralizing influences, manifesting extraordinary talent in the government of a great state, when he had climbed to the throne by acts of unscrupulous bloodshed.'

The 'Macedonian', or more correctly, Armenian dynasty founded by Basil I lasted for nearly two centuries. It is considered to be one of the most glorious and successful in Byzantine annals. It is interesting that some others who seized the imperial power during this epoch were also Armenians: for instance, Romanus Lecapenus (919–44) co-emperor with Constantine VII Porphyrogenitus, and also the warlike John Tzimisces (969–76), famous for his victories over the Russians and Bulgarians, and also over the Saracens.

The Armenian element was also prominent in the intellectual life of Byzantium, which underwent a notable revival in the ninth century. Prominent in this movement were such figures of part-Armenian blood as John the Grammarian, Caesar Bardas, and Leo the Philosopher, who helped with the re-establishment of the University of Constantinople, housed in the Magnaura Palace, and for that reason known as the School of Magnaura. Also of partial Armenian descent was Patriarch Photius (820–93), whose stormy patriarchate marked the beginning of the schism between the Eastern and Western Churches. Photius helped to initiate the conversion of Bulgaria and the beginnings of Byzantine Christianity in Russia. He wrote an astonishing number of important works of learning and theological speculation, including a Lexicon of rare Greek words, homilies, biblical commentaries, polemical treatises and juristic studies. Professor Robert Browning has concluded: 'Photius is one of the greatest intellectual figures of the Middle Ages, at the very centre of the Byzantine renaissance of learning, whose effects were felt all over Europe.'

Armenians also played a distinguished role in public affairs in the great rival of Byzantium, namely the Umayyad and later the 'Abbasid caliphate. Some of them were converted, outwardly at least, to Islam, while others managed to retain their Christian faith. One leading figure in Caucasian affairs was the Amir 'Ali al-Armani, or 'Ali the Armenian, who died in 863, soon after being appointed by the caliph to be governor of Armenia and Azerbaijan. Armenians were particularly successful in the service of the Tulunid and Fatimid sultans of Egypt. An Armenian slave named Badr al-Jamali rose to be Vazir or chief minister in Cairo from 1073 to 1094. Another Armenian Vazir in Egypt, Bahram or Vahram by name, remained openly a Christian while attaining the highest dignities of state. He was awarded several titles usually reserved for the defenders of the Faith of Islam, and his funeral in Cairo was attended by the sultan himself; the biography of Bahram is given in the *Encyclopaedia of Islam*.

Not all Armenians of merit emigrated abroad. Two princely families were especially prominent in ninth-century Armenia, and benefited by the gradual weakening of the power of the caliphs. These were the Ardsrunis and the Bagratunis. The Ardsrunis held vast domains in the south and south-east of Armenia; they ruled over the entire province of Vaspurakan, and their power extended to the province of Ayrarat on the north, and to Lake Urmia in Azerbaijan in the east. The Bagratunis or Bagratids, who were also powerful in Georgia, had been ousted from Vaspurakan, and then established themselves in the region of Mount Ararat and the Araxes valley.

The shrewd, calculating Bagratids exploited the fears awakened in the minds of the Arabs by the rise of the Ardsrunis. The Bagratuni prince Ashot IV received from the caliph the title of Presiding Prince of Armenia, and reigned from 806 to 826, during which time he extended and consolidated his domains by attacking rebel Arab amirs. He made a number of conquests in north-western Armenia, as well as in the province of Taron. After the death of Ashot IV, his dominions were divided between his children, and the power of the Bagratuni dynasty waned for a time. Between 852 and 855, Armenia was ravaged from end to end by an Arab army 200,000 strong, under Bogha the Turk.

A revival took place under Ashot V, known as 'the Great', a grandson of Ashot

IV. This famous leader of the Armenian people was High Constable from 856. Six years later, in 862, the caliph granted him the title of 'Prince of Princes of Armenia, of Georgia, and of the lands of the Caucasus'. Ashot the Great succeeded in winning the trust both of the Arabs and of his own compatriots. Urged by the catholicos of Armenia, the Armenian nobles ultimately sank their differences and resolved to appoint Ashot as their king. The caliph of Baghdad ratified their choice in 885, by sending Ashot a royal crown, and naming him 'King of Kings'. The Byzantine emperor soon followed suit and also sent Ashot a crown and royal gifts.

The Caliphate might show goodwill towards the new Armenian monarchy, but local Muslim rulers were far from being reconciled to its existence. The Muslim dynasty of the Sajids, nominally vassals of the caliph, were building themselves a powerful state in Azerbaijan, which Armenia found to be an implacable foe. The reign of Ashot's son, King Smbat I the Martyr (890–914), was occupied with struggles against the *amirs* of Dvin and of Manazkert, as well as with dynastic quarrels with his uncle, the High Constable Abas of Siunia and Vaspurakan. Smbat was harassed by the repeated incursions of the Sajid amirs Afshin and Yusuf, treacherously egged on by the Ardsruni princes of Vaspurakan. In 908, Amir Yusuf proclaimed the Ardsruni prince Khachik-Gagik of Vaspurakan as king of Armenia, so that the country was divided into two rival monarchies. Eventually, the Amir Yusuf invaded Armenia at the head of an army, and besieged King Smbat in his fortress. In 913, King Smbat capitulated to Yusuf under promise of amnesty and good treatment, but the perfidious amir cast the king into a dungeon and crucified him the following year, after inflicting inhuman tortures upon him.

Even these tragic events could not reverse the economic and social revival of Armenia, which had gathered momentum under Ashot the Great. According to the chronicler Asoghik:

'In the days of Smbat I and in those of the rule of his father, peace reigned everywhere in our land, and each one, in the words of the Prophet, dwelt safely under his vine and under his fig-tree. The fields became settlements, and the settlements cities in their population and wealth, so that even the shepherds began to appear in silk garments.'

Naturally the reference by Asoghik to shepherds in silk garments is pure hyperbole, but this general optimism is shared by another historian, John the Catholicos:

'And in those days the Lord showed benevolence to our land of Armenia, he defended her and favoured her in all good undertakings. At that time all dwelt in their inherited possessions, and having appropriated the land, they set out vineyards and planted olive trees and gardens, they ploughed up fields among the thorns and gathered a harvest an hundred fold. The barns were filled with wheat

53. Gaiané Church at Echmiadzin

54. General view of Aghtamar Church

after the harvest and the cellars overflowed with wine after the gathering of the grapes. The mountains rejoiced since the herds of cattle and of sheep multiplied on them. Our chief *nakharars*, feeling themselves safe from plundering raids, built stone churches in isolated spots, villages and settlements and covered them heavily with whitewash.'

The son and successor of the martyred Smbat, King of Kings Ashot the Iron (914–28) rid the country of Muslim marauders and re-established public order and security. Armenia reached the apogee of power, prosperity, and cultural achievement under his successors: Ashot's brother Abas I (928–52), who set up his capital at Kars; the son of Abas, Ashot III the Merciful (952–77), who transferred the capital to Ani; and then the sons of Ashot the Merciful, Smbat II, the Conqueror (977–89) and Gagik I (989–1020).

However, there were already signs of potential fragmentation and decay of the body politic. Ashot the Merciful split off the district of Kars-Vanand and granted it, with the title of King, to his younger brother Mushegh. In 970, Smbat of Siunia proclaimed himself king of the north-eastern marches. The kingdom of the Ardsrunis of Vaspurakan, centred on the Aghtamar and Lake Van region, was further partitioned into several apanages. The division spread into the realm of the Church, so that from 969 until 972 there were simultaneously two rival catholicos-patriarchs, each one supported by a different Armenian king.

For close on a century and a half, the Armenians were at least recognized as masters of the greater part of their native land. The kings erected churches and palaces, hospitals and other buildings of public utility. At Ani, the capital of the Bagratids, surrounded by a double line of massive fortifications, there were so many sacred buildings that the historians call it the 'city of a thousand and one churches'.

Thomas Ardsruni, a scion of the royal house of Vaspurakan, describes the wealth and splendour of the reign of King Gagik, founder of the dynasty. The walls of King Gagik's palace on the island of Aghtamar, or Lake Van, were decorated with paintings of 'gilt thrones, on which are seated, in gracious majesty, the king surrounded by young pages with resplendent faces, groups of musicians and marvellous maidens. There are also companies of men with bared swords; wrestlers fighting with one another; lions and other fierce animals; birds with varied plumage. In short, if one wanted to enumerate all that can be seen, it would be hard work both for the narrator and for the listeners.'

Nobody who today gazes at the ruins of Ani, Dvin, old Van, Kars, Artsn near Erzurum, and other towns which figure in the Armenian annals of this period would guess that they once sheltered up to a hundred thousand souls each, and were renowned entrepôts of trade, and the centres of royal or viceregal courts. However, the results of archaeological investigations over the last half century have provided indisputable evidence of this, in the shape of foundations and ruins of important buildings, and innumerable specimens of pottery, glassware, metal-work, coins and other items of material culture, the best of which are now displayed in the Historical Museum of Armenia in Erevan, the Hermitage Museum in Leningrad and the Russian Historical Museum in Moscow.

During this period, the fertile soil of the Armenian plateau was once more cultivated and irrigated with skilful care. Industry and commerce flourished, through being linked up with two great economic systems: that of the Islamic world, including Bukhara and Samarkand in central Asia, Tabriz in Azerbaijan, and Baghdad and Damascus; and that of the Byzantine Empire, comprising the Black Sea region, Asia Minor and Georgia. Armenia exported its own products and those from further east to Constantinople via Erzurum and Trebizond; to the countries of Islam, the main routes lay through Van-Bitlis-Mosul, and Dvin-Nakhchevan-Tabriz. Armenia offered a variety of native products and manu-factures. Among these were exquisite fabrics, textiles and carpets; metal work and armour; jewellery and fine intaglio work; horses and cattle; also salt, cereal pro-ducts, wine, honey, timber, leather and furs.

Comprehensive data on the urban life and industrial development of Bagratid Armenia are given by the late Professor H. A. Manandian.[1] He concludes that these medieval Armenian cities, like other urban centres in the Muslim Near East, consisted basically of three sections: the citadel or acropolis with the royal palace; the *shahristan* (in Armenian *shahastan*), which was the city proper, and contained the residences of the merchants and ruling class; and the *rabad* or suburbs, which extended far outside the city walls, and contained the cottages and hovels of the lower classes of the populace, with their own markets and living quarters assigned to various crafts and guilds. The fact that a large part of the population lived outside the main city walls is important for understanding the layout and organization of these medieval Armenian towns. The inner ramparts of these cities could certainly not have accommodated permanently the large numbers of workers and townsfolk whose toil enabled the cities to prosper, as they did during the apogee of Bagratid rule in Armenia. Most of these workers and minor bazaar employees lived in poverty and squalor, as has always been the case in towns of the Near East. The size of these city populations at the height of Armenia's medieval prosperity is confirmed by the discovery of a vast cemetery, more than a square kilometre in area, outside Ani's city walls; a figure of around one hundred thousand inhabitants for Ani seems quite plausible and acceptable.

Medieval Arabic authorities on geography and commerce list the products exported from Armenia during the period of the Bagratid kingdom. Dried and salt fish from Lake Van, Lake Sevan, and various rivers, were available in the markets of Shirvan, Syria, Iraq and Persia. Among the items of annual tribute paid to the caliphs figure such items as 20 rugs, 10,000 pounds of salt fish, 200 mules and 30 falcons. Armenian horses and mules were highly prized in Khurasan,

[1] *The Trade and Cities of Armenia*, trans. Garsoian, pp. 135–172.

Iraq and Syria. The country was much more thickly wooded than in modern times. Trees of enormous thickness were sought in Armenian forests, and walnut trees were prized for construction purposes.

The Armenian historian Ghevond speaks of the discovery of a new silver mine in the Sper region. Iron, copper, borax, and arsenic were exploited commercially. Natron, or native sesquicarbonate of soda, was obtained around Lake Van, and exported to the Near East for the use of bakers. The salt mines of Kulp were constantly worked, while other sources of revenue included mountain resin, mercury, copper sulphate, silver and lead. Armourers and goldsmiths flourished in the cities, while a wide variety of excellent mineral and vegetable dyes were exported, and used locally for the manufacture of high quality silks, rugs and cotton goods.

This lost golden age of Armenian freedom is conjured up by that eloquent historian, Aristakes of Lastivert, who lived in the eleventh century.[1]

'The country once displayed to the traveller the aspect of a happy garden of woodlands, abounding in foliage, fertile and verdant, and laden with fruit. Happy princes, clothed in vivid colours, sat on their princely thrones, and witnessed the colourful parade of soldiers that resembled the flowers of spring; they heard only joyous songs and cheerful words, where the sound of trumpets, cymbals and other instruments brought happiness and merriment to the listeners.

'The elders sat in the public squares, their venerable heads crowned with white hair, while mothers held their children in their arms, sheltering them with heartfelt maternal tenderness as doves shelter their fledgelings, and in the fullness of their joy they had forgotten the ordeals of travail. And what should one say of the brides in their bridal chambers, and of the tender love of the newly wed?

'But let us elevate the subject of our discourse and revert to the patriarchal throne and the splendour of the royal dignity.

'The one, endowed with the graces of the spirit, like clouds laden with dew, shed the dew of life upon the garden of the Church, which enriched it and made it fruitful and placed upon its ramparts vigilant guardians consecrated by itself. As for the King, he was the cynosure of all eyes when he left the city in the morning, like a bridegroom emerging from the nuptial chamber or as the morning star in its ascent which attracts the eye of every creature; in his resplendent garments and pearl-encrusted crown, he caused all eyes to turn to him and to marvel; his white thoroughbred horse, trotting beneath him, caparisoned in gold, glittered in the sunshine and dazzled the eyes of the spectators. And the army of soldiers marching before him in close formation surged in succession like the waves of the sea. The desert regions were also filled and crowded with the ranks of religious men; while in the villages and hamlets, people, prompted by a desire for good deeds, built dwellings for the holy men. Our country had all of these things, and

[1] Extracts from Aristakes, in a translation by Miss S. A. Essefian, are given by Robert H. Hewsenian in his article, 'The Coming of the Turk', in *Ararat*, VII, no. 1, 1966, pp. 36–42.

v The Ascension, from the Mlke Gospels
    A treasure of the Echmiadzin Cathedral Library

VI Eighteenth-century Kazak rug
Borjalu Kazak rug

much more. I wrote this because when I describe the opposite I shall move every-one to tears.'

This happy era of the independent Armenian kingdoms was not destined to last long. It owed its existence to a power vacuum in the Near East, due to the decay of the Caliphate, dissensions within Byzantium, and the failure (in spite of the ravages of local potentates like Amir Yusuf) of the Muslims to establish a powerful and united regime in Iran. Soon all this was to change. To begin with, the Byzantines began a massive campaign to recover from the Arabs their lost territories in northern Syria and the former Armenian kingdoms of Sophene and Commagene. In this, they were aided by local Christian populations, and also by the services of Armenian battalions led by highly skilled and energetic Armenian officials and generals. The key event in this Byzantine resurgence was the capture of Melitene (Malatya) on the Euphrates in AD 934, the Byzantine army being led by an Armenian general named John Curcuas. Melitene was not strictly speaking Armenian country, though at the time of its capture some Armenians lived there. However, through immigration from the east, it was not long before Melitene became a regular Armenian town.

To these territories the Byzantines added in 966 the ancient and glorious Armenian province of Taron, situated in the regions where the Arsanias River is joined by its tributary, the Qara Su, which rises in the mountains of Nimrud Dagh to the west of Lake Van. Its capital is the city of Mush, and it contains many shrines of ancient Armenian heroes and the founders of Christianity in Armenia. The country was ceded under relentless pressure from Constantinople by the two Armenian brothers, Princes Gregory and Bagrat, who had inherited it from their father; Gregory and Bagrat were now compensated by grants of land elsewhere in the Byzantine Empire.

The loss of territory by the independent Armenian kingdoms led to increased emigration, particularly to Byzantine Asia Minor. This was particularly marked during the patriarchate of Catholicos Khachik (972–92). The Armenian his-torian Asoghik notes that during the pontificate of Khachik, 'the Armenian nation scattered and spread itself to the countries of the West, to such an extent that he appointed bishops for Antioch of Syria, Tarsus of Cilicia, Soulndah (or Lulnday) and for all those regions.' Soulndah is the important fortress of Lulon situated south of Tyana, and commanding the strategic road which led through the Cilician Gates. Other Armenians settled in the regions of Sebastia or Sivas, Kharput, Mezré, and Caesarea (Kayseri), where their descendants remained and flourished for close on a thousand years, until rooted out and massacred by the Ottoman government in its death throes in 1915.

Ironically enough, the downfall of Armenian statehood in the eleventh century was occasioned not only by Muslim aggression, but by the encroachments of a Christian empire, that of Byzantium. The death of the Bagratid ruler of Ani,

55. The Battlements of Ani: general view

56. Statue of King Gagik I, from Ani

57. Ani Battlements, close up

58. Castle of Hoshap, south-east of Lake Van

Gagik I, took place in 1020. This event opened the final chapter in Greater Armenia's national history during the medieval period. The Bagratid domains, now reduced to the province of Shirak or Siracene, were divided between Gagik's two sons, the phlegmatic John-Smbat III, and the more energetic Ashot IV the Valiant. Very soon the Daylamites from Azerbaijan invaded Armenia (1021), while the first bands of Seljuq Turks made their appearance in Vaspurakan, around Lake Van.

All Armenia's traditional foes entered the arena. These now included the Byzantine Empire. Instead of aiding these hard-pressed outposts of Christendom against Muslim pressure from the east, the Emperor Basil II thought mainly of enlarging his own domains at their expense. Basil II is usually known as 'Bulgaroktonos' or 'the Bulgar-slayer'. It is worth noting that his leading foe, King Samuel of Bulgaria (997–1014), was himself of Armenian descent. In 1014, Basil II overwhelmingly defeated King Samuel's Bulgarian forces, which he celebrated by blinding the 15,000 prisoners and leaving a single one-eyed man to every hundred to lead them back to their tsar, who fainted and expired at the sight.

This left Basil free to turn his attention to Georgia and Armenia. In 1021, he invaded Georgia, and annexed several districts bordering on Armenia, notably Tao, Kola, Ardahan and Javakheti. He forced King Sennacherib-John of Vaspurakan to cede his kingdom to the Byzantine Empire; this kingdom comprised 10 cities, 72 fortresses, and around 4,000 villages. King Sennacherib was awarded the Byzantine title of Magister, and domains in Cappadocia, to which he retired with some of his vassals. Vaspurakan, now the Byzantine province of Basparacania, was placed under the authority of a Greek governor or *catepan*. H. F. B. Lynch relates how the tomb of King Sennacherib at the monastery of Varag near Lake Van was despoiled by the Abbot, the future Catholicos Khrimean Hayrik, as a sign of contempt for this unworthy monarch.[1]

Next to be swallowed up was the Bagratid kingdom of Armenia itself, comprising Ani and part of the province of Shirak. King John-Smbat sought to appease Emperor Basil II by designating him as heir to the Armenian monarchy. In return for this gesture, John-Smbat was granted the titles of Magister and Archon of Ani and Great Armenia; later on he received the hand of the niece of Emperor Romanus III. John-Smbat died childless in 1040, and the new Emperor of Byzantium, Michael IV, claimed the inheritance. Several high personages, like Catholicos Peter, and the Vestes Sargis Siuni, sided with the Constantinople party, and favoured annexation by Byzantium. However, Prince Vahram Pahlavuni rallied the Armenian nobility and army to the cause of John-Smbat's nephew, who was proclaimed king as Gagik II (1042-5).

The imperial throne in Constantinople had meanwhile changed hands yet again, and was occupied by one of the most formidable of the emperors, Con-

[1] Lynch, *Armenia. Travels and Studies*, I, p. 237; II, p. 115.

stantine IX Monomachus (1042–55). This sovereign determined to enforce the cession of all Armenia to Byzantium, and even incited the rival Armenian king of Lori, as well as the Shaddadid *amir* of Dvin, to attack Gagik II in Ani. Eventually the treacherous courtier Sargis Siuni prevailed on Gagik to go to Constantinople, where he was bullied into abdication. In return, Gagik received extensive domains in Asia Minor, as well as a palace in Constantinople itself.

Byzantine rule over Armenia proved oppressive. Instead of the traditional feudal dues and military service, the Greeks extorted from the population large sums of money by way of taxation. Rather than pay, both nobles and peasantry began to flee the country. Instead of loyal garrisons of tough Armenian knights and soldiers, the strategic points were manned by indolent Greek mercenaries, who had little interest in defending Armenia from outside aggression, and thought only of retiring to the fleshpots of Greece, Thrace and western Asia Minor.

The bitterness felt by the Armenians at their betrayal by the Greeks, with nostalgia for their lost liberties, is vividly expressed by the contemporary historian Aristakes of Lastivert:[1]

'Populous towns turned into the abode of beasts and their fields became pasture for game animals. Much-coveted, spacious, and high-vaulted mansions became storehouses and the dwelling place of satyrs, as the lament of the Holy Prophets over the desolation of Israel: "There shall the porcupine raise and feed her young, without fear." Monasteries became dens of robbers along with the churches therein, which had resembled the firmament by virtue of their magnificent style and exquisite adornments, their ever-burning lights and lamps radiating their brilliance into the air as they swung to and fro like the waves of a tranquil sea rippling in the gentle breeze; and the sweet fragrance of the clouds of burning incense, the votive offerings of generous donors, resembled the mist that settles on mountaintops in the springtime and veils the rays of the sun . . . . All of these were in the past, and now they look empty and bleak, shorn and robbed of their splendour. Instead of sweet-voiced songsters, owls and buzzards are the choristers now; and instead of psalmodies, turtle-doves and pigeons coo and – as the prophet says – tenderly call their young.'

The Byzantine Empire did not long benefit by its annexation of Armenia. From 1045 onwards, the land was subject to repeated attacks by the Seljuq Turks, who had swarmed out of central Asia, and were strongly entrenched in Persia. A notable setback for Armenia was the capture and destruction in 1048 of the important but unfortified trading centre of Artsn, a few miles from Erzurum. In the words of Aristakes of Lastivert:

'The crowds of infidels arrived like famished hounds and besieged the city, they came like harvesters of fields, they took the sword and reaped until they depleted

---

[1] *Ararat*, VII, no. 1, 1966, p. 39.

the city of all living creatures. And those who fled into their homes or churches were set afire and burned mercilessly . . . . The weather was also helpful on that fatal day, because a strong gust of wind fanned the flames until the smoke reached the sky and the blazing jets of fire eclipsed the rays of the sun. It was a most pitiful and terrifying sight, for the entire city was covered with the bodies of the victims who fell in the market places, on the streets, and in the large halls. And who can count the people who were scorched to death? For all those who escaped the glittering sword and took refuge in their houses were charred to death. And the priests, whom they captured in the churches, were killed by fire; and some of them were killed outdoors and large hogs were placed in their laps as an outrage to us, and as objects of ridicule for the spectators.'

Armenia's death throes lasted another two tragic decades. In 1064, the city of Ani, now a Byzantine outpost, fell to the Turks. The same year, the last Armenian king of Kars, Gagik-Abas, tried to save his realm by ceding it to the Byzantine emperor, but this province too was soon snatched by the Seljuqs. The crowning disaster occurred at the battle of Manzikert or Manazkert north of Lake Van, in 1071, when the Byzantine Emperor Romanus Diogenes was defeated and captured by the Seljuq Sultan Alp Arslan. Within a few decades, the Turks had overrun two-thirds of Asia Minor, founded the Sultanate of Iconium, and appeared on the shores of the Aegean and the Mediterranean. A few local Armenian princes and minor kings struggled on in their highland strongholds, until most of the country fell under the dominion of the Muslim Shah-Armen dynasty. Later, in the twelfth and thirteenth centuries, the warlike Armenian house of the Zachariads or Mkhargrdzeli ('Long-armed') ruled in northern Armenia at Ani, Lori, Kars and Dvin under the aegis of such Georgian sovereigns as Queen Tamar (1184–1213).

The last word in this tragic tale belongs again to the pen of Aristakes of Lastivert:

'Where are the thrones of our kings? They are seen nowhere. Where are the legions of soldiers that massed before them like dense cloud formations, colourful as the flowers of spring, and resplendent in their uniforms? They are no more, they are nowhere to be seen. Where is our great and marvellous pontifical throne? Today it is vacant, deprived of its occupant, denuded of its ornaments, filled with dust and spider webs; and their heir to the throne removed to a foreign land as a captive and a prisoner. The voices and the sermons of the *vardapets* (doctors of theology) are silent now. The chandeliers are extinguished and the lamps dimmed, the sweet fragrance of incense is gone, the altar of Our Lord is covered with dust and ashes. At the gates, boys holding tablets in their hands used to sing the Psalms of David; today they are out in the demon-haunted caverns which they call the mosque. They prance as they learn the teachings of Muhammad. The virtuous and chaste women, who were reluctant even to accept marriage to their lawful husbands, have today learnt to practise wanton promiscuity.

'Now, if all that we have related has befallen us because of our wickedness, then tell heaven and all that abide in it and above it, tell the earth and those that dwell on it, tell the mountains and the hills, the trees and the dense woodlands, that they too may weep over our destruction.'

Chapter IX

CILICIAN ARMENIA AND THE CRUSADES

THE amazing resilience of the Armenian people is nowhere better illustrated than in the saga of Cilician Armenia. This artificial entity, founded under conditions of the utmost difficulty in an alien land, managed to survive and often to flourish for nearly three centuries, outliving most of the Crusader states of the Franks, and leaving behind pockets of Armenian culture and population which exist up to the present day.

Cilicia is a land of immense strategic importance, extending along the Mediterranean coast south of the Taurus and Anti-Taurus mountain systems, and including the Gulf of Alexandretta and such cities as Tarsus, the birthplace of St Paul. Much of it is rugged mountainous country, formed by the spurs of Taurus, which often terminate in rocky headlands with small sheltered harbours – a feature which, in Classical times, made the coast a resort of pirates, and, in the Middle Ages, attracted Genoese and Venetian traders. There were a number of forests, supplying timber to Egypt and Syria. The eastern part of the country is studded with isolated rocky crags, ideal for military defence, and crowned by ruins of ancient strongholds. The low-lying plain country is well watered and extremely fertile. From the military and political viewpoint, control of Cilicia was vital for free communication between Asia Minor and Syria, since the famous Cilician Gates running through a narrow pass between walls of rock provided the most convenient and sometimes the only practicable route from Constantinople and western Asia Minor to the great cities of Syria, Egypt and Mesopotamia.

Cilicia had belonged to Byzantium prior to the rise of Islam. During the seventh century, it was overrun by the Arabs, to be recaptured by Emperor Nicephorus II in 965. The Greeks found the country largely depopulated, and appointed some Armenians as governors of important cities, entrusted them with command of local armies, and ceded large tracts of land to them. Gradually, these chieftains assumed hereditary status, and set up independent enclaves and baronies of their own, with only nominal allegiance to Constantinople. As Greater Armenia was annexed piecemeal by the Greeks, and then overrun by the Seljuq Turks, the trickle of Armenian immigrants into Cappadocia, Cilicia and northern Syria became a flood.

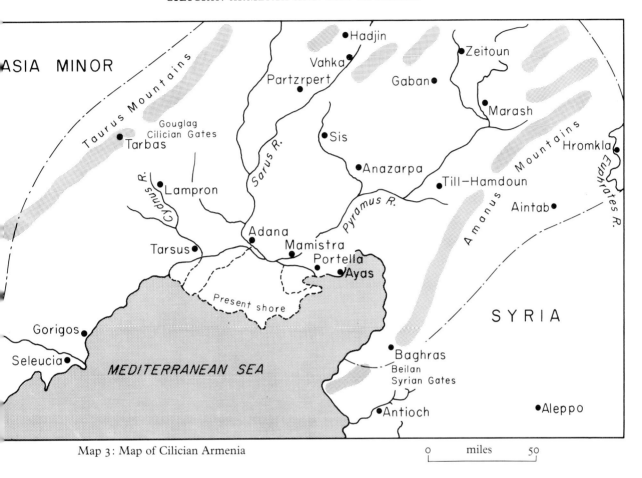

Map 3: Map of Cilician Armenia

0   miles   50

Between 1078 and 1085, an Armenian chieftain named Philaretus even united under his authority a vast area which comprised the cities of Melitene, Marash, Edessa and Antioch, though this agglomeration was dissolved at his death.

Thus it was that when the princes and knights of the First Crusade had broken through the Seljuq field armies near Nicaea in 1097, they were pleased and surprised to find themselves welcomed by a largely Christian population. The 'country of the Armenians' extended virtually as far north as Caesarea of Cappadocia; when the Crusaders reached Comana and Coxon they were welcomed by the Armenian population of these cities.

After passing through the Cilician Gates, the Crusaders received help from many Armenian chieftains. The governor of Melitene (Malatya), Gabriel, was an Armenian of the Greek Orthodox faith, whose daughter Morfia married Baldwin of Le Bourg. The Armenian Constantine was lord of Gargar. Tatoul had been appointed governor of Marash by the Emperor Alexius Comnenus, and was confirmed in this position by the Crusaders. The Armenian element was especially numerous at Edessa, the governor of which, Toros, received the high dignity of Kuropalates or 'Guardian of the Palace' from Emperor Alexius Comnenus.

A leading spirit among the Armenian adventurers of this era was a certain Ruben or Roupen, who established himself around AD 1080 in the castle of Bardzrberd[1] in the Cilician mountains. Ruben, founder of the dynasty of the Rubenids, was succeeded by his son Constantine I (1095–1100), in whose time the first waves of Crusaders arrived on the scene. The Armenians actively assisted the Crusaders by supplying them with provisions and military equipment for the siege of Antioch. Constantine's son, Theodore or Toros I (1100–23) felt himself sufficiently strong to emerge from his mountain fastnesses, and capture the upper valley of the Pyramus, with the cities of Sis and Anazarbus, from the Byzantines. By this time, also, the Armenians were beginning to play a part in the internal struggles of the Crusaders. Toros helped Baldwin II of Edessa in his wars against the Amir of Mosul. When Baldwin became King of Jerusalem, Joscelin de Courtenay succeeded him; Joscelin was the brother-in-law of Toros, and their relations were friendly. On the other hand, Toros was obliged to war against Tancred, who dreamt of establishing a Norman kingdom in Cilicia. Under later Rubenid princes, the Byzantines made determined efforts to recover Cilicia for the Empire. Emperor John II overran Cilicia in 1137, capturing the ruling Baron Levon I and two of his sons, one of whom died after being blinded. In 1162, a prince of the Rubenid house was captured by the Byzantine governor of Lower Cilicia, and boiled alive.

By a mixture of military prowess and diplomatic guile, the Armenian Rubenids survived these setbacks, and consolidated their domains with consummate skill; dynastic marriages with leading Crusader families played a part in the Rubenids' success, while contact with the commercial centres of the Mediterranean enabled them to engage in profitable trade. With Levon I the Great (1186–1219) and his son-in-law, Hetum I (1226–69), Cilician Armenia reached international status, becoming a kingdom whose alliance was courted even by the Pope and the Holy Roman Emperor.

The prowess of the Armenian knights of Cilicia is evinced by the fact that no less a personage than the Emperor Frederick Barbarossa made overtures to them on the eve of the Third Crusade, while Pope Clement III wrote to both Levon I and to the Armenian Catholicos Gregory IV, urging the Armenians to grant financial and military help to the Crusaders. Frederick left Regensburg in May 1189, at the head of a splendid army, and having overcome the hostility of the Byzantine Emperor Isaac Angelus, marched into Asia Minor. When the Emperor approached the Armenian territories of Cilicia, Levon sent an embassy escort. Meanwhile, on June 10, 1190, Frederick was either bathing in or attempting to cross the River Calycadnus or Gök-Su, near Seleucia (Selefke), when he was accidentally drowned. A second Armenian embassy, headed by the distinguished

[1] The Western Armenian form 'Partzrpert' is also commonly found.

bishop and author Nerses of Lampron, arrived too late to see the emperor alive, and returned to Tarsus with the emperor's son, the clergy, and the German army. Frederick had made a solemn promise that he would reward Levon's fidelity with a royal crown, so that his death came as a rude shock to the Armenians. However, Levon gave full support to the Crusaders; his troops were present at the siege of Acre and he joined Richard the Lionhearted of England in the conquest of Cyprus.

Eventually, Levon's tenacity was rewarded. Armenian embassies sent to the new Holy Roman Emperor, Henry VI, and to Pope Celestine III, met with a favourable response, especially as the Armenians held out prospects of an eventual reunion with the Catholic Church. In 1197, the Imperial Chancellor, Conrad of Hildesheim, left for the east, carrying two crowns, one for Amalric of Cyprus, another for Levon of Armenia. In spite of difficulties over the religious question, Levon's coronation ultimately took place at Tarsus on January 6, 1199, being consecrated both by the Papal Legate Cardinal Conrad of Wittelsbach, and by the Armenian Catholicos Gregory VI Pahlavuni.

Although Levon failed in his aim of winning Antioch for Cilician Armenia, his reign marked the apogee of Armenian statecraft in Levant. His kingdom extended from the Amanus to Isauria. He was a wise politician and a skilled diplomat, and established useful alliances with contemporary rulers, such as Amalric of Lusignan, King of Cyprus and Jerusalem, whose son-in-law Levon became by his second marriage. Levon wedded his daughter Rita, also known as Stephanie, to John of Brienne, King of Jerusalem. Levon's niece Philippa became the consort of Theodore I Lascaris, Emperor of Nicaea. Levon lived through the epoch of the sack of Constantinople in 1204 by the army of freebooters and miscreants who styled themselves the Fourth Crusade. Seeing the ascendancy of the Papacy and the Western adventurers, Levon ceded considerable territories to the Hospitallers and the Teutonic Knights, in the hope that these would help him to keep the Seljuq Turks of Anatolia at bay.

The coronation of Levon I brought promise of political stability and commercial prosperity. Genoa and Venice hastened to send ambassadors seeking trade agreements and privileges. In March 1201, a treaty of commerce was signed between Levon and the Genoese envoy, Ogerio di Pallo. Cilician Armenia became an important entrepôt for the exchange of exotic products from central Asia, which were brought by caravan from beyond the Caspian Sea, and manufactured goods from western Europe. The Genoese were granted the right to have residences and commercial establishments in Sis, Mamistra and Tarsus, with their own churches, and consular officials. Soon afterwards, similar privileges were granted to the Venetians.

A number of sources testify to the commercial importance of Cilician Armenia.[1]

---

[1] These are cited in W. Heyd's *Histoire du commerce du Levant* (2 vols., new ed., Leipzig, 1936), and more recently, in Paul Z. Bedoukian's *Coinage of Cilician Armenia* (New York: American Numismatic Society, 1962).

The chief customs house was at Portus Pallorum, though its importance was gradually overshadowed by that of Ayas, ten miles to the east. The important city of Adana was situated on the Sarus, a short distance from the sea, while Mamistra on the Pyramus was also on navigable waters. Records indicate that as late as 1322, Tarsus too could be approached by water. Nowadays, most of the former ports of Cilician Armenia are far removed from the coast line, which has been extended many miles to the south into the Mediterranean by the rapid accumulation of silt brought down by rivers from the Taurus mountains. In particular, Cilicia became an international centre for the spice trade. Other commodities mentioned in contemporary documents include sugar, brazil wood, cotton, iron, copper, tin, silk, linen and hides. Caravans linked the country by land with Konya and Constantinople on the north west, and Marash and Tabriz on the east.

Levon paid great attention to the administrative and legal organization of his realm. He modelled his court on Frankish models, introducing many French titles for offices and institutions, for instance, bailiff, marshal, seneschal, and so forth. The ancient feudal system of Armenia was modified in imitation of Western feudalism. The unruly *nakharars* or hereditary princes were brought to heel and obliged to repeat the oath of fealty to their monarch. Many Armenian peasant immigrants established themselves as freeholders, but the local Cilician peasantry was reduced to serfdom. The judicial system was organized on Western lines. The High Court was established at the royal capital of Sis; modelled on the Assizes of Antioch, this royal court held a monopoly of the 'High Justice' once held by the great barons. There was also a Lower Court, for the burgesses. It is interesting that the law code known as the Assizes of Antioch has survived only in its Armenian recension, which was made about 1265 by High Constable Smbat, brother of King Hetum I. There were also special courts under the jurisdiction

of the Latin knightly orders, such as the Hospitallers at Isaurian Seleucia, and the consular tribunals of the Genoese and the Venetians; the Armenian catholicos had his own ecclesiastical tribunals.

The events of Levon's reign are faithfully recorded in his magnificent coinage which

59. Coins of King Levon I

exists in gold, silver and copper. The chief mint was as Sis. On the obverse of all the silver coins of Levon I, apart from the special coronation issue, the king is portrayed seated on a throne ornamented with lions' heads. He wears a crown and a royal mantle on his shoulders, usually holds a cross in his right hand, and a fleur-de-lis in his left. On most silver coins, the king's feet rest on a footstool. In some particulars, this design is modelled on the coinage of the Holy Roman Emperor Henry VI. A special type of silver coin was issued to mark Levon's coronation in 1199. These coins show Christ standing, and Levon, wearing the royal mantle, kneeling with the crown upon his head. Between the head of Christ and the king there is sometimes a ray of light descending from the sky, or the figure of a dove; occasionally there is an arm or hand stretched out, pointing towards the king's crown. The reverse of most of Levon's silver *trams* (*drachms*) has an unusual design – a cross between two lions rampant regardant; other varieties show a lion walking or holding a cross. Levon was fond of making a punning use of his name – Leo, 'the lion'. Often the lions on his coins have human features, and wear crowns. This feature is very pronounced on his copper coinage, where the king's face is purposely shown with leonine traits. Levon also issued a few gold coins; genuine specimens are extremely rare, but around 1960, forgeries began to come on the market originating in a jeweller's shop in Antioch (Antakya).

When Levon I died in 1219, he left no male heir. He had named his young daughter Isabel as his rightful heiress, though this choice was unacceptable to many of the leading princes and barons. Eventually, after several palace plots and gruesome murders, a solution was found to the succession problem by the marriage of Isabel to Prince Hetum, a scion of the influential Hetumid family of Lampron (AD 1226).

Hetum I reigned for over forty years, and showed great adroitness in face of overwhelming odds: among his foes were the mighty Mamluks of Egypt and the Seljuq Sultans of Konya. The hold of the Crusaders on the Levant was greatly weakened at this time. The entire situation in the Near East was complicated by the sudden influx of Mongol hordes from central Asia, who overran Persia, Russia, Georgia and large areas of Anatolia and Mesopotamia. The Armenians of Cilicia managed to propitiate the Mongols by means of diplomacy and offers of alliance and supplies, but not before the Altaic hordes had wreaked terrible havoc in Greater Armenia itself, which lay on their direct invasion route. One of the chief sources on the Mongol invasions is the thirteenth century Armenian chronicler Gregory of Akner, who composed a valuable work entitled *History of the Nation of the Archers*.[1] Gregory vividly conveys the terror inspired by the Mongol and Tatar hordes, which matched that inflicted by the Seljuq Turks two centuries previously:

'Now, however, we shall also tell what these first Tatars resembled, for the

---

[1] Trans. and edit. by Robert P. Blake and Richard N. Frye, Harvard, 1954.

first who came to the upper country were not like men. They were terrible to look at and indescribable, with large heads like a buffalo's, narrow eyes like a fledgling's, a snub nose like a cat's, projecting snouts like a dog's, narrow loins like an ant's, short legs like a hog's, and by nature with no beards at all. With a lion's strength they have voices more shrill than an eagle. They appear where least expected. Their women wear beautiful hats covered at the top with a head shawl of brocade. Their broad faces were plastered with a poisonous mixture of gum. Death does not appear among them, for they survive for three hundred years . . . .

'They themselves, according to their resources and ability, came with their cavalry with them on raids, and took the unconquered towns and castles, plundering and taking captives. They killed without mercy men and women, priests and monks, making slaves, taking the deacons as their slaves, and plundering the churches of the Christians without fear. Stripping the precious relics of the holy martyrs and the crosses and holy books of their ornaments, they cast them away as of no value.'

60. Coins of King Hetum I

Once the initial fury of the Mongol onslaught had died down, the Armenians were able to take stock of the situation and profit by certain favourable dispositions of the Mongol leaders towards the Christian population of the Near East. Prior to the official adoption of Islam by Ghazan Khan around AD 1300, the Mongols regarded the Muslim powers as their chief enemy. The Great Khans even opened negotiations with the Papacy, with the result that several Western embassies reached the Mongol capital at Karakorum. There seemed hope of renewal of the Crusades with Mongol support. This prospect was especially attractive to King Hetum of Cilician Armenia, hard pressed as he was by his Muslim neighbours. Indeed, between 1233 and 1245, Hetum had found it necessary to strike silver coins jointly in his own name, and that of the Sultans Kai-Qobad I and Kai-Khusrau II of Konya, who had invaded Cilicia and imposed a tribute upon the Armenians.

King Hetum set out in 1253 to visit the Great Khan Möngke in Karakorum. He was the first foreign sovereign to come to the Mongol court of his own accord, and was received with high honour. Möngke promised to free from taxation the

Armenian churches and monasteries in Mongol territory. Hetum's dominating idea was to free the Holy Land once more from the Muslims, with the help both of the Mongols and of the Western Catholic powers. With this in view, he cultivated dynastic alliances with the Frankish princes. His sister Stephanie married Henry I of Cyprus; another sister of Hetum's, Maria, married John of Ibelin, count of Jaffa. Hetum further married his daughters to various Crusading dynasts: Sibyl to Bohemond VI of Antioch; Euphemia to Julian, count of Sidon; and Maria to Guy of Ibelin, son of Baldwin, seneschal of Cyprus.

The Armenians at first benefited considerably from their alliance with the Mongols. Hetum even defeated the Seljuq Sultan of Rum, Kilij Arslan IV, in 1259; he routed the Turcomans established on the western borders of Cilicia, and mortally wounded their leader, Karaman (1263). But the Armenians soon experienced the disadvantages of their alliance. After the Mongol leader Hulagu Khan destroyed Aleppo in 1260, he had to return to Karakorum to take part in the election of a new Supreme Khan. The command of the Mongol army in Syria was left to Kitbogha, a Nestorian Christian Mongol. Although Damascus surrendered to Kitbogha in the same year, the Mongols suffered a crushing defeat near Nazareth in September 1260, at the hands of Kutuz, the Mamluk Sultan of Egypt, and his general Baybars. A few weeks later, Baybars murdered his liege lord Sultan Kutuz, and seized the throne of Egypt for himself; the Mongols retreated from Syria and Palestine into Persia and Anatolia.

The Armenians were among the first targets of Baybars' wrath. Deprived of their defensive shield of Mongol cavalry, the Armenians were unable to put up much of a resistance. The Mamluks surged into Cilicia in 1266, sacking Mamistra, Adana, Ayas, Tarsus, and several smaller towns. At the royal capital of Sis, they set fire to the cathedral after looting the treasury of all the gold and valuables gathered there. King Hetum had been in Tabriz, seeking support from the Mongol Il-Khan of Persia; on his return, Hetum found his country in ruins, and abdicated in favour of his son, who reigned as King Levon II (1270–89).

For a few years, the attention of the Mamluks was occupied elsewhere, affording Levon II respite to heal the ravages caused by the Egyptian invasion. Fresh privileges were granted to the Venetians, and the port of Ayas was rebuilt. When Marco Polo visited Ayas in 1271, he found it 'a city good and great and of extensive trade', adding that 'all the spicery and the cloths of silk and of gold and of wool from inland are carried to this town'. However, Cilicia soon suffered fresh Mamluk attacks, while internal dissension and revolts by some of the barons added to Levon II's problems. The Mongol Il-Khans of Persia invaded Syria with Armenian support, in 1281, but were unable to vanquish the Mamluks. Thereupon Levon II concluded a peace treaty with Egypt, but on very onerous terms, including payment of a million dirhems, of which part was to be paid in horses, mules and iron ingots.

After Levon II's death in 1289, his five sons fought among each other for the succession, and at one time or another, each managed to occupy the throne. Of Levon II's four daughters, Isabel was given in marriage to Amalric, brother of King Henry II of Cyprus, while Rita married Michael IX, son and associate of the Emperor Andronicus II Palaeologus of Byzantium. Internecine strife among the Armenian princes gave the Egyptians the chance to storm the patriarchal see of Armenia at Hromkla. This was a strongly fortified place on the Euphrates, north of Bira; it is known in Muslim sources as Qal'at al-Rum. The Armenian catholicos-patriarchs had been resident at Hromkla since 1151, when the chateau was offered to them by Beatrice, wife of Joscelin II of Courtenay. In spring of 1292, the Sultan al-Ashraf marched on Hromkla and took the citadel by assault after a siege of thirty-three days. Terrible slaughter followed and the Catholicos Stephen IV was carried off into captivity. The Egyptians looted the churches and the patriarchal residence and stole or destroyed the precious relics and church treasures.

Encouraged by the disruptions, various Armenian barons and feudal lords rose in rebellion. Armenian society became divided by antagonism between the pro-Western faction, who remained faithful to the Papal and Frankish alliance, and a nationalist group, who detested everything which differed from the ancient traditions associated with St Gregory the Illuminator. (This dualism remains a potent factor in Armenian affairs even in our own times, in the twentieth century.) It is sometimes alleged that in 1307 the anti-Western party encouraged a Mongol general, Bilarghu, in his murder of King Hetum II and his nephew King Levon III, together with a number of lords in their entourage. However, Sirarpie Der Nersessian challenges this tradition, which is not based on any contemporary sources.[1]

Under the last two kings of the Cilician royal line, Oshin (1308–20) and Levon IV (1320–42) palace intrigues and secret murders became the order of the day. Repeated appeals to the Pope and the King of France for help against the Infidels led to nothing, and the Armenian kings were forced to become once more tributaries of the Egyptian Sultans. Levon IV was assassinated in August 1342, by a nationalist faction which opposed any further rapprochement with the Latins and the Papacy.

Levon IV was the last of the direct descendants of the Rupenid Queen Isabel, and the Hetumid King Hetum I. He had designated as his successor his cousin Guy de Lusignan, who was the son of Levon's aunt Isabel, widow of Amalric of Lusignan, Prince of Tyre. Guy arrived from Constantinople with 300 soldiers and knights, and was crowned, assuming the royal style of King Constantine II. However, the palace soon took on the appearance of a Latin court, the king surrounding himself with French-speaking favourites who took little interest in Armenian national traditions. It is interesting that Guy-Constantine continued to use the French form of his name ('Gi') on his silver and copper coinage. Although Guy-Constantine was a brave warrior, who upheld Armenian national interests

[1] See *A History of the Crusades*, vol. II, edit. Wolff and Hazard, Philadelphia, 1962, p. 658.

11 Goradis carpet
    Shusha-Karabagh carpet

VIII 'Waterfall' by Arshile Gorky, *c.* 1943 *(Tate Gallery)*

in the face of Muslim coercion, he soon fell a victim to the intrigues of the Armenian nationalist cabal, and was assassinated in November 1344.

In this atmosphere of violence and treason, which reminds one of the Sicilian Vespers, or the Rome of the Borgias, the maintenance of royal power in Cilician Armenia could hardly endure for long. The Armenian nobles now chose as their king a candidate outside the royal line in the person of Constantine III (1344–63), son of Baldwin of Nigrinum, Marshal of Armenia. During the reign of Constantine III, the last important port, Ayas, fell to the Mamluks of Egypt (1347), as a result of which the kingdom was reduced to a land-locked enclave in Muslim territory, devoid of international importance. Furthermore, Cilicia was in the direct line of the spread of the Black Death from Asia to Europe, and the population was decimated during Constantine III's reign by this most terrible of scourges.

The situation was further complicated by the pretensions of the King of Cyprus, Peter I, who had ambitions of becoming king of the Armenians himself, or of ruling through the intermediary of one of the Lusignan princes, nephews of the dead King Guy. To secure Papal support, Peter set out for Avignon in 1362, taking with him Prince Bohemond, Guy's elder nephew. When Bohemond fell ill and died in Venice on the way, Peter transferred his patronage to Bohemond's younger brother, Levon. According to some accounts, Levon, who was to be the last king of the Armenians, was illegitimate.[1] At all events, Levon V occupied the throne of Cilician Armenia twice: first for a few months in 1363–4, and again, in 1374–5. Faced by the hostility of the leading barons, and besieged in his capital of Sis by 30,000 troops under the command of the Mamluk viceroy of Aleppo, Levon V Lusignan held out manfully for several months against overwhelming odds. Finally, he capitulated, and was taken a prisoner to Cairo, along with his queen, Margaret of Soissons, and their two children.

Eventually, through the intercession of the king of Castile and of Armenian notables in Cairo, and also through the efforts of his faithful confessor Dardel, Levon V was freed by the Egyptians, and allowed to retire to Paris. Levon died there in November 1393, and was buried in the Célestins. His monument is now in the Cathedral of Saint Denis. It is interesting that the Sainte-Chapelle in Paris bears a stone relief showing Noah's Ark and the Deluge, with Mount Ararat and the Armenian cathedral of Zvartnotz in the background.

Despite the gruesome cruelties, betrayals and murders which disfigure the annals of Cilician Armenia, the achievement of its rulers, knights and citizens was no mean one. Cilicia outlived most of the Frankish kingdoms of the Levant, and has left behind it a durable heritage in architecture, art, miniature painting, poetry, historical writing and legal and administrative codes. It was Cilicia which gave birth to that sublime poet Nerses Shnorhali and the theologian and scholar, Nerses of Lampron (d. 1198). It was here that the two masters of the Armenian miniature, Sargis Pitzak and Toros Roslin, created their elegant and matchless

[1] See Count W. H. Rüdt-Collenberg, *The Rupenides, Hethumides and Lusignans*, Paris, 1963, p. 76.

paintings. Virtually all modern books on Crusader castles include a large number which are in fact Armenian. Outstanding among these are such masterpieces of feudal building as the fortress at Anamur, which was chosen to illustrate the second volume of the University of Pennsylvania's *History of the Crusades*.[1]

With Levon V, the political history of Armenia came to a close for over five centuries – until the proclamation of the Armenian Republic in 1918. Cilicia formed part of the Mamluk domains until the sixteenth century, when it was taken over by the Ottoman Empire. The title of King of Armenia was inherited by the Lusignans of Cyprus, and then passed from them to the House of Savoy. Only in Caucasian Armenia did some remains of the old structure of feudal monarchy linger on in the Karabagh district, bordering on modern Azerbaijan: here the *meliks* or local kings retained their sovereignty right up to the Russian annexation in 1805.

Cilicia had provided the Armenians with a door to the Western world. Through this door they were to pass into the Mediterranean and Western lands in increasing numbers, and instal themselves in strength in Cyprus, at Cairo and Smyrna, and as far afield as Venice and Marseilles. Under Ottoman rule, their community flourished in Constantinople right up to the terrible events of Abdul Hamid's reign and the régime of the Young Turk junta. In Jerusalem, the Armenian Patriarchate is still a power to be reckoned with, in religion, culture, and in the political affairs of the Near East. Armenians also settled in Holland, and operated a printing press in Amsterdam from the seventeenth century onwards. It was an Armenian named Pascal who introduced coffee to the Parisians. He founded the first Paris café at the Foire Saint-Germain in 1672, during the reign of Louis XIV. Later on, Pascal installed himself at the Quai de l'École, where he sold coffee at 2 sols 6 deniers per cup. Failing to prosper in Paris, Pascal eventually moved to London, where coffee houses were all the rage in the reign of King Charles II. A few years later, another Armenian named Maliban opened a new Paris café in the Rue de Bussy, near the Jeu de Paume de Metz, close to the Abbey of St Germain. In modern times, of course, this district has become one of the most famous tourist attractions and renowned café quarters in the world.

Armenians also moved northwards into Rumania, Poland, Hungary, and later, into Russia, where they became numerous in the region of Rostov on Don, with their own town of New Nakhchevan. In the Middle Ages, the free Armenian towns of Poland and of Hungary were great centres of activity and social and industrial progress.

In Caucasian Armenia, great misery and suffering was caused by the incessant wars between the Ottoman Turks and the Persian dynasty of the Safavis, between 1500 and 1722. The Turks and Persians carved up Armenia into two spheres of influence, the larger part around Lake Van falling to the Turks, and the smaller part, including Erevan and Lake Sevan, to the Persians. Shah Abbas I (1587–1629)

[1] Published in 1962: see Plate 1B, facing p. 325.

deported large numbers of Armenians from the Nakhchevan and Julfa region to the outskirts of his own capital city of Isfahan, where they settled and prospered, in their cathedral city of New Julfa. In taking this step, Shah Abbas was motivated partly by a desire to quell separatist trends in the Armenian homeland, but also by a realization that the Armenians were excellent businessmen, who could help Isfahan to flourish, and would forge trading links with the Persian Gulf, India, and even Malaya and the Far East.

India with its vast and teeming centres of population presented a tremendous challenge to Armenian enterprise and ingenuity. The Mogul emperor Akbar (1542–1602) invited Armenians to come and settle at his court, with the result that a flourishing Armenian colony sprang up at Agra. At the emperor's express wish, an Armenian church was erected there in 1562. One of Akbar's queens, Mariam Zamani Begum, was an Armenian, as was Akbar's chief justice (Mir Adl) and the lady doctor in charge of the royal seraglio, Juliana by name. Armenians were instrumental in procuring from the Mogul government the rights and privileges which enabled Job Charnock to establish the port and trading metropolis of Calcutta in 1690. In the dark days succeeding the sack of Calcutta and the tragedy of the 'Black Hole', it was a humane Armenian merchant, Khojah Petrus Arathoon, who secretly provisioned the British fugitives who had taken refuge in their ships down the river at Fulta, prior to the arrival of the army of retribution from Madras under Admiral Watson and Colonel Clive, in January 1757.

From 1760 onwards, the Indian armament industry was largely in Armenian hands, outstanding masters in this craft being Shah Nazar Khan, who worked for Ahmad Shah Durrani in Lahore, and his fellow countryman, Gurgin Khan, the Armenian minister and commander-in-chief of Nawab Mir Kassem of Bengal (1760–63). At Dacca, Armenians were pioneers of the jute trade, while they were also numerous and influential in Bombay. It is worth noting that the first Armenian journal in the world, *Azdarar*, appeared at Madras from 1794 to 1796, edited by the Reverend Arathoon Shumavon. Edward Raphael, a Roman Catholic Armenian, was one of the founders of the Carnatic Bank, the first joint stock bank founded in Madras, which opened its doors on June 1, 1788. It is interesting to note that Edward Raphael's son, Alexander, succeeded in entering the House of Commons as a Catholic Tory for St Albans. He had been the Sheriff of London for 1829, and was the first Armenian to have a seat in the British Parliament.

Chapter X

CHRISTIAN ARCHITECTURE AND
THE ARTS

LIKE the Urartians before them, the Armenians, who inhabit one of the most picturesque countries in the world, are blessed with a strong aesthetic sense. Their art and architecture throughout the ages combine the beautiful and the useful to an outstanding degree. Domestic pottery and textiles are almost invariably notable for their decorative qualities. The twentieth-century visitor, however intent on studying the effects of modern technology on the industry, agriculture and education of Soviet Armenia, can scarcely stir a mile without being brought face to face with a fine church, a ruined castle, or an ancient bridge. Modern public buildings in Erevan and elsewhere retain the ancient Armenian tradition of high quality masonry in tufa of various colours – gray, purple, pink, even orange – and blocks of apartments are often decorated with carved stone friezes reproducing the intricate patterns found in such classic monuments as the temple at Garni, or the church of Aghtamar.

The architecture and art of pre-Christian Armenia have been discussed in preceding chapters, in relation to the historical phases which gave birth to them. In this chapter, we shall concentrate briefly on the rich heritage of medieval Christian Armenia. This field is becoming quite well known in the English speaking world, first through the provocative and stimulating writings of the Viennese art historian Josef Strzygowski, more recently, through the works of Professor Sirarpie Der Nersessian, author of a superb monograph on Aghtamar, of the Edinburgh scholars David and Tamara Talbot Rice, and of Professor John Carswell, who has produced the definitive work on the Armenian churches of New Julfa, near Isfahan. We are fortunate also in having at hand the results of several missions undertaken by the enterprising Paris architect and engineer, Edouard Utudjian, who superintended the restoration of the patriarchal Cathedral in Echmiadzin, and has published an indispensable illustrated guide to buildings of historical interest.[1]

---

[1] *Les Monuments arméniens du IVe siècle au XVIIe siècle*, Paris: Éditions Albert Morancé, 1967.

Broadly speaking, Armenian churches fall into two categories, those with, and those without a dome. When St Gregory the Illuminator undertook the conversion of pagan Armenia, he found in existence two major types of religious edifice: the Hellenistic temple with a pitched, or gabled roof, and the Zoroastrian fire temple, which was a domed tower-like structure. The Hellenistic temple was represented *par excellence* by the superb shrine at Garni, the only such monument to survive into relatively modern times – it was destroyed by an earthquake in the seventeenth century. Indeed this gabled style of temple was even represented in Urartian times, by the shrine at Musasir destroyed by Sargon.

The Hellenistic temple gave rise to the Christian basilica. Although basically simple in design, to the point of being barn-like at times, the basilica had great possibilities, and could be developed by the addition of side aisles, with colonnades surmounted by elegant arches; it could be made beautiful by a carved timber ceiling or by splendid mosaics.

There are several references in the historical sources to the adaptation by St Gregory and his disciples of pagan temples for use as Christian shrines, and there can be no doubt that a number of these were adapted and elaborated as basilicas. Some of these Caucasian basilicas originally had open-sided outer walls, built above colonnades, as are sometimes met with in Italy. These are unsuited to Armenia's cold winters, and were discontinued in favour of solid walls, though these often have multiple apertures and side ingresses.

Sirarpie Der Nersessian considers that 'the vaulted basilica, without a dome, was an alien type and it disappeared from Armenia as soon as the Greek and Syrian influences waned'.[1] Reference to Syria is apt here, in view of the multiple links which united Syrian and Armenian Christianity in the early days. Syria gives us essential clues for study of such masterpieces of early Armenian architecture as the Ereruk basilica, situated four kilometres from the ancient royal city of Ani. Ereruk was originally a pagan temple, built in the first or second century AD, and transformed into a Christian basilica in the fifth and sixth centuries; this grandiose shrine, even in its present ruined state, amazes by the refinement of its decorative motifs and the technical mastery of its finely chiselled masonry. Links with the Classical world are affirmed in doorways flanked by Corinthian columns and surmounted by graceful arches with elegant pediments. Ereruk is the true counterpart of such masterpieces of Syrian architecture as the quadruple basilica built between AD 476 and 490, and dedicated to St Simeon Stylites by the Emperor Zeno; of this monument, Father Jules Leroy has written:[2]

'With its triple porch, surmounted by triangular frontons raised on fluted columns, with the wall of its south entrance (now minus its pignon) still pierced by four windows framed in the rolls of the moulding, with its semicircular apses and the

---

[1] *Armenia and the Byzantine Empire*, p. 58.
[2] *Monks and Monasteries of the Near East*, London, 1963, p. 143.

great round arches of the octagon, with all these elements, St Simeon's may well be said to contain the seed of romanesque art; indeed, may one not imagine that it was in this far-distant sanctuary that Western architects at the time of the Crusades found the inspiration for their Romanesque basilicas which lie along the great pilgrim-routes to Rome, Jerusalem and St James of Compostella?'

Ereruk for its part continues to impress, in spite of its ruined condition. The barrel vaults of the nave and of the side aisles were strengthened by salient arches forming ribs. On the west end, two towers flanked the portico or narthex; this feature, besides the clerestory, a rare feature in Armenia, confirms the links with Syrian architecture. Ereruk marked the high point of the basilican type of church in Armenia, though this pattern retained a surprising popularity in neighbouring Georgia. Thus, the delightful church of Parkhal in Tao-Klarjeti is a straight-forward basilica, and dates from the period of Bagratid power in the ninth and tenth centuries. In both Armenia and Georgia, a number of early basilicas were furnished at a later date with one or more domes, to accord with prevailing architectural fashion.

In the sixth and seventh centuries, the Armenians and their Georgian neighbours became preoccupied with the problem of the church with a central dome or tower superimposed upon the vaulted roof. Some scholars have credited the Armenians with the invention of the architectural devices known respectively as the squinch and the pendentive. The squinch makes it possible to raise a circular dome above the square central space of a roofed edifice, the strain being taken by the outer walls. With pendentives, the dome rests on four corner pillars or buttresses. However, it must be recalled that the Babylonians were already employing elliptical vaulting around 1500 BC. The Parthians were adept at chamber-roofing which consisted of a peculiar 'squinch-vault', a direct forerunner of later Sasanian domes on squinches that were used in fire temples and other important buildings. The palace of Ardashir Papakan, founder of the Sasanian dynasty, built at Firuzabad around AD 225, already contains examples of squinch vaulting in rough cobble stones and mortar. Where the Armenians excelled was in transmitting the crude and perishable mud brick prototypes into perfectly chiselled, durable and scientifically assembled masonry, which would not crumble away, but would stand the test of time.

The technical problems connected with the dome challenged characteristic Armenian inventiveness and preoccupation with technical perfection. Apart from this, the soaring, pointed dome also appeals to a people surrounded by high, snow-covered mountains, who were ever intent on drawing spiritually closer to God in heaven. The Urartians also had excelled in lofty, tower-like structures built on to their temple shrines and rearing up towards heaven. At such sites as Kayalidere, where the mud-brick superstructure has long since collapsed, the size and height of the original Urartian temple tower can still be estimated, since it was built in brick of a special reddish colour, which can be distinguished and isolated from the surrounding brownish crumbling clay. For the Christian too, the dome enabled the believer looking upward to gain an illusion of gazing at the firmament of heaven. Not for nothing do so many Byzantine churches contain the impressive image of the risen Christ looking down in majesty at the faithful assembled beneath.

The earliest and basic type of domed church built in Armenia is the so-called 'apse-buttressed' or 'niche-buttressed' square. Cruciform within, this type has four principal axial buttresses, and often four lesser ones in the corners. A semi-circular niche opens out in the middle of each of the four sides, the eastern niche behind the altar serving as an apse. The dome, resting on squinches, covers the entire central space. This popular design of church is found almost simultaneously in Armenia at Avan (c. 600) and at St Hripsimé in Echmiadzin built by the Catholicos Komitas in 618, and in Georgia, at the Jvari monastery on a high hill above Mtskheta (c. 605). A little later, need for a larger inner space dictated the introduction of four free-standing piers to support the central dome. Barrel vaults were introduced to intervene between the base of the dome, and the supporting buttresses. A good example of this development is the Cathedral at Bagaran, built between 624 and 631; the ground-plan of this monument resembles a Greek cross inscribed in a square.

Once they possessed technical mastery of the erection of central domes, the Armenian architects showed enormous virtuosity in ringing the changes on the basic cruciform pattern. Sometimes they would elongate the western barrel-vault in a church of the Bagaran type, producing a 'trefoil' pattern, with a nave complete with aisles. Again, an extra niche could be introduced between each of the four principal niches, producing a double quadrilobe, or eight-pointed star effect, as at the seventh century church of Irind. At a later stage, in the tenth century, ingenious hexagonal churches, with six apse-buttresses, make their appearance at Ani. For large-scale churches and cathedrals, both the eastern and western ends of the cruciform plan building could be greatly lengthened, and the north and south apses extended to form transepts. The effect then is of two basilicas intersecting, with the dome rising above the junction. We see a prototype of this kind of construction in the Cathedral of Talish built by Grigor Mamikonian between 662 and 685. This form of church became popular and widespread in the tenth and eleventh centuries in both Armenia and Georgia; fine examples are the main monastery churches at Haghpat and Sanahin, in a mountainous region of northern Armenia, as well as the church of Oshki in Tao, south-western Georgia. The wide variety of plans available to Armenian architects enabled them to avoid monotony when planning monastic or urban ensembles. Thus, an important monastery often includes a cathedral with two or three smaller churches grouped round it, all harmonizing in quality of stonework and decoration, but each subtly different in layout and proportions. Of thirteen surviving churches at Ani described in a recent publication, no two have a precisely matching ground-plan or exterior design.[1]

The apotheosis of this flowering of Armenian Christian architecture in the seventh century is undoubtedly the palace church of Zvartnotz erected by the Catholicos Nerses III of Ishkhan, 'the Builder', between 643 and 652. This fine construction is now in ruins. However, the remains of the walls and the foundations can still be seen, two miles from Echmiadzin; the relief carved upon the Sainte-Chapelle in Paris, and the church erected by King Gagik I at Ani in imitation of Zvartnotz, provide enough evidence to enable one to accept with confidence the reconstruction proposed by Toros Toromanian (1904). Zvartnotz was a circular, domed church, built in three storeys of truly monumental proportions. Inside, the sanctuary was cruciform, but only the apse niche had a solid wall. The other three niches were open exedrae, each with an arcade supported by six columns. This feature ensured free access to the circular ambulatory between the inner shrine and the outer wall.

The proportions of this magnificent structure were phenomenal. According to Toromanian's calculations, the height was 45 metres, while the diameter was close on 36 metres. The capitals of the pillars were carved with the splendid eagle of Zvartnotz, also with spirals and intricate geometrical designs. At intervals around the outer walls we come upon little portraits of the master builders, executed in stone relief, each bearing a set-square or similar tool of his craft. Between the inner and outer walls of finely cut masonry, the structure was reinforced by a core of rubble and concrete. The mortar was, according to Armenian tradition, mixed with the yoke and white of eggs, imparting special strength to the masonry. When the cathedral was destroyed during a Saracen raid late in the tenth century, the invaders had to light an immense pyre in the middle of the shrine to crack and buckle the arches and supports, and then to employ six hundred slaves for several weeks before the site could be levelled to the ground.

The Arab occupation of Armenia beginning around AD 650 imposed a halt upon church building which lasted for almost three centuries. During this period, the Armenians in spite of their religious differences, imbibed much of the culture and art of the Umayyad and 'Abbasid caliphates, centred on Damascus and Baghdad, the local representatives of which sat in the Armenian metropolis of Dvin. When Armenian architecture came to life once more, early in the tenth century, native traditions were supplemented by many new motifs and techniques for which we must seek parallels in the Arab world, even as far afield as Moorish Spain, in Granada and Cordoba.

The first great flowering of the Armenian architectural renaissance, following the Saracen domination, gave birth to the church of Aghtamar, built on a small island at the south-eastern corner of Lake Van. Aghtamar, later the seat of an autonomous Armenian catholicos, began as the palace church of the Ardsruni

[1] *Architettura Medievale Armena*, Rome, 1968, nos. 50–8, 66–9.

kings of Vaspurakan, being built for King Gagik by the architect Manuel between 915 and 921. This explains the exceptional richness of the external friezes and bas-reliefs, which embody many features not usually associated with ecclesiastical architecture. The basic structure of Aghtamar lacks originality, and belongs to the epoch of the St Hripsimé church in Echmiadzin, dating from a period three centuries earlier. It has the traditional plan of a square central chamber roofed with a dome, and flanked by the usual four apse-like exedrae. The sculptures, which are the chief glory of the building, hold a central position in the art history of the Middle East; they are of special importance for the understanding of Christian and Islamic art of the period.[1]

To give a few examples, the engaging upper frieze of the grape-harvest, a vine-scroll peopled by peasants, and invaded by wild animals including some sinister and insistent bears, goes back on the one hand to a familiar theme of Graeco-Roman decoration; on the other, it has parallels in the Umayyad stucco reliefs of Khirbat al-Mafjar. There are several striking resemblances to themes of contemporary Muslim art. An example is the prince seated cross-legged in the vineyard, and drinking from a wine cup; also the biblical king of Assyria, represented as a turbaned Arab prince, recalling many an episode from the popular epic of David of Sassoun. Again we have historical and biblical figures depicted in cross-over brocade overcoats and elaborate belts, and once even a turban. Armenian princes wearing turbans, incidentally, figure in sculptured donor reliefs on a number of churches, including the monastery of Haghpat, and the figure of King Gagik I from Ani. No less interesting from the viewpoint of dress and equipment is the representation of Goliath with combined chain-mail and scale armour, a round buckler, and the straight sword with forward-projecting quillons known from later Arab contexts. St Theodore is depicted as a Byzantine cavalryman. Intertwined peacocks and a harpy are treated in Islamic fashion, but other mythological beasts and birds try to revive ancient Iranian models from the Sasanian epoch: such are Jonah's whale, in the guise of a winged sea-lion; a griffin; a fantastic bird wearing jesses, a collar and bull's horns; a lion and an eagle with their prey.

Links and parallels with Islamic architecture naturally became increasingly frequent in later phases of Armenian church building, especially in areas where the Armenians were a minority amid a largely Muslim population. Stalactite vaulting, often attributed to the Seljuqs, was equally well developed by the Armenians, as seen in the famous church of Geghard, with its series of chapels and halls carved out of the living rock. Here too can be seen prayer niches closely resembling the Muslim *mihrab*. The free-standing tomb (*gunbad*, or *kümbet*), found all over Anatolia and in parts of Iran, looks like the dome of an Armenian church, detached and set upright upon the ground. It is interesting to see how the

---

[1] See the analysis by Dr A. D. H. Bivar, in *Bulletin of the School of Oriental and African Studies*, London, XXX, pt. 2, 1967, pp. 409–10.

outer hall or narthex, a regular feature in later Armenian churches, sometimes took on an interior layout resembling that of a mosque. Intricate patterns of crossed and intersecting arches, splaying out close to the ground from squat column bases, are a characteristic feature here. Armenians made a considerable contribution to Muslim architecture, as planners, designers, and masons; among those who have stressed this achievement is Professor Sir Archibald Creswell, author of the standard *Early Muslim Architecture* (1932–40) and *The Muslim Architecture of Egypt* (1952–9).

If Armenian architecture sometimes looked backwards towards the Orient, it also gazed prophetically towards the West. Nowhere is this better seen than in the churches and public buildings of the Bagratid capital of Ani, now situated right on the Soviet-Turkish border.

Ani had its period of glory under King Gagik I (989–1020), who was brilliantly served by the world-famous Armenian architect Trdat or Tiridates, whose biography has been written by Dr K. L. Oganesian.[1] The city of Ani, frequently devastated and rocked by earthquakes, still impresses the visitor. Built on a rocky peninsula overhanging the rapid waters of the Arpa Chai, Ani was designed both as a royal residence and a fortified stronghold.

The city of Ani was shaped like a rough triangle, defended on the east by steep cliffs, and on the west by a dry ravine of considerable breadth, containing hundreds of tombs and caverns. These two valleys meet at the apex of the triangle, which is at the southern end. The base of the triangle, facing towards the north, was defended by massive walls defended by numerous round towers, and extending right across the isthmus. In 1836, W. J. Hamilton estimated these walls as being between 40 and 50 feet high; much of the fortification system still survives at the present time. Many bastions have the device of the Cross incorporated in their design, a challenge to the Infidel, who was finally to prove victorious.

The main glory of the city of Ani is the cathedral, the dome of which has long since fallen in. This is the work of the illustrious Armenian architect Trdat, and was commissioned by King Smbat II shortly before his death in 989. The erection of this masterpiece of world architecture was delayed by the king's death, and by the simultaneous collapse of the dome of the Cathedral of St Sophia in Constantinople, due to an earthquake. Such was the renown of the Armenian master-builder that he alone was deemed capable of restoring the metropolitan church of the Byzantine Empire, and reinforcing its dome to survive up to the present day. St Sophia was built during the reign of Justinian (527–65), but both the two first domes collapsed soon after construction. It is only with the building of the present dome by the Armenian master Trdat that the circle of forty windows around the base was introduced, which not only lightens the weight of the dome, but also furnishes a beautiful illumination for the interior. Trdat's colossal dome is 100 feet in diameter, with a crown 180 feet above the floor.

[1] *Zodchy Trdat*, Erevan, 1951.

61. Aghtamar wall carvings:
(1) King Gagik offering a model of the church to Christ

62. (2) Biblical scenes

63. (3) Detail: Jonah a
    the Whale

64. (4) Christ enthroned and the
    Virgin and Child

65. (5) Samson

66. (6) David and Goliath

With this experience behind him, it is not surprising that Trdat's creation of the Cathedral at Ani turned out to be a masterpiece. Even without its dome, the cathedral amazes the onlooker. Technically, it is far ahead of the contemporary Anglo-Saxon and Norman architecture of western Europe. Already, pointed arches and clustered piers, whose appearance together is considered one of the hallmarks of mature Gothic architecture, are found in this remote corner of the Christian East. The rigorous simplicity of design, like a Mozart symphony, gives Ani Cathedral a stately and sublime quality. The rectangular, oblong outer walls are of delicate rose-pink stone. The external decoration is simple and harmonious. False arcades rise almost up to roof level, and embrace niches on three of the walls. Within the edifice, the lofty arches of the arcades curve gracefully to form a delicate horseshoe; the niches have vaulting shaped like Chinese silk fans or peacocks' tails. Among the other noteworthy churches of Ani are the citadel church; that of the Holy Apostles; the Holy Saviour church; St Gregory Abughamrents; St Gregory of King Gagik I; St Gregory of Tigran Honents; and the exquisite Shepherd's Chapel, outside the city walls. Several churches have the remains of frescoes within, mostly faded and peeling.

The Armenians, perforce, were great experts on fortification and military architecture generally. Of much interest in this connection is the seventh-century castle of Amberd, on the south-eastern slopes of Mount Aragats, not far from the modern observatory of Byurakan. Close to the castle is the picturesque church of Amberd, built in 1026 for Prince Vahram Vachutian. Favoured sites for castles were isolated rocky crags, and long, inaccessible ridges commanding large stretches of open country. These commonly afforded very little ground area, with the result that the necessary magazines and offices had to be quarried out of the solid rock, or else built in multi-storeyed tiers on the steep slopes.

These characteristics also affected Armenian castles and fortresses in Cilicia. Armenian castles have a compact and vertical silhouette which appears even more impressive to the eye than their more spacious Frankish counterparts:

'The castles of Lesser Armenia also differ from contemporary Frankish and Arab defensive complexes in numerous details of fortification. While the structure of curtain-walls is similar, discounting frequent variations in stonemason's technique and fineness of finish imposed by local materials, there is a distinct difference in the shape and disposition of towers. In contrast to the generally rectangular towers and bastions of Frankish and Arab castles, Armenian builders (possibly influenced by Byzantine tradition) favoured semicircular towers, most of which projected a far distance so as to enfilade the long curtain-walls and protect exposed points. The strong donjon or keep, a widespread feature of Frankish fortification, is rarely found in Armenian castles'.[1]

It is significant, however, that towards the end of the independent existence

[1] W. Müller-Wiener, *Castles of the Crusaders*, London, 1966, p. 32.

67. Ani: the Cathedral

68. Ground-plan of the Cathedral of Ani

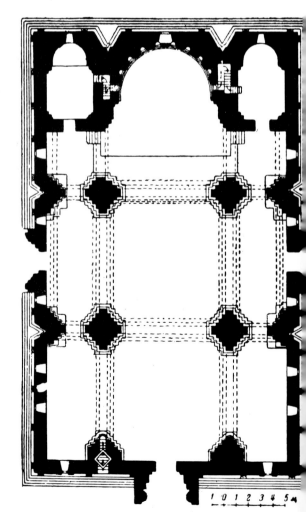

69. Ani: Church of St Gregory of Tigran Honents

70. Ani: Chapel of St Gregory Abughamrents

of Cilician Armenia, when Frankish alliances and cultural trends were an important factor at the royal court, the design of Armenian castles also underwent certain changes. This was particularly the case in the fourteenth century, under the short-lived house of Lusignan. Consequently, a few later castles, such as Anamur and Corycus, display features evidently deriving from the Crusader castles of the Franks, and also Italian influences.

We have already had occasion to remark on the achievements of the Armenians in the realm of sculpture. Until modern times, sculpture was virtually the servant of architecture. The Armenians made little attempt to emulate the Greeks and Romans in the realm of statuary, nor did they contribute any vital element to the sculpture in the round of Renaissance Italy. They made up for this by the wonderful friezes and bas-reliefs carved on churches, by their imaginative and splendidly carved *khachkars* or memorial stones, indeed by the loving care lavished on every detail of thousands of memorable buildings, ranging from wayside fountains and caravanserais to king's palaces and metropolitan cathedrals.

Many motifs used in Armenian sculpture were inherited from Hellenistic times; others, as mentioned in discussing Aghtamar, take one back to Sasanian and Islamic models. However, the resulting synthesis is wholly Armenian. Masterly use of Corinthian and Ionic capitals, together with the acanthus and the vine scroll, is combined with figure sculpture full of imaginative touches, having naturalistic and occasionally even humorous features. The façades of churches are adorned with figure sculpture, from the sixth century onwards. Thus, at Ptghavank, two flying angels, flanked by three busts of saints in medallions, decorate the archivolt of a window on the south façade. To the left, below the archivolt, a rider armed with bow and arrows, sallies forth against a lion; to the right, a man is thrusting his lance into a griffin. At the church of Mren, dating from the seventh century, we encounter two angels occupying the upper part of the tympanum, while, in the lower part, Christ and three saints holding books stand on the sides of a double cross. Accurate representation of costume is already a feature: the founder of the church, David Saharuni, and his wife, are seen advancing towards the central group, wearing a long tunic over which is a heavy, probably fur coat, with long narrow sleeves hanging loosely at the sides.

Many of the subjects treated by Armenian sculptors are common to the arts of the peoples of western Asia, some even having their roots in the ancient civilizations of Mesopotamia. Among these widespread subjects are the lion 'passant', with head turned so as to appear full-face; lions in pairs, affronted or back to back; pursuits of one creature by another and combats; horsemen and other figures depicted in symmetrical pairs, on either side of a tree; fantastic winged quadrupeds, and birds. Some of the best examples of the Armenian animal style are comparatively late. No traveller should miss the opportunity of a visit to the Monastery of the Holy Lance at Geghard, thirty-eight kilometres east of Erevan, which has a whole series of fascinating buildings, including hermit cells carved from the solid rock. The arms of the princely family of the Proshians, who owned the monastery during the thirteenth century, dominate the underground mausoleum, and embody a whole group of fantastic beasts and birds, carved almost in the round.

Particular care was lavished on the surrounds of doors and windows. Following the Seljuq conquests of Armenia, we find enormously elaborated arches, with geometrical patterns recalling Muslim models, surrounding comparatively small doors. Drums of churches are adorned with delicate blind arcades, having trefoil arches again derived from Islamic sources. These drums later undergo considerable elaboration. The conical roof, instead of being circular where it meets the drum, sometimes develops an elaborate zig-zag edge and has rich sculptured ornament at the juncture.

One of the glories of medieval Armenian sculpture is the profusion of carved *khachkars* or memorial stones, which are found in their hundreds in graveyards and around the leading monasteries and cathedrals. These slabs are rectangular in shape, the cross motif being carved in relief in the central panel. Often the cross is shown entwined with elaborate interlace carving, suggesting the Tree of Life with its sinuous strands, accompanied by flowers and leaves. Birds and animals abound. Customary types include Christ, the Virgin and Child, angels and saints; sometimes one sees such scenes as Daniel in the lions' den, the sacrifice of Isaac, and the Nativity and the Baptism of Christ. Inscriptions commemorate the name and family of the deceased, often complete with date and pious inscription. The variety of the *khachkars* is infinite; even in places like Julfa, where they run into thousands, scarcely any are duplicated by one another.

Some archaic *khachkars* are much simpler, as at Talin, Haridj and Adiaman.[1] These primitive examples have archaic carvings of divine and biblical personages, strongly resembling those found on ancient Irish high crosses, such as can be seen at Clonmacnoise, Kells and elsewhere. Parallels between Armenian and Celtic sculpture and interlaced work have been drawn by several scholars. There seems to be some shadowy evidence of early evangelization of Ireland by monks and missionaries from Armenia. However, it seems more likely that the similarities remarked on arise from a common fund of artistic taste rooted in the people, and a similar naive and reverent approach to the problems of Christian iconography.

In the modern period, sculpture in the round has made great advances in Armenia. A pioneer in the field is the most eminent of living masters, Ervand Kochar, creator of the equestrian statue of David of Sassoun. This original and spirited masterpiece rears up in the centre of the square in front of Erevan's main railway station, a fitting symbol of Armenia's national renaissance, and her agelong defiance of her foes. Soviet Armenia also has a flourishing group of avant-garde primitive sculptors. One of the best representatives of this movement is

[1] Sirarpie Der Nersessian, *Armenia and the Byzantine Empire*, Plate IX.

Arto Chakmakchan (b. 1934) a former graduate and staff member of the Erevan School of Arts. One of Chakmakchan's most striking creations is called 'Hiroshima': it rises gauntly from a desolate wilderness – a sculptured human head, 50 feet high, cupped in one hand. One eyeball swings in an empty socket in the wind, giving a hollow thud from time to time.[1] Modern as Chakmakchan's work seems, it is based ultimately on the art of ancient Armenia and Urartu, as found in the ancient temples and friezes – an art, he points out, 'both monumental and intensely expressive'. Chakmakchan's work shows familiarity with sculptors as diverse as Rodin and Henry Moore; his monument to the most famous Armenian composer, Komitas, was unveiled in Erevan in 1968.

Closely allied to sculpture in stone is the art of the wood carver. Here again, the Armenians have always excelled. Several masterpieces in the form of column capitals and church doors are up to a thousand years old. Outstanding is a wooden capital from one of the Lake Sevan churches, which is adorned with confronted peacocks and ducks. Tamara Talbot Rice makes a case for comparing the treatment of these bird figures with that on an Achaemenid gold disc from the Akhalgori hoard, found in Georgia.[2] Again, one can see in Erevan a magnificent carved wooden door from a church in Mush. This door, with its delicate ornamentation, dates from 1134; it was saved during the Ottoman pogroms of 1915 by the self sacrifice of the local inhabitants, and brought safely to its present place of exhibition.

Of related interest is the art of carving in ivory. An outstanding example of this is exhibited in the public showroom of the Matenadaran Manuscript library in Erevan – the ivory cover of the Echmiadzin Gospels. Older than the gospel manuscript itself, the ivory cover is dated to the sixth century AD. It is fully comparable with the best examples of Byzantine ivory work, and has a series of panels showing the Virgin and Child, the Flight into Egypt, the Adoration of the Magi, the Entry into Jerusalem and other episodes from the life of Christ. Both front and back plates show a pair of angels, bearing up a wreath in which is framed a cross.

This is also the point to consider briefly Armenian metal and repoussé work, in particular reliquaries, triptychs and book covers with raised reliefs. The Armenians are known to this day as skilful craftsmen in silver, gold and fine jewellery. Unfortunately, the ravages of time and greedy invaders have destroyed virtually all the earliest examples of Armenian metal work, prior to the thirteenth century. Of what remains, the best collections are in the museum at the rear of Echmiadzin cathedral; in the State Historical Museum of Armenia, Lenin Square, Erevan; in the treasury of the Armenian patriarchate of Jerusalem; and in that of the catholicosate of Cilicia, now established at Antelias, close to Beirut in the Lebanon. The finest pieces of this latter historic collection are illustrated in the

[1] Reproduced in *Soviet Weekly*, August 10, 1968, p. 11.
[2] *Ancient Arts of Central Asia*, London, 1965, p. 232.

71   Kars: the Cathedral

72. Chapel and memorial stone at
     Sanahin Monastery

73. Geghard: Monastery of the Holy Lance

74. Geghard: stalactite vaulting

75. Monastery of Haghpat

76. Geghard: sculpture over doorway

77. Memorial stone *(khachkar)* dated 1308, from Amaghu

Album of the Catholicosate of Cilicia, published at Antelias in 1965; a copy was presented to the present writer by His Holiness Khoren I on his visit to London, on May 16, 1967. Of the Antelias collection, we must single out the silver cover of the Gospels of Catholicos Constantine I, made in 1248, and showing Christ enthroned, on the front plate, and Christ crucified, on the back plate. Both these compositions are surrounded by small crosses and medallions depicting the Holy Virgin, saints and also symbolic figures of winged beasts, forming an ensemble of indescribable beauty. Another book cover belonging to Catholicos Constantine, dating from 1255 and fashioned from silver-gilt, is now in Erevan. Dedicatory inscriptions frame two large compositions: the Deesis figures upon the front plate, and four standing Evangelists on the back one. As seen on some Byzantine ivories of the eleventh century, Christ stands between the Virgin and St John the Baptist, instead of being enthroned according to the more usual pattern of the Deesis.

In the view of Sirarpie Der Nersessian the finest example of Armenian metal work is the silver gilt reliquary, in the form of a triptych, presented to King Hetum II by the Catholicos Constantine II in 1293.[1] This famous masterpiece, known as the Reliquary of Skevra, has been frequently illustrated. The central panel shows St Gregory the Illuminator and the Apostle Thaddeus on either side of a large cross. The apostles Peter and Paul are shown in bust, in circular medallions, together with four saints, one of whom is St Vardan Mamikonian, the hero of the Battle of Avarayr. The wings of the triptych represent the Annunciation, while there is a medallion framing the figure of King Hetum II kneeling in the attitude of a pious suppliant.

Every major Armenian church and cathedral had a fine collection of altar furnishings in gold and silver. Jewelled tabernacles, censers, pontifical mitres adorned with precious stones, embroidered silk on cloth of gold, silver doves wherein is contained the Holy Chrism, pontifical crosses, and ornamented golden chalices are some of the articles on which the greatest skill and craftsmanship are lavished. Among the relics of Antelias is an embossed silver chest, in which are kept the bones of the right hand of St Gregory the Illuminator. In both Echmiadzin and Antelias, we see a number of relics comprising the right hands of saints, enclosed in silver or gild cases shaped like hands, giving the appearance of gauntlets. There are several items of Armenian ecclesiastical regalia in the Victoria and Albert Museum in London, including so-called 'Tau crosses', the head being shaped like a letter 'T', often entwined with fantastic embellishments in guise of serpents and other forms.

Besides architecture, sculpture and metal work, the Armenians excel in the art of painting. It is true that one of the great genres of medieval painting of the Byzantine world – fresco painting – is scantily represented in Armenia, but this is because the stone construction lent itself better to carved than to painted

---

[1] *Armenia and the Byzantine Empire*, p. 98.

78. Carved wooden door from Tatev Monastery (date 1253)

79. Yeghvart: carved bull

decoration, and also because so many ruined churches have remained roofless for centuries, so that rain and snow have washed away the original frescoes. In areas under Muslim domination, paintings representing human figures were frowned on by the populace and the governing class; even in Holy Echmiadzin Cathedral itself, we see a largely stylized pattern of flowers and foliage. The Russians had a mania during the nineteenth century for whitewashing the interiors of churches and this example was sometimes followed by certain over-zealous Armenian prelates.

However, several seventh century churches still show traces of mural painting, as well as of decorative mosaics. Ancient Armenian mosaics found in Jerusalem have floral designs, as well as a representation of Orpheus, a pagan subject carried over into early Christianity. Around 610, the Armenian theologian Vrtanes Kertogh wrote that many Christian scenes were depicted in churches, including the Virgin and Child; the martyrdom of St Stephen; the tortures inflicted on St Gregory the Illuminator by King Tiridates; portraits of the martyred virgins Gaiané and Hripsimé, and their companions; the miracles of Christ and scenes from his life and ministry. Vrtanes further states that 'all that the Holy Scriptures relate is painted in the churches'. The famous church of Aghtamar is rich in mural paintings dating, like the structure itself, from the tenth century, and showing a complete cycle of episodes from the life of Christ, from the Visitation and the Nativity, to the Crucifixion and the Ascension. The historian Stephen Orbelian speaks of the rich paintings which adorned the churches of Siunia, in north-eastern Armenia, during the tenth century, while the illustrious sacred poet Gregory of Narek praised the portraits of saints in the church of the Holy Cross founded by Stephen of Mokk in 983.

Even after the Seljuq invasion of Armenia, fresco painting continued to flourish in Greater Armenia, under the patronage of the Georgians, who were great exponents of mural painting and established a protectorate over Armenia during the twelfth and early thirteenth centuries. The best surviving example is undoubtedly the church of St Gregory at Ani, built by Tigran Honents in 1215. The interior walls are covered all over with dignified and impressive fresco paintings, right up to roof level and including the dome.[1] The subjects include the conversion of Armenia by St Gregory, as well as the Dormition of the Virgin and other conventional themes. Inscriptions in Georgian, and also a distinctly Greek flavour in the treatment of the human figure, betoken a departure from the exuberant Armenian national tradition in favour of more conventional and stylized modes.

An even better conception of Armenian medieval painting is to be gained from manuscript illumination, in which field the nation produced masters of world stature. The Armenian alphabet was invented early in the fifth century by St Mesrop-Mashtotz, and the Gospels and other liturgical and sacred texts were

[1] Tamara Talbot Rice, *Ancient Arts of Central Asia*, Plate 215.

80. People's Artist Ervand Kochar in his studio

81. Statue of David of Sassoun by Kochar

82. Ivory cover of the Echmiadzin Gospels (6th century)

83. Detail from a silver triptych of 1300

84. Decorated page from a gospel manuscript (Chester Beatty Collection, Dublin)

85. The Annunciation, by Toros Roslin

86. A page of miniatures showing the Annunciation, visit of the Magi,
etc., from an Armenian *Menologium* in the British Museum

87. Illuminated headpiece, showing ornithomorphic letters
(B.M. Or. 12550)

soon being translated into Armenian, primarily from Syriac, and also from Greek. The Syrians were skilled illuminators; many naturalistic and also some exotic, oriental traits found in archaic Armenian illuminations undoubtedly stem from Syria. Illuminated manuscripts were already being produced in Armenia around AD 600, since the theologican Vrtanes Kertogh is quoted by Sirarpie Der Nersessian as writing:

'We also see the book of the Gospels painted, and bound not only with gold and silver but with ivory and purple parchment; and when we bow before the Holy Gospel, or kiss it, we do not worship the ivory or the red paint, which has been brought for sale from the land of the barbarians, but we worship the word of the Saviour written on the parchment.'

While this text might indicate that sets of coloured miniatures were imported from abroad, and then incorporated into Armenian manuscripts copied locally, it is certain that the art of manuscript illumination was well understood in Armenia itself by this early date. The best proof of this is the set of four miniatures bound in at the end of the Echmiadzin Gospels of AD 989, and generally available for study since they were reproduced in Mme. Lydia Dournovo's work on *Armenian Miniatures*.[1] These miniatures have parallels with Armenian frescoes of the sixth and seventh centuries, and are clearly of local workmanship. They have a severe style and generally monumental character; we must admire the richness of the architectural settings, and the wonderfully expressive features of the human and divine personages, with their dark, staring eyes. There is a frame of highly original design surrounding the scene of the Baptism of Christ: a pelican stands on a gold chalice adorned with precious stones, which is set in turn upon an ornate paten. This motif has, of course, profound eucharistic significance, and takes us right back to the religious symbolism of the early Church.

As in the case of architecture, the liberation of Armenia from the Saracens, and the foundation of the Bagratid kingdom in Ani and the Ardsruni monarchy in Vaspurakan, provided a powerful stimulus to the creative originality of Armenian miniature painters. The vast majority of the ninth and tenth century illuminated manuscripts are Gospels, these being the most sacred and generally used book of the Christian Church. The decorations are concentrated on the initial folios, which contain the Epistle of Eusebius to Carpianus, explaining the concordance between the four Gospels. The concordances or canon tables are adorned with elaborate arcades, the general composition resembling a church porch. Animal, floral and geometric motifs fill the lunettes of these arcades, which have birds and flowers painted all round them. In most cases, the canon tables are followed by a full-page decoration, which imitates a small circular temple or *tempietto* adorned with birds and cypresses. Then we may expect to find Gospel scenes and portraits of the Virgin and Jesus Christ. The four Evangelists regularly feature, each painted on a separate sheet, and shown in the act of writing with a

[1] London: Thames and Hudson, 1961.

88. Title page of St Mark's Gospel (Chester Beatty Collection)

desk in front of him, and usually a church in the background. The sacrifice of Isaac was another favourite theme. Characteristic Gospel scenes would include the Nativity, the Entry into Jerusalem, the Last Supper and the Crucifixion, and the Ascension.

One of the most admired examples of early Armenian illuminated Gospels are those once belonging to Queen Mlke of Vaspurakan, consort of Gagik Ardsruni, written in 862, and presented to the monastery of Varag, not far from Van. This famous codex is No 1144 in the manuscript collection of the Armenian Mekhitarist monastery of San Lazzaro, at Venice. The crocodile hunts which decorate the Epistle of Eusebius prove that the Armenians had some knowledge of life in Egypt, or at least of the early Alexandrian school of art. Octopuses and other sea fish are included in the frame of the second canon table. The bold impressionistic style of the Evangelist portraits, and of the Ascension, place this manuscript in the front rank of medieval miniature painting. Well known to generations of art historians, the wonderful miniatures of the Mlke Gospels, with many others from the Venice collection, are presented to the world in the great album, with a detailed and scholarly introduction, published at the Armenian printing press of San Lazzaro in 1967, under the direction of Father Mesrop Janashian.

As early as the twelfth century, profane and mundane motives begin to penetrate the classic religious themes in Armenian Gospel miniatures. In the miniatures of the Haghpat Gospels, copied in 1211 at the Horomos monastery near Ani, the artist ignored the generally accepted traditions of sacred iconography, and depicts the Entry of Christ into Jerusalem in a highly original manner. The painter shows a handsome, many-storied house, similar to a contemporary mansion in Ani itself, with the wealthy owner coming out to receive his honoured guest, and bidding his servant to spread out a carpet for Christ as he dismounts his ass. On the balcony, a number of youths are engaged in friendly converse with young ladies. Several joyful townspeople holding axes and matchets have climbed up into willow trees; they are chopping down the branches from palms and willow trees to strew in Christ's path, and are watching the happy scene. In another miniature of these Gospels, a man is sitting in a garden under a tree, and playing a *saz*, which is a guitar-like Armenian instrument. The *saz* is accompanied by the song of a thrush perched on a tree. From such realistic touches as these, it is only a few steps to the later manuscripts, in which Christ is even depicted in medieval costume, wearing wide trousers and leather boots.

One very delightful feature of Armenian manuscript illumination of the middle and later periods is the frequent appearance of birds with human heads, which occur in manuscripts copied in Greater Armenia and even more frequently, in those from Cilicia. The origin of this kind of ornament goes back to Egyptian usage, where the soul figures as a bird, and to Greece, where in Attic days, there were sirens with the bust and head of a woman. The motif is not unknown in Byzantine art. The Armenian anthropomorphic birds are in fact close to the

242

Byzantine type; often the Armenian variety are both winged and crowned. There are examples of quadrupeds with human head; also figures of a bird with the bust of a woman. Similar motifs are used in Armenian medieval architecture, notably on a capital and in a frieze of one of the tenth century churches at Ani. Other favourite stylized ornaments include a bouquet, a heart, an oval, a cup or chalice, a candelabrum, and ornamented crosses – often adorned with elaborate motifs of palms, acanthus, lobes, scrolls and spirals, sometimes overloaded to the point of obscuring the basic outline of the design.

Splendid as are the illuminated codices of Greater Armenia from the ninth century onwards, it is to Cilicia that we must turn for the apogee of Armenian miniature painting, which occurred during the zenith of royal power there under kings Levon I and Hetum I. A pioneer of the Cilician school was Kirakos, who worked at Drazark and at Hromkla, and is named by his disciple, the great Toros Roslin, as 'the magnificent scribe'. Kirakos flourished around 1240, and several of his works are preserved in the libraries at Vienna, Venice, Antelias and Erevan. The immortal Toros Roslin worked at Hromkla and at Sis, mostly between 1260 and 1270. Toros Roslin had a vigorous artistic temperament, gifted with lively imagination, of excellent taste in the harmony of colours, and a refined sense of design. He doubtless travelled a great deal, though his biography is little known. Byzantium and Italy enlarged his artistic horizons, but his sense of the beautiful was inborn and instinctive. His iconography is perfect in proportion; the style is virile and refined; and his decorations are precise and fertile in the motifs utilized. In the works of Toros Roslin appear all the perfections achieved by his precursors and contemporaries, enhanced by a superiority of technique all his own. Toros Roslin has been justifiably hailed as a precursor of the Italian Renaissance; though of miniature proportions, his art approaches the perfection of a Giotto or a Cimabue, and assures him an honoured place in the history of world art.

All but two of the masterpieces of Toros Roslin are preserved in the library of the Armenian Patriarchate in Jerusalem. The Western public had an unexpected opportunity of admiring two of the superb master works of Toros Roslin, when a group of twenty-three valuable manuscripts from the Armenian Patriarchate in Jerusalem were stolen, allegedly by a gang of art thieves, and brought to London for sale by auction in March 1967. One of the two Roslins was the famous 'Hetum Gospels' manuscript, written at Hromkla in 1268–9, with eighteen full-page miniatures; the other, copied and illuminated in 1262, is distinguished by the double portrait of Prince Levon of Armenia, and his wife, Princess Keran, a rare example of Armenian secular portraiture. The circumstances of the transfer of the manuscripts to London suggested to well-informed authorities that one or more of the thieves may have had legitimate access to the inner Treasury of the Jerusalem Patriarchate. Prompt action by Armenian communities throughout the world, and by British friends of Armenia, secured the return of the manuscripts to Jerusalem, though not before a sumptuous sale catalogue had been prepared, with twenty plates, three of them in colour.[1]

The second great master of the Cilician school of Armenian miniature painting is Sargis Pitzak, who flourished during the fourteenth century, over a period of fifty years. The surname 'Pitzak' signifies 'bee'; tradition has it that his father, the scribe Grigor, found Sargis painting a bee in a highly skilled and realistic manner, and gave him this nickname as a result. Alternatively, the name could have been won by the singular industry and indefatigable energy of Sargis Pitzak, whose competent and highly skilled works are found in many of the principal collections of the world, including Erevan, San Lazzaro in Venice, Jerusalem, the Pierpont Morgan library in New York. It may be that Sargis Pitzak lacked the genius and imagination of Toros Roslin. However, his works testify to a technical mastery beyond compare. His tastes go to the Eastern motifs, rather than to the Greek and Italianate refinements of Roslin. The subtle blending of naturalism and stylization in the drawings of birds and animals has largely disappeared; contours are simplified, and forms are heavier, being often subordinated to definite geometrical shapes. One work decorated by Sargis Pitzak which has special historical relevance is the Armenian recension of the Assizes of Antioch, translated by Smbat the High Constable. The Venice codex, No. 107 of San Lazzaro, contains an illuminated page representing King Levon IV on his throne, in a judgement scene where the figures wear contemporary dress.

Whenever Armenians settled abroad, they set to work with devout and loving care to produce illustrated manuscripts of great beauty. As early as 1007, before the fall of the Bagratid monarchy, a fine Armenian Gospel manuscript was written and illuminated at Adrianople (Edirne), on the Bulgarian frontier, for the Protospatharios John, a high Armenian official in the Byzantine service. In the public gallery of the Matenadaran in Erevan, you may see miniatures executed at Tabriz in Persia in 1337, illuminated Gospels from Theodosia in the Crimea (1649), a Bible executed at Lvov in Poland in 1619, and another illuminated at Constantinople between 1654 and 1660. Interesting local schools grew up in Asia Minor and Greater Armenia under Ottoman domination, such as the schools of Van, Erzinjan, Khizan, Melitene or Malatya, Karin or Erzurum, and Sebastia or Sivas, also Nakhchevan, and New Julfa close to Isfahan in the Persian zone of influence. The Khizan school, centred in the region south of Lake Van, was active during the sixteenth century, and produced many valuable and interesting works; bright colouring in reds, orange and gold, helped to make up for a certain lack of anatomical definition in depicting the human form, where we sometimes see gaunt, twisted figures reminiscent of the art of Hieronymus Bosch. In addition to sacred books, profane stories were also illustrated, notably the 'Romance of Alexander the Great,' by the Pseudo-Callisthenes.

[1] Sotheby & Co., *Catalogue of Twenty-three Important Armenian Illuminated Manuscripts*, London, 1967. See also Arpag Mekhitarian and others, *Treasures of the Armenian Patriarchate of Jerusalem*, Armenian Patriarchate, Jerusalem, 1969.

The overwhelming impression left behind by Armenian illuminated manuscripts is one of masterly design, supported by complete technical success in the preparation and use of coloured pigments. Many of the miniatures, in spite of the ravages of damp, frost, ants, mould, and constant liturgical use, are almost as bright as when they were painted. Armenians were great chemists and mixers of rare pigments. As early as the seventh century, Vrtanes Kertogh was laying down the ingredients needed for successful manufacture of ink and paints for use in manuscripts: the pigments for writing the text were vitriol, gall, and gum; the materials used for the figures included milk, eggs, arsenic, azure, verdigris, lime and other ingredients, some animal, some mineral, and others vegetable. This knowledge which placed the Armenians well ahead of their neighbours in medical knowledge during the Middle Ages, was turned to good account in illuminating precious manuscripts.

Unlike Armenian architecture, to study which necessitates a lengthy trip to the Near East, it is easy to acquire knowledge of and love for Armenian miniature paintings. We have mentioned the excellent publications by Madame Lydia Dournovo, by Professor Sirarpie Der Nersessian, and by the Mekhitarist Fathers in Venice. The King's Library in the British Museum keeps almost constantly on view a selection of fine Armenian illuminated manuscripts; the same is true of the Chester Beatty Library in Dublin. In America, we have the Pierpont Morgan library in New York, as well as the important collection at the Freer Gallery in Washington. Driven pitilessly from their homeland, the Armenians have scattered these priceless treasures of beauty and pious toil for the delight of countless generations all over the civilized world.

The advance of European power and Western cultural influences into the Near East from the eighteenth century onwards could not fail to influence the character of Armenian art and civilization generally. Both among the Armenians of Constantinople, and those of the Russian Empire, the monopoly of the Church in art and literature was undermined. Painting emerged from the monastic cell into the fashionable salon. Following the Russian annexation of Caucasian Armenia in 1828, aspiring Armenians found the way open to the academies of St Petersburg, and to patronage by the wealthy Russian aristocratic and merchant class. The development of a wealthy cosmopolitan society centred on the Russian viceregal court in Tbilisi (Tiflis) provided fresh opportunities, of which Armenian artists were not slow to take advantage.

Among Armenian painters of the nineteenth century, the most remarkable was certainly Hovhannes (in Russia, Ivan Konstantinovich) Aivazovsky (1817–1900), a native of Theodosia in the Crimea. Aivazovsky is one of the world's most thrilling masters of the marine picture, as well as one of the most prolific. Four thousand canvases are attributed to him, though it is sometimes alleged that he was in the habit of signing those of his more talented pupils, produced in his atelier. Early in his life, Aivazovsky's imagination was stirred by the Greek

War of Independence, and especially the Battle of Navarino. In later years he wrote: 'The first pictures which I saw at the time when the spark of passionate love for painting was catching fire within me, were lithographs depicting the exploits of the heroes of the late 1820s, fighting the Turks for the liberation of Greece. Later on I discovered that sympathy for the Greeks as they shook off the Turkish yoke was expressed by all the poets of Europe: Byron, Pushkin, Hugo, Lamartine.... The thought of that great country haunted me, in the shape of battles fought on dry land and at sea.'

Aivazovsky's outstanding talent won early recognition. In 1833, he was admitted to the Academy of Fine Arts at St Petersburg, where he won several medals. Six years later, we find him taking part in a naval expedition to the Black Sea shores of the Caucasus. From 1840 to 1844, Aivazovsky was sent abroad to finish his studies in Italy where he painted many delightful Venetian scenes, after which he set out with Admiral Litke on a voyage round Asia Minor and the islands of the Greek archipelago. One of the fruits of this trip was his great canvas, the 'Battle of Cheshme', evoking with brilliant effect the naval victory of Catherine the Great's fleet over the Turks in 1770. Together with his taste for historical drama, Aivazovsky developed a great feeling for the dramatic and tragic aspects of the sea. Eloquent of this is his painting, 'The Ninth Billow', in which we see a forlorn group of shipwrecked voyagers clinging to fragments of a vessel in the first livid rays of dawn; before their horrified eyes, an enormous wave is gathering strength to burst upon their fragile support, and consign them to a watery grave.

Aivazovsky was an incorrigible romantic. He belonged to the European age of Delacroix, Berlioz and Victor Hugo, to the Russia of Pushkin and Lermontov. His favourite subjects – storm scenes, thunder and lightning at sea, naval battles – were such that he could not remain peacefully in his studio and paint from nature. 'The artist who does nothing but copy nature', he once declared, 'becomes her slave. The movements of the living elements elude the brush: to paint lightning, a gust of wind, the splash of a wave, from nature is unthinkable. The artist must store them up in his mind.... The subject for a picture takes shape in my memory as in that of a poet; after making a rough sketch on a scrap of paper, I set to work and do not leave my canvas until I have expressed my vision upon it with the brush.'

In 1869, Aivazovsky went to Egypt to take part in the ceremonial opening of the Suez Canal. As a result of this experience, he painted a general panorama of the canal and a series of pictures depicting the landscape of Egypt and the customs of the people, with a background of pyramids, sphinxes and camels. The next year was the fiftieth anniversary of the Russian discovery of the Antarctic, and Aivazovsky was called upon to execute a rapid volte-face from the tropics to the eternal snows for his painting, 'The Ice Mountains'. During the 1870s Aivazovsky painted many nocturnes, showing the play of the moon over the sea. Ever and again he would return to his favourite marine landscape, that of the Black Sea, the subject of an impressive painting executed in 1881, where all the brooding, dark and tempestuous nature of the Euxine is superbly conjured up. At the age of eighty-one, in 1898, Aivazovsky completed his masterpiece 'Amid the Waves', free from all extraneous elements such as shipwrecked mariners or rocky headlands – a pure, abstract vision of the eternal mystery of the ocean.

A member of five academies, Aivazovsky exhibited his works as far afield as London. His favourite canvases he bequeathed to the art gallery which he founded in his natal town of Theodosia, in the Crimea. What a happy paradox, that an offspring of land-locked Armenia should attain the summit of renown in a genre of painting which depends on complete personal surrender to the genius of the deep, combined with consummate mastery of the technical arts of marine painting!

When we come to the art of Soviet Armenia, one name is quoted everywhere as the quintessence of the national genius and rebirth. It is that of Martiros Sarian, born at New Nakhchevan, near Rostov-on-Don, in 1880, and universally known today as 'The Master'; his portrait hangs in many Armenian homes and humble workshops. Sarian's talent was developed in the Moscow School of Painting, Sculpture and Architecture, where he was taught by Serov, Korovin, Levitan, Arkhipov, Kasatkin, Korin, Stepanov and Pasternak. From about 1907, Sarian came under the influence of the so-called 'Blue Rose' group of avant-garde painters, who are today stigmatized by Soviet critics as 'formalists' and 'decadents'. A journey to Turkey, Egypt and Persia from 1910 to 1913 opened Sarian's eyes to the exotic charm and mysterious atmosphere of the Orient, and inaugurated a distinctive phase in his long and many sided career.

From his early youth, Sarian had hoped and planned to live and work in Armenia, the land of his ancestors. In his own words, he 'was fascinated by the Southern Caucasus. It was there that for the first time I saw the sun and felt its warmth intensely. Camel caravans and tinkling bells coming down the slopes of the hills, shepherds with sun-browned features leading their flocks of sheep, cows, horses, donkeys and goats; street life; Turkish women gliding away in their black and pink veils and violet pantalettes and wooden sandals; Armenian women with large black almond-shaped eyes; these and many more things were the realities I had dreamed of since my early childhood. I felt that nature was my house, my only solace, that my admiration for it was entirely different from that for the manifestations of art, because the latter are short-lived and elusive. Nature – many-faceted, multi-coloured and infused with a wonderful and incomprehensible force – was my only teacher.'

During World War I, Sarian worked among the starving refugees from the Ottoman pogroms, and along with such friends of Armenia as Valery Bryusov and Maxim Gorky, threw all his energies into relieving the distress of his fellow countrymen. Beginning with these early years in Armenia, Sarian became immersed in the technique of recreating the natural beauties of his native land. 'First I was carried away by the fantasy-like manifestations of nature. It was necessary for me to find a form and pattern and the means to reproduce them on canvas in order to be able to express my inner thoughts. I began to search for durable, simple colours and forms to bring out the essence of a picturesque reality. My purpose was to avoid superfluities, to free myself from half-tones and grays, and I am of the firm belief that I have gained partial success.' Sarian was captivated by the sun-covered hills of Armenia, by its wild waterfalls, by swiftly running rivers, by expansive plateaus and luxuriant green pastures. His 'Armenia', a huge, multi-coloured landscape considered to be one of his masterpieces, and 'Noonday Calm', also of this period, were exhibited in his first show at Venice in 1924.

It is hard to classify Sarian to any school or movement of painting. He stands by himself, embodiment of the artistic genius of the Armenian nation. With his bold vision, firm brushwork, and uncanny mastery of light, shade and colour, Sarian challenges comparison with the French Impressionists – a kind of Armenian Cézanne or Matisse.

Sarian has worked in almost every genre open to his unique gifts – book illustration, still lifes, portrait painting, even stage designing. Worthy of mention are his scenic creations for the revival of the opera *Almast* by the national composer A. A. Spendiarov, produced with éclat in 1939. Sarian designed the state emblem of the Armenian Soviet Socialist Republic, with Mount Ararat in the background and sunrays spreading symbolically from behind the summit to spread all over resurgent Armenia. Sarian's portraits combine uncanny truth to life, with inexorable analysis of the character of his sitter, warts and all. Among his best known portraits are those of the fiery revolutionary poet Eghishe Charentz, with his bold, rebellious mien and primeval energy; Nelson Stepanian, aviator and hero of World War II; the architect Alexander Tamanian, who transformed Erevan from a village of mud huts into a bustling modern city; Avetik Issahakian, the modern master of Armenian poetry. His gallery of celebrities further contains composer Aram Khatchaturian; the astronomer Victor Ambartsumian; the art historian Iosef A. Orbeli, Director of the Leningrad Hermitage Museum; the poet Nikolai Tikhonov – in short, virtually all those who have won renown in Armenia's public and intellectual life, and many other well known Soviet figures besides. Few would not consider it an honour to be immortalized on canvas by Martiros Sarian, whose brush is guided by a psychologist's brain and an uncanny gift for characterization.

A legend in his life time, Sarian has been honoured with the titles of People's Artist of the Armenian Soviet Socialist Republic (1926) and Academician of the Academy of Arts of the USSR (1947). He served several times as deputy to the Supreme Soviet of the USSR, and received the Order of Lenin on two occasions. Modest and unspoilt, Sarian and his family have lived for some years in Erevan, in the gallery and studio devoted to his works. To be received there and enjoy the intimacy of the dedicated family, as was my privilege in April 1968, is an unforgettable experience.   248

89. Martiros Sarian with Avetik Issahakian

90. 'Street In Tabriz' by Akop Kojoyan (born 1883)

In spite of the restrictions of Socialist Realism, Soviet Armenia has a flourishing school of young avant-garde painters. Many of these work unofficially, though a number of private collections are being built up, which will doubtless be treasured as national heirlooms in future years.

Outstanding among modern Armenian abstract painters was Arshile Gorky (1904–48), whose family name was Adoyan. Born in Armenia, Gorky emigrated to the United States in 1920, moving to New York around 1925. Over the next fifteen years, Gorky's talent developed under the influence of the European Cubist and Surrealist painters, notably Picasso; from 1940, his work is sometimes reminiscent of Kandinsky, Miró and the Chilean artist Matta. His last period is marked by increasingly abstract work – highly emotional, fragmented images, related both to the world of the unconscious and to nature. Besides New York, Gorky had a studio at Sherman, Connecticut. Cut off prematurely in his prime, Arshile Gorky is revered today as a pioneer of Armenian Abstract Expressionism, one of his best works being in the Tate Gallery, London.

Even at its most sophisticated, the art of Armenia scarcely ever loses its roots in the consciousness of the people. From professor to peasant, all share a common pride in the artistic heritage handed down from past ages. Metalwork, tapestries, ceramics, all reflect the aesthetic sense of this uniquely talented nation. Arabic authorities a thousand years ago extolled the quality of Armenian textiles, and this tradition has been carried on into modern times in the form of rugs and carpets which enjoy wide renown in the markets of the world.

The most common trade names for Armenian carpets and rugs are 'Kazak' and 'Karabagh', and these in turn can be classified into several well-defined categories, usually named after the individual villages and districts where they are made. Not all carpets from Armenia are actually made by Armenians: local Kurds and Tatars are also highly qualified producers of good class rugs. To distinguish their own products, Christian Armenians sometimes embody a religious symbol into the design of their carpets, such as the Armenian letter 'T' for 'Ter', or 'Lord God'.

Thanks to the work of such specialists as Dr Ulrich Schurmann,[1] we now have a fairly detailed classification for Armenian carpets of various periods and provenance. The earliest preserved examples, dating from the fifteenth century, are the so-called 'dragon carpets'. In these examples, the area is divided up into lozenge shapes by lancet-patterned leaves. In the resulting polygons, dragons and scenes of animal fights are depicted. The design is thought to have arisen from contacts with the Far East during the time of Marco Polo. The earliest scenes of dragon and animal fights were very realistic, but before long they degenerated into conventional and indistinct designs. The 'dragon' style was not peculiar to Armenia, being also produced in the Daghestan area, in north-eastern Caucasia.

[1] *Caucasian Rugs*, Brunswick and London, c. 1965.

The 'dragon carpets' were succeeded by rugs with floral patterns, some Armenian examples being up to 6 or even 8 metres in length. These patterns were either ascending in character, or else arranged, lozenge-shaped, around a central point. In the eighteenth century, a new trend began the south Caucasian weaving areas of Kazak, Ganja, Shirvan and Karabagh. Ornaments deriving from plant and animal life were stylized in such a way as to give the impression of an abstract painting. Much attention was paid to the elaboration of ornamental borders, which include trefoil, leaf, flower and tendril and other designs; in some old carpets, a beautiful border of linked lyre-shaped instruments is encountered.

Modern Kazak rugs are generally distinguished by their large, bold designs and clear uniformity of colour. A high pile combined with thick weave make for a hard-wearing product. The warp is of natural coloured wool, and is most commonly in three-ply. The weft is also of wool, either natural gray or dyed red. Two weft threads are normally inserted after every row of knots. The ends are finished off in a number of different ways. As Dr Schurmann explains,[1] a loop forms the beginning of the rug, that is to say, the free ends of the warp threads are not cut, but drawn back to the other end of the rug. This is done by placing a baton across the warp threads, and looping the threads round the baton. When the rug is complete, the baton is removed, leaving the looped ends. At the opposite end of the rug, the free warp threads are either knotted, or laid parallel to the weft in plait-like patterns. Often there are no fringes, but the *kelim* (a band of weaving formed by the warp and the weft, but without pile) about 2 or 3 centimetres wide is turned under and sewn to the back of the rug.

The length of the pile depends upon the district in which the rug is woven. The higher the place of production, the longer the pile, for the rug often serves as a means of keeping the family wrapped up and warm in winter weather. In Armenian Kazaks, the average length of the pile ranges from 8 to 12 millimetres. Usually the handle of Kazak rugs is heavy and 'meaty', giving the feel of substantial body.

Among the Kazak family of carpets the following regional types are distinguished in the trade:

1. Lambalo, a village close to the Ganja region, producing rugs of low pile, and fine and silky to the touch. The wool is beautifully dyed, and the design includes geometrical flowers in the border. The ground or field is often plain, without any ornament whatever. In size, Lambalo rugs seldom exceed 130 × 210 centimetres.

2. Shulaveri, in southern Georgia, produces rugs woven with fine wool, and coloured with excellent dyes. One good example, illustrated by Dr Schurmann, has highly unusual medallions consisting of a multitude of narrow borders and many small coloured corner motifs. The yellow staff pattern surrounding the medallions in this case recalls similar patterns in early Anatolian carpets, especially Ushaks.

[1] *Caucasian Rugs*, p. 37.

3.   The Borchalo district, also on the Georgian-Armenian border, is famous for its silky wool and bold designs, usually an all-over pattern of hexagons with a reciprocal, trefoil border in white wool on a black or brown ground. Sometimes remarkable designs of octagonal, balloon-like ornaments, or hexagons filled with cruciferous flowers are encountered, the best examples dating from the nineteenth century.

4.   The mountainous region of Lori-Pambak is characterized by high-pile Kazaks, recognized by their starkly impressive design. A massive central medallion is often surrounded by a large field in plain colours.

5.   At the town of Karaklis, on the Erevan-Tbilisi railway line, carpets of a black-brown ground colour are produced; rich flower and bird decorations are favoured.

6.   The little town of Idjevan, north of Lake Sevan, produces carpets similar to Lori-Pambaks, being stark in design and sombre in colouring.

7.   From Fakhralo, west of Shulaveri, come rather loosely woven rugs, often with polygonal designs in the centre, framed by a prayer-arch or *mihrab*. Calyx and leaf outer borders are found, while patterns of stylized tulips provide effective bands for the inner surround.

8.   The village of Karachopf, near Lake Sevan, exports particularly splendid large, square Kazaks. A lovely green is used for the ground colour; to the touch, these carpets are silky and tight woven. Often, small, star-filled squares with light coloured grounds are grouped around a central square or octagon. Prayer-arches are incorporated at each end of the field.

Whereas the area of Kazak rug production is centred to the north and north-west of Lake Sevan, the other great Armenian carpet region, that of Karabagh, is situated east and south-east of the lake.

The technique of manufacture in the Karabagh mountains is similar to that of the Kazak carpets, though the pile is often closer, and the stitch finer. The wool used in the warp is usually brown. Since the region almost borders on Persian Azerbaijan, the ornamentation betrays Persian influences. Designs are less stylized and geometrical than in the Kazak rugs; freer, flowery designs are favoured; in addition to Caucasian motifs, the purely Persian Herati pattern is often reproduced here. Again following Dr Schurmann, we may distinguish several local variations in the Karabagh group:

1.   The village of Chelaberd is the home of the famous Eagle Kazaks, so called because of the radial design of the central medallion, with projecting spurs suggesting the feathers and wings of a large bird. These carpets are well known among collectors, and highly prized.

2.   From Khondzoresk come the striking 'cloud-band' Kazak rugs, so called because of the sinuous whitish motifs which recur throughout the field of the design. A central place is occupied by square medallions, each one containing a swastika.

3.   The ancient city of Shusha, capital of mountainous Karabagh, produces some of the most striking and individual rugs of the area. Their filigree ornamentation is full of imaginative touches. The areas of plain colour are chiefly in the Karabagh cochineal red, but there are some with an ivory coloured ground. Partly with an eye to the market among Russian officers and administrators, the Shusha Armenians used to produce rugs with medallions filled with bouquets of roses; these matched Western European furniture introduced into Caucasia by Russians and by European settlers.

4.   From Goradis, in the extreme south of the Karabagh, come rugs, sometimes woven with a cotton weft, showing an unusual pattern of stylized scorpions in white and red on dark blue ground. A well-worked leaf border in turquoise and gray on a cochineal red ground surrounds the field.

5.   Other striking types of Karabagh carpets are classified as Lampa-Karabagh, or Karadagh, with certain affinities towards Persian rugs; Khan-Karabagh, which are mostly prayer rugs; Kazim Ushag carpets, made by Kurds, and having plants and geometrical forms in many colours; and Channik rugs, which often have a blue-black ground colour and fine stitch.

We turn now to another intensely original branch of the arts as practised in Armenia – that of music. There is no doubt that chants and hymns played a prominent part in the cults of pagan Armenia; the priests and priestesses of Anahit and the other national deities were accomplished singers. Music also featured in the theatrical performances given by such cultured rulers as King Artavazd at the Armenian royal court. Ancient sculptures and friezes show musicians performing on various instruments, while medieval manuscripts often feature quaint little figures playing pipes and flutes, and apparently prancing up and down in the margins of the page.

An important link with Armenia's ancient musical past is provided by the minstrels who are called *gusan* – in the eighteenth century, also known as *ashugh*. Now the word *gusan* is Parthian, and takes us back to the musical world of the Arsacid kings of pre-Christian Armenia. The Georgian form is *mgosani*, which is in common use even today in the sense of a singer, bard or professional reciter of dirges at a funeral.[1]

There are several ancient Persian texts, going back to the Parthian period, and witnessing to the role of the minstrel in ancient Iran and Armenia. The romance of Vis and Ramin, which was popular throughout Iran and as far afield as Georgia, contains an episode where a *gosan* recites an allegory about King Mobad, his wife Vis, and her lover Ramin, who is the king's own brother. Even more interesting is a text discovered by Sir Harold Bailey, concerning one of the half legendary kings of ancient Iran:

[1] The whole question of the ancient Iranian and Armenian *gosans* or *gusans* has been studied by Professor Mary Boyce in an article in the *Journal of the Royal Asiatic Society* for 1957, under the title 'The Parthian *gosan* and Iranian minstrel tradition'.

'Bahram Gur enquired ever of the state of the world, and found none with any pain or distress, except that men used to drink their wine without minstrels. Therefore he bade write to the king of the Indians, and asked of him *gosan*; and in the Pahlavi language, *gosan* means 'minstrel'. Then there came from India twelve thousand singers, men and women. The Luris of today are their descendants. And he (Bahram) gave them goods and animals, that they might without charge make minstrelsy for the poor.'

From this text we gather that in ancient Iran, and presumably in pre-Christian Armenia also, to eat one's dinner without music was regarded as a distinct hardship. Certainly this view is held in modern Armenia, where drinking songs and musical toasts are the order of the day in banquets held in the traditional style.

The ancient *gusans* used to compose and sing lays about the Iranian and Armenian heroes of old. A Manichaean text discovered by the late Professor W. B. Henning, and dating from about the fourth century AD, contains the phrase: 'Like a gosan, who proclaims the worthiness of kings and heroes of old, and himself achieves nothing at all.' The role of the *gusans* in perpetuating the renown of the ancient Armenian monarchs is shown by many passages of the history by Moses of Khorene, which derive from ancient lays and ballads. Moses specifically refers to 'information about ancient Aram, lacking in books, being derived from the chants and popular songs of certain obscure gosans'.

From the early Christian period of Armenian history come several more references to *gusans* and other kinds of singers and musicians. In AD 368, we hear of the eunuch Drastamat, like Blondel in search of Richard the Lion-hearted, waiting on his imprisoned master, King Arshak II, and 'encouraging and consoling him and making him glad with *gusans*'. The downfall and murder of King Pap in AD 374 is also associated with music: the tragedy occurred at a banquet while Pap was 'gazing at various groups of *gusans*', accompanied by drummers, pipers, lyrists and trumpeters. The Roman historian Ammianus Marcellinus records independently that this assassination took place while 'the great building rang with the music of strings, songs, and wind-instruments'.

Musical instruments used in Armenia in early medieval times also included the pipes of Pan, and local equivalents of such European instruments as the fithel, nakers, hurdy-gurdy, shawm, pipe and tabor, minstrel's harp, bagpipes, and organ. Singers often accompanied themselves on the *saz*, a form of guitar.

The Armenian Christian Church was hostile to secular music, which rivalled the appeal of ecclesiastical chants. Early Christian writers condemn profligates who gave themselves up to prostitutes, dancing girls and *gusans*, whose art was stated by one irate cleric to have been 'invented by the grandsons of Cain'. Since minstrels were associated with mimes and theatrical performances, they naturally became included in general condemnations of actors and profane spectacles. The *gusans* were sometimes employed at funerals instead of regular priests, which led a fifth century authority on Church law to lay down:

'Of those who mourn for the dead, let the head of the household and the *gusans* be found and taken to the king's court and punished; and let not their families dare to lament afterwards.'

Another Church authority commands: 'Let not priests, abandoning pious songs, receive *gusans* into their houses', while an Armenian prayer book contains the confession: 'I have sinned by attending comedies, I have sinned by entertaining *gusans*.'

This hostility to frivolous songs and light music generally was common throughout medieval Christendom, and does not imply any general hatred of music as an adjunct of religion. Indeed St Sahak the Great, who flourished around AD 400, was stated by his contemporaries to be 'perfectly versed in singers' writing', by which we understand some early form of musical notation. From the ninth and tenth centuries onwards, we find in hundreds of sacred manuscripts a system of musical signs known in Armenian as *khaz*, which are written in above the line to help the priest in chanting the divine service. The *khaz* signs were used to mark the pitch, nuance, rhythm and cadence of various forms of recitative and plain-song used in the medieval church liturgy, as well as the beautiful hymns or *sharakans* which give the Armenian divine service so much of the character of an oratorio. The *khaz* system is the Armenian equivalent of the neumes used in Western plain-song, to indicate the note or group of notes to be sung to a syllable.

The *khazes* do not provide a complete system of musical notation: they assume that the singer knows the basic melody already. It is therefore very difficult to reconstruct ancient Armenian Church music from the *khaz* markings in manuscripts except where these relate to traditional airs which have been handed down orally to the present day. The most famous of Armenian musicologists, Komitas, is thought to have deciphered a large part of the *khaz* system before he was tortured into insanity by Turkish gendarmes in 1915, and his library burnt by the police. From a recent article by Robert Atayan,[1] we learn that scholars in the Armenian Academy of Sciences at Erevan are currently planning to break down the *khaz* musical code system with the aid of computers.

Among the most famous composers of hymns and sacred melodies in medieval Armenia was Gregory of Narek (945–1003) in Greater Armenia, while in Cilicia, pride of place belongs to Nerses Shnorhali (1101–73), whose surname means 'the Gracious'. Usually for a single voice, these vocal compositions astonish the present-day listener with their harmony of form, depth of thought and diversity of mood. A striking feature of medieval Armenian church music is its flowing melodic line, which never ceases to delight.

Another feature of medieval and modern Armenian music is the close connection between the art of the professional musician and the spontaneous songs and melodies of the popular masses. This is seen both in the *sharakans* or hymns of the Church, and in the highly sophisticated ballets of modern composers like

[1] 'Armenian Systems of Musical Notation', in *New Orient*, Prague, October, 1967, pp. 129–31.

Aram Khatchaturian. There are many types of Armenian popular music – the *horovels* or ploughing and harvesting songs, where a gentle cantilena is interrupted from time to time by abrupt, staccato rhythms as the oxen are prodded into greater exertion; love songs, tender, and often pathetic and tragic; heroic lays, such as the melodies used for recitations of episodes from the David of Sassoun cycle; wedding choruses, and drinking songs, of which there is a great variety; and the intensely emotional songs of the exiles or *antuni*, which breathe the passionate devotion of the Armenian people for their homeland.

Archbishop Bessak Toumayan kindly informed me that some of the finest Armenian hymns, with music by St Nerses Shnorhali, were originally composed by the saint as popular songs for his palace guards at Hromkla, when St Nerses resided there as Supreme Catholicos. These guards distressed the saint by their addiction to Turkish and Arab ditties of a profane character, but St Nerses soon converted them to his own beautiful Armenian melodies.

Outstanding pioneer work in recovering and recording the treasury of ancient Armenian music done by Hambartsum Limonjian (1768–1839), who set down many volumes of church and popular music in a new system of notation, which combined the ancient Armenian neumes with standard Western methods of musical transcription.

During the nineteenth century, several outstanding Armenian composers made their mark on the musical scene in Istanbul, St Petersburg, and also Tbilisi (Tiflis) in the Caucasus. In the Turkish capital, Tigran Chukhajian (1837–98) earned the title of the 'Armenian Verdi' with his masterpiece, the grand opera Arshak II, recalling the heroic days of early Christian Armenia under the Arsacid kings. This splendid piece, first produced in 1868, is in the permanent repertory of the Armenian National Opera in Erevan, and of other opera houses in the Soviet Union and abroad. Another classical opera composer was Armen Tigranian (1879–1950), whose lyric drama *Anush* is taken from the poem by Hovhannes Tumanian.

Of all Armenian composers, the most popularly loved and revered is Komitas, the pseudonym of Solomon Solomonian (1869–1935). Born at Kutina in western Anatolia, Komitas studied music and philosophy in Leipzig and Berlin, before becoming a *vardapet* or learned doctor in the Armenian Church. Komitas was one of those rare combinations – a composer of genius who was also a scholar, versed in the languages and musical traditions of the leading countries of Europe and the Near East. He collected more than three thousand Armenian, Kurdish, Turkish and Iranian folk songs and melodies, of all kinds, and was the first non-European member of the International Musical Society, founded in 1899. As singer, conductor, and teacher, Komitas won universal renown as the indefatigable champion and renewer of the national musical traditions of Armenia. His original compositions, including brilliant songs, choral works, and compositions for

256

91. Armenian sazandari band in nineteenth-century Tbilisi
92. Erevan Opera House

93. Tigran Chukhajian

94. Scene from opera *Arshak II* by Chukhajian

95. Komitas

96. Alexander Spendiarov

97. The Prima donna Gohar Gasparian

98. The Komitas Quartet

orchestra and solo instruments, are currently being published in Erevan in a twelve-volume edition under the direction of Robert Atayan.

The vocal works of Komitas never cease to amaze and impress by their nobility of style, rich harmony, and sublime musical inspiration. Claude Debussy once declared that one song of Komitas – 'The Homeless' – was enough to assure him a place in the company of the great composers.

The last public appearance of Komitas in western Europe was in 1914, in Paris, where he gave demonstrations of Armenian music at an international conference of musicologists, with great effect. In the following year, he was arrested in Istanbul and tortured by the Ottoman gendarmerie. His personal sufferings, and his distress for the million and a half Armenians murdered by the Young Turk junta, led to his mind breaking down completely. Saved from death by a compassionate German officer, Komitas ended his days at an asylum in Paris; his mortal remains were repatriated to Soviet Armenia, and lie in state for ever in Erevan, where his grave is a national shrine.

The work of Komitas was continued and extended by the versatile composer Alexander Spendiarov or Spendiarian (1871–1928), a pupil of Rimsky-Korsakov and a friend of Glazunov. Spendiarov inherited much of Rimsky-Korsakov's talent for harnessing the exotic brilliance of Eastern music to the classical forms of the concert hall. He was equally at home in orchestral pieces, choral odes, symphonic poems and operatic writing. He set to music the poems of Lermontov, and revised and elaborated the songs of the great eighteenth-century Armenian bard Sayat-Nova. In 1915, at the time of the Ottoman extermination of the Turkish Armenians, he wrote his hymn, 'To Armenia', with words by Hovhannes Hovhanessian. He devoted the last years of his life to a splendid opera *Almast*, first produced posthumously in 1930. The title role immortalizes a heroic Armenian princess of the eighteenth century, who devoted her life to fighting against the Persian oppressors; the libretto is taken from the poem by Hovhannes Tumanian, 'The Taking of Tmkabert'. Spendiarov is revered together with Komitas as the joint founder of the modern national school of Armenian music, and his name is embodied in that of the national opera house in Erevan.

To Western listeners, 'Armenian music' today means primarily the varied and exuberant works of Aram Khatchaturian. Born in Tbilisi in 1903, Khatchaturian came of a peasant family from the Nakhchevan district; his father was a book-binder, and built up a substantial business. At the Tbilisi Opera House young Khatchaturian had the chance of hearing the superb national opera *Abesalom and Eteri* by Zakaria Paliashvili, the father of modern Georgian music. This work made an indelible impression on him: such was the beauty of harmony, the variety of instrumental timbres and the vivid evocation of the romantic, tragic world of Caucasian chivalry, that, as he recalls: 'All next day I went about in a daze!' From that time onwards, Khatchaturian never wavered in his determination to devote his life to music.

Khatchaturian's great opportunity came in 1921, when he was entered as a student at Moscow University. He also enrolled at the Gnesin School of Music, where he studied under Mikhail Gnesin and Nikolai Myaskovsky. In 1929, he gained admission to the Moscow Conservatoire. The young Armenian musician's earliest works already bear the unmistakable stamp of his individuality, with such compositions as the Song-Poem for violin and his Trio. His First Symphony and Piano Concerto made Khatchaturian's name known abroad. Well-known foreign conductors and soloists began to perform his works. In search for novel musical media, Khatchaturian drew on the wealth of melodies and rhythms of Armenian folk music. He studied assiduously the technique of Glinka, Borodin and Rimsky-Korsakov, whose compositions were so much enriched by the musical treasury of the East.

From the 1930s onwards, Khatchaturian went from strength to strength. He was elected in 1937 Chairman of the Moscow branch of the Union of Soviet Composers, and has since occupied many public positions in the official musical hierarchy as well as winning the Order of Lenin. Great acclaim was accorded his Violin Concerto, first performed in 1940 with David Oistrakh as soloist. He became increasingly well known internationally with the ballet *Gaiané*, first performed in 1942; his Second Symphony (1943) has strong echoes of war, and reflects the struggle for victory of good over evil. A visit to Italy in 1950 provided him with inspiration for one of his most successful works, the ballet *Spartacus*, with its revolutionary social overtones, set in the slave-owning society of ancient Rome. First performed at the Kirov Opera and Ballet Theatre in 1956, the work was revised and presented in a new version at Moscow in 1968.

Brash, breezy, full of ebullient emotions and love of contrasts, Khatchaturian is one of the most stimulating figures in the Soviet musical scene. For making Armenia's popular musical heritage known all over the world, his homeland pays him well deserved acclaim.

In a single day in Moscow, one may hear on the radio the young soprano Lucine Zakarian, and go to listen to the Moscow Chamber Orchestra directed by Mikheil Terian, who was for twenty-five years a member of the renowned Komitas Quartet. The soprano Gohar Gasparian has appeared as a guest artist on many of the principal operatic stages of the world. Indeed, Armenia seems fated to supply glorious voices to the major musical centres of the West. These Armenian prima donnas often pay visits to their homeland, and are welcomed warmly by an appreciative public; Lucine Amara from the Metropolitan Opera in New York is a good example, and there are several others. Among instrumentalists, outstanding as a harpist is Shushanik Miltonian, who lives in Belgium and has carried off several international awards, as well as visiting Erevan with great success in 1968. From this, it should be clear that in spite of their modest numerical strength, Armenians play a remarkable role in the musical life of the Soviet Union today, as well as in a number of countries overseas.

Chapter XI

LITERATURE AND LEARNING

CHRISTIAN Armenia was the heir to a long tradition of ancient lore and learning. From prehistoric times, Armenia had been a meeting place for the civilizations of East and West, and a market place for the exchange of the products of Europe and Asia, after being a focal point of important Neolithic and Bronze Age cultures. It was not surprising that the great empires of the ancient world sought constantly to extend their sway into the Armenian highlands. Among the greatest of these empires were the Sumerians, the Hittites, the Babylonians and the Assyrians. From the west came the impact of the civilizations of Troy and of the Aegean world, while the highly evolved culture of Urartu was largely the product of the inventive genius of ancestors of the Armenians of today.

The origins of writing, of learning, and of technology in Armenia go back further than is generally realized. A key site is the village of Metzamor, a few miles to the west of Echmiadzin, and within sight of both Mounts Ararat and Aragats. Close to the village is a great rocky hummock, perhaps half a mile in circumference, with several outcrops of craggy stone. This hummock is riddled with caves, underground storage vaults, and prehistoric dwellings. There were hollows carved from the solid rock surface, for the mixing and storage of phosphorus made from ground bones and liquid clay. This phosphorus was used in the preparation of metal alloys, of which fourteen different kinds were identified from slag left on the site. This busy centre of ancient metallurgy seems to have been in more or less continuous operation from about 2800 BC until Classical times, while later sporadic occupation continued until the Middle Ages.

Adjoining this ancient factory city was a temple, with an altar of baked clay, surmounted by massive tridents. Hollows in the altar surrounds were shaped for the reception of blood from sacrificial victims. A short distance from the main rock city, out in the open plain, stands a rugged outcrop of brownish stone. On top of this is a roughly hewn platform, to which a flight of steps carved in the rock gives access. The structure is carved with a series of mysterious, cabbalistic signs. One series of patterns appears to point out over the plain to the spot where Sirius, the dog-star, would have made its heliacal and cosmical rising in ancient times.

From this evidence, Miss Elma Parsamian, of the Byurakan Observatory of the Armenian Academy of Sciences, has deduced that we have here one of the ancient astronomical observatories of the Near East, dating back perhaps to the third millennium BC.[1]

Hieroglyphic writing in Armenia goes back to very early times, perhaps to the New Stone Age. All over Armenia, we find pictograms or petroglyphs, carved or scratched on rocks, caves and cliff faces, and showing simplified human and animal figures. There is little doubt that these served as means of communication, as well as of ritual and artistic self-expression. A modern parallel can be drawn with the well-known Conan Doyle story of Sherlock Holmes and the Dancing Men. Other forms of hieroglyphs and codes of conventional signs developed during the Bronze Age, under the stimulus of cultural contacts with the Hittites, who used both picture-writing and cuneiform script. The Urartians, of course, were highly literate with their numerous monumental inscriptions, while Assyrian and later, Achaemenid Persian systems of writing also spread into the territory of Armenia.

Enough has been said in earlier chapters to show the wealth of literary and religious texts in various languages, which existed in pagan Armenia during the Artaxiad and the Arsacid periods. We have spoken about boundary stones inscribed in Aramaic characters, of Armenian kings composing plays in Greek, about minstrels composing love songs in the Armenian vernacular, and of high-priests intoning the praises of Anahit in hymns handed down by the initiate from generation to generation. Little is left of this splendid pre-Christian culture, which was thoroughly rooted out by St Gregory and his successors, but what remains is enough to give the impression of a land full of creative and intellectual vitality.

The official adoption of Christianity by King Tiridates III in AD 301 inaugurated a new phase in the intellectual and spiritual life of the Armenian people.

Like many a missionary of modern times, the founders of the Armenian Church had to set themselves the task of translating the New Testament and essential prayer books into the language of the people. Originally, prayers and chants were conducted either in Greek or in Syriac, and largely by foreign preachers with little or no knowledge of the Armenian tongue.

The main obstacle to the spreading of Christian knowledge in Armenia was, of course, the fact that the language had as yet no alphabet of its own. Like Georgian, Armenian has a number of consonants which cannot be expressed by a single sign in either Latin, Greek, or any Semitic alphabet. The difficult but vital task of inventing an alphabet for the Armenian language was ultimately achieved by Mesrop-Mashtotz, whom the Armenian Church reveres among her saints.

Little is known about Mesrop's early life. His main biographer is Koriun, one of Mesrop's first and ablest disciples. Mesrop-Mashtotz was born in the

[1] See *Sky and Telescope*, November, 1967.

264

99. Petroglyph, showing men wrestling
    with serpents

100. Urartian inscription from Karmir-Blur,
     mentioning the town of Erebuni – Erevan

101. Armenian alphabet: capital letters and
     small letters with scientific transcription

^dHal-di-e EN ŠU i-ni i-si-qi ^{giš}ša-e-i ^IAr-gi-iš-ti-i-še
^IMe-nu-a-ḫi-ni-še za-du-ni i-u ^{alu}Ir(Er)-bu-ni-ni ši-du-iš-tu-ni

Ա Բ Գ Դ Ե Զ Է Ը Թ Ժ Ի Լ Խ Ծ Կ Հ Ձ Ղ Ճ Մ

ա բ գ դ ե զ է ը թ ժ ի լ խ ծ կ հ ձ ղ ճ մ

a b g d e z ē ə t' ž i l x c k h j ł č m

Յ Ն Շ Ո Չ Պ Ջ Ռ Ս Վ Տ Ր Ց Ւ Փ Ք Օ Ֆ Ու

յ ն շ ո չ պ ջ ռ ս վ տ ր ց ւ փ ք օ ֆ ու

y n š o č' p ǰ ṙ s v t r c' w p' k' aw f u

265

year 361, in the province of Taron, and graduated from one of the schools established by Catholicos Nerses the Great. As a man of exceptional ability who had mastered Greek, Syriac, Persian and other languages, he was soon appointed to be a royal secretary at the city of Vagharshapat or Echmiadzin, then the capital of Armenia. After a few years of government service, Mesrop resigned his post and entered the Church.

Mesrop was some forty years of age when he first began his preachings in different parts of Armenia. It was during these tours that he conceived the idea of inventing Armenian characters and translating the Bible, thus marking the beginning of the national literature. The invention of a national alphabet, he considered, would not only help to propagate the Christian Faith, but would also establish a strong tie to bind together Armenians living in eastern and western Armenia and elsewhere; since the Persians and Byzantines had partitioned the homeland between themselves in AD 387, this was obviously an urgent task.

Mesrop's project met with the approval of Catholicos Sahak, the saintly head of the Church, and himself an erudite scholar. The King of Eastern Armenia, Vramshapuh, also expressed keen interest, and told Mesrop that he had once seen in Mesopotamia a set of characters which had been devised for Armenian by a certain Bishop Daniel the Syrian. These were promptly sent for, but proved unsuitable for rendering the complicated phonetic system of Armenian. No doubt Daniel's system was based on Syriac, which is written from right to left, and has basically the same twenty-two characters as Hebrew. The Syriac alphabet fails to provide a complete system for writing the vowels. Since the Armenian alphabet as invented by Mesrop and his disciples was found to need thirty-six characters, it is hardly surprising that Syriac failed to provide an adequate basis for writing Armenian.

Mesrop and his pupils now set to work to devise a fresh system for Armenian. They decided to write the characters from left to right, as in Greek. They retained a number of Greek letters, and altered others to fit in with the aesthetic pattern which they had adopted. As far as possible, Mesrop retained the order of the Greek alphabet, while interpolating a number of new and hitherto non-existent signs, which had to be devised to render those sounds which occur in Armenian and in Georgian, but not in Greek. The work was completed in Samosata, probably in AD 404 or 406. Later on, Mesrop and his group of disciples devised alphabets for the Georgians and for the Albanians of the Caucasus. The Armenian and Georgian alphabets have continued in use up to the present day, with the original sets of characters, though nowadays written in modern, cursive script. This fact is a great tribute to this remarkable pioneer, who passed away at a ripe old age in the year 440.

Mesrop is buried in the crypt of the church at Oshakan, not far from Echmiadzin itself. The shrine is guarded to this day by a lineal descendant of Mesrop's patron and protector, Vahan Amatuni, *Hazarapet* and Great Prince (*Ishkhan*) of the Armenians; the Amatunis were, from time immemorial, hereditary lords of Oshakan, which is the Auzacana of the geographer Ptolemy.

The Armenian classical language, as written down by St Mesrop and his disciples, is known as *grabar*, or 'book language'. From the fifteenth century onwards, poets and scribes began to use the popular spoken idiom of the people, known as *ashkharabar*, and to write it down. During the nineteenth century, there were developed two main spoken and literary languages, Eastern Armenian, based on the Armenian of the Ararat region, and Western Armenian, based on the idiom of the Armenians of Istanbul.

The original Armenian alphabet was written in large capital letters or uncials, of a monumental character and size. Between the tenth and eleventh century, we find a type of curved uncials, called *boloragits yerkatagir*, or 'iron capitals'. The 'middle' *yerkatagir* of the eleventh and twelfth centuries has more straight lines, and there is also a small *yerkatagir* script. Sometimes a combination of more than one style of *yerkatagir* occurs, referred to as 'mixed letters'. From the thirteenth century onwards, the predominant script is the small *bolorgir* writing, which closely resembles most Armenian printing of the present day. In the eighteenth century, a form of cursive writing was developed, under the name of *notrgir*.

Mesrop's example was followed by a brilliant school of disciples, who set out to create a new Christian literature, systematically covering all the main fields of knowledge and including theology, philosophy, history, geography and astronomy. These classic writers of the fifth century are often known as the 'interpreters', because they brought knowledge to the people.

Eminent among these pioneer writers was Eznik of Kolb, a much admired author who wrote a polemical treatise under the title *Against the Sects*. Here he champions the Christian faith against Zoroastrianism, and also confounds Manicheeism and Gnosticism. The information conveyed by Eznik concerning the pagan beliefs of the Armenian people, and the astronomical, mythological and religious beliefs of the followers of Zoroaster, is of vast interest.

Eznik's work is complemented by that of the distinguished Armenian Neo-Platonist of the fifth to sixth centuries, David Anhaght, or 'the Invincible', so styled because nobody could overcome him in argument. Three main philosophical works come from David the Invincible's pen, namely *A Definition of Philosophy, An Analysis of the Introduction by Porphyrius* and *An Interpretation of Aristotle's Analytics*. Such was the interest aroused by David the Invincible's speculative thought that almost 500 manuscripts containing the text of his works, as well as commentaries and interpretations, are found in the Matenadaran Manuscript Library in Erevan alone.

The fifth century also saw the beginnings of Armenian historiography. The Armenians early showed themselves highly gifted chroniclers, though with a natural patriotic bias towards their own fatherland. A particularly valuable feature of Armenian historical writing is the light which it throws on events in neighbouring countries, particularly Sasanian Iran, also Byzantium, the Arab Caliphate, Georgia and Caucasian Albania.

The earliest Armenian historian is apparently the rather shadowy figure known as Agathangelos, who purports to have been a contemporary of King Tiridates III and an eye-witness of the conversion of Armenia by St Gregory the Illuminator. In fact, he probably lived about the middle of the fifth century. His account of the evangelization of Armenia was translated into Greek, as well as Syriac, Coptic, Arabic and Georgian.

The struggle of the Armenian people against the Persians and the Byzantines is vividly narrated by such chroniclers as Faustus of Buzanda, who concentrated on the period between AD 330 and AD 387; his continuator, Lazarus of Pharpi, who carried on the narrative up to the year 486; and Eliseus the Vardapet, whose *History of the Vardanians* is our best source for the revolt against the Great King of Iran, led by Prince Vardan Mamikonian, and culminating in the battle of Avarayr in 451. For the seventh century, a prime source is Bishop Sebeos, who wrote a history of the Byzantine Emperor Heraclius and his age, covering the period from about AD 590 to AD 660.

Of great importance, as containing much of the ancient, pre-Christian historical tradition of the country, is the work on the Armenian antiquities going by the name of *The History of Armenia*. The author of this work is known as Moses of Khorene. For many years, Moses of Khorene was regarded as an author of the fifth century AD, but there are a number of indications which show that he lived somewhat later, probably in the eighth century. For this reason, he is sometimes known as the pseudo-Moses of Khorene, especially as much of his historical data has been shown to bear a legendary character. Latterly there has been a tendency to rehabilitate Moses of Khorene, especially as he undoubtedly used authentic ancient sources including Armenian pagan traditions, and Greek and Syriac authorities. Certainly he is a most delightful and imaginative writer, who made a vital contribution to ancient Armenian folklore and mythology, as well as to history in the narrower sense.

By this time, Armenian men of letters were already making their mark in Constantinople and the lands of western Europe. At the Matenadaran Manuscript Library in Erevan, one can read of a certain pupil of Mesrop-Mashtotz, named Paruir Haykazn, who emigrated to Rome in the fifth century. There he became renowned as an orator, under the name of Proieresius. Such was his fame that the city erected a statue to this Armenian rhetor, with the inscription: 'From Rome, the king of cities, to Proieresius, the king of orators'.

One of the most original Armenian writers of this early period was Ananias of Shirak or Anania Shirakatsi (c. 600–70). Born in the Armenian province of Shirak or Siracene, Ananias travelled to Erzurum and to Trebizond in search of knowledge and information. He was a kind of early Armenian Newton, combining enthusiasm for geography and astronomy with an interest in metaphysics, chronology and mathematics. He was an innovator, who refuted the ancient belief that the world was flat and surrounded by the ocean; also refused to believe that the earth was supported on the back of a large number of elephants. Rather, it was held up by the atmosphere and the winds: 'The earth is in the centre, all round the earth is the air, and the heavens surround the earth on every side'.

The world – and here Ananias was unable to free himself from conventional beliefs – was composed of four elements: fire, air, earth and water. These elements were indissolubly linked by a predestined pattern of interlocking and interaction. The world was undergoing a constant process of movement and of evolution. 'Birth is the beginning of annihilation, and annihilation in its turn is the beginning of birth. From this immortal paradox, the earth derives its eternal existence.'

One of the best Armenian treatises on geography, formerly attributed to Moses of Khorene, is now generally ascribed to Anania Shirakatsi. This work makes use of some fifteen ancient sources, including the works of Ptolemy. In the first part of his *Geography*, Shirakatsi presents general information on the roundness of the earth, its relief, climatic zones, seas and oceans. The second and more extensive portion deals with the three continents then known – Europe, Libya (Africa) and Asia. The part covering Europe is divided into twelve countries, Libya into eight, and Asia, into thirty-eight. In describing each country, Shirakatsi takes note of the boundaries, the location, the inhabitants and their customs, the names of the seas, mountains and rivers, also natural resources, flora and fauna. As might be expected, Shirakatsi is especially well informed on the countries of south-western Asia, namely Persia, Mesopotamia, Asia Minor, Georgia and the Caucasus. Such is the wealth of data provided on Armenia itself that the best ethnographic and historical atlases of ancient Armenia are based extensively on Shirakatsi's information.

During the fifth and following centuries, Armenian literature was enriched by many translations from Greek and other languages. Naturally enough, great attention was paid to rendering the Bible and early Church Fathers into Armenian, for use in the divine service. However, many classics of ancient philosophy were also translated, without regard to their pagan content. In many cases, the originals have perished, and the Armenian versions are the only ones to survive. For instance, much interest was aroused by the discovery of the lost treatise *On Nature* by Zeno of Citium (335–263 BC), the founder of the Stoic school; this work was identified in 1949 by Academician L. Khachikian of Erevan. In the Erevan Matenadaran alone, 300 manuscripts contain various works by Aristotle, with commentaries on them. Then again, we find Armenian redactions of works by such obscure or forgotten writers as Theon of Alexandria (first century AD), author of a treatise on the science of rhetoric; Hermes Trismegistus, the fictitious divine author of a large body of religious writings which date in their present form from the third century AD; Dionysius Thrax (born 166 BC), the Greek grammarian; Porphyry (AD 233–305), the pupil of Plotinus, and a neo-Platonist critic of Christianity; Timothy Aelurus, fifth-century Monophysite Patriarch of Alexandria, whose *Polemica* exist solely in Armenian translation; and Olympiodorus the Younger, a neo-Platonist philosopher who flourished at Alexandria during the sixth century, in the reign of Justinian.

The Arab invasions, as has been noted in an earlier chapter, greatly hindered the evolution of literature and learning in Armenia, though the work of national enlightenment was worthily carried on by such patriots as Catholicos John III of Otsoon, called Imastaser, 'the Philosopher' (consecrated 717, died 728), and Catholicos John V of Draskhanakert, called Patmaban, 'the Historian' (consecrated 898, died 929). Particular interest attaches to the *History of the House of Ardsruni* by Thomas Ardsruni, in which we find a detailed chronicle of the chequered fortunes of the great house of Vaspurakan, up to the tenth century.

One of the spiritual glories of the province of Vaspurakan, and indeed of Armenia generally, is the mystical writer Gregory of Narek, author of the *Book of Lamentations*, available in a French translation by Isaac Kechichian.[1] Gregory of Narek was born about 945, and was educated at the monastery of Narek, south of Lake Van. Gregory's father, Khosrow the Great, Bishop of Antsevatsik, was also a well-known ecclesiastical writer, author of a Commentary on the Armenian Liturgy. At Narek, Gregory was placed under the care of his great-uncle Anania, and grew up in an atmosphere of great intellectual and religious fervour, in contact with the best products of Greek and also perhaps of Arabic philosophy.

Gregory of Narek is considered one of the great, spontaneous mystical geniuses of medieval Christendom. His writings include a Commentary on the Song of Songs; a panegyric on the Virgin Mary; a panegyric on the Twelve Apostles and Seventy-Two Disciples; a panegyric on St James of Nisibis; anthems in honour of the Holy Ghost, the Holy Church and the Holy Cross; hymns and sacred odes. Gregory of Narek's hymns have been set to music by some of Armenia's best composers, and are regarded as models of their kind.

Gregory of Narek's most famous work is, of course, the *Book of Lamentations* (or: *Prayers, Elegies*). This consists of ninety-five separate Lamentations or canticles, put together rather like the Psalms of David to form a connected whole. The Lamentations are written in rhythmic prose, sometimes free verse, and are breathless and tumultuous in their passionate outpouring. Sometimes Gregory appears to be wrestling with his God, like some doughty Jacob of old; sometimes he is imploring a Deity who seems to have left him lonely and forsaken, like Job abandoned in the land of Uz. But the final tone of the Lamentations is optimistic, even triumphant.

---

[1] *Le Livre de Prières*, Paris, 1961.

I

O Sun of Justice,
Blessed ray of light,
Archetypal radiance;
Ardently desired,
Exalted, impenetrable,
Powerful, infallible;
Joyfulness of good things,
Hope realized,
O Praised and Celestial One:
King of Glory,
Christ the Creator,
Eternal life proclaimed!
Deign now to make good the defects
    and failings of my feeble tongue,
Wretch that I am,
By thine own all-powerful Word,
And present my prayer as acceptable
    supplications to Thy Father Almighty:
Since it is for my sake that Thou didst
    come to suffer the ordeal of malediction,
Having assumed my own human likeness in very truth . . .

II

And because of Thy precious blood continually offered,
In accordance with the will of Him who sent Thee,
Let all perils be taken from me, condemned
    sinner that I am,
My debts forgiven,
My shame effaced;
Let my disgrace be forgotten,
Sentence of judgement quashed on appeal,
The worm of hell trampled underfoot;
Let tears be dried,
Calmed, the gnashing of teeth;
Let lamentation cease,
Weeping be stilled;
To mourning make an end;
Let darkness turn to light,
And anger's fire be quenched,
All instruments of torture cast away!

III

Let thy compassion rest upon us,
O Thou who dost dispense life to all men
    according to Thy will;

271

Make rise the shining sun,
Hasten Thy redemption,
Send Thy succour to us;
Advance the hour of Thy visitation,
Sprinkle swiftly the dew of Thy mercy:
Let it fall to refresh the dried up
    pasture of my bones,
Which misfortune has plunged into death's abyss!
Let the celestial cup of Thy life-giving blood
Make the soil of my body flower and yield
    up fruit,
Having been prepared for the day of light,
Blood inexhaustible, for ever offered up
    by way of sacrifice,
As a memorial of life and redemption
For the souls which have gone to their eternal
    rest,
And thus my soul, mortified by my sinful body,
Shall be confirmed in Thee by Thy grace,
O merciful One,
And I shall be renewed by Thee,
Cut off from sin by life immortal
At the resurrection of the righteous,
And Blessed of Thy Father.
Together with Him, to Thee be glory,
And praise to Thy Holy Spirit;
Let grateful thanks be offered up
Now and for evermore
And for ever and ever, Amen.

Following the fall of the Bagratid and Ardsruni kingdoms, the tradition of Armenian spirituality was worthily carried on in Cilician Armenia by such remarkable figures as St Nerses Shnorhali, or 'the Gracious', and his kinsman, Archbishop Nerses of Lampron.

St Nerses Shnorhali was the younger brother of the Armenian Catholicos Gregory III Pahlavuni, who was elected to be supreme pontiff of the Armenians in 1113, at the age of twenty. For nearly fifty years, Nerses the Gracious was the right hand of Catholicos Gregory III, following him faithfully from one refuge to another to escape the raids and vexations of the Turks and Saracens. When Gregory retired from the office of Catholicos, Nerses was unanimously elected to succeed him (1166) and occupied the catholicosate for seven years, until his death in 1173.

St Nerses Shnorhali was a prolific poet and theologian. He wrote a verse history of the Armenian nation, a long elegy on the fall of the city of Edessa to the

Saracens, a panegyric of the True Cross, and a vast poem on the Life of Christ, under the title: *Jesus, Only-Begotten of the Father*. Nerses Shnorhali is the author of many commentaries on the holy scriptures, as well as on the lives of the Saints; he enriched the Armenian liturgy with hymns, anthems, sacred poems and prayers, which are in use to this very day.

Nerses of Lampron was born in 1153; his father was Prince Oshin of Lampron, and his mother, Princess Shahandukht, niece of St Nerses Shnorhali. At the age of twenty-two, Nerses of Lampron was appointed Archbishop of Tarsus. He was also the Abbot of the Monastery of Skevra, and is often referred to by his contemporaries as the 'modern St Paul', or 'Doctor Universalis'. Nerses of Lampron was versed in Greek, Syriac and Latin, and was constantly employed in diplomatic missions on behalf of his sovereign lord, King Levon II. He was instrumental in securing the support of Emperor Frederick Barbarossa for the young Armenian state of Cilicia, and in preparing the way for winning a royal crown for the Rupenid dynasty. He died at the age of forty-four, in 1198, just too soon to witness the fruition of his political plans.

Nerses of Lampron left behind him a wonderful literary heritage, comprising more than thirty major theological writings, including treatises, sermons, homilies, hymns, and epistles, one of these being a letter to the future King Levon on the perils of court life. His panegyric on the Assumption of the Virgin Mary is much admired. Nerses of Lampron was a strong advocate of reunion with Rome, and translated into Armenian the monastic rules of St Benedict, the Catholic Mass, and various Papal Bulls addressed to the Armenian nation.

In spite of the Seljuq invasions, intellectual life was by no means at a standstill in Greater Armenia itself. The outstanding figure here at this period was Mkhitar Gosh (1133–1213), equally celebrated as a law-giver, and as the author of a book of fables which deserve to rank with those of Aesop or La Fontaine. The nickname 'Gosh' means 'scanty of beard', and is an allusion to the famous writer's puny physique and insignificant personal appearance. However, Mkhitar Gosh made up for these disadvantages by his exceptional versatility and mental energy. For instance, when the Monastery of Getik was destroyed by an earthquake in 1190, Mkhitar Gosh persuaded the local prince, Ivane, to endow a new abbey, Nor-Getik, on the site of the old. Here Mkhitar became abbot, and founded a veritable monastic academy with a brilliant galaxy of teachers and acolytes.

Mkhitar Gosh's brilliant and witty fables, full of moral and philosophic wisdom, were studied and translated into Russian by the late Academician Iosif Orbeli. Mkhitar's code of laws, completed in 1184, consists of three parts: Introduction, Church Law, and Civil Law. Half a century later, the Code was translated into colloquial Armenian, and introduced into the Armenian kingdom of Cilicia. Such was its authority that other Armenian communities of the diaspora adopted the Mkhitar Code as their own, so that it was translated into Latin, Polish, Georgian, Russian and even Qipchak. In 1519, the Polish King Sigismund I sanctioned the application of the Mkhitar Code for the internal jurisdiction of the Armenian community in Poland.

The art of the fabulist was further developed by that outstanding medieval writer, Vardan of Maratha, who flourished in Cilicia around 1220. Vardan's fables were edited, with a Russian translation, by Academician Nikolai Marr in 1894–9. Far away in Siunia there lived, also during the thirteenth century, another talented author of a popular character, who wrote under the pseudonym of Frik, perhaps a diminutive of Frederick. Frik composed militant verses against social inequality:

> . . . . Why should one man rule the land,
> Another be in want of bread?
> One be king and favoured,
> Another poor and sad?

Frik railed against fickle fortune who 'gilds the houses of the evil, while the good are sent to beg for crumbs'.

> . . . O fortune, how can we in thee trust?
> Today the favoured wears a golden crown,
> Tomorrow, he is dethroned and trampled in the dust.

Frik seems himself to have had an unhappy life. He lost his home and family, probably in some Mongol invasion, and wandered off into exile, eventually reaching Cilician Armenia. There the homesick poet appeals to the flying crane for tidings of his homeland:

> Crane! whence hast thou come?
> I long to hear your call.
> Crane! Hast thou any news of home?
> Stay! You'll quickly reach your flock.
> Crane! Hast thou any news of home?

> . . . O God! pity him who lives in exile!
> The wanderer's breast is full of sorrow, his heart is sore.
> Bitter is the bread he eats, the water vile.
> Crane! Hast thou any news of home?

> Autumn is nigh, you are on the wing
> And have gathered a flock thousands strong.
> You gave me no answer, but flew straight on.
> Crane! Fly from our land, take to the wing!

However, Frik was not too depressed to enjoy the good things of life when they came his way. He celebrated earthly passion in a number of eloquent love lyrics.

I

Luna, you boast of illumining the world.
Here in my embrace lies an earthly moon.
I shall unveil the beauty if you doubt,
But fear you too will be enamoured
And clothe the world in gloom.

II

—— Thou sleepest 'neath the stars, thou bosom lighting the stars,
Take me unto thee, or else let me go home.
—— I can neither take thee unto me, nor let thee go home,
But must abide here and wait for the break of dawn.

Frik was the forerunner of scores of medieval Armenian lyric poets and bards, some of them musicians as well. The most renowned was Sayat-Nova (1712–95). The specimens of poetry collected at the Erevan Matenadaran come from the pens of some five hundred *gusans* – minstrels and troubadours. Detailed studies of much of this material were made by the Russian symbolist poet Valery Bryusov, who concluded that 'medieval Armenian lyric poetry is one of the most wonderful conquests of the human spirit ever known in the annals of world literature'.

Not even the Seljuq and Mongol invasions could arrest the progress of education and enlightenment in Armenia. From Classical times, academies and seminaries had existed in Armenia, attached to the principal shrines, both pagan and then Christian, as well as to the courts and palaces of the kings. In Greater Armenia, noted centres were at Vagharshapat and then at Ani, also in the northern marchlands, at the monasteries of Haghpat and Sanahin. In Cilician Armenia, the patriarchal see of Hromkla had a noted seminary, while schools flourished at the royal city of Sis.

Special renown attaches to two centres in the north-eastern province of Armenia, Siunia. These are Tatev and Gladzor. The monastery of Tatev was founded in 895 by Bishop John on a rocky promontory, at the foot of which the River Tatev flows through a valley 'full of vineyards and gardens filled with flowers of paradise', to quote the historian Stephen Orbelean. Bishop John took care to build a number of underground strongholds and hidden cells, to store precious manuscripts and other church treasures in the event of enemy raids. This gave the monastery the aspect of a veritable citadel, and accounts for its survival throughout a series of political and military disasters which overtook medieval Armenia. At one time, Tatev contained 500 monks, scribes, students, musicians, painters. The academy was organized on the most advanced lines; as well as preparing young men for priesthood, it was a productive centre for copying manuscripts and the diffusion of learning generally.

The scriptorium even had its own factory and workshop, where parchment, ink, and leather and gilt bindings could be manufactured on the spot. During the Cilician renaissance, Tatev was temporarily eclipsed as the metropolis of Armenian learning, but it regained its old splendour in the fourteenth and fifteenth centuries. In 1400, the library contained around 10,000 volumes. Tatev is famous as the home of one of Armenia's most renowned philosophers and polemists, Grigor Tatevatsi (1340–1411), author of the *Book of Questions*, a kind of encyclopaedia in the form of a catechism, covering such subjects as philosophy, pedagogy, chemistry, physics and anatomy; he was also a prolific writer on theological topics, and had many brilliant students and disciples.

The other great centre of learning in Siunia, that of Gladzor, flourished for only sixty years, from 1280 to 1340, but left behind it a rich intellectual heritage. Under the patronage of the local Prince Proshian, Gladzor grew rapidly into a regular university, housing 363 monks and students. Contemporary writers speak of Gladzor as 'the seat and school of our holy doctors', 'glorious second Athens', 'metropolis of all forms of learning', and 'celebrated holy monastery and University'. In the courtyard was a tower 15 metres high, at the foot of which certificates and diplomas of the degree of *vardapet* or learned doctor were handed to successful candidates. The leading teachers were Nerses of Mush, and his disciple Isaiah Nichetsi. After the latter's death in 1338, the monastery and academy fell into decline and were subsequently sacked and ruined. The history of Gladzor university continues to arise interest among Armenian scholars, as shown by the interesting doctoral dissertation by L. G. Khacherian on 'Isaiah Nichetsi and the Gladzor University', which was defended at Erevan University on April 20, 1968.

It should not be thought that education in medieval Armenia was confined to theology and such traditional studies as history and mathematics. Science and especially medicine were very well developed, following the example of the seventh century experimental philosopher Anania Shirakatsi. In medicine, there are several outstanding names. The first is that of Mkhitar Heratsi, author of a celebrated treatise, *Relief from Fevers* (1184). Mkhitar Heratsi mastered the technique of surgical operations, and used silk thread for sewing up wounds. He employed mandragora for an anaesthetic. He carried out experiments on animals, and was aware of the value of special diets in treating disorders, and of music and psychotherapy for the relief of nervous complaints. For the first time in the history of medicine, Mkhitar Heratsi introduced the notion that typhoid, malaria and septic fevers were infectious 'mouldy' fevers, as he aptly termed them. Heratsi abandoned the use of the classical *grabar* tongue, in favour of colloquial Armenian, with the result that his researches became available to the masses of the population. There are more than 850 medical manuscripts in the Erevan Matenadaran alone.

In one fifteenth-century manuscript, one may read about the physiological activities of the brain and the five senses:

'The head (brain) perceives and discerns the objects of the outer world which penetrate it by means of the senses. The head functions with the help of the five senses: for instance, the eye discerns colours, the sense of smell distinguishes odours, the sense of touch judges heaviness and lightness. With the aid of these five senses, thoughts are conducted to the mind of each individual human being.'

The distinguished Armenian doctor Amirdovlat Amasiatsi (1416–96) was personal physician to the Sultans of Turkey. He wrote a number of treatises under such titles as *For the Benefit of Medicine* and *Things unnecessary to the Ignorant*; in the former he criticized the errors of the Jewish philosopher and physician Maimonides (1135-1204). Amirdovlat Amasiatsi left behind him 300 original recipes for drugs and medicines. Over the centuries, Armenians and Greeks between them attained a dominant position in the medical profession throughout the Ottoman Empire, as well as in Persia, Egypt and other countries of the Levant.

The diffusion of knowledge was greatly stimulated by the invention of printing. The first Armenian printed book was published at Venice as early as 1512; it was a *parzatumar* or calendar. In the course of the next century, Armenian printing presses were set up in Constantinople, Livorno, Marseilles, Rome, and Amsterdam.

A further revival in Armenian culture and learning began during the eighteenth century under the aegis of the Armenian Catholic order of the Mekhitarists, who are still pursuing their dedicated and highly useful activities at the present time. The founder of the order was Abbot Mkhitar of Sebastia (Sivas, in Turkey). Born in 1676, Mkhitar entered the priesthood at an early age, and soon came under the influence of the Roman Catholic Church. Although he won fame as a preacher in Constantinople, he was suspect in the eyes of the authorities of the Armenian national Church, and resolved to set up a new Armenian brotherhood, directly subject to Rome. Mkhitar and his brethren began by settling in the Morea, under the protection of the Venetians. However, hostilities between Venice and the Ottoman Porte soon led the young congregation to seek refuge in Venice itself, where they were given the island of San Lazzaro out in the bay, close to the shore of the present-day Lido.

Mkhitar and his disciples set themselves the task of acting as intermediaries between Armenia and the advanced countries of the West, in preparation for the day when Armenia's ancient territories would be liberated from their Muslim overlords. To this end, they set up their own printing press, and founded a magnificent library, filled with the treasures of Armenian calligraphy and learning. They worked out their own form of Catholic Mass and liturgy, in the Armenian language. In the nineteenth century, Lord Byron visited San Lazzaro to learn Armenian, and one can still see the stone table in the monastery garden where he used to sit and study within sight of the Cathedral of San Marco. Two of the greatest Armenian historians belonged to the Venice congregation: Michael Chamchian (1738–95), and L. Alishan (1820–1901), the latter famous for his unsurpassed histories of the various Armenian provinces, including Cilician Armenia. Since 1843, the Venice Mekhitarists have been issuing a journal of Armenian historical studies, called *Pazmaveb*, besides a series of editions of major classics of Armenian literature. The San Lazzaro fathers also staff the Armenian High School in the city of Venice.

Following Mkhitar's death in 1749, dissension broke out among the Venice Fathers, and a portion seceded, to found a separate monastery in Trieste (1773). Following the invasion of Italy by Napoleon, the Armenian Fathers were driven from Trieste, and took refuge in Vienna, where they were accommodated by the Austrian government in the former Capucin monastery close to the city centre (now District 7, Mechitaristengasse 4). Since their installation in Vienna in 1811, the Austrian Mekhitarists have rivalled their Venice colleagues in learning and patriotic zeal. Their library and printing press (now run on commercial lines as a firm of general printers) are justly famous, while the Vienna journal of Armenian philology, *Handes Amsorya*, has been appearing regularly since 1887. Father Nerses Akinian of Vienna has attained international renown as an authority on ancient Armenian literature and history. The former head of the Vienna Congregation, the late Archbishop Mesrop Habozian, was an outstanding expert on ancient Armenian coins and an active promoter of Armenian studies all over the world, to whom the present writer is personally much indebted.

Another noted Armenian seat of learning abroad was the Lazarev Institute in Moscow. Founded in 1815 by an Armenian family from Persia, the Lazarev Institute became a leading Russian centre for oriental studies. The original building still exists, and is now the Institute of the Peoples of Asia and Africa of the Soviet Academy of Sciences. The Institute's address is 2, Armyansky Pereulok, or Armenian Lane; the left wing of the building houses the Armenian High Commission in Moscow, while to the right is the Oriental Publishing House of the Soviet Academy. An obelisk in the centre of the front garden commemorates the original Armenian founders of the Institute.

As we approach modern times, the history of Armenian literature and intellectual life becomes rapidly more dynamic and many-sided. In Constantinople, Tbilisi, and also in Russian and Turkish Armenia, a galaxy of talented writers stimulated the revival of Armenian national self-confidence which is such a feature of the late nineteenth century.

The father of the modern Armenian intelligentsia was Khachatur Abovian (1805–48), who studied in Dorpat, and became a school inspector in Erevan. Abovian was the author of the patriotic novel *The Wounds of Armenia*, fables, lyrics and short stories. Above all, he never ceased to stress the need for educating the people, and reviving their pride in Armenia's glorious past. This patriotic zeal led to his dismissal by the Tsarist Ministry of Public Instruction, after which Abovian died in mysterious circumstances, possibly as a result of murder or suicide. His work was carried on by Michael Nalbandian (1830–66), famed as a

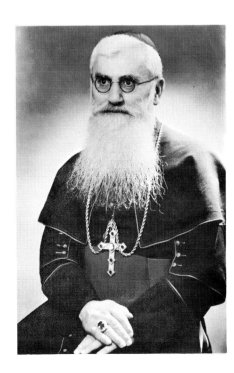

102. Page from a gospel manuscript in Bolorgir writing

103. Abbot Mkhitar (1676–1749)

104. Archbishop Mesrop Habozian

105. Catholicos Khrimean Hayrik (1820–1907)

106. The Matenadaran Manuscript Library, Erevan

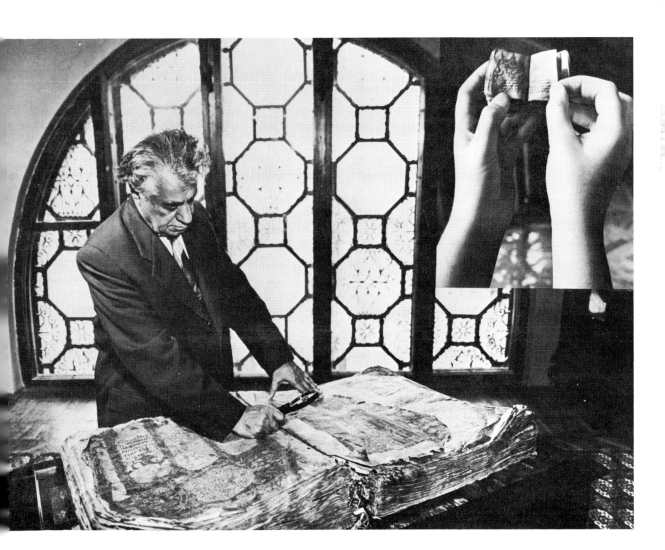

107. Contemporary novelist Garegin Sevunts

108. The largest and the smallest: studying two manuscripts in the Matenadaran Library

poet and novelist, and as one of Armenia's early educators and social reformers; he was imprisoned for three years under Tsar Alexander II, and contracted tuberculosis from which he died.

In the Armenian Church, a leading personality was Bishop, later Catholicos Mkrtich Khrimean, known as *Hayrik*, or Little Father. Born at Van in 1820, Khrimean began his career as a teacher, and then entered the Church, becoming Abbot of Varag and Bishop of Van. He founded a printing press in Van, where from 1856 he published a patriotic journal called *Eagle of Vaspurakan*, as well as founding several schools in the district. In 1869, Khrimean was elected Patriarch of Constantinople, but held this dignity for only four years, before the jealous suspicions of the Turkish government obliged him to resign. In 1889, the eloquent preacher and patriot was sent into honourable exile in Jerusalem, but was three years later elected to the primacy of the Armenian Church in Echmiadzin. Catholicos Khrimean Hayrik died in 1907, and is revered to this day as an outstanding architect of Armenian spiritual revival.

Among dramatists, the noted name is that of Gabriel Sundukian (1825–1912), regisseur and playwright, and for many years the life and soul of the flourishing Armenian theatrical life of Tbilisi, in Georgia. Best known of nineteenth-century novelists is Raffi, the pen-name of Akop Melik-Akopian (1835–88), a native of Salmas, in Persian Azerbaijan. This prolific writer is known for his historical novels, as well as for his gripping panoramas of Armenian life during his own time. Several of Raffi's novels have been translated into Russian, French, English, German, Czech and Georgian. Among a galaxy of poets, we should single out Hovhannes Tumanian (1869–1923), whose House Museum is one of the monuments of present-day Erevan. Tumanian provided the poetic themes for two of Armenia's most famous operas: *Anush* by Armen Tigranian, and *Almast* by Alexander Spendiarov.

Among the numerous Armenian intelligentsia of Constantinople, we may single out two figures whose lives were cut short in 1915 by the indiscriminate murder policy of the Young Turk junta: Daniel Varuzhan and Siamanto, the latter being the pen-name of Atom Yarjarian. Varuzhan studied in Belgium, at the University of Ghent, where a monument has been erected to this talented poet, who perished at the age of thirty-one. Varuzhan is celebrated for his patriotic poems, such as *The Heart of the Nation*, devoted to the agelong struggle of the Armenian people, and *The Shepherd*, in which the poet's grandfather comes down from the hills with his flock in winter-time, and tells many a story of times gone by. Other poetic masterpieces by Varuzhan are *Pagan Songs* and *The Song of Bread*. Siamanto was a poet of highly original technique, sometimes branded as 'decadent'. His poems are pessimistic, cataclysmic even; such is his *Agony and Torch of Hope*, dealing with the Adana massacre of 1909 in which many thousands of Armenians perished. Siamanto also celebrated the heroic struggle of such Armenian partisan fighters as Andranik, Albiur, Christaphor and others.

A poet who spanned the gap between the old and the new Armenia was Avetik Issahakian (1875–1957). Born in Alexandropol, the modern Leninakan, Issahakian studied in Germany and lived for many years in France. He returned to the Soviet Union in 1928 and was awarded the Order of Lenin in 1945. A close friend of the composer Komitas, Issahakian could claim to be the spiritual descendant of such beloved national bards as Sayat-Nova, the eighteenth-century prince of Armenian troubadours, court poet of King Erekle II of Georgia. Issahakian was a man of immense erudition, though capable of complete simplicity and spontaneity in his lyric verse. Peasant blood ran in his veins. To the end of his long life, he never forgot how as a barefoot boy, he would run about the hot Shirak Steppe, dipping sun-parched lips in the spring waters descending from Mount Aragats, and then on winter nights listen to wise old men of the village retelling traditional stories of Armenia's ancestor, Haik, of Queen Shamiram and Ara the Fair, of David of Sassoun and his magic horse, Jalali. Intensely loyal to his native land, Issahakian was one of those rare Armenian poets who could merge his national aspirations and yearnings with those of humanity at large. In this way, Issahakian attained a true universality, a philosophical depth of thought which sets him apart from his contemporaries. The finest example of Issahakian's world vision is his long poem *Abulala al-Maarri*, in which the poet takes on the symbolic guise of one of the classics of Arabic literature, in order to give vent to his own deeply moving vision of the destiny of man. First published in 1909, *Abulala al-Maarri* was translated into Russian by Valery Bryusov, into French by Jean Minassian, into Czech by Vladimir Holan and Ludmila Motalova.

With the foundation of the Soviet Socialist Republic of Armenia in 1920, and the achievement of universal literacy throughout the country, opportunities for writers became enormously improved. One of the pioneers of Soviet Armenian literature who is especially dear to the modern reader is Eghishe Charentz (1897–1938). After going through the usual Symbolist phase of 'elusive emotions', 'wavering dreams' in a world 'sunk in lack-lustre sleep', Charentz saluted the Revolution of 1917 with enthusiasm and embarked on a new phase of poetic creation, and of propaganda for the new Soviet Armenian homeland. He wrote a number of poems about Lenin, and won the nickname of 'the Armenian Mayakovsky'; he was also active in the creation of an Armenian Society of Proletarian Writers. He wrote patriotic and love poems of rare beauty. All this failed to save Charentz from the holocaust of the Stalin and Beria terror of the 1930's, which claimed exceptionally numerous victims among the intelligentsia of Armenia, as also of Georgia. Proportionately, the number of élite writers who perished in the Caucasian republics far exceeded those who died in European Russia.

However, enough Armenian writers survived to ensure the onward transmission of the country's literary heritage, so that the intellectual scene in Soviet Armenia today is a varied and exciting one. Since we are mainly concerned in this book with Armenia's ancient and classical culture, we confine ourselves to mentioning among present-day authors the lively and original Garegin Sevunts, whose novel *Teheran* has been translated into twenty languages. In 1966, it was in his company that my wife and I first set eyes on Lake Sevan.

There are of course several well-known Armenian authors writing in English and other foreign languages. One of the most original of these was Michael Arlen, the pen-name of Dikran Kouyoumdjian, who died in 1956. Arlen's most famous work was the novel *The Green Hat*, first published in 1924; it was not reprinted until 1968, when it aroused considerable interest, as a satirical chronicle of the scandalous life of the 'Smart Set' of the 1920s. The story concerns the green hat worn by a lively lady named Iris Storm, dressed *pour le sport*, and seated in her yellow Hispano-Suiza, in which she finally commits suicide by crashing the car into a tree when her life has crashed around her. The book was considered highly shocking when it first appeared. The literary critic Alan Pryce-Jones recalls that, as a youth, he presented it to his father, who was staying at the time at a seaside resort in Yorkshire.

'With the gesture of Perseus slaying the dragon, my father, having hurled it into a burning grate (very necessary in a Yorkshire August by the seaside), held it in the flames with a poker. The gesture was splendid but not effectual. After a minute or two he exchanged the poker for tongs. The edges of the binding were slightly charred. We did not speak of the matter again'.

It is alleged that Stalin attributed the suicide of his second wife to the corrupting influence of Michael Arlen's *The Green Hat*. The book scarcely has power to alarm us nowadays. Frivolous, brittle, but oh so nostalgic, it is amusing to read and a mine of detail for social historians of the period.

An émigré Armenian writer who could never have alarmed or corrupted anyone is William Saroyan, born in 1908, and still going strong. Saroyan is much admired by a wide circle of readers, and has of course made a great deal of money by his plays and short stories. He has a roseate view of human nature, and writes a whimsical, half-humorous, half-sentimental type of prose which appeals to the great American public.

As to whether Saroyan writes great literature, only posterity will be able to tell.

Within Soviet Armenia, the general advance in education and learning over the last half century is phenomenal. There are today 1,600 schools of various kinds, with more teachers than there were pupils in pre-Revolutionary times. Universal compulsory ten-year education is the accepted norm. Particular attention is paid to training qualified specialists. The Armenian Soviet Socialist Republic has twelve institutions of higher education, and forty-five specialized secondary schools, which train 70,000 students. In Armenia, there are 177 students for every 10,000 inhabitants; in Erevan itself, there are more than twice as many students today than the entire population of the city in 1914.

Many of the lecturers and professors of Erevan State University, whose Rector is Professor Mkrtich Nersessian, are known far beyond the boundaries of the Soviet Union. Of the 480 faculty members, 10 are Academicians, 25 Doctors of Science, and 250 Masters of Science. The University has housed such outstanding figures as Professor H. A. Manandian, unsurpassed as the historian of ancient Armenia, and Manouk Abeghian, who revolutionized the study of the history of Armenian literature.

The Armenian Academy of Sciences, established in the hectic war years, in 1943, is the leading centre of scientific reserach. It has some thirty subsidiary institutes. For many years, Victor Ambartsumian, the prominent astrophysicist, has been the Academy's President. Ambartsumian's cosmogonical discoveries have earned him a great name among astronomers, and he has built up the young Byurakan Observatory into a leading scientific centre, where visitors from all leading countries of the world are regularly welcomed.

The Institute of Physics in Erevan has a unique electronic accelerator of elementary particles. Armenian physicists have many achievements to their credit, particularly in the fields of cosmic rays and high energy physics. Armenian geologists have been instrumental in discovering and exploiting many fresh metals and minerals on the territory of the republic, which have contributed to developing the country's present sophisticated economy. The workers of the Institute of Fine Organic Chemistry have synthesized a number of medicinal substances, including such useful preparations as gangleron, quateron and ditilin.

Armenian scientists and scholars make their mark far outside the frontiers of the Armenian Soviet Socialist Republic. For instance, the mathematician Sergei Mergelian became a Doctor of Science at the age of twenty, and six years later, was elected a Corresponding Member of the Soviet Academy of Sciences. The son of Stephan Shaumian, the Baku Commissar and friend of Lenin, is chief editor of the *Great Soviet Encyclopedia.*

The two brothers Orbeli, Leon Abgarovich, born in 1882, and his brother Iosif Abgarovich, born in 1887, are another case in point. Leon became one of the leading Soviet physiologists, Colonel-General in the medical service, Director of the Institute of Physiology named after I. P. Pavlov, three times winner of the Order of Lenin, and an Academician of the Soviet Academy of Sciences. His brother Iosif, also a member of the Soviet Academy, was Director of the Leningrad State Hermitage Museum, President of the Armenian Academy of Sciences from 1943 to 1947, and one of the greatest experts on Armenian, Caucasian and Muslim art, architecture, metal-ware and medieval literature. Such remarkable careers are rare; but in leading intellectual centres of the Soviet Union, and in many countries abroad, Armenian scholars will be found, who combine exceptional brilliance with the dogged perseverance which has enabled their race to survive so many perils right up to the present day.

Chapter XII

DEATH AND RESURRECTION

The quarter of a century from 1895 to 1920 was the most tragic in the long and chequered history of the Armenian people. Stirred by the example of the Greeks and the Bulgarians, the Armenians in Turkey had begun to put forward modest claims for regional autonomy for those districts of Armenia which were under Ottoman rule. Delegations were sent to the Berlin Congress of 1878, and two patriotic societies formed, the Dashnaks and the Hunchaks.

Conditions in Turkish Armenia under Sultan Abdul-Hamid II (1876–1908) went from bad to worse. Forbidden to carry arms, the Armenians were classed as second-grade citizens, a prey to Kurdish marauders and Ottoman tax-gatherers alike. However, in Istanbul, they enjoyed considerable privileges. Under the jurisdiction of the Armenian Patriarch, they formed a separate *millet* or national community, and enjoyed a measure of communal self-rule. The Ottoman civil service and banking system was largely staffed by Armenians, as well as Greeks; their superior culture and industry made them an object of jealousy on the part of the sluggish peasant population and bazaar masses.

The Ottoman government, with some justification, saw the Armenians as the tools of European imperialist powers, who desired to carve up the Ottoman Empire among themselves. After the war of 1877–8, which brought liberation for Bulgaria, the Russians annexed large districts of former Turkish Armenia, which was added to the Russian viceroyalty of the Caucasus. The districts annexed included the strategic fortresses of Kars and Ardahan, which controlled the access route to Erzurum and on towards Ankara and to the Mediterranean. Through mission schools, many Armenians had acquired an attachment to English and American culture, while the Armenian catholics tended to look towards Rome and France for salvation. In view of the open boasts of Russian and British statesmen, who talked of carving up the 'Sick Man of Europe', and of the humiliating Capitulations or extra-territorial rights enjoyed by many foreign residents in Turkey, the Ottoman sultans became morbidly suspicious of their Armenian subjects, whom they went out of their way to alienate by every form of discrimination and petty persecution.

Matters came to a head in 1895, when Abdul-Hamid began to put into effect his 'final solution' of the Armenian problem. Special armed troops, called *Hamidiya* after the Sultan, were formed to massacre the Armenian populations in Sassoun, Erzurum, Trebizond, Van, Kharput, Istanbul and Marash. Armenian revolutionaries retaliated by seizing the Ottoman Bank in Istanbul, and appealing to the European powers for help. This was the signal for a general onslaught, in which some 300,000 Armenians perished, and another 80,000 fled to other countries. Most Western countries angrily condemned this monstrous crime, the most vocal being the British statesman Gladstone. However, Kaiser Wilhelm II of Germany, with an eye to German projects such as the Berlin-Baghdad railway, paid a state visit to Istanbul and publicly embraced the slavering Commander of the Faithful.

To be impartial, it must be stated that the situation of Armenians in Russian Transcaucasia was sometimes no more enviable than that of the Turkish Armenians. In 1903, the Russian government confiscated most of the landed property of the Armenian national Church, and closed down Church schools and libraries. During the Revolution of 1905, terrible massacres of Armenians by Tatars, often aided and abetted by local Russian governors, took place in Baku, Elizavetpol (Ganja) and other districts. Armenians like Kamo (Ter-Petrossian) were active in underground Bolshevik organizations. In 1912, a mass trial of Armenian nationalist leaders was held before the Russian Senate in St Petersburg, fifty-two individuals receiving sentences of imprisonment and exile, though relatively light ones.

In 1908, a revolution occurred in Turkey, headed by the so-called 'Committee of Union and Progress', or 'Young Turks'. The Committee proclaimed an end to the oppressive policy of Abdul-Hamid II, and a new deal for racial minorities in the Ottoman Empire. The Armenians loyally supported the Young Turk movement, and participated in the formation of a new government. However, a terrible massacre soon occurred in Adana, where over 15,000 Armenians perished.

Within the Young Turk movement, a ruling junta soon came into being, headed by Enver Pasha, Minister for War; Talaat Pasha, Minister of the Interior and later Grand Vizier; and Jemal, Military Governor of Istanbul and later Minister of the Marine. These individuals became increasingly subservient to German influence, as well as to the new racialist doctrine of Pan-Turkism. They dreamt of annexation of the ancient Turkic lands of central Asia, and the formation of a vast Turanian empire stretching from Istanbul to Samarkand and beyond. The main obstacle to this was the Armenian race, still some three million strong on Ottoman territory, and forming an ethnic barrier between Asia Minor and the Caspian Sea. In several secret conferences of the 'Committee of Union and Progress', held in Salonica from 1910 onwards, the elimination of all Armenians was adopted as a central object of Young Turk policy.

With a view to the annihilation of the Armenian population, various provincial governors were removed from their posts, and replaced by persons subservient to the Young Turk junta. In 1914 Turkey entered World War I on the German side. Almost immediately, Turkey found itself squeezed between a massive Russian invasion from the direction of Tbilisi, Kars and Ardahan, and the ill-fated British landings at Gallipoli, very close to Istanbul itself. These events sealed the doom of Turkey's Armenian population. With the tacit connivance of Liman von Sanders, the German Inspector-General of the Ottoman army, and of Freiherr Hans von Wangenheim, the German ambassador in Istanbul, the master-plan for destroying the Armenians was put into effect.

It is difficult to convey the horror of the events of 1915, as the Ottoman government set into action its design for genocide. In April 1915, the Armenian intellectual and community leaders in Istanbul were rounded up and transported in ships to their doom; among the victims were a number of priests, poets, doctors, and the great composer Komitas. Able-bodied Armenian males throughout the Ottoman empire had already been rounded up into labour battalions, though not issued with arms. They did sterling work for the Ottoman army, and built many roads and railways. They were now set upon by the Turkish units, and shot down or bludgeoned to death almost to the last man.

Even more tragic and horrible was the fate reserved for the Armenian civil population. Infants were forcibly removed from their families to 'orphanages', which turned out to be pits dug in the ground, into which the children were hurled alive, to be covered up with piles of stones. Women and old people were formed up into caravans, and forced to march on foot for hundreds of miles towards Aleppo and other concentration points in Syria. On the way, they were waylaid by bands of ruffians, who were given *carte-blanche* by the government to kill deportees and steal their possessions. Neither food nor water was provided for the deportees, who soon went mad and died of thirst. In the night-time, the gendarme escorts would amuse themselves by stripping any good looking girls who took their fancy, and forcing them to indulge in various forms of sexual perversion. These usually ended with the victims being disembowelled, and their breasts sliced off; many such corpses were thrown into the Tigris and Euphrates, and washed up in towns farther downstream. A few women and children were spared to be sold into slavery, or taken into Turkish families and hidden. Some of Talaat Pasha's provincial viceroys evolved novel ways of carrying out his orders. The governor of Trebizond, for instance, would offer his official launch to panic-stricken Armenian refugees, promising to convey them to safety further down the coast. As soon as they were well out into the Black Sea, the Armenian passengers were thrown into the water and left to drown amid the jeers of the Turkish crew.

In spite of these bestialities, many thousands of Armenians managed to flee into Russian territory, though a large number starved to death during the famines which followed the Revolution of 1917. Others were herded together in the desert wilderness of northern Syria, the district called Deir al-Zor, and left to die of

288

starvation and exposure. About one and a half million Turkish Armenians were physically eliminated out of the pre-war total of nearly three million.

That the extermination was deliberately planned and ordered by the Young Turk junta cannot be denied. The secret directives of Talaat Pasha were found in central and provincial chancelleries after World War I; they give the most stringent and detailed orders for the physical extermination of all Armenians. Public documents, of course, used euphemisms like 'resettlement of the population', 'reallocation of personnel' and so forth, as was the practice under the Hitler régime at the time of the extermination of the Jews.

The question of German connivance in this crime is a controversial one. Certainly, individual German officers and consuls protested, and tried to save some of the victims, but their efforts were nullified by Wagenheim and Liman von Sanders, as well as by the Berlin government. Press reports of the massacres were suppressed by the German censors, though the humanitarian Lepsius, and the distinguished orientalist Joseph Marquart (Markwart) refused to be silenced. General Ludendorff was heard to complain that the Ottoman army seemed more interested in killing unarmed Armenians than well-armed Russian and British soldiers, though the German General Staff officially turned a blind eye to these gruesome happenings.

Among the many foreign eye-witnesses to these horrible events was the American Ambassador Henry Morgenthau, who remained steadfastly at his post, and did everything he could to alleviate the sufferings of the victims. He made no secret of his sympathy for the sufferings of the Armenians: Ottoman officials seemed surprised that Morgenthau, a Jew, should concern himself with the problems of Christians. On one occasion, Talaat Pasha, with unparalleled cynicism, applied to Morgenthau for the insurance monies in respect of dead Armenians who had insured their lives with American companies; the Grand Vizier argued that since all the families of these Armenians had also perished, the money now belonged rightfully to the Ottoman state. America played a leading part in relief work among the destitute Armenians, many of whom found new homes in the United States of America. There are today many flourishing Armenian communities in such American cities as New York, Boston, Detroit and, particularly, Fresno in California; most have their own churches.

Following the collapse of Tsarist Russia in 1917, the Armenians were able to set up an independent republic in Erevan. However, the Ottoman régime was still pursuing its ruthless drive eastwards to Baku and central Asia. It was truly said that, in setting the boundaries for their new state, the Turks allowed the Armenians only enough room for a mass cemetery. The independent Armenian republic was dominated by the nationalist Dashnak party, though internal policy was largely social-democratic in character.

In view of the catastrophic economic condition of the country, a close association with the Soviet Union presented the only feasible way out of the economic

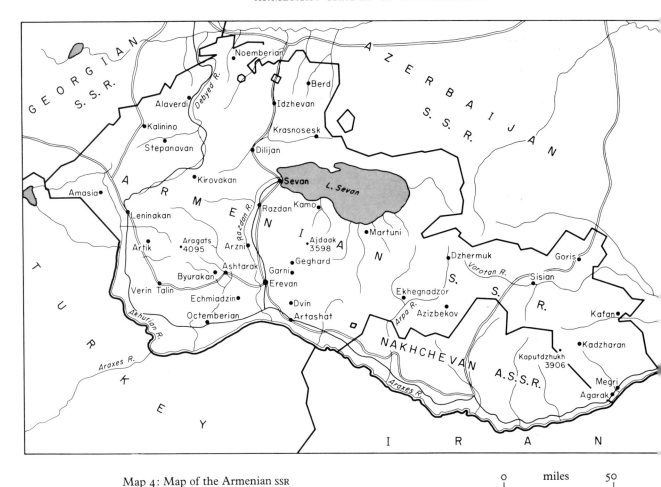

Map 4: Map of the Armenian SSR

0   miles   50

and political difficulties facing the country. The Red Army, aided by local Communist sympathizers, advanced into Armenia on November 29, 1920 and set up a Soviet régime there. On January 30, 1922, the First Congress of Soviets of Armenia adopted the constitution of the Armenian SSR, and elected a Central Executive Committee to carry on government between Congress meetings. A Soviet of People's Commissars was also formed. Later that year, the Transcaucasian Soviet Republics of Armenia, Georgia and Azerbaijan united to form the Transcaucasian Soviet Federative Socialist Republic, which existed until 1936. In that year, each republic became a constituent republic of the Soviet Union.

Naturally, inclusion within the USSR did not take place without a measure of opposition. The collectivization campaign, and the five-year plans which got into full swing from 1928 onwards, brought hardship as well as economic progress.

A leading role in Soviet, as well as in Armenian affairs, was played by A. I. Mikoyan, now one of the most respected of Soviet elder statesmen. However, even Mikoyan was powerless to counteract the excesses of the Stalin terror of 1936 and 1937. In accordance with directives from the bloodthirsty NKVD chiefs Yezhov and Yagoda, L. P. Beria decimated the leading Party cadres of Armenia, as well as the Armenian intelligentsia, just as he did in Georgia and Azerbaijan.

In spite of these negative features, the social and economic life of Soviet Armenia made rapid strides, both before and especially after World War II. Pre-revolutionary Armenia had been an agrarian country, with poorly developed industry. Agriculture accounted for 75 per cent of its output. Its most important industries – copper, wine and cognac-making – were in the hands of foreign or Russian capitalists. Such industry as there was vanished almost completely during the terrible events of World War I and the aftermath of revolution and famine. It was not until 1928 that the volume of industrial production in Armenia reached the 1913 level once more.

Soon the natural genius of the Armenian people for hard work and inventive effort found an outlet in the modernization of the Republic. A carbide plant – the first in the Soviet Union – was put into operation in Erevan in 1927, and another important factory, making synthetic rubber, was opened there in 1940. Following World War II, new factories and research laboratories have been opened up almost every month. Hydroelectric power stations have harnessed the energy of Armenia's rivers, and new roads and railways have been built. The machine-building industry produces metal-cutting lathes, generators, electric motors, power transformers, mobile power stations, electric welding equipment, electric lamps, and cables. In the *Daily Telegraph* on June 9, 1967, the British science correspondent Angela Croome wrote, after a tour of 10,000 miles through the Soviet Union:

'Most astonishing was to find a whole family of locally built large memory computers ('Razdan') using transistors and printed circuits in Armenia, which is still only twenty years from the veil'.

At the present time, no one visiting Erevan, Leninakan and other cities of Soviet Armenia can fail to be struck by the general air of bustle, and the active pace of industrial and domestic construction works continually in progress. Such sophisticated processes as the manufacture of transistor radios are rapidly acclimatized here, alongside traditional occupations such as fruit and vine growing.

The repatriation of many thousands of Armenians from abroad has led to pressure on living space and agricultural resources throughout the Republic. Many new regions have been reclaimed, the stones being often carried by hand from the land to be tilled. The fact that several traditional Armenian ethnic areas, such as Nakhchevan and the Karabagh, remain under the jurisdiction of Soviet Azerbaijan sometimes leads to friction, while there is a contested claim for territories in southern Georgia, notably in Javakheti and Samtskhe provinces.

As noted in preceding chapters, advances in sciences and technology in Armenia have been fully matched by progress in the cultural field. Soviet Armenia has two film studios, and successful films are assured of an all-Union audience of up to fifty million. The Erevan State Conservatory named after Komitas assures a high level of musical life throughout the country, and sends many ensembles and soloists abroad. Such are, for instance, the noted Komitas String Quartet, and the ever popular operatic prima donna Gohar Gasparian.

Naturally, the official ideology of Soviet Armenia is Marxism-Leninism. This does not prevent the Armenian national Church from being held in high esteem – a factor in this being the personality and enlightened patriotism of the present Supreme Catholicos, His Holiness Vazken I. An example of Catholicos Vazken's exceptional ability to win the devotion even of non-Armenian Christians occurred in 1966, when he was invited to celebrate the Armenian liturgy in the Protestant Cathedral in Geneva – the first non-Calvinist prelate to perform such an act of worship since the days of Calvin himself.

Echmiadzin, situated almost beneath the shadow of Mount Ararat, still remains the spiritual centre of all Armenian worshippers. In view of the strong attachment of all Armenians to the land of their fathers, Echmiadzin plays a strong unifying role in the political sphere – a fact recognized by the privileges granted by the Soviet Government to the Holy See of Echmiadzin, and to foreign Armenian bishops and delegations who come constantly to visit the shrine. Forty students are housed at the Echmiadzin Theological Seminary, in preparation for graduation to the priesthood.

Other Armenian Church centres today include the Cilician catholicosate of Antelias, a suburb of Beirut; the Armenian patriarchates of Constantinople and Jerusalem; the French eparchy, with its seat in Paris; the eparchy of Southern France, with its seat in Marseilles; the Iranian eparchy, with seats in Isfahan, Tehran and Tabriz; the North American (Eastern) and Canadian eparchy, centred on New York; the North American (Western) eparchy including Mexico, and having its seat in Los Angeles; the South American eparchy, centered on Buenos Aires; the Rumanian and Bulgarian eparchy, with its headquarters in Bucharest; the Egyptian eparchy, covering also Ethiopia and the Sudan, and centred on Cairo; the Indian and Far Eastern eparchy, with its seat in Calcutta; the Iraq eparchy, whose head resides in Baghdad. Besides these, there are two Armenian ministries in London, another in Geneva, one in Vienna and another in Milan.

In spite of the westernization of large areas of Armenian family life, many national traditions are still observed. In fact, the flowering of Soviet Armenian culture has led to an intensified interest in ancient costumes, dances and folk beliefs. Marriages are attended by many picturesque rites. On holidays too, peasants bring their sheep to Holy Echmiadzin, slaughter them as a token sacrifice to the Church,

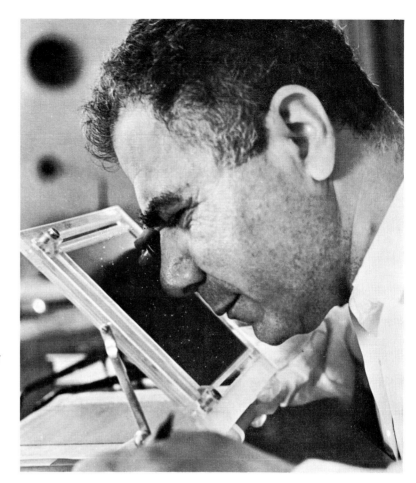

99. Professor Victor Ambartsumian

10. The Byurakan Astrophysical Observatory

111. National emblem of the Armenian Soviet Republic

112. At the silk factory named after Lenin

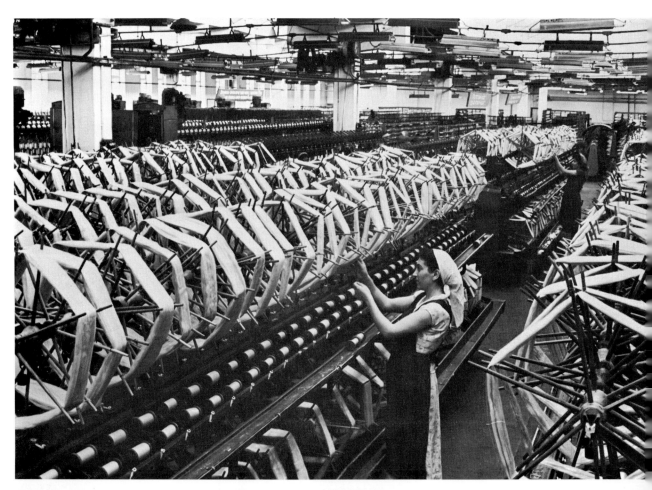

and then enjoy a picnic close to the Cathedral grounds. The people still celebrate pagan and Christian holidays and ceremonies, which have often long since lost their original religious meaning. One of these is the *trindez*, celebrated at the onset of summer. Singing songs with torches in their hands, young people light numerous bonfires; then they jump over the fire to 'purify' themselves in the flames.

Again, at the beginning of August, when the heat is particularly oppressive, and the fields are dry from want of rain, the *vardavar*, or 'bearing of roses' holiday, is celebrated. On that day, everyone is liable to be sprinkled with water – no offence can be taken. Then popular games and contests are held. Young men and boys show their prowess in horsemanship, wrestlers match their strength. The singers' contest always attracts the crowds who come to listen to improvization in the form of ballads and witty riddle songs.

In October 1968, the Armenian people celebrated the 2,750th anniversary of the foundation of Erevan by the ancient Urartian king who built a citadel there and called it Erebuni. This jubilee was attended by many thousands of Armenians from all over the world, and turned into a spontaneous demonstration of national pride and solidarity. All this augurs well for the future destiny of this remarkable people and their much ravaged but ever hallowed land – a veritable cradle of human civilization.

BIBLIOGRAPHICAL NOTES AND SUGGESTIONS FOR FURTHER READING

Since this book is intended mainly for non-specialist readers who may not know Armenian or Russian, nor have ready access to large reference libraries, I have kept footnotes and bibliographical details to a minimum.

For the older period, two works are of outstanding value for reference purposes:

LYNCH, H. F. B. *Armenia. Travels and Studies.* 2 vols., London, 1901. Reprinted by Khayats Booksellers and Publishers, Beirut, 1965. Bibliography in vol. 2, pp. 471–96.

MIANSAROV, M. M. *Bibliographia Caucasica et Transcaucasica*, tom. I, sections 1 and 2. St Petersburg, 1874–6 (no more published). This work is now again available in reprint form.

I list below, chapter by chapter, the principal sources which have been drawn upon in writing this book, also other works and articles recommended for detailed study. Preference is given to items in Western languages, though titles in Armenian and Russian are included where these contain information not available elsewhere.

CHAPTER I

GABIKIAN, KARAPET. *Flora of Armenia* (in Armenian). Jerusalem, 1968.

GRAVES, SIR ROBERT WINDHAM. *Storm Centres of the Near East.* London, 1933.

GROUSSET, RENÉ, *Histoire de l' Arménie.* Paris, 1947.

LEHMANN-HAUPT, C. F. *Armenien einst und jetzt*, 3 pt. Berlin, Leipzig, 1910–31.

MACLER, FRÉDÉRIC. *Trois conférences sur l'Arménie, faites à Bucarest.* Paris, 1929.

MASON, K., and others. *Turkey, vol. I* (Naval Intelligence Geographical Handbook Series), 1942.

MEILLET, A. *Esquisse d'une grammaire comparée de l'Arménien classique.* 2nd ed., Vienna, 1936.

MORGAN, JACQUES DE. *Histoire de peuple arménien.* Paris, Nancy, 1919.

MOVSESIAN, S. A. *Armeniya vchera, sevodnya, zavtra* ('Armenia yesterday, today and tomorrow'). Erevan, 1966.

NANSEN, FRIDTJOF. *L'Arménie et le Proche Orient.* Paris, 1928.

OVNANIAN, S. V. *Armyano-bolgarskie istoricheskie svyazi i armyanskie kolonii v Bolgarii vo vtoroi polovine XIX veka* ('Armeno-Bulgarian historical links and the Armenian colonies in Bulgaria during the second half of the nineteenth century'). Erevan, 1968.

REVUE DES ÉTUDES ARMÉNIENNES. Series 1, Paris, 1920–33; series 2, Paris, 1964, etc.

RIKLI, MARTIN. *Natur- und Kulturbilder aus den Kaukasusländern und Hocharmenien.* Zurich, 1914.

SANDERS, A. (pseudonym of Alexander Nikuradze). *Kaukasien. Geschichtlicher Umriss.* Munich, 1942.

SURMELIAN, LEON. trans. *Daredevils of Sassoun.* London, 1966.

CHAPTER II

CLARKE, GRAHAME. *The Stone Age Hunters.* London, 1967.

KRUPNOV, E. I. 'Kavkaz v drevneishei istorii nashei strany' ('The Caucasus in the most ancient history of our country'), in *Voprosy Istorii* ('Problems of History'), no. 5, 1966, pp. 27–40.

LYUBIN, V. P. 'Paleolit Turtsii i problema rannego rasseleniya chelovechestva' ('The Palaeolithic cultures of Turkey and the problem of the early migration of humanity'), in *Sovetskaya Arkheologiya* ('Soviet Archaeology'), XXVII, 1957, pp. 71–90.

MONGAIT, ALEXANDER. *Archaeology in the USSR.* Moscow, 1959.

MORGAN, JACQUES DE. *La Préhistoire orientale,* tom. III. Paris, 1927.

NIORADZE, G. K. *Paleolitichesky chelovek v peshchere Deviskhvreli* ('Palaeolithic man in the cavern of Devis-Khvreli'). Works of the Georgian State Museum, no. 6. Tbilisi, 1933.

OAKLEY, KENNETH P. *Man the Tool-Maker.* 5th ed., London, 1965.

PANICHKINA, M. Z. *Paleolit Armenii* ('The Palaeolithic cultures of Armenia'). Leningrad, 1950.

SARDARIAN, S. A. *Paleolit v Armenii* ('The Palaeolithic cultures in Armenia'). Erevan, 1954.
Primitive Society in Armenia (in Armenian, with Russian and English summaries). Erevan, 1967.

VERESHCHAGIN, N. K. *The Mammals of the Caucasus,* trans. Lerman and Rabinovich. Jerusalem, 1967.

CHAPTER III

ACADEMY OF SCIENCES OF THE USSR. *Kratkie soobshcheniya Instituta Arkheologii* ('Brief communications of the Institute of Archaeology'), Moscow. Many issues have material on Armenia, including nos. 46 (1952), 66 (1956), 93 (1963) and 108 (1966).

ACADEMY OF SCIENCES OF THE USSR. *Materialy i Issledovaniya po Arkheologii SSSR* ('Materials and Researches on the Archaeology of the USSR'), Moscow. Many volumes have material on Armenia, including nos. 67 (1959) and 125 (1965), with articles by O. A. Abibullaev and others on the Nakhchevan Kül-Tepe and other Bronze Age sites.

ACADEMY OF SCIENCES OF THE USSR. *Ocherki istorii SSSR* ('Studies in the History of the USSR'), volume on 'Primitive-Communal Society and most ancient states on the territory of the USSR', edit. P. N. Tret'yakov and A. L. Mongait, Moscow, 1956.

ACADEMY OF SCIENCES OF THE USSR. *Sovetskaya Arkheologiya* ('Soviet Archaeology'), Moscow. Many valuable articles on Armenia.

ANATI, EMMANUEL. *Palestine before the Hebrews*. London, 1963.

BURNEY, CHARLES A. Articles in *Anatolian Studies, Iraq*, etc.

BURTON BROWN, T. *Excavations in Azarbaijan, 1948*. London, 1951.

CHILDE, GORDON. *What Happened in History*. London, 1942.

CHUBINISHVILI, TARIEL. *Amiranis Gora. Materials on the ancient history of Meskhet-Javakheti* (in Georgian). Tbilisi, 1963.
Mtkvrisa da Araksis ormdinaretis udzvelesi kultura ('The most ancient culture of the Kura and Araxes river valley region'). In Georgian, with Russian summary, Tbilisi, 1965.

COLE, SONIA. *The Neolithic Revolution*. 3rd ed., London, 1965.

FORBES, R. J. *Metallurgy in Antiquity*. 2nd. ed., in 2 vols., Leiden, 1964.

GOETZE, ALBRECHT. *Kleinasien (Handbuch der Altertumswissenschaft)*. 2nd ed., Munich, 1957.

HEHN, VICTOR. *The Wanderings of Plants and Animals*. London, 1888.

HYAMS, EDWARD. *Dionysus. A Social History of the Wine Vine*. London, 1965.

KHANZADIAN, EMMA. *The Culture of the Armenian Highlands in the 3rd millennium BC*. (Armenian and Russian texts.) Erevan, 1967.

KUFTIN, B. A. 'Urartsky "kolumbarii" u podoshvy Ararata i Kuro-Arakssky eneolit' ('The Urartian "Columbarium" at the foot of Ararat and the eneolithic stage of the Kura-Araks basin') in *Bulletin of the Georgian State Museum*, XIII-B, Tbilisi, 1944, pp. 1–171.

LANG, D. M. *The Georgians* ('Ancient Peoples and Places'). London, 1966.

MELLAART, JAMES. *Earliest Civilizations of the Near East*. London, 1965.

MARTIROSIAN, A. A. *Armeniya v epokhu bronzy i rannego zheleza* ('Armenia in the period of Bronze and Early Iron'). Erevan, 1964.

MAYRHOFER, MANFRED. *Die Indo-Arier im alten Vorderasien*. Wiesbaden, 1966.

PIOTROVSKY, B. B. *Arkheologiya Zakavkaz'ya* ('The Archaeology of Transcaucasia'). Leningrad, 1949.

SCHAEFFER, CLAUDE F. A. *Stratigraphie comparée de l'Asie Occidentale*. Oxford, 1948.

SOLLBERGER, EDMOND. *The Babylonian Legend of the Flood*. London; British Museum, 1962.

WOOLLEY, C. LEONARD. *Ur of the Chaldees*. London, 1929.

CHAPTER IV

ADONTZ, NICHOLAS. *Histoire ancienne de l'Arménie*. Paris, 1946.

AKURGAL, E. *Urartäische und altiranische Kunstzentren*. Ankara, 1968.

ARUTYUNIAN, N. V. *Novye urartskie nadpisi Karmir-Blura* ('New Urartian inscriptions from Karmir-Blur'). Erevan, 1966.
Zemledelie i skotovodstvo Urartu ('Agriculture and stock-breeding in Urartu'). Erevan, 1964.

AZARPAY, G. *Urartian art and artifacts*. California University Press, 1968.

BARNETT, RICHARD. Articles in *Anatolian Studies*, and in *Iraq*, 1950 and 1954.

BURNEY, CHARLES A. 'A first season of excavations at the Urartian citadel of Kayalidere', in *Anatolian Studies*, XVI, 1966, pp. 55–111. And many other valuable articles on Urartu.

JENNY, WILHELM A. 'Schamiramalti', in *Praehistorische Zeitschrift*, XIX, nos. 3/4, Berlin, 1928, pp. 280–304.

KÖNIG, F. W. *Handbuch der chaldischen Inschriften.* Graz, 1955.
Vorchristliches Armenien. Vienna, 1955.

MARR, N. Y., and SMIRNOV, YA. I. *Les Vichaps.* Leningrad, 1931.

MELIKISHVILI, GIORGI. *Nairi-Urartu.* Tbilisi, 1954.

NYLANDER, CARL. 'Remarks on the Urartian Acropolis at Zernaki Tepe', in *Orientalia Suecana*, XIV-XV, 1966, pp. 141–54.

OGANESIAN, K. L. *Arin-Berd.* tom. I, Erevan, 1961.
Erebuni. K 2750-letiyu osnovaniya Erevana ('Erebuni. On the 2750th anniversary of the foundation of Erevan'). Erevan, 1968.

ÖZGÜÇ, TAHSIN. *Altintepe. Architectural monuments and wall paintings.* Ankara, 1966.

PIOTROVSKY, B. B. *Iskusstvo Urartu* ('The Art of Urartu'). Leningrad, 1962.
Karmir-Blur. toms. 1–3, etc. Erevan, 1950, etc.
Urartu: the Kingdom of Van and its Art, trans. and edit. by Peter S. Gelling. London, 1967.
Vanskoe Tsarstvo ('The Vannic kingdom'). Moscow, 1959.

SAYCE, A. H. Articles in *Journal of the Royal Asiatic Society*, various issues, between 1882 and 1932.

SETON LLOYD, H. F. *Early Highland Peoples of Anatolia.* London, 1967.

CHAPTER V

DYAKONOV, I. M. *Predystoriya armyanskogo naroda* ('The prehistory of the Armenian people'). Erevan, 1968.

HERODOTUS. *The Histories of Herodotus of Hallicarnassus,* trans. and introduced by Harry Carter. London, 1962.

INGLISIAN, VAHAN. *Armenien in der Bibel.* Vienna, 1935.

JEREMIAH, THE PROPHET. *The Book of the Prophet Jeremiah : Old Testament.*

MOSES OF KHORENE. *History of Armenia.*

SARKISIAN, G. KH. 'Ueber den chronologischen Zusammenhang in der "Geschichte Armeniens" von Moses Chorenazi', in *Proceedings* of the 25th International Congress of Orientalists, Moscow, 1960.

SEYRIG, HENRI. Articles in *Revue Numismatique*, 1955, etc.

STRABO. *The Geography*, trans. H. L. Jones. (Loeb Classical Library.)

STRONACH, DAVID. 'Urartian and Achaemenian Tower Temples', in *Journal of Near Eastern Studies,* vol. 26, no. 4, Oct., 1967, pp. 278–88.

TOUMANOFF, PRINCE C. L. *Studies in Christian Caucasian History.* Georgetown, 1963.

XENOPHON. *The Anabasis; The Cyropaedia.*

CHAPTER VI

ANANIKIAN, M. H. *Armenian Mythology.* Boston, 1925.

ASLAN, KÉVORK. *Études historiques sur le peuple arménien.* 2nd. ed., Paris, 1928.

CHAUMONT, MARIE-LOUISE. 'Le culte de la déesse Anahita (Anahit) dans la religion des monarques d'Iran et d'Arménie au Ier siècle de notre ère', in *Journal Asiatique*, tom. CCLIII, 1965, pp. 167–81.
'L'ordre des préséances à la cour des Arsacides d'Arménie', in *Journal Asiatique*, tom. CCLIV, 1966, pp. 471–97.

COLLEDGE, MALCOLM A. R. *The Parthians.* London, 1967.

DER NERSESSIAN, SIRARPIE. *The Armenians.* London, 1969.

EREMIAN, S. T. 'Proiskhozhdenie nekotorykh orudii pashennogo zemledeliya v drevnei Armenii' ('The origin of certain agricultural implements in ancient Armenia') in *Materialy po istorii sel'skogo khozyaistva i krest'yanstva Armenii* ('Materials on the history of agriculture and the peasantry in Armenia'), tom. I, Erevan, 1964, pp. 9–27. Also many other valuable articles and monographs in Armenian and Russian journals and symposia.

GOELL, T. 'Throne above the Euphrates', in *National Geographic Magazine*, vol. 119, 1961, no. 3.

MACLER, F. *Contes, légendes et épopées populaires d'Arménie*, tom. II. Paris, 1933.

MANANDIAN, H. A. *Tigrane II et Rome.* Lisbon, 1963.

NEUSNER, JACOB. 'The Jews in pagan Armenia', in *Journal of the American Oriental Society*, vol. 84, 1964, pp. 230–40.

PLUTARCH. 'Antony', Crassus', 'Lucullus', in *Plutarch's Lives* ('The Dryden Plutarch', revised by A. H. Clough, Everyman's Library.)

SARKISIAN, G. KH. 'Obozhestvlenie i kul't tsarei i tsarskikh predkov v drevnei Armenii' ('Deification and the cult of the king's ancestors in ancient Armenia') in *Vestnik Drevnei Istorii* ('Journal of Ancient History'), 1966, no. 2, pp. 3–26.
Tigranakert. Moscow, 1960.

STARK, FREYA. *Rome on the Euphrates.* London, 1966.

TREVER, K. V. *Nadpis' o postroenii armyanskoi kreposti Garni* ('The inscription about the building of the Armenian fortress of Garni'). Leningrad, 1949.
Ocherki po istorii kul'tury drevnei Armenii ('Studies in the history of the culture of ancient Armenia'). Moscow, Leningrad, 1953.

WIDENGREN, G. 'Recherches sur le féodalisme iranien', in *Orientalia Suecana*, V, 1957, pp. 79–181.

CHAPTER VII

ATIYA, AZIZ S. *A History of Eastern Christianity.* London, 1967.

LANG, D. M. *Lives and Legends of the Georgian Saints.* London, 1956.

MÉCÉRIAN, JEAN. *Histoire et institutions de l'Église arménienne.* Beirut, 1965.

MOSES, DASKHURANTSI. *The History of the Caucasian Albanians*, trans. C. J. F. Dowsett. Oxford, 1961.

ORMANIAN, PATRIARCH MALACHIA. *The Church of Armenia.* New ed., London, 1955.

PASDERMADJIAN, H. *Histoire de l'Arménie.* 2nd ed., Paris, 1964.

SARKISSIAN, KAREKIN. *The Council of Chalcedon and the Armenian Church.* London, 1965.

TOUMANOFF, PRINCE C. L. 'Armenia and Georgia', being Chapter XIV of *Cambridge Medieval History*, IV, 1: *The Byzantine Empire*, Cambridge, 1966, pp. 593–637.

CHAPTER VIII

ACADEMY OF SCIENCES OF THE USSR. *Ocherki istorii SSSR* ('Studies in the history of the USSR'), Third to Ninth centuries, ed. B. A. Rybakov. Moscow, 1958; Ninth to Thirteenth centuries, ed. B. D. Grekov and others. Moscow, 1953.

ADONTZ, NICOLAS. *Études arméno-byzantines.* Lisbon, 1965.

ARISTAKES OF LASTIVERT. Extracts of his Chronicle, trans. by S. A. Essefian, in the article by Robert A. Hewsenian, 'The Coming of the Turk', in *Ararat*, VII, no. 1, 1966, pp. 36–42.

CHARANIS, PETER. *The Armenians in the Byzantine Empire.* Lisbon, 1963.

COMNENA, ANNA, PRINCESS. *The Alexiad.* Trans. Elizabeth A. S. Dawes. 2nd ed., London, 1967.

CONSTANTINE PORPHYROGENITUS, Byzantine Emperor. *De Administrando Imperio.* Ed. and trans. Gy. Moravcsik and R. J. H. Jenkins, Budapest, 1949; commentary, by Jenkins and others, London, 1962.

DER NERSESSIAN, SIRARPIE, *Armenia and the Byzantine Empire.* Harvard, 1945.

GARSOIAN, N. G. *The Paulician Heresy.* The Hague, 1967.

LAURENT, J. *L'Arménie entre Byzance et l'Islam.* Paris, 1919.

MANANDIAN, H. A. 'Marshruty persidskikh pokhodov Imperatora Irakliya' ('The itineraries of the Persian campaigns of the Emperor Heraclius') in *Vizantiisky Vremennik* ('Byzantine Chronicle'), III, 1950, pp. 133–153. *The Trade and Cities of Armenia in relation to ancient world trade.* Trans. Nina G. Garsoian, Lisbon, 1965.

MARKWART, JOSEPH. *Südarmenien und die Tigrisquellen.* Vienna, 1930.

MUSHEGIAN, KH. A. *Denezhnoe obrashchenie Dvina po numizmaticheskim dannym* ('The monetary circulation of Dvin, according to numismatic data'). Erevan, 1962.

MUYLDERMANS, J. *La Domination arabe en Arménie.* Louvain, 1927.

TOUMANOFF, PRINCE C. L. 'The background to Mantzikert', in *Proceedings* of the Thirteenth International Congress of Byzantine Studies, Oxford, 1966.

VASILIEV, A. A. *Histoire de l'empire byzantin.* 2 vols. Paris, 1932.

CHAPTER IX

BEDOUKIAN, PAUL Z. *Coinage of Cilician Armenia.* New York: American Numismatic Society, 1962.

DER NERSESSIAN, SIRARPIE. 'The Kingdom of Cilician Armenia', in *A History of the Crusades*, vol. II, edit. Wolff and Hazard, Philadelphia, 1962, pp. 630–59.

GREGORY, OF AKNER. *History of the Nation of the Archers*. Trans. and edit. by Robert P. Blake and Richard N. Frye, Harvard, 1954.

HEYD, W. *Histoire du commerce du Levant*, 2 vols., new ed., Leipzig, 1936.

MANANDIAN, H. A. *Critical history of the Armenian people* (in Armenian) tom. III. Erevan, 1952.

MIKAELIAN, G. G. *Istoriya kilikiiskogo armyanskogo gosudarstva* ('History of the Cilician Armenian kingdom'). Erevan, 1952.

MÜLLER-WIENER, W. *Castles of the Crusaders*. London, 1966.

RUDT-COLLENBERG, COUNT W. H. *The Rupenides, Hethumides and Lusignans*. Paris, 1963.

SANJIAN, AVEDIS K. *The Armenian communities in Syria under Ottoman dominion*. Harvard, 1965.

SETH, MESROVB JACOB. *Armenians in India from the earliest times to the present day*. Calcutta, 1937.

YAKOBSON, A. L. *Srednevekovy Krym* ('The medieval Crimea': with an account of the Armenian churches and other remains in the Crimea.) Moscow, Leningrad, 1964.

CHAPTER X

ARCHITETTURA MEDIEVALE ARMENA. – Roma, Palazzo Venezia, 10–30 giugno 1968. (A richly illustrated descriptive guide.) Rome, 1968.

ARUTYUNIAN, V. M. and OGANESIAN, K. L. *Arkhitektura Sovetskoi Armenii* ('Architecture of Soviet Armenia'). Erevan, 1955.

ARUTYUNIAN, V. M. and SAFARIAN, S. A. *Pamyatniki armyanskogo zodchestva* ('Monuments of Armenian architecture'). Moscow, 1951.

ATAYAN, ROBERT. 'Armenian Systems of Musical Notation', in *New Orient*, Prague, October, 1967, pp. 129–131.

AZARIAN, L. R. *Kilikiiskaya miniatyura XII–XIII v. v.* ('Cilician miniature painting of the 12th–13th centuries.' In Armenian). Erevan, 1964.

BABENCHIKOV, M. V. *Narodnoe dekorativnoe iskusstvo Zakavkaz'ya* ('Popular decorative art of Transcaucasia'). Moscow, 1948.

BARSAMOV, N. S. *Ivan Konstantinovich Aivazovsky*. Moscow, 1965.

BOYCE, PROFESSOR MARY. 'The Parthian *gosan* and Iranian minstrel tradition', in *Journal of the Royal Asiatic Society*, 1957, pp. 10–45.

CARSWELL, JOHN. *New Julfa. The Armenian churches and other buildings*. Oxford, 1968.

CHEGODAEV, A. D. *Martiros Sergeevich Sarian*. (An illustrated appreciation of the Armenian national painter.) Moscow, 1961.

CILICIA, CATHOLICOSATE OF. *Album of the Catholicosate of Cilicia*. Antelias, 1965.

DAVTIAN, SERIK. *Armyanskoe kruzhevo* ('Armenian lace'. Armenian, Russian, French and English texts). Erevan, 1966.

DER NERSESSIAN, SIRARPIE, *Aght'amar. Church of the Holy Cross.* Harvard, 1965.

Armenian Manuscripts in the Freer Gallery of Art. Washington, 1963.

The Chester Beatty Library. A catalogue of the Armenian Manuscripts. 2 vols., Dublin, 1958.

DOURNOVO (DURNOVO), LYDIA A. *Armenian Miniature Painting* (Armenian, Russian and French texts). Erevan, 1967.

Armenian Miniatures. London, 1961.

Armyanskaya naboika ('Armenian printed textiles'). Moscow, 1953.

Drevnearmyanskaya miniatyura ('Ancient Armenian miniature painting'). Erevan, 1952.

Kratkaya istoriya drevnearmyanskoi zhivopisi ('Brief history of ancient Armenian paintings'). Erevan, 1957.

ECHMIADZIN, *Album* (Armenian and English texts). Echmiadzin, 1962.

EREVAN. – State Historical Museum of Armenia. *Putevoditel'* ('Illustrated Guide to the Museum'), ed. by K. G. Kafadarian and G. Kh. Sarkisian. Erevan, 1963.

HARVEY, JOHN H. 'The Origins of Gothic Architecture' in *The Antiquaries Journal*, 1968, pt. I, pp. 87–99.

JANASHIAN, MESROP, AND OTHERS. *Armenian Miniature Paintings.* Venice, 1967.

KAFADARIAN, KARO G. *Haghpat* (An archaeological and architectural study of the Armenian monastery complex. In Armenian). Erevan, 1963.

LEROY, JULES. *Monks and Monasteries of the Near East.* London, 1963.

MNATSAKANIAN, A. SH. *Armenian decorative arts* (Armenian text). Erevan, 1955.

OGANESIAN, K. L. *Zodchy Trdat* ('Biography of the Armenian architect Trdat'). Erevan, 1951.

ORBELI, I. A. *Izbrannye trudy* ('Selected works'), tom. I. Erevan, 1963.

Izbrannye trudy v dvukh tomakh ('Selected works in two volumes'). Moscow, 1968, etc.

PARSAMIAN, R. *Gosudarstvennaya kartinnaya Galereya Armenii* (Illustrated handbook to the State Picture Gallery of Armenia). Moscow, 1960.

PATRIK, ARAKEL. *Armenian costume from ancient times to the present day* (in Armenian). Erevan, 1967.

SARXIAN, WARDAN. *Sacred Music of the Armenian Church.* 2 vols., New York, 1966.

SCHURMANN, ULRICH. *Caucasian Rugs.* Brunswick and London, *c.* 1965.

SHNEERSON, GRIGORY. *Aram Khachaturyan.* Moscow, 1959.

SOTHEBY and CO. *Catalogue of Twenty-Three Important Armenian Illuminated Manuscripts.* London, 1967.

STRZYGOWSKI, JOSEF. *Die Baukunst der Armenier und Europa.* 2 vols., Vienna, 1918.

Origin of Christian Church Art. Oxford, 1923.

TALBOT RICE, TAMARA. *Ancient Arts of Central Asia.* London, 1965.

TOKARSKY, N. M. *Arkhitektura Armenii, IV-XIV vv.* ('Architecture of Armenia from the 4th to the 14th century'). 2nd ed., Erevan, 1961.

Gegard (Armeniya) (A description of the monastery and church.) Moscow, 1948.

UTUDJIAN, EDOUARD. *Mission technique en Arménie.* Paris, 1962.
> *Les Monuments arméniens du IVe siècle au XVIIe siècle.* Paris, 1967.

VARDANIAN, SOLOMON. *Arkhitektura armyanskikh narodnykh zhilykh domov* ('Architecture of Armenian traditional dwelling houses'. In Armenian.) Erevan, 1959.

YARALOV, YU S., general ed. *Arkhitektura respublik Zakavkaz'ya* ('Essays on the architecture of the Transcaucasian Republics'). Moscow, 1951.

CHAPTER XI

ABEGHIAN, MANOUK. *Collected writings on Armenian literary history* (in Armenian). Tom. I, etc. Erevan, 1966, etc.

ABGARIAN, G. W. *The Matenadaran.* Erevan, 1962.

ACADEMY OF SCIENCES OF THE ARMENIAN SSR – Museum of Literature and Theatre Art. *Vystavka po istorii armyanskogo teatra* ('Exhibition on the history of the Armenian theatre'). Erevan, 1958.

ACADEMY OF SCIENCES OF THE USSR – Institute of World Literature. *Istoriya Armyanskoi Sovetskoi Literatury* ('History of Armenian Soviet Literature'). Moscow, 1966.

AKOPIAN, AKOP. *Stikhotvoreniya i poemy* ('Verses and poems', trans. into Russian by various hands). Ed. A. Salakhian. Leningrad, 1961.

ANANIAS, OF SHIRAK (ANANIA SHIRAKATSI). *Kosmografiya* ('The Cosmography'). Russian trans. by K. S. Ter-Davtian and S. S. Arevshatian. Erevan, 1962.

ANASIAN, A. S. *Armyanskaya bibliografiya, V-XVIII vv.* ('Armenian bibliography, from the 5th to the 18th century'). Tom. I, etc. Erevan, 1959, etc.

ARARAT. *A Quarterly Magazine.* No. 1, etc. New York, 1959, etc.

BOYAJIAN, ZABELLE C. *Armenian legends and poems.* 2nd. ed., London, 1958.

BRYUSOV, VALERY. *Ob Armenii i armyanskoi kul'ture* ('On Armenia and Armenian culture'). Erevan, 1963.
> *Poeziya Armenii* (An anthology of Armenian poetry, in Russian trans. by various hands). Moscow, 1916; reprinted, Erevan, 1966.

CHALOYAN, V. K. *Armyansky Renessanc* ('The Armenian Renaissance'). Moscow, 1963.
> *Istoriya armyanskoi filosofii* ('History of Armenian philosophy'), Erevan, 1959.

CONYBEARE, F. C. *The Key of Truth.* Oxford, 1898.

DAVID, THE INVINCIBLE. *Opredeleniya filosofii* ('A definition of philosophy'). Russian trans. by S. S. Arevshatian. Erevan, 1960.
> *Tolkovanie Analitiki Aristotelya* ('Interpretation of Aristotle's Analytics'). Russian trans. by S. S. Arevshatian. Erevan, 1967.

EREVAN. – Matenadaran Library. *Vestnik* ('Bulletin'). Toms. 1–9, etc. Erevan, 1941—.

ETMEKJIAN, JAMES. *The French influence on the Western Armenian Renaissance.* New York, 1964.

305

EUROPE, Revue mensuelle. no. 382–383. 'La littérature arménienne'. Paris, 1961.

EZNIK, OF KOLB. *Kniga oproverzhenii* ('Against the Sects'). Russian trans. by V. K. Chaloyan. Erevan, 1968.

FEYDIT, F. *Considérations sur l'alphabet de Saint Mesrop*. Vienna, 1964. *David de Sassoun: épopée en vers* (trans. Feydit). Paris, 1964.

GALSTIAN, A. G. *Armyanskie istochniki o mongolakh* ('Armenian sources about the Mongols'). Russian trans., Moscow, 1962.

GOYAN, GEORG. *2000 let armyanskogo teatra* ('Two thousand years of the Armenian theatre'). Moscow, 1952.

GREGORY, OF NAREK. *Le Livre de Prières*, trans. Isaac Kechichian. Paris, 1961.

GULBEKIAN, E. V. *Armenian Press Directory*. London, 1967.

INGLISIAN, VAHAN. 'Die Armenische Literatur', in *Handbuch der Orientalistik*, Abt. I, Bd. VII, Leiden, 1963, pp. 156–250.

ISSAHAKIAN, AVETIK. *Stikhotvoreniya i poemy* ('Verses and poems', trans. into Russian by various hands). Moscow, 1960.

KARST, JOSEF. *Armenisches Rechtsbuch*. 2 Bd., Strassburg, 1905.

KASPER, ROBERT E. *Hundertfünfzig Jahre Mechitaristen-Buchdruckerei*. Vienna, 1961.

KHACHATRIANTS, YA. trans. *Armyanskie skazki* ('Armenian folktales'). Leningrad, 1930.

KHACHERIAN, L. G. *Esai Nichetsi i Gladzorsky Universitet, XIII-XIV vv.* ('Isaiah Nichetsi and the Glazdor University in the 13th and 14th centuries'). Erevan, 1968.

KORIUN. *The Life of Mashtots*. Trans. by Bedros Norehad. New York, 1964. *Zhitie Mashtotsa*. Russian trans. by Sh. V. Smbatian. Erevan, 1962.

MARKWART, J. *Über den Ursprung des armenischen Alphabets*. Vienna, 1917.

MEILLET, A. *Études de linguistique et de philologie arméniennes*. Lisbon, 1962.

MKHITAR, HERATSI. *Uteshenie pri likhoradkakh* ('Relief from Fevers', Russian trans. ed. by S. S. Arevshatian). Erevan, 1968.

OGANESIAN, L. A. *Istoriya meditsiny v Armenii* ('History of medicine in Armenia'). Erevan, 1946.

PERIKHANIAN, A. G. 'K voprosu o proiskhozhdenii armyanskoi pis'-mennosti' ('On the question of the origin of Armenian writing'), in *Peredneaziatsky Sbornik* ('Near Eastern Symposium'), Moscow, 1966, pp.103–33.

RAFFI, (AKOP MELIK-AKOPIAN). *Zolotoi Petukh, Roman; Bezumets, Roman*. (Two novels, trans. into Russian by S. Khitarova.) Moscow, 1959.

RHODES, ERROLL R. *An annotated list of Armenian New Testament Manuscripts*. Tokyo, 1959.

SARKISSIAN, KAREKIN. *A Brief Introduction to Armenian Christian Literature*. London, 1960.

SAYAT-NOVA. *Stikhotvoreniya* ('Verses', trans. into Russian by various hands, and ed. with introduction by Suren Gaisarian). Leningrad, 1961.

SEVAK, GURGEN. *Mesrop Mashtots*. (A monograph on the creator of the Armenian alphabet.) Erevan, 1962.

SIMEON, LEHATSI. *Putevye zametki* ('Travel sketches'). Russian trans. by M. O. Darbinian. Moscow, 1965.

SOVIET LITERATURE. No. 3, Moscow, 1966. Issue devoted to Literature and Art of Soviet Armenia.

SURMELIAN, LEON. *Apples of Immortality. Folktales of Armenia*. London, 1968.

THOROSSIAN, H. *Histoire de la littérature arménienne*. Paris, 1951.

VAHRAM RABUNI. *Analiz 'Kategorii' Aristotelya* ('Analysis of the Categories of Aristotle'). Armenian text with Russian trans., ed. by G. O. Grigorian. Erevan, 1967.

ZARIAN, RUBEN. edit. *Shakespearakan. An Armenian year-book of Shakespeare*. Vol. I, etc. Erevan, 1966, etc.

CHAPTER XII

ACADEMY OF SCIENCES OF THE ARMENIAN SSR. *Atlas of the Armenian SSR* (in Armenian). Erevan, 1961.

ARMENIAN SSR. – SUPREME SOVIET. *Armyanskaya SSR – Administrativno-territorial'noe delenie* ('Armenian SSR – Administrative and territorial divisions'). 3rd ed., Erevan, 1964.

BRYCE, JAMES, LORD. *Transcaucasia and Ararat*. London, 1877.

ENCYCLOPAEDIA OF ISLAM, articles 'Anadolu', 'Arminiyya', etc.

GREAT SOVIET ENCYCLOPAEDIA, article 'Armenian SSR', and separate articles on Armenian personalities, towns, rivers, etc.

HAXTHAUSEN, AUGUST VON. *Transkaukasia*. 2 vols., Leipzig, 1856.

HOVANNISIAN, RICHARD G. *Armenia on the Road to Independence, 1918*. University of California Press, 1967.

LEPSIUS, JOHANNES. *Deutschland und Armenien, 1914–1918*. Potsdam, 1919.

LUKE, SIR HARRY. *Cities and Men. An Autobiography*. Vol. II, London, 1953.

MORGENTHAU, HENRY. *Ambassador Morgenthau's Story*. New York, 1918.

NAIM BEY. *The Memoirs of Naim Bey. Turkish official documents relating to the deportations and massacres of Armenians*. 2nd. ed., Pennsylvania, 1964.

NALBANDIAN, LOUISE. *The Armenian Revolutionary Movement*. University of California Press, 1963.

NOVOSTI PRESS AGENCY. *Armenian Soviet Socialist Republic*. Moscow, 1967.

SURMELIAN, LEON. *I Ask You, Ladies and Gentlemen*. London, 1946.

SUTHERLAND, DR JAMES KAY. *The Adventures of an Armenian Boy*. Ann Arbor, 1964.

TOTOVENTS, VAHAN. *Scenes from an Armenian Childhood*, trans. Mischa Kudian. London, 1962.

TOYNBEE, ARNOLD, ed. *The Treatment of the Armenians in the Ottoman Empire*. London, 1916.

INDEX

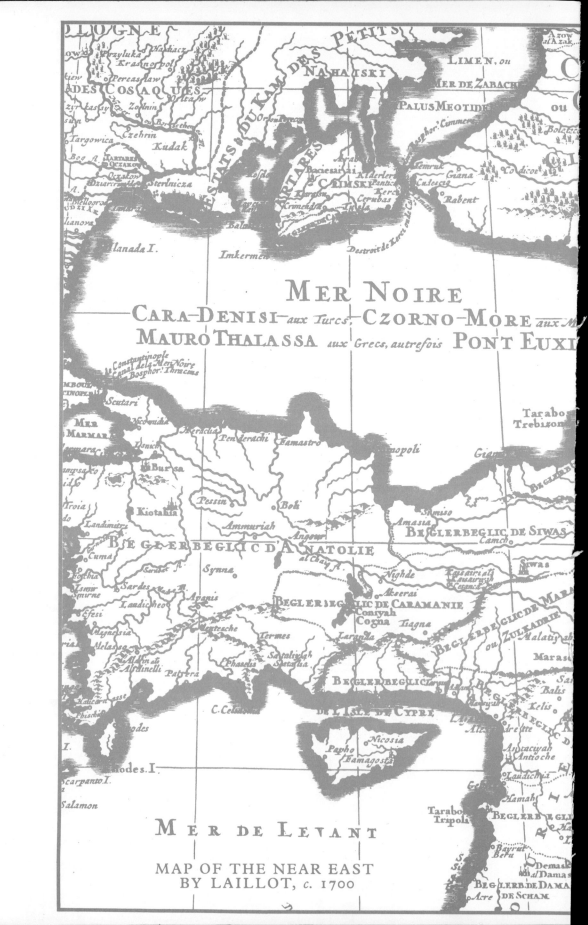

MAP OF THE NEAR EAST
BY LAILLOT, c. 1700